HITLER'S
BENEFICIARIES

HITLER'S
BENEFICIARIES

PLUNDER, RACIAL WAR, AND
THE NAZI WELFARE STATE

GÖTZ ALY

Translated by Jefferson Chase

A Holt Paperback
Metropolitan Books / Henry Holt and Company
New York

Holt Paperbacks
Henry Holt and Company, LLC
Publishers since 1866
175 Fifth Avenue
New York, New York 10010
www.henryholt.com

Originally published in Germany in 2005 under the title *Hitlers Volksstaat* by S. Fischer Verlage, Frankfurt.

Library of Congress Cataloging-in-Publication Data

Aly, Götz, 1947–
    [Hitlers Volksstaat. English]
    Hitler's beneficiaries : plunder, racial war, and the Nazi welfare state / Götz Aly;
translated by Jefferson Chase.
        p.   cm.
    Includes bibliographical references and index.
    ISBN-13: 978-0-8050-8726-0
    ISBN-10: 0-8050-8726-5
    1. Germany—Economic policy—1933–1945.   2. Germany—Politics and
government—1933–1945.   3. National socialism—Philosophy.   4. World War, 1939–1945—
Destruction and pillage—Europe.   5. World War, 1939–1945—Economic aspects—Switzerland.
6. Jewish property—Europe—History—20th century.   7. Holocaust, Jewish (1939–1945)—
Economic aspects.   I. Title.

HC286.4.A613 2007
330.943'086—dc22   2006046672

Henry Holt books are available for special promotions and
premiums. For details contact: Director, Special Markets.

Originally published in the United States in 2007 by Metropolitan Books
First Holt Paperbacks Edition 2008

Designed by Meryl Sussman Levavi

Printed in the United States of America
D   10   9   8   7

Contents

Part IV
CRIMES FOR THE BENEFIT OF THE PEOPLE

Acknowledgments

The J. B. and Maurice C. Shapiro Foundation Award of the Center for Advanced Holocaust Studies at the United States Holocaust Memorial Museum allowed me to work in archives and libraries in and around Washington, D.C. This book was also written with the help of grants from the Köhler Foundation—part of the Association of German Research Foundations—and the S. Fischer Foundation. The assistance of all of the above was a mark of their support for the basic idea of this book, and for that I thank them. I am also grateful to the many individuals who offered constructive criticism and encouragement, helped to clear up specific questions, and intervened to prevent mistakes.

TRANSLATOR'S NOTE

In the interests of rendering an extraordinarily complex historical investigation more comprehensible to an American audience, this book occasionally deviates from the text of Götz Aly's German original. All changes have been made in consultation with the author.

HITLER'S
BENEFICIARIES

Preface

One of the inspirations for this book was the series of negotiations carried out by Stuart E. Eizenstat to recover damages from the Swiss and German governments on behalf of victims of persecution during World War II. Eizenstat was, of course, entirely right to demand compensation for the stolen gold and confiscated bank accounts of those murdered in the Holocaust, as well as for the slave labor performed by survivors. Nonetheless, his highly public negotiations gave rise to a distorted picture of history. The fact that the names of large Swiss and German banks—together with those of world-famous companies like Daimler-Benz, Volkswagen, Allianz Insurance, Krupp, the Bertelsmann publishing group, and BMW—were constantly in the news gave the impression that prominent German capitalists, occasionally in alliance with major Swiss banks, were the main culprits behind the terrible crimes of Nazi Germany.

There is no question that many leading German industrialists and financiers were complicit in Hitler's regime. But it would be wrong to conclude that primary responsibility for the Holocaust or other Nazi crimes lay with the elite of the German bourgeoisie. Eizenstat's efforts, as well as those of the Jewish Claims Conference, indirectly, if unintentionally, encouraged such a conclusion. And indeed many Germans had a stake in seeing the public's attention focused on the captains of industry and finance, since it shifted the burden of blame for Nazi barbarism to a handful of individuals.

This book was conceived as an attempt at redressing the balance, at redirecting public attention toward the potential advantages everyday Germans derived from the Nazi regime. In so doing, it uncovered a "missing link" that was better able than previous historical arguments to explain the widespread, if always temporary, satisfaction most Germans felt with their government during the Third Reich. Precisely because so many Germans did in fact benefit from Nazi Germany's campaigns of plunder, only marginal resistance arose. Content as most Germans were, there was little chance for a domestic movement that would have halted Nazi crimes. This new perspective on the Nazi regime as a kind of racist-totalitarian welfare state allows us to understand the connection between the Nazi policies of racial genocide and the countless, seemingly benign family anecdotes about how a generation of German citizens "got through" World War II.

I myself heard many such anecdotes. I was born in 1947 and still have vivid memories of the first two decades of postwar Germany. People often talked about how they had suffered from food shortages in 1946–47. "We were well off during the war," they complained. "Food deliveries always went smoothly." It was the "organizational incompetence of the Allies" after the war that "made us go hungry." My mother told me that my portly grandfather suddenly became thin in 1946 and regained his weight only in 1950. Recounting their experiences in the Wehrmacht, my teachers—some of whom were missing an arm or a leg—never spoke of suffering. Rather, their stories made the war sound like the ordinary man's travelogue, full of adventure and funny incidents. They recalled Italy, France, and Poland. They reminisced about the things they enjoyed in those countries, things they had never known before—foods, goods, amenities. In contrast, the American care packages that helped Germans survive the early years after the war were dismissed as little more than chicken feed. (German housewives back then were no great fans of corn.)

It was only when I began work on this book that the truth behind these stories became clear to me. The women of the Third Reich were accustomed to far better than chicken feed. The packages their husbands had constantly sent back from the German-occupied countries between 1941 and 1944 contained staple and gourmet items that supplied well beyond the minimum calories necessary for human survival. This discovery prompted me to ask my relatives some pointed questions. One aunt cheerfully recalled: "I had a real shoe fetish. My fiancé, Fritz, sent me sixty pairs of shoes from the African front." She was still wearing some of those shoes during the 1950s. An older cousin remembered her godfather sending her a gold-embroidered down quilt from Paris. My mother received nothing—my father was sent to the Eastern Front in early 1943 and was wounded after only a few weeks. But she, too, remembered that her older sister Dora "got a package every few days from her husband in Romania, which contained everything she could possibly want. He also sent ham and honey from Russia. But she never shared anything." I once asked my mother whether she could recall Hermann Göring's speech on October 4, 1942. Without hesitation, she shot back: "He said we'd be getting more to eat and other extra rations for Christmas. And we got them!" In fact what Göring had said was: "If someone has to go hungry, let it be someone other than a German."

As I was writing this book, I found I could no longer take pleasure in several beautiful pieces of antique furniture in my home. My wife and I had inherited them from my in-laws in Bremen, whose house had been bombed during the war. As I now know, Germans bombed out by Allied air raids on Bremen were resupplied with furniture taken from Dutch Jews who had been deported and murdered. In Bremen alone, many hundreds of freight cars and dozens of ships full of furniture were unloaded. Their contents, which ran the gamut from the basic to the luxurious, were handed out to Germans according to social class for refurnishing their homes. My in-laws are now dead, but the uneasy question remains: what are these heirlooms that I have in my own home? In Germany even now antique furniture can be a troubling legacy from the past.

Such material benefits suggest how the regime maintained its popularity during the war. Indeed, concern for the people's welfare—at any cost—was a mark of the Nazi system from its inception. Between 1933 and 1935, the leadership owed its domestic support to its efficient campaign against unemployment. However, the regime succeeded in combating joblessness only by incurring a fiscally irresponsible level of state debt. Later the regime would require a not particularly popular war to keep government finances afloat. But Hitler was able to maintain general morale by transforming Germany's military offenses into an increasingly coordinated series of destructive raids aimed at plundering other peoples. The Nazi leadership established a framework for directly sharing the spoils of its military victories with the majority of Germans—the profits derived from crippling the economies of occupied and dependent countries, the exploitation of work performed by forced laborers, the confiscated property of murdered Jews, and the deliberate starvation of millions of people, most notably in the Soviet Union. Those benefits, in turn, made the recipients amenable to Nazi propaganda and gave them a vested interest in the Third Reich.

Although the Nazi crimes were unprecedented, there is no reason to think that the circumstances in which they arose were completely extraordinary. However understandable it may be for subsequent generations to want to distance themselves from the Third Reich by classifying the regime as an extreme aberration, the evidence uncovered in this book undermines various attempts by historians, past and present, to reduce Nazi guilt to this or that specific group. It also belies the optimistic conviction that we today would have behaved much better than the average person did back then. Readers of these pages will encounter not Nazi monsters but rather people who are not as different from us as we might like them to be. The culprits here are people striving for prosperity and material security for themselves and their children. They are people dreaming of owning a house with a garden, of buying a car of their own, or of taking a vacation. And they are people not tremendously interested in the potential costs of their short-term welfare to their neighbors or to future generations.

IN AIMING to shed light on the symbiotic relationship between the Nazi *Volksstaat* (or people's state) and the regime's crimes against humanity, this book departs from the usual historical approach of separating the manifestly vicious side of National Socialism from the political programs that made Hitler's regime so attractive to the majority of Germans. My goal is to locate Nazi barbarism within the broader context of twentieth-century

German history. The genesis of the Holocaust is not to be found solely in the official files devoted to the "Jewish question." My alternative approach in no way lessens the achievements of historians who have focused directly on the phenomenon of genocide. On the contrary, I was inspired to undertake this book by a fundamental issue raised by their works: what were the preconditions that made the Holocaust and other Nazi crimes possible in the first place?

The chapters that follow address the simple but still unanswered question of how Nazi Germany could have happened. Or, to put it another way, what drove ordinary Germans to tolerate and commit historically unprecedented crimes against humanity, in particular the murder of millions of European Jews? Without doubt, state-propagated hatred of "inferior peoples"—of Poles, Bolsheviks, and Jews—was a major factor. But ideology alone is not an adequate explanation. In the decades preceding the Hitler regime, Germans were no more malicious toward or resentful of Jews than other Europeans were, nor was German nationalism more racist than that of other nations. There was no specific German deviation from "normal" cultural development that led to Auschwitz. Nor is there any empirical basis for the proposition that a special exterminatory anti-Semitism and xenophobia took root early on in German history. It is a mistake to assume that an especially catastrophic aberration must have extraordinary, long-term causes. The Nazi Party rose to and consolidated power because of a constellation of factors situated in a specific historic context. The most important of these factors are to be found in the years after—and not before—1914.

In consolidating their authority, the Nazis certainly relied on propaganda depicting Jews as "parasites," "traitors," and "subhumans." But anti-Semitic ideology rarely functioned in isolation. Even the traditional anti-Jewish pogroms in medieval Europe were not always based on religious hatred alone. Often, anti-Semitism was combined with plunder for plunder's sake. To cite just one of many examples from the nineteenth-century historian Heinrich Grätz's *History of the Jews*: "In Nördlingen in 1384, the entire community, including women and children, were killed. Throughout the region of Swabia [today part of southwestern Germany],

Jews were persecuted, and in Augsburg, they were imprisoned in dungeons until they paid the sum of 20,000 guilders." Emperor Wenceslas, Grätz continues, had ordained that "all Jewish claims upon Christians—in terms not only of interest, but also of capital—[were to be] erased and all instruments of debt handed over. The imperial decree was announced (in September 1390) from every pulpit, and the cancelation of debt [evoked] great jubilation." In addition, Grätz records, the emperor "declared all property acquired by Jews to be his own and forbade them from transferring it or giving it away." The ideological justification for this instance of plunder and murder conformed to the Christian hostility to Jews typical of the era. "The Jews concerned deserved their fate," it was proclaimed, "because they were seen outside their homes on Easter Sunday."¹

The Nazi war on the Jews was similarly complex. The widespread enthusiasm for the Nazi campaign of "Aryanization," for example, was not easily reduced simply to the anti-Semitic predilections of those involved. Indeed, such enthusiasm can generally be observed whenever a part of society claims the right to nationalize other people's property, justifying that act with the rationale that the beneficiaries make up a homogeneous and theretofore underprivileged majority, the "people" itself. The eagerness with which individuals have assumed this position is a fundamental element in the history of twentieth-century violence. While anti-Semitism was a necessary precondition for the Nazi attack on European Jews, it was not a sufficient one. The material interests of millions of individuals first had to be brought together with anti-Semitic ideology before the great crime we now know as the Holocaust could take on its genocidal momentum.

ANY INVESTIGATION into Hitler's ascent must thus examine the give-and-take relationship between the populace and the Nazi leadership. It is a matter of historical record that the party hierarchy was, from its earliest days, extremely unstable. The mystery is how it managed to stabilize itself, if only temporarily, so that the regime could survive for twelve spectacularly destructive years. Solving this mystery requires a more precise rephrasing of the general question "How could Nazi Germany have happened?" Namely, how did National Socialism, an obviously deceitful, megalomaniacal, and criminal undertaking, succeed in persuading the great majority of the German people that it was working in their interest?

One answer is that as harshly as the Nazi leadership applied its racist ideology to Jews, the handicapped, and other "undesirables," their domestic policies were remarkably friendly toward the German lower classes, soaking the wealthy and redistributing the burdens of wartime to the benefit of the underprivileged. These "social" policies are the focus of part I of this book.

Moreover, once the Nazi state undertook what became the most expensive war in world history, the majority of Germans bore virtually none of the costs. Hitler shielded the average Aryan from that burden at the cost of depriving others of their basic subsistence. To ensure contentment among its own people, the German government destroyed a number of foreign currencies—most notably the Greek drachma—by forcing other countries to pay ever-increasing contributions and tributes to their occupiers. To maintain living standards, the Wehrmacht plundered millions of tons of food to keep German soldiers well fed, then shipped what was left over back to the fatherland. And while the Third Reich was gorging itself on food from the countries it occupied, the German army paid its operating costs in the devalued local currency. Officials in Berlin were guided by two iron principles: if someone had to starve in the war, then better them than us, and if wartime inflation was inevitable, let it happen everywhere, but not in Germany. Part II of this book examines the financial tricks and techniques that were devised to achieve those ends.

The German war chest was also filled with billions of reichsmarks garnered from the dispossession of European Jews. That is the focus of part III, which traces how Jewish property was stolen in Germany, in allied states, and in countries occupied by the Wehrmacht. These chapters proceed by example, without any claim to encyclopedic completeness. The same holds true for the chapters describing the methods used by Germans in World War II to plunder other nations; the emphasis is on specific instances that were typical of the larger procedure.

By exploiting material wealth confiscated and plundered in a racial war, Hitler's National Socialism achieved an unprecedented level of economic equality and created vast new opportunities for upward mobility for the German people. That made the regime both popular and criminal. The cascade of riches and personal advantages—all derived from crimes against humanity, for which ordinary Germans were not directly responsible but from which they gladly profited—led the majority of the populace to feel that the regime had their best interests at heart. Conversely, the Nazis' genocidal policy gained momentum from the fact that it also improved the material welfare of the German people. The lack of significant internal opposition to Hitler as well as ordinary Germans' later refusal to acknowledge any personal culpability for the crimes of the Third Reich arise from one and the same historical constellation. That is the subject of part IV.

So complex an answer to the question of how Nazism could have happened does not lend itself to mere antifascist sloganeering or the didacticism of museum exhibits. It is necessary to focus on the socialist aspect of National Socialism, if only as a way of advancing beyond the usual projections of blame onto specific individuals and groups—most often the delusional, possibly insane Führer but also the cabal of racist ideologues or the members of a particular class, like bankers and business tycoons, or certain Wehrmacht generals or the elite killing units. The chief problem with such approaches is they all suggest that a special group of evil "others" bears culpability for Nazi crimes. At the very least the present volume attempts to break through this comforting proposition by showing how everyday people, acting on ordinary calculations of self-interest, could become complicit in a government-driven program of larcenous genocide.

THE FOLLOWING chapters are necessarily full of numbers: budget figures, property calculations, tax revenues, occupation costs, currency values, and so on. A table of exchange rates set by the German government for foreign currencies can be found on page 333. To get an idea of the actual value of the sums discussed, a good rule of thumb is that one reichsmark was roughly equivalent to 12 dollars in 2006 terms; 200 reichsmarks represented a better-than-average gross monthly income in 1939, and a monthly pension of 40 reichsmarks was standard. In autumn 1942, when the price for fifty kilos of potatoes went up to 75 pfennigs, the rise led to "scattered discontent" among the populace.

Relative to general living standards at the time, wartime expenditures reached dizzying proportions. But readers should also remember the costs *not* included in the billions of reichmarks discussed in this book. The figures include only expenditures on the German side for weapons, fortifications, transport, food, wages, and family income support. The costs incurred by those people who had to defend themselves against German aggression and by wounded veterans or the families of fallen soldiers cannot be taken into account. The incalculable sums that went to rebuilding Warsaw, Rotterdam, Kharkiv, and tens of thousands of other war-damaged cities and towns are likewise omitted, as are the postwar costs of repairing destroyed bridges, industrial facilities, railways, roads, and dams and of restoring fields and forests. Lastly, there is no place for human casualties in the balance sheet of war.

Part I

POLITICAL OPPORTUNISTS IN ACTION

CHAPTER 1

The Dream of a "People's Empire"

Heady Days

The National Socialist German Workers Party was founded on a doctrine of inequality between races, but it also promised Germans greater equality among themselves than they had enjoyed during either the Wilhelmine empire or the Weimar Republic. In practice, this goal was achieved at the expense of other groups, by means of a racist war of conquest. Nazi ideology conceived of racial conflict as an antidote to class conflict. By framing its program in this way, the party was propagating two age-old dreams of the German people: national and class unity. That was the key to the Nazis' popularity, from which they derived the power they needed to pursue their criminal aims. The ideal of the *Volksstaat*—a state of and for the people—was what we would now call a welfare state for Germans with the proper racial pedigree. In one of his central pronouncements, Hitler promised "the creation of a socially just state," a model society that would "continue to eradicate all [social] barriers."[1]

Like all other revolutionaries, the predominantly youthful members of the Nazi movement had an urgent, now-or-never aura about them. When Hitler came to power in 1933, Joseph Goebbels was thirty-five years old. Reinhard Heydrich was twenty-eight; Albert Speer, twenty-seven; Adolf Eichmann, twenty-six; Josef Mengele, twenty-one; and Heinrich Himmler and Hans Frank, both thirty-two. Hermann Göring, one of the eldest among the party leadership, had just celebrated his fortieth birthday. And a decade later, in the midst of World War II, Goebbels could still conclude from a statistical survey: "According to the data, the average age of midlevel party leaders is 34, and within the government, it's 44. One can indeed say that Germany today is being led by its youth." At the same time, Goebbels nonetheless called for a continuing "freshening of the ranks."[2]

For most young Germans, National Socialism did not mean dictatorship, censorship, and repression; it meant freedom and adventure. They saw Nazism as a natural extension of the youth movement, as an antiaging regimen for body and mind. By 1935, the twenty- to thirty-year-olds who set the tone for the party rank and file viewed with open contempt those who advocated caution. They considered themselves modern men of action with no time for petty, individual concerns. "The philistines may fret," they mocked, "but tomorrow belongs to us." In January 1940, one ambitious young Nazi wrote of Germany's standing on the threshold of "a great battle" and declared confidently that, "no matter who should fall, our country is heading toward a great and glorious future." Even as late as March 1944, despite the terrible costs Germany had incurred, the faithful were still cheerfully gearing up for "the final sprint to the finish in this war."[3]

In a diary entry from 1939, a thirty-three-year-old described his decision to apply for a position helping resettle ethnic Germans from Eastern Europe in the expanding German empire: "I didn't need to think about it for a second. It's a once-in-a-lifetime opportunity. I hope they'll be able to use me and will accept my application. It would get me out of the confines of my office, which has grown very stale." Two weeks later he noted: "I'm awed by the size of the task. I've never been given such great responsibility before."[4] Female university students spent semester breaks in occupied Poland, staffing the provisional day care centers that freed German settlers to bring in the harvest. One student later wrote enthusiastically: "It made no difference which school we were from. We were united in one great mission: to apply ourselves during our break in Poland with all our strength and whatever knowledge we had. It was truly an honor to be among the first students allowed to do such pioneering work."[5]

In 1942, twenty-seven-year-old Hanns Martin Schleyer—later a leading industrialist and president of the Employers' Association in the Federal Republic of Germany—was working in the Nazi administration of occupied Prague. There he complained about older bureaucrats dragging their feet and contrasted their hesitancy with the gung-ho attitude of his own generation: "We learned at a young age during the movement's days of struggle to seek out challenges, instead of waiting for them to come to us—this and our constant efforts for the party, even after it took power, made us ready to take on responsibility much earlier than usual."[6] In May 1941, Hans Schuster, who would go on to become a senior editor of the liberal *Süddeutsche Zeitung* after the war, was made economic attaché to the German mission in Zagreb. Although only twenty-six, he was charged with helping to establish Croatia as a Nazi satellite state. Earlier, having written his Ph.D. dissertation on "The Jewish Question in Romania," he had worked for the German embassy in Bucharest, where he was involved in various conspiratorial endeavors. In a letter from January 1942 to his friend Hellmut Becker, another influential figure in postwar Germany, Schuster wrote with the breathless enthusiasm of a true believer:

> I would really like to move on soon. The past year here has been too good to me. Things have gone almost too smoothly, though conditions have been very tense and, for weeks on end, quite dangerous. [We had] the coup d'état in Belgrade, followed by the war and our coup here in Agram [Zagreb]. I've had the good fortune to be assigned to help with the difficult task of building up this country. For a full six months, I've been working under the excellent command of envoy Kasche [an SA squadron leader] and have been given a lot of responsibility. The circumstances are especially fortuitous thanks to our good relations with the present government before it came to power.

Schuster was granted his request for a transfer, and later, as a soldier, he expressed his gratitude that "the variety of this life, the constant excitement, the challenge of making independent, if minor, decisions that require a modicum of imagination and initiative" had protected him against "the side of war that dulls the senses."[7]

These young men and women were living out the perennial dream of people in their twenties: independence, opportunity, and jobs that demanded pioneer spirit, satisfying their need for improvisation and constant physical and mental challenges. Disdaining the small-minded culture of everyday office work, they wanted to test their limits, enjoy themselves, and experience the thrill of the unknown and the intoxication of taking part in a fast-paced, modern war. Elated by feelings of unlimited possibility, they embarked on a search for an identity all their own.

Among those who took power in 1933 were many recent university graduates and students. Their ranks included the rebellious sons of old elite families and the increasingly self-assertive lower classes, who had profited from the Social Democrats' reforms in the Weimar Republic. They overcame differences in background through their collective struggle for a National Socialist utopia, a utopia at once romantic and technologically modern. Viewing themselves and their peers as the avant-garde of the "young *Volk*," they disdained their more experienced, skeptical elders as "cemetery vegetables." To members of the new generation, veteran civil servants, with their devotion to rules and principles, were "ossified old geezers."[8] The movement's activists and the far greater number of cautious but curious sympathizers looked beyond the constraints of the present toward the dawning of a new, *völkisch* age. The burden of what would soon become enormous daily challenges was easy to bear when one's gaze was fixed so firmly on the future. Goebbels considered calling his 1941 book of war speeches "Between Yesterday and Tomorrow." (The actual title of the volume, when published, was *An Unprecedented Age*.)[9] For all these reasons, National Socialism can be seen as a dictatorship of youth. Within only a few years, it developed into the most destructive generational project of the twentieth century.

Another source of the Nazi Party's popularity was its liberal borrowing from the intellectual tradition of the socialist left. Many of the men who would become the movement's leaders had been involved in communist and socialist circles in the waning years of the Weimar Republic. In his memoirs, Adolf Eichmann repeatedly asserted: "My political sentiments inclined toward the left and emphasized socialist aspects every bit as much as nationalist ones." In the days when the movement was still doing battle in the streets, Eichmann added, he and his comrades had viewed Nazism and Communism as "quasi-siblings."[10] Also typical of his generation was Wolfgang Hillers, a leftist writer and art critic, who declared: "The 'I' has to be subjugated to a 'we,' and new German art can only be nourished from the wellsprings of this 'we.' "[11] Before Hitler's rise to power, Hillers had collaborated with socialist authors Bertolt Brecht and Johannes R. Becher on *The Great Plan*, a choral work celebrating the achievements of the industrialization of the Soviet Union under Stalin. After 1933, Hillers needed only to substitute the word "German" for "proletariat" to conform to the new political spirit. He'd already made the journey from "I" to "we," and his recognition "that the new spirit of collectivism could best be expressed in choral form" was easily transferable. The new Germany envisioned by the Nazis gave their former opponents in the demonstrations, debates, and public battles of the Weimar Republic ample opportunity to make their own personal peace with the Third Reich.[12]

GERMANY'S RAPID military defeat of France in 1940 was accomplished by violating Belgian and Dutch neutrality—a transgression against international law that Hitler dismissed as "meaningless." The Führer impressed upon his supporters, and gradually upon the German people as well, a maxim that was soon to justify any and all sorts of crimes: "No one will ask questions, once we've achieved victory."[13]

That year, while temporarily confined to a sickbed, Reich Deputy Finance Minister Fritz Reinhardt wrote to his boss, Count Lutz Schwerin von Krosigk: "I'm looking forward to the great tasks that will have to be accomplished soon. . . . We can be enormously glad to live and work in these heady days. Paris in German hands, France on the verge of capitulation! In such a short span of time! It's hard to believe!"[14]

It is pointless to ask whether any of the Nazis' grandiose plans for the future were anything more than propaganda. The extraordinarily feverish tempo, the youthful élan with which Germans jettisoned their moral scruples are what make the twelve short years of Nazi rule so difficult for us to comprehend. Nazi society drew its extreme intensity from the regime's ability to merge opposites: rational and emotional political goals, old and new elites, the interests of the people, the party, and the government bureaucracy. Huge bursts of energy were released wherever the Nazi Party apparatus conjoined contradictory elements: the preservation of putative traditions with the desire for technological achievement; antiauthoritarian glee at the toppling of the old order with the authoritarian devotion to a new utopia in which Germany would finally assume its place in the sun. Hitler combined the prospect of national revival with the risk of absolute collapse, the ideal of communal class harmony with minutely organized genocidal violence.

The Seismic Shift

The Nazi leadership had little patience with lawyers, judges, career diplomats, general staff officers, and other stolid members of the old order. But it was to the party's advantage to give such people time to conform to the new order. Equally useful to the party were civil servants within the Reichsbank and the Ministries of Finance and Economics, shrewd men who had gathered their first political and professional experience in Wilhelmine Germany and the early years of the Weimar Republic. Many had fought in World War I, and they came from all walks of life, as did the members of most university institutes, private and semiprivate economic think tanks, academic societies, newspaper editorial staffs, and economics divisions of large commercial banks.

Their expertise was crucial to the success of the Nazi leadership's criminal undertakings. Between 1939 and 1945, under the leadership of Ministerial Director Gustav Schlotterer, civil servants within Division III of the Ministry of Economics plundered much of Europe with a thoroughness that is difficult to imagine today. Division III was founded in 1920 to fulfill Germany's obligations under the Treaty of Versailles. Helpless to resist French, Belgian, and British demands for reparations, this generation of civil servants received an introductory lesson in the art of subjugation, looting, and blackmail. Later, they would turn this involuntarily acquired know-how back on their teachers, bolstering it with a German talent for bureaucratic organization. In their minds, the myriad techniques they applied to exploit their fellow Europeans were just compensation for previous humiliations.

Civil servants were also instrumental in advancing the Führer's anti-Semitic agenda. The Nuremberg Laws, which were broadly and somewhat hastily proclaimed by Hitler at the annual Nazi Party conference in September 1935, mandated the preservation of "German blood" against threats from Jews. But they did not even define who was to be considered Jewish. It was up to legal experts to transform Hitler's vague ideas of protecting German blood and of "breeding out" the characteristics of "inferior" races into practicable regulations that bureaucrats could implement. Only once this had been done could the government issue the first ordinance of the Reich Citizenship Law (*Reichsbürgergesetz*), which defined who was to be considered Jewish and how to classify people in cases of mixed parenthood and marriage. In formulating that legislation, the party's legal experts ignored the fine racial distinctions worked out by German geneticists and simply decreed that the religious affiliation of an individual's grandparents, which could be easily ascertained from registration documents, would be the legal basis for deciding hundreds of thousands of cases of disputed ethnicity. This created an automatic procedure for social exclusion.

Civil servants played an equally key role in the "atonement payment" (*Judenbusse*) of one billion reichsmarks that Hermann Göring, in a fit of anti-Semitic fervor, ordered Jews to pay in 1938. The Finance Ministry translated this demand into a 20 percent levy on personal assets, to be paid in four installments over the course of a year. In the end, the money raised significantly exceeded Göring's original figure.

These so-called special measures, now regarded as the first steps toward the Holocaust, could only be put into practice with the help of precise work by bureaucrats and civil servants. After Nazi Germany's conquest of Central and Eastern Europe, for example, the Reich General Auditor's Office monitored the confiscation of Jewish property in Belgrade, the management of the deportation centers for Dutch Jews, and the operations of the German administration of the Lodz ghetto in Poland.[15] Economic logic was a motor that drove the Holocaust. The Ministry of Economics charged the National Board for Economy and Efficiency with producing a cost-benefit analysis of the Warsaw ghetto. The board issued a number of reports that cautioned against maintaining such prisonlike but economically unviable "Jewish areas of residence."[16]

These examples illustrate how the impulsive, populist, and often improvised actions of the Nazi movement were supported by an experienced bureaucracy. As willing as civil servants were to serve the national cause, however, they were never keen to relinquish control over their traditional instruments of power. The General Auditor's Office and the civil court system, for instance, continued to operate much as they had before 1933; the leadership of both institutions retained considerable autonomy, and the multitiered bureaucracy worked with notable efficiency. The Nazi gauleiters (district leaders), whose ideal form of rule was a nonbureaucratic dictatorship directly translating popular will into action, were constantly frustrated by civil servants who insisted that fiscal questions be decided in strict accordance with national budgetary guidelines. Friction, irritation, and conflict were unavoidable, especially when government bureaucrats sought to impose financial limits on political or military maneuvers. Yet the polycratic organizational structure of the Nazi state did not, as is often claimed, lead to chaos. The strength, however precarious, of the regime was its capacity for resolving conflicts of interest and deciding on an appropriate course of action. This capacity allowed the state to avoid administrative gridlock while it developed and implemented ever more radical policies. Such was the genesis of Nazi Germany's ultimately homicidal mixture of political volunteerism and functional rationality.

THE COOPERATION between professional experts, political leaders, and the majority of the populace was facilitated by Hitler's willingness to carry through overdue reforms, many of which had been derailed during the Weimar Republic by special-interest squabbling. In its hunger for action, the National Socialist bureaucracy simply jettisoned a lot of what it considered useless, outmoded ballast. In 1941, a directive prohibited the use of traditional German *Fraktur* (broken-script typeface) in favor of Latin lettering—a reform originally called for by Jacob Grimm in 1854.[17] Article 155 of the Weimar constitution had done away with entailments, a medieval form of communal property inheritance common in northeastern Germany and considered antithetical to modern capitalism. But whereas the Weimar Republic had been unable to enforce the ban, which had been on the political agenda since 1849, entailments were simply eradicated by a Reich law dated July 6, 1938, and signed "Adolf Hitler, Berchtesgaden."

The Nazi leadership gave Germans their first taste of what it might be like to own an automobile. It introduced the previously almost unknown idea of vacations. It doubled the number of days off for workers and began to develop large-scale tourism in Germany. The Berlin regional warden of the German Labor Front was particularly energetic in his promotion of such benefits: "In 1938 we want to devote ourselves more and more to reaching all those comrades who still think that vacation travel isn't something for blue-collar workers. This persistent misconception must finally be overcome."[18] At the time, a fourteen-day trip through Germany cost between 40 and 80 reichsmarks, roughly equivalent to between 480 and 960 dollars in today's terms.

From its earliest days in power, the Hitler regime privileged families over single people and childless couples, and it insured farmers against the vagaries of the weather and the world market. Nazi-era policies paved the way for many postwar reforms, everything from European Union agricultural policy, joint tax returns for couples, and compulsory liability insurance for drivers to state child-support allowances, graduated income tax, and the beginnings of environmental conservation. Nazi civil servants drafted the outline for a pension system that anticipated the one adopted in 1957 by the Federal Republic of Germany. The 1939 system tried to end the poverty faced by retirees and decreed that "the living standards of veterans of the workforce should not deviate dramatically from that of currently employed comrades."[19]

A number of Nazi leaders came from humble origins and had direct personal experience with court officers arriving at the front door to repossess their family belongings. Not surprisingly, some of the first measures enacted after the Nazis came to power were aimed at alleviating the threat, felt by the majority of Germans in the wake of the Depression, of eviction and repossession. Several early Nazi laws restricted the rights of creditors vis-à-vis debtors so as to prevent "the impoverishment of the [German] people." The 1938 Old Debt Eradication Law invalidated hundreds of thousands of titles to collectible debts. The Law for the Prevention of Misuse of Repossession, passed in late 1934, was directed against what was seen as the "nearly unlimited freedom enjoyed by creditors" in the past.[20] As was typical for the Nazi style of rule, the law granted officers of the court broad powers of discretion in carrying out individual court orders.[21]

The German trade journal for court officers, the *Deutsche Gerichtsvollzieher-Zeitung*, set the tone for how this new freedom should be interpreted: "A court officer with a social conscience will not have the heart to subject his comrades to absolute destitution, to rob them of their last possessions, their trust in the protecting state, and their love of their fatherland. [Germans] are entitled to believe that they will be allowed to live with a modicum of comfort." In a *Volksstaat*, the officer of the court was to develop "a sense of true social solidarity" and at all costs "avoid becoming hardened" to his ethnic comrades' plight. He had to "spare no effort and accept possible personal disadvantage in order to live up to social ideals." Finally, he was told to remain ever conscious of his ethnic duty "in light of the close connection between the social and the national concept."

Another issue of the same journal cited an early maxim of "the people's chancellor," Adolf Hitler: "Germany will be at its greatest when its poorest citizens are also its most loyal."[22] Göring seconded this sentiment: "The property owner who displays a pitiless lack of scruples and turns his poorer ethnic comrades out on the street over insignificant [debts] has forfeited his right to protection by the state." That dictum applied even when the property owner had "the appearance of legality" on his side, if he violated "the basic laws of ethnic solidarity."[23] Meanwhile, court officers were also called upon, as a matter of course, "to take the harshest steps" against "malicious debtors," whom the author referred to as "parasites on the German people."[24]

With the start of World War II on September 1, 1939, a Nazi directive prevented creditors from repossessing the belongings of draftees and their families. An announcement in the court officers' journal read: "All procedures requiring the auctioning off of nonliquid personal assets are suspended or postponed by law, regardless of whether the compulsory auction was ordered before or after [this] directive came into force." The Nazi regime also strengthened rent-control and tenants'-rights laws to benefit soldiers and their families. Although the government later took a harder line toward debtors, protection of their rights remained one of the courts' central responsibilities. This policy, the *Deutsche Gerichtsvollzieher-Zeitung* stated, "contributes in a fundamental way to the victory of our people, who are engaged in a fierce struggle for their survival."[25]

On October 30, 1940, the regime issued a similar directive, giving indebted Germans increased protection against having their wages seized. All wages earned from working overtime—as well as vacation pay, Christmas bonuses, state child-rearing allowances, and retirement pensions for those injured on the job—were declared off-limits to creditors. The regime also exempted most wages from being garnished by using net rather than gross income to calculate what debtors could afford to repay and by creating exemptions they could claim for family members. To increase equality among the German populace, this directive also annulled the special protection from creditors enjoyed by civil servants and clergymen, a privilege dating back to the early days of German capitalism.[26] Laws such as these made the "national socialism" of the Third Reich immensely popular among many Germans.

CULTURAL AND even state institutions retained a remarkable degree of internal diversity. To many people—from intellectuals to civil servants and engineers—it seemed as if institutional paralysis had been overcome and that a seismic shift in society, an explosion of technical expertise unfettered by party politics and class restraints, was at hand. In this moment of tension between change and continuity, specialists of all sorts, drawing on their expertise to take advantage of the new opportunities for career advancement, voluntarily turned themselves into instruments of Nazi rule. Whatever their role in the new system, public employees were never compelled to betray their personal convictions. Unlike Communism, National

Socialism did not demand absolute devotion. Instead it called for closeness to the common man—an antielitist stance that held considerable appeal for twentieth-century European intellectuals.

The cooptation of civil servants allowed for the peculiar combination of populist opportunism, selective government manipulation, and premeditated genocide that characterized the Third Reich. This constellation, rather than any particular German fondness for bureaucracy or Prussian subservience, helps explain the success of the Nazi movement. Despite the regime's self-image as a state with an omnipotent central Führer, National Socialism deemphasized vertical chains of command in favor of more modern, horizontal decision-making processes. In this sense the Nazi bureaucracy was more advanced than its democratic precursor in the Weimar Republic. The regime unleashed the force of individual initiative in both long-standing and newly created government agencies. It broke through the rigidity of established hierarchies. The drudgery of merely following procedure was replaced by meaningful work, in which people were encouraged to think for themselves—and to plan for the future.

This was the spirit in which the Nazis' finance minister, Schwerin von Krosigk, organized a brainstorming session for his staff in the summer of 1935. The goal was to maximize the amount of money squeezed out of Jews by the tax system. The participants were instructed to rate various proposals as "recommended," "possible but not recommended," and "definitely not recommended." Acting on their own, without pressure from above, they suggested eradicating dozens of tax credits provided that they also benefited Jews. Mindful of the various ordinances in place, they argued that, where Jews were concerned, "an expedient that contravenes the law is already an option today."[27]

In April 1938, the finance minister held a second meeting on the subject, forwarding the ideas suggested to Minister of the Interior Wilhelm Frick. Tax officials debated the merits of denying Jews—either all Jews or only minor dependents—the allowable exemptions from the wealth tax. They questioned whether guide dogs for Jews who had been blinded fighting in World War I should continue to be exempt from the tax on dogs. One participant drafted legislation imposing a special premium on income and assets taxes for Jews alone. The proposal stipulated that the amount of the premium was "to be flexible so that it can be increased in special cases such as malicious behavior by individual Jews toward the people as a whole."[28] These initiatives required original thought and belied the cliché that Germans were reflexively obedient to arcane bureaucratic procedure.

Hitler's inner circle quickly warmed to representatives of the old elite, such as Finance Minister Schwerin von Krosigk, who took a constructive attitude toward Nazi anti-Semitism. At the beginning of each new phase of radicalization, Goebbels noted in his diary, von Krosigk may have been "somewhat shaky," but in the end he always proved reliable. In terms of personality, Goebbels added, von Krosigk was "the sort of civil servant we definitely need in our state."[29] In 1937, Hitler awarded him the golden insignia of honorary Nazi Party membership. Thereafter, von Krosigk used the official Nazi form of address "Esteemed Party Comrade" when the occasion called for it and didn't object when he, too, was addressed in that way instead of by his aristocratic title. In 1939, the honorary Nazi earmarked 450,000 reichsmarks (the equivalent today of $5 million) in the national budget for a ministerial apartment befitting his social status.[30]

Count Lutz Schwerin von Krosigk was born in Anhalt in 1887 and was later adopted by an aristocratic Prussian family. He studied at Lausanne and Oxford and received his law degree in Halle, where he passed the German equivalent of the bar exam. Highly decorated in World War I, he retired as a lieutenant colonel. In 1919, von Krosigk joined the reconstituted Finance Ministry and rose rapidly through the ranks. Ten years later he was put in charge of its budget division. Although he wasn't affiliated with any political party, Chancellor Franz von Papen appointed him finance minister in 1932, and Papen's successors, Kurt von Schleicher and Adolf Hitler, honored his financial expertise by retaining him in that post. Von Krosigk stayed loyal to the inner circle of the Nazi regime even through the final days of World War II. On May 2, 1945, Hitler's successor, Admiral Karl Dönitz, named him director of the short-lived government that negotiated Germany's surrender. After the war he was given a sentence of ten years in prison, which was commuted in 1951. He died in 1977.[31] An undisputed master of state finances, von Krosigk was known for the ease with which he countered critics, in freely dictated, multiple-page letters explaining the intricacies of the Third Reich's wartime budget.

Von Krosigk's deputy, Fritz Reinhardt, came from an altogether different background. The son of a Thuringian bookbinder, Reinhardt was born in 1895 in far more humble circumstances. He attended trade school in the town of Ilmenau and became a salesman. After the outbreak of World War I, Reinhardt was arrested in Riga as an enemy alien by the Russian army and deported to Siberia. Freed after the war, he founded a school for export trade in 1924 in the Bavarian town of Herrsching am Ammersee. The school received little support from the Weimar Republic's educational bureaucracy, and two years later a disillusioned Reinhardt joined the Nazi Party and started a booking agency for party speakers. An expert in budgetary politics, Reinhardt was later appointed the party's financial spokesman. He was elected to the Reichstag as a Nazi deputy in 1930.

Reinhardt served as deputy finance minister from 1933 to 1945. A diligent worker with vast specialized knowledge, he expounded his political goals in hundreds of speeches, pamphlets, and articles. Driven by a desire for greater equality in German society, he introduced countless tax breaks for lower- and middle-class Germans, many of which remained in effect after 1945. Ordered by the Nazi labor minister in 1941 to narrow the gap in pensions between blue-collar and white-collar workers, Reinhardt responded simply, "Good!"[32] He lowered the standards for entrance into various branches of the civil service and introduced mandatory supplemental training for Finance Ministry employees, taking the unprecedented step of founding a series of government-run financial "academies."[33] "Reinhardt may be an irritatingly pedantic little schoolmaster in his approach to problems," Goebbels remarked, "but by and large he knows how to solve them."[34]

The duo in charge of the Finance Ministry represented a marriage of opposites typical of National Socialism: the aristocratic and apolitical minister who had enjoyed the finest education and his parvenu deputy who had acquired his expertise as a conscientious, politically driven autodidact. Reinhardt saw himself as embodying progress toward a more egalitarian, classless, social welfare state. Von Krosigk, on the other hand, represented thousands of civil servants, military officers, scientists, and intellectuals who succeeded, working from the inside, in rationally codifying the nebulous and self-contradictory ideology of National Socialism.

National Integration

Contrary to what is generally assumed today, and despite his intolerance of socialists, Jews, and nonconformists, the German people perceived Hitler not as a strident social divider and excluder but rather as a great integrator. The peace treaties of Versailles and St. Germain, which prohibited Austria and Germany from merging into one state, were widely seen as unjust. When Nazi Germany defied those treaties and incorporated Austria in March 1938, the dream of a Greater Germany, which had existed since the failed revolutions of 1848, was finally realized. The new German nation-state was not, of course, the liberal one envisioned in the nineteenth century, but its formation was nonetheless greeted with considerable popular enthusiasm. Though this period in German history is often interpreted as a deviation from "normal" development, in the late 1930s it was seen, equally broadly, as a difficult, even torturous process toward the national unification of a linguistic and cultural community, not unlike what had taken place in many other European states.

It was in the spirit of nationalist enthusiasm that the Judenstrasse ("Street of the Jews") in the Spandau district of Berlin was renamed for Carl Schurz, a leading revolutionary of 1848. (A second street was named for Schurz's fellow nationalist Gottfried Kinkel.) Hitler always defined himself not just as German chancellor but as leader of the entire German people, including ethnic Germans living outside the boundaries of the state he ruled. On March 15, 1938, Hitler proclaimed in Vienna: "As leader and imperial chancellor of the German nation, I announce before history the entry of my homeland into the German Reich." A short time later in Frankfurt, the city that had hosted the failed German national assembly of 1848, Hitler presented himself as the man who had finally achieved the German people's age-old dream: "The great work for which our forefathers struggled and shed their blood ninety years ago can now be considered complete."[35]

The euphoria into which the nation was whipped only increased with Nazi Germany's early military triumphs. Germany's catastrophic defeat in World War I seemed to have been a blessing in disguise. Victory in 1918, many Germans felt, would merely have preserved the outmoded Habsburg and Hohenzollern monarchies, at the cost of millions of war casualties. (Hitler liked to refer to the Austro-Hungarian empire as "the Habsburg state-cadaver.")[36] Now it was the revolutionary young nation-state of Greater Germany that was achieving victory, led by a representative of the common people who had risen up through the social ranks. Suddenly the incalculable human suffering of World War I and the years that followed no longer seemed to have been in vain. Defeat was reinterpreted as a prelude to a grandiose triumph. In November 1939, when Hitler called together his generals to prepare for the blitzkrieg against France, he did so with the words "All in all, this represents the completion of the world war, not a specific campaign."[37]

German troops had occupied Prague on March 15 of that year. Hermann Voss, a professor of anatomy who was later the recipient of numerous honors in Communist East Germany, noted in his diary: "Charles University—the oldest German university and the mother of the one in Leipzig—once again in German hands! It's hard to believe. What a blow for the Slavs and what a boon for us. We are living in a great age and should feel privileged to experience such things. What does it matter if butter is in short supply, coffee is sometimes unavailable, or you sometimes have to do one thing or another that you don't completely approve of? Weighed against such progress, these problems are laughably trivial."[38]

Germany's early series of military triumphs, combined with the appearance of economic recovery, decisively weakened opposition to Hitler on the home front. Protests against his policies by pragmatists like army chief of staff Ludwig Beck, Reichsbank director Hjalmar Schacht, and former Leipzig mayor Carl Friedrich Goerdeler faltered, their appeals to moderation and compromise no match for Hitler's wildly popular invocation of a bold, historic transformation, of a high-stakes battle between polar opposites. The Third Reich was not a dictatorship maintained by force. Indeed, the Nazi leadership developed an almost fearful preoccupation with the mood of the populace, which they monitored carefully, devoting considerable energy and resources toward fulfilling consumer desires, even to the detriment of the country's rearmament program.[39]

To put the level of Nazi state coercion of its citizens into perspective: Communist East Germany would later employ 190,000 official surveillance experts and an equal number of "unofficial collaborators" to watch over a populace of 17 million, while the Gestapo in 1937 had just over 7,000 employees, including bureaucrats and secretarial staff. Together with a far smaller force of security police, they sufficed to keep tabs on more than 60 million people. Most Germans simply did not need to be subjected to surveillance or detention. By the end of 1936, four years after the Nazis had become Germany's largest political party and once their initial period of terror and violence against opponents was over, only 4,761 people—some of whom were chronic alcoholics and career criminals— were incarcerated in the country's concentration camps.

Although the financial basis for Germany's economic upswing was precarious, Hitler's popularity grew with each seemingly effortless triumph, soon spreading beyond the party rank and file and further undermining the opposition. By 1938, what Mussolini aptly called *democrazia totalitaria* had been established. After many years of civil strife, class hatred, and political obstructionism, Germans were united in their yearning for popular community.

In his memoirs, my grandfather Wolfgang Aly described his experience of World War I at great length. The recipient of a doctorate in Germanic linguistics (his father had overruled his wish to become a mathematician), he had served in the war as an artillery commander. In 1917, a particularly capable staff sergeant caught his attention. "He was entirely without fear," my grandfather wrote. "I wanted to promote him to senior officer and ordered him to report to me. When he learned of my plan, he answered: 'My father is a tailor. I'd rather stay a junior officer. I don't fit in with that sort of company.' Nonetheless," the account concluded, "he was awarded the Iron Cross, First Class."[40] This social dynamic, set in motion during World War I, was taken up and exploited by National Socialism. The party appealed to thousands of men who had left their class identification behind them in the grime of trench warfare. It drew in left-leaning blue-collar workers, artisans, and office workers who hoped their children would enjoy upward social mobility. They were joined by those who had already profited from the educational reforms of the Weimar Republic and wanted to continue their rise in status. These groups sought not a new class dictatorship but rather the sort of meritocracy we take for granted today: a society in which the circumstances of one's birth have relatively little influence on one's eventual career and social standing.

THE NAZIS' racist teachings have been read solely as encouragement for hatred, violence, and murder, but for millions of Germans their appeal lay in the promise of real equality within the ethnic community. Externally, Nazi ideology emphasized differences; internally, it smoothed them over. Hitler demanded "the highest degree of social solidarity and maximum educational opportunities for every member of the German race; toward others, however, [we assume] the standpoint of the absolute master."[41] For all those who legally belonged to the German racial community—about 95 percent of the population—social divides became ever smaller. For many people, the regime's aim of leveling out class distinctions was realized in the Hitler Youth, the National Labor Service, the major party organizations, and ultimately even in the Wehrmacht. The Nazis' fondness for uniforms is today seen as a manifestation of its militarism. But uniforms, whether worn by schoolchildren or Boy Scouts or sports teams, are also a way of obscuring differences between the well-off and their less fortunate peers.

The goal of reducing class differences also motivated the Nazis to launch, between 1939 and 1942, a series of increasingly ambitious plans to settle Germans in Eastern Europe. Designed to give Germans more living space, greater access to natural resources, and better opportunities for self-advancement, the most extreme proposal envisioned forcibly relocating 50 million Slavs to Siberia. (For years, the German Research Foundation also supported the development of technocratic plans for the slaughter of millions of people. Funds for research in this area were still allocated in the Nazis' final budget for the fiscal year 1945–46.) In domestic terms, the General Eastern Settlement Plan was promoted as a driving force behind an assurgent lower-class movement in Germany. Party officials were well aware of the plan's advantages on the home front. Himmler spoke of a "socialism of good blood." Hitler declared enthusiastically: "We can take our poor workers' families from Thuringia and the coal mining mountains and give them vast stretches of land." The German Labor Front hoped that in this way "at least 700,000 economically unviable, small agrarian enterprises can be gotten rid of."[42] Academic studies were commissioned to look into "settler reserves" within the German population, and all made reference to Marx's term for excess labor, "the industrial reserve army." These were precisely the sorts of people who in an earlier period would have emigrated to the United States, driven by poverty.

By 1942 German children were staging imaginary gunfights on the "black soil" of central Russia, while hundreds of thousands of soldiers' wives dreamed of owning country estates in Ukraine. Even Heinrich Böll, who would go on to receive the Nobel Prize for Literature in 1972 and who was certainly not one of Hitler's willing executioners, wrote to his parents on December 31, 1943, from a frontline hospital: "I long to return to the Rhine and to Germany, yet I often also think of the possibility of a colonial existence here in Eastern Europe once the war has been won."[43] Children's writers Thea Haupt and Ilse Mau conceived of a primer "for beginning readers" that would "acquaint small children with the ideas behind the settlement plan and transfer the cowboys-and-Indians romanticism [of the American West] to Eastern Europe." They concocted the following flights of fancy: "Let us now borrow Tom Thumb's magic boots and take a walk through a foreign land. We'll need them if we hope to get there. . . . Here we are in the fruitful terrain of black soil. . . . The corn rustles alongside the wheat and rye."[44]

This land of milk and honey in Eastern Europe was to be conquered not for the benefit of landed Prussian Junkers and powerful industrialists but to provide ordinary people with a real-world utopia.

The Trauma of 1918

Utopian dreams represented a pointed contrast to Germans' experience of World War I. Three memories were particularly traumatic: the food shortages caused by the British naval blockade, the devaluation of the currency, and the civil unrest that followed defeat. More than 400,000 people starved to death during the war—a number that does not include those who died prematurely of tuberculosis and other infectious diseases made worse by malnutrition.[45] Currency devaluation made runaway inflation a part of daily life. On average, the cost of food doubled in Germany during the war, and in isolated parts of the country, the rise was even more dramatic.[46] In the absence of effective government price-control mechanisms, inflation placed most of the economic burden on ordinary people, few of whom possessed savings or material assets. Price rises continued to torment Germany after the war. The hyperinflation of 1923 led to the de facto impoverishment of the nationalistically inclined middle classes.

In many Germans' memories of the two final years of World War I, the humiliation of defeat was combined with a hatred of those perceived to have profited from the people's desperation. The popular view held that traitors to the nation had stirred up discontent and defeatism among an otherwise patriotic public. What else could explain Germany's failure to achieve victory on the Western Front, after it had defeated Russia and its other enemies in the East? Only after internal unity had collapsed, many believed, was the fatherland finally subdued on the battlefield, a calamity that led to the trauma of the communist uprising of November 1918. Hitler deftly exploited this widespread sentiment. Point 12 of the National Socialist Party platform read: "With respect to the enormous sacrifice of life and property that every war demands of the populace, wartime profiteering must be considered a crime committed against the people. We therefore demand that all profits from war, without exception, be confiscated."

Popular anxieties about wartime profiteers and revolutionaries were easily projected onto a phantom propaganda enemy: the "Jewish plutocrat" whose greed played into the hands of the equally rapacious "Jewish Bolshevik." While the former was accused of destroying the middle classes and enslaving agricultural and industrial workers in the service of big-money capitalism, the latter was blamed for "the complete dissolution of order" and the erosion of public respect for religion, morality, property, and the rule of law.[47]

Using this propagandistic foundation, the instigators of anti-Semitic state policies invariably justified their measures against "the Jews" as acts of self-preservation. The concluding chapter of *Mein Kampf* is entitled "The Right to Self-Defense." A landmark piece of anti-Semitic legislation, the April 1933 Law for the Restoration of the Professional Civil Service, was justified on the same grounds and initiated the gradual exclusion of Jews from public life. When the Finance Ministry drafted legislation paving the way for the partial dispossession of German Jews in the summer of 1937, the draft was titled the Law Concerning the Reparation of Damages Caused to the German Empire by Jews.[48] The longer the war went on, the more one-dimensional German propaganda depicted it as the struggle of "Aryan resistance" against the aggression of "global Jewry," with its threefold aspirations to world dominance: "firstly as Jew, secondly as member of a plutocratic Jewish clan, and thirdly as Jewish Bolshevik."[49]

The Nazi doctrine of Germans as a master race fit in seamlessly with these schematic divisions. Despite all the bluster about German superiority, the doctrine was grounded in the anxiety that humanity's worthiest representatives—as defined by racialist pseudoscience—would inevitably come under attack by their inferiors and be forced to defend themselves. The socialist worldview contained a similar, if less paranoid, element in its doctrine, whereby the proletariat, the inevitable victors of history, were under siege by the bourgeoisie, an inferior class condemned to extinction. That affinity eased the transition of many Germans from one salvation doctrine (Communism) to the other, especially given that National Socialism presented itself as the more open and pragmatic ideology and was indeed capable of appealing to extremely diverse segments of German society. Civil strife and class antagonisms had spelled the end for the Weimar Republic. In its wake, the Nazi movement seduced its followers with the dream of a "third way." Nazi politicians promised the populace that justice would be restored and that they would fight against all forms of social "disintegration," whether liberal-capitalist or doctrinaire-Bolshevik in nature.

IN CONTRAST to the Germany of 1939, that of 1914 could look back on three successful wars. Waged between 1864 and 1871, they coincided with Prussian chancellor Otto von Bismarck's successful creation of an imperial German nation-state. Forty years of peace followed, bringing economic growth and bourgeois prosperity. At the beginning of World War I, German warehouses were full with stockpiled necessities valued at about 40 billion reichsmarks. In 1940, Germany possessed only 5 billion reichsmarks in available reserves in case of a blockade, and the purchasing power of the reichsmark was dramatically lower than in 1914. Furthermore, while on the eve of World War I the Reichsbank could draw on holdings of 1.4 billion marks to procure supplies from neutral countries and the value of its gold reserves was 2.5 billion marks, Germany's public and clandestine gold reserves on September 1, 1939, amounted to only around 500 million reichsmarks.[50]

Yet although Germany was in better fiscal shape at the start of the First World War than at the beginning of the Second, World War II proved to be better financed. From September 1939 to September 1944, 50 percent of war expenditures (considered a golden ratio) were covered by existing revenues. From 1914 to 1918 that figure was only 13.1 percent. "Floating debts," which were paid by printing more money, covered 24.8 percent of expenditures, while the remaining 62.1 percent were financed via long-term war bonds bought by the German people. The nine series of war bonds issued between 1914 and 1918 brought in 98.2 billion marks. By comparison, Great Britain covered 28 percent of its costs in World War I with tax receipts.[51]

Germany's difficulty in raising revenues between 1914 and 1918 was not just a failure of political will. It was caused primarily by the fact that the individual states within imperial Germany retained most of the control over the tax system. The imperial government lacked its own financial administration. In 1913, the gross national product totaled 40 billion marks, from which the imperial government was able to raise only 2.3 billion in taxes. Three-quarters of that sum went for military expenditures. By today's standards, the proportion of state revenues relative to GNP appears laughably tiny. Wilhelmine Germany was hardly the centrally organized colossus it is often depicted as.[52]

The wartime truce declared by Germany's political parties in 1914 prevented any serious debate about how the state could bolster its tax revenues. Alone among the leading parties, the Social Democrats called for levies on war-related profits. But they were outnumbered. The only remaining option was to incur long-term debt in the form of war bonds. It wasn't until 1919, when the Weimar Republic created a centralized tax system as part of its overall finance reform, that the German state was able to increase—gradually but continually—the share of GNP it raised in taxes. The Weimar Republic thus set a precedent that allowed the Hitler regime, during World War II, to collect taxes in amounts that scholars agree would have been dismissed as utterly unworkable in 1914.[53]

Along with requiring deficit spending, both world wars took a heavy toll on Germany's economic infrastructure. Commodity reserves were used up; machinery, buildings, industrial facilities, and means of transportation were left in need of repair; and forests and arable land were badly depleted. Between 1914 and 1918, the average German's standard of living declined by almost 65 percent, with the majority of the populace hovering just above the minimum required for survival. That decline was viewed by financial strategists in the Third Reich as "deeply unsettling." In 1941, one young economist wrote: "History has shown us that once this level of deprivation has been reached, the people can bear no more. The collapse of the home front was the price paid for shoring up the front lines abroad." But in contrast to their experience in World War I, the author hastened to add, the citizens of the Third Reich had no reason to fear such a "deterioration of their standard of living."[54]

CHAPTER 2

The Accommodating Dictatorship

The Appearance of Economic Improvement

Upon taking power in 1933, Hitler promised, above all, to put Germany's 6 million unemployed back to work. He was able to achieve this goal within five years. In one twelve-month period alone, the number of jobless fell from more than 2.5 million people to 1,610,000.[1] Examined closely, however, the turnaround was largely an illusion. Wages and pensions stagnated at the paltry levels of the Depression. In 1928, the best economic year of the Weimar Republic, total wages paid in Germany amounted to 42.6 billion reichsmarks. In 1935 that figure was 31.8 billion. It took three more years before wages regained their previous level, and hourly and individual wages, as well as pensions, remained lower than in the 1920s.[2] Furthermore, annual revenues from agriculture in Nazi Germany lagged considerably behind those of 1928–29.[3]

The public's belief, however, that decisive authoritarian action had produced an economic recovery was enough to secure the National Socialist government the loyalty of the vast majority of Germans. By late 1933, after an initial wait-and-see period, most middle-class citizens were convinced. "Trust is growing," wrote Leipzig anatomist Hermann Voss. "We're coming to believe that there will be an economic upswing in Germany under this government."[4] In 1936, the Socialist Workers' Party smuggled

Willy Brandt, later chancellor of the Federal Republic, from Norwegian exile into Germany to gauge the mood of working people in Berlin. He characterized it as "neither euphorically nor especially proregime," but "definitely not antiregime."[5]

In a free plebiscite in 1935, despite the best efforts of antifascist activists, the people of the Saar region, claimed by both Germany and France, voted overwhelmingly to rejoin the German Reich. The reintroduction of compulsory military service and the remilitarization of the Rhineland—in violation of the Treaty of Versailles and the spirit of the Locarno Pact—followed quickly upon that vote. Meanwhile, the Wehrmacht was rapidly being rearmed with state-of-the-art weaponry. The regime in Berlin had officially abrogated the Treaty of Versailles in 1935, two years after withdrawing from the League of Nations. Both these moves had increased the government's popularity. In the eyes of the vast majority of Germans, they showed that the regime was willing to stand up to those who had burdened post–World War I Germany with the "lie of culpability" and "a shameful peace" and who had subjected the country to constant harassment and humiliation in the 1920s. The early years of Hitler's rule gave a desperate, belligerent, and self-destructive people satisfaction for perceived past affronts.

When Hitler assumed the daily business of running the government in 1933, the Depression had already bottomed out. It was the perfect moment for his financial experts to promote the incipient economic recovery. They increased the state's short-term debt in order to combat unemployment and to boost domestic spending. That move freed the state from welfare payments, which took money out of government coffers, and offered the promise of increased revenues in the near future.

Indeed, tax revenues increased by 25 percent, or 2 billion reichsmarks, between 1933 and 1935. At the same time, unemployment-related expenditures dropped by 1.8 billion. Viewed narrowly, some 3.8 billion reichsmarks' worth of public debt paid for itself in a relatively short period. The regime's policy of borrowing against future prosperity seemed to be literally paying off. Nazi propaganda trumpeted what it called a German financial miracle.[6] At the same time, respected economists began publishing essays with titles like "A Time of Exceptional Performance in Reich Public Finances."[7]

Yet with additional expenditures exceeding additional revenues by almost 300 percent, public debt increased in the first two years of the Nazi regime by 10.3 billion reichsmarks.[8] The only major tax increase enacted between 1933 and the beginning of World War II to cover the spiraling deficit was in the corporate income tax, which had been introduced nationally in 1920 under the Weimar Republic. In four stages between August 1936 and July 1939, the base rate of that tax was doubled from 20 to 40 percent. The hike was aimed particularly at corporate enterprises that profited from rearmament, and the government increased the taxable base for enterprises by reducing the possibility of tax depreciation.[9] By 1938, corporate tax revenues, which had amounted to 600 million reichsmarks in 1935, had increased to 2.4 billion marks, and the proportion of total state tax revenues they accounted for rose from 7 to 14 percent.[10] Though not nearly enough to close the budget gap, transferring the tax burden to corporations earned the leadership in Berlin considerable political capital, as the government keenly registered. The 1938 annual report of the Main Security Office, an organ of state surveillance, noted: "The increase in corporate income tax has made a favorable impression, especially on the working classes." This was interpreted as proof that the costs of rearmament should be financed "via a socially just sharing of the burden," in which "the huge profits of large corporations are duly taken into account."[11]

Populist social and tax policies benefited families. The income tax law of October 1934 dramatically raised the basic exemption, bettering the lot of low-income wage earners. But because the law stipulated that the tax reform should not lead to a decrease in government revenues, the shortfall had to be made up "by increasing the proportion of the burden on single people, married couples without children, and, in certain higher income brackets, couples with up to two children." Family and child tax credits, marriage loans, and home-furnishing and child-education allowances were among the measures with which the state tried to relieve the financial burden on parents and encourage Germans to have more children. Yet in absolute terms, the level of funding the regime devoted to such programs before 1941 was relatively low, amounting to just over 3 billion reichsmarks.[12]

BUT THERE was a budget crisis in the making. Between 1933 and mid-1939, the Third Reich spent at the very least 45 billion marks on the military, an astronomical sum for the time and more than three times the amount of total state revenues for the fiscal year 1937. Consequently, by August 1939 the national debt had reached 37.4 billion marks.[13] The reemployment of millions of jobless and the rearmament of German military forces had been financed by borrowing gigantic sums of money. Even Goebbels, who otherwise mocked the government's financial experts as narrow-minded misers, expressed concern in his diary about the exploding deficit.[14]

In January 1939, the directors of the Reichsbank sent a letter to Hitler, calling upon him to intervene:

> The unlimited expansion of state expenditures flouts every attempt to draw up an orderly budget. It has brought state finances, despite the drastic tightening of tax legislation, to the brink of collapse and threatens now to destabilize both the national bank and the currency. No financial recipes or systems—no matter how ingenious or well thought out—and no institutions or set of fiscal mechanisms can suffice to rein in the disastrous consequences of unbridled deficit spending on the currency. No national bank is capable of propping up the currency against the inflationary spending policies of the state.[15]

The authors of the letter had facilitated the state's early policy of deficit spending with a broad range of fiscal tricks, yet their warnings that it could not continue led only to the forced resignation of the bank's president, Hjalmar Schacht, along with a number of its directors. Walther Funk, who had already taken charge of the Economics Ministry from the insufficiently compliant Schacht, assumed the top position at the Reichsbank, while Emil Puhl, a gentlemanly but politically inexperienced currency specialist, became its managing vice president. In that capacity he was responsible, together with hundreds of highly qualified experts, for running the daily activities of the bank, whose scope soon encompassed all of occupied Europe. Puhl quickly became known for his occasional sarcasm about the competence of the Nazi government, but he served its interests well until 1945. To Puhl, a consummate economics professional, protecting the German currency was an end that justified any and all means.

In 1939, the regime needed an estimated 16.3 billion reichsmarks to cover civilian expenditures, while military outlays claimed 20.5 billion. An additional 3.3 billion marks of the total regular state revenues of between 17 and 18 billion marks went toward interest payments on past debts.[16] Carl Friedrich Goerdeler, later a leader of the anti-Hitler resistance, characterized the expenditures as "financial insanity." In a memorandum written on July 1, 1940, as Nazi Germany was celebrating its military triumph over France, he remarked dryly: "The Reich's finances are in shambles," adding that, if the war dragged on to the end of 1941, "three-fifths of annual revenues . . . will go to pay off past debt. That means that the Reich's indebtedness is already so great that our obligations can no longer be met by current revenues, and debt will now increase automatically on its own."[17]

Hitler bridged what he and his leadership knew to be a precarious financial situation with military adventures that had terrible consequences for millions of people. Dispossession, deportation, and mass murder became major sources of state income. In 1942, Deputy Finance Minister Reinhardt issued a blanket order: "The contributions that have been allocated to paying off the interest and principal on the national debt must henceforth be covered by *current* revenues earned from the economic exploitation of the eastern territories."[18] The Nazi regime required the constant military destabilization of the periphery in order to maintain the illusion of financial stability at the center of the Reich. "Gigantic arms and construction projects are already being planned," wrote Goerdeler in 1940. "The German people have been promised that they will receive comprehensive state care in their old age. With the increase in the territory under our control, we will get involved in even bigger construction and development plans."[19]

Aryanization for War

Another major source of stop-gap revenues to fund Hitler's popular tax and rearmament policies was Germany's—and later much of Europe's—Jewish population. By late 1937, civil servants in the Finance Ministry had pushed the state's credit limit as far as it could go. Forced to come up with ever more creative ways of refinancing the national debt, they turned their attention to property owned by German Jews, which was soon confiscated and added to the so-called *Volksvermögen*, or the collective assets of the German people. The ideologically charged concept of collective assets, which was by no means restricted to German society, implied the possibility of dispossessing those considered "alien" (*Volksfremden*) or "hostile" (*Volksfeinden*) to the ethnic mainstream.

Prior to 1937, Jewish civil servants, businesspeople, doctors, and white-collar employees had been the targets of discriminatory legislation. Many people lost their jobs, careers were ruined, flourishing businesses were forced into emergency liquidation, and Jewish participation in commercial life became subject to constant harassment in a variety of locally specific forms. All these measures were intended to convince Jews to leave Germany. Wherever finance and customs authorities could, they exploited the state-created plight of German Jews with punitive emigration levies and ever tighter restrictions on taking currency, stocks, stamps, jewelry, gold, silver, precious stones, artworks, and antiques out of the country. Meanwhile, private citizens were busy "Aryanizing" Jewish-owned businesses and real estate, buying them up in deals that were partially voluntary and partially forced by state-encouraged and societal terror. But up until late 1937 it would be incorrect to speak of a systematic dispossession of Germany's Jewish citizens. Jews retained control over their life insurance policies and stock portfolios, and they were still allowed to choose how to invest their money. What they faced was an increasingly well-organized though piecemeal state confiscation of assets, made worse by the willingness of tens of thousands of ordinary Germans to exploit the suffering of a disadvantaged minority.

Following the *Anschluss* of Austria in March 1938, the confiscation of

Jewish property progressed with furious rapidity. On March 19, Hitler's personal economic adviser, Wilhelm Keppler, was appointed Reich commissioner for Austrian affairs. That same day, Göring presented Keppler with three key tasks: exploiting Austrian natural resources, bringing wage and price levels under control, and Aryanizing Jewish-owned businesses. "The Aryanization of economic enterprises in Austria," Göring wrote, "will likely be required on an even larger scale than in the old Reich." Carrying out this process "quickly and professionally," Göring emphasized, would be crucial to the success of Germany's arms buildup.[20]

A glance at the general state of the Reich's finances in early 1938 shows that German armament programs were underwritten to a significant extent by 12 billion marks' worth of promissory notes. The notes were signed not by the government but by a fictional private enterprise, the Metallurgic Research Association, to conceal the extent of the debts the state was running up.[21] The trick was the brainchild of Hjalmar Schacht in his dual capacity as economics minister and Reichsbank president. The notes were scheduled to come due in 1939, and funds thus had to be allocated from the budget or borrowed to pay off the short-term obligations. At the same time, the Wehrmacht was demanding 11 billion reichsmarks from the 1939 budget for military expenditures. That overtaxed the capital market. To cover the Third Reich's running costs, the finance minister hastily began to issue treasury bonds, which, in turn, came due six months later.[22]

These sorts of tricks couldn't go on indefinitely. As a first step in getting the state out of its self-created financial jam, the government issued the edict of April 26, 1938, requiring Jews to declare all personal assets in excess of 5,000 reichsmarks to local tax authorities. This was to happen within six weeks, and at the very latest by June 30, although the date had to be moved back to July 31 because the government had difficulty delivering the necessary forms. The declarations allowed the state to monitor the investment and flow of Jewish-owned assets. A short time later, the chief legal adviser for the Ministry of Economics, Alf Krüger, characterized the edict as the "forerunner to a complete and definitive removal of Jews from the German economy."[23] Krüger divided the reported assets into different categories. The holdings of foreign Jews in Germany, as well as those of gentile spouses of German or stateless Jews, were declared "unassailable." But more than 7.1 billion reichsmarks in "seizable" assets remained. In the summer of 1938, Krüger reported that "according to official surveys" German and Austrian Jews "possessed wealth worth around 8 billion marks."[24] Apparently, that figure included either some of the "untouchable" assets or assets that fell under the 5,000 reichsmark limit.

Despite the size of these sums, German Jews in general were not particularly wealthy. In Hamburg, for example, only 16 percent of German Jews possessed assets that exceeded the limit. But even less-affluent Jews, like many other German citizens, contributed to pension plans and health, life, and disability insurance funds. If we assume that half the 700,000 Jews living in Germany and Austria in 1938 had claims to personal entitlements averaging 1,500 reichsmarks, more than a half billion marks in "Jewish entitlements" fell to the Aryanized social welfare state after forced emigration and deportation. The state could then use this money to reduce subsidies to social benefits programs or raise benefit levels for the German population.

Only two of the many paragraphs in the 1938 edict dealt with issues beyond the formalities of how Jews were to declare their assets. One empowered Göring to direct a four-year plan to "coordinate the integration of reportable assets with the needs of the German economy." The next paragraph laid out possible sanctions—expropriation of personal wealth and up to ten years' incarceration—that could be imposed if Jews tried to conceal their holdings. The edict required Jews to "voluntarily" submit to the Aryanization of their assets by tax authorities.[25] Simultaneously, in May 1938, the Economics Ministry issued the following policy statement: "The development of legislation concerning Jews will lead to increased efforts to emigrate." Subordinate authorities were instructed to "take prompt preemptive measures" with respect to Jewish wealth when they had reason to believe Jews were preparing to leave the country.[26] As the Dutch historian A. J. van der Leeuw has pointed out, this instruction "laid the groundwork so that the largest possible proportion of Jewish-owned assets would flow into the state's coffers."[27]

Three days after the edict was issued, on April 29, 1938, Göring called a conference of government ministers. The topic under discussion was how to achieve "the definitive removal of Jews from economic life," with the goal of "transforming Jewish wealth in Germany into assets that will deny [the Jews] any economic influence." In practice, this somewhat cryptic formulation meant that Jews would be forced to exchange most of their assets for government stocks and bonds. The conference participants hoped that this initiative would play well abroad since German Jews would be, at least on paper, compensated for lost assets—"in the form best suited to the purpose, the issuing of government bonds."[28]

Those responsible for the finances of the Third Reich saw a number of advantages in the compulsory exchange of Jewish-owned personal assets for government securities. In mid-June 1938, the government was forced to redeem 465 million reichsmarks of its own bonds to prevent the currency from plummeting. With such emergency interventions, which entailed nothing more than the central bank's printing more money to cover the state's exorbitant debts, the Finance Ministry hoped to conceal Germany's precarious financial situation from global markets. Officials also hoped the buyback would allow them to issue new bonds in the future, "which would otherwise be difficult and perhaps completely impossible." On September 1, 1938, Schwerin von Krosigk informed the Führer that within the month state coffers would run dry. Issuing more bonds, von Krosigk insisted, was not an option, since potential investors favored tangible assets. "We are heading for a grave financial crisis," von Krosigk warned. "The initial signs of it have already attracted attention abroad to the weakness of our economy and have led to a worrisome loss of confidence at home."[29]

With Germany's financial situation worsening by the day, the Nazi leadership in Berlin was keen to forge ahead with its annexation of Czechoslovakia and its domestic pogroms against Jews. The state treasury needed money. Despite various accounting tricks, the government was just barely avoiding bankruptcy; if nothing was done, Germany's financial problems would quickly be laid bare. The only hope was to go on the offensive.

Looking back a few days after the anti-Jewish pogroms of November 9–10, 1938, Göring recalled the discussions of "removing the Jews from the economy, entering them into the ledger sheet, and letting them live on the interest." Göring was referring to the interest on the government bonds for which Jews had been forced to exchange their property: "The Jew is being driven from the economy and is surrendering his economic assets to the state. In return he is being compensated. His compensation is noted in the ledger sheet and accrues a certain amount of interest. That is what he has to live on."[30] The assets of Germany's Jews, converted into government bonds, would provide the country's war chest with a cushion of several billion reichsmarks. In contrast to the seizing of church property during the French Revolution, the Foreign Office noted in a communiqué to its embassy staff abroad entitled "The Jewish Question as a Factor in Foreign Relations for the Year 1938," compensation was being provided for the confiscated wealth: "The Jew whose assets have been expropriated receives imperial bonds bearing interest, to which he then has access."[31]

In a speech to gauleiters on December 6, 1938, Göring emphasized the connection between Germany's arms buildup and the nationalization of Jewish-owned property. Individual businesses, warehouse stocks, furnishings, and works of art, he told them, were to be sold off locally. An oil painting seized from a Jewish household in Stuttgart, for example, should preferably be offered for sale to a Stuttgart museum. The same procedure applied to cars, which were to be placed on the local market at the going price. But Göring hastened to add that the proceeds from the sale of businesses, paintings, or cars, whether "in Munich or Nuremberg, in Stuttgart, Karlsruhe, or Hamburg," belonged not to the cities, local states, or districts but "exclusively to the Reich central government."

Disavowing any interest in the Jewish question, Göring explained why he was getting so deeply involved: "I know no other way to keep my Four-Year Plan and the Germany economy going." He cautioned the gauleiters against confiscating Jewish-owned belongings for their own personal gain: "The proceeds from Aryanization are to go solely and exclusively to the Reich. That means to its administrator, the finance minister, and to no one else. Only in this way is it possible to carry out the Führer's rearmament program." Interior Minister Wilhelm Frick was equally clear in warning local authorities and personal profiteers: "Assets currently in Jewish hands are to be regarded as the property of the German people. Any destruction of or decrease in their value means a decrease in the collective assets of the German people."[32] An edict issued by Göring that month further decreed that the proceeds from the expulsion of Jews from the German economy would go exclusively to the Reich.[33] The pogroms of November 9–10, 1938, accelerated the process of turning what had been a vague policy statement into reality. Backing fiscal policy with terror made it possible to implement the long-standing idea—among bureaucrats at the Reichsbank, the Finance Ministry, and elsewhere—of forcing Jews to convert a sizeable proportion of their assets into government bonds.

This process served as the model for ambitious Aryanizers throughout Europe. Citizens were soon able to purchase confiscated Jewish property not just in Stuttgart but in Prague, Amsterdam, and Paris. Aryanized assets were usually sold off to residents by local authorities, and most of the proceeds were directed, in accordance with the 1938 model, into German state coffers.

The intense interest of finance experts in having Jewish assets converted into government bonds is evident in the debate over the atonement payment of one billion reichsmarks levied on German Jews on November 12, 1938, in the immediate wake of the pogroms. To raise this sum, Jews would clearly have to sell off holdings, including real estate, stocks, and even government-issued bonds. That prospect drew protests from Reichsbank board member Karl Blessing, who feared "that next week the Jews will begin to sell off hundreds of thousands of Reich bonds to procure the necessary funds." The levy would be counterproductive, he argued, since such a mass sale would either undermine the value of future bond issues or compel the finance minister to buy back bonds to protect their credibility. Blessing's objections were answered by a prohibition against the Jews' selling off their bonds.[34]

GÖRING HAD a second problem in 1938. Along with figuring out how the government could secure credit, preferably on a long-term basis, he also needed hard currency to import raw materials for the arms buildup and foodstuffs to meet both Germany's immediate and future requirements, including stores of grain for the impending war. Thus, on July 25, six days before the extended submission deadline, Göring instructed tax authorities to scour Jewish asset declaration forms "with maximum haste" for foreign securities. The holders of these securities were to be ordered "to offer and, if asked, sell them" to the Reichsbank "within a week."[35] Here, too, Jews were to receive nominal compensation in the form of government bonds. A few days later Hans Fischböck, the minister responsible for economic affairs in what had been Austria, requested that a Reichsbank manager be assigned to the currency division of the Jewish Emigration Bureau, an agency created by Adolf Eichmann to help force Jews to leave the country.[36]

The atonement payment increased state revenues by 6 percent. The money was earmarked to help the government bridge the acute financial shortfall. Earlier that year Schwerin von Krosigk had threatened to freeze expenditures, halt new construction projects, and decrease already allocated budgets to prevent state finances from spiraling out of control. He rallied those affected by the potential cutbacks by quoting Göring: "Solving the problems that face us will be easier if we act as quickly and decisively as possible to ensure the vitality of our nation against all eventualities."

Walther Bayrhoffer, the Finance Ministry representative within the Reichsbank leadership, warned in his annual report for 1938 that the state of government finances in November was "catastrophic." "In terms of cash flow," he wrote, "there is a deficit of 2 billion reichsmarks. There is an immediate danger that the Reich won't be able to pay its debts."[37] This was precisely the juncture at which the atonement payment was ordered. The financial crunch also spurred the government to insist that the banks involved in "appropriately" selling off Jewish-owned stocks provide the Reich with emergency credit. The desperate need for funds prompted Alf Krüger, the official responsible for Jewish affairs at the Economics Ministry, to focus on liquid assets in his calculations of reported Jewish wealth. Such assets—which excluded real estate and business assets—totaled 4.8 billion reichsmarks and could be easily confiscated.[38] On November 18, 1938, a Foreign Office representative jotted down the following bullet points during a speech Göring gave there: "Reich's finances in extremely critical condition. Short-term relief firstly from the billion demanded of Jews and also state profits from Aryanization of Jewish businesses."[39]

The specifics as to how Jews were to make the atonement payment quickly followed. In a decree on November 21, 1938, the finance minister ordered all German Jews required to declare their assets under the 5,000 reichsmark rule to hand over 20 percent of all holdings. "Without receiving special notification," they were to pay local tax authorities in four installments, on December 15, 1938, and the fifteenth of February, May, and August 1939.[40] The resulting 1.1 billion reichsmarks that flowed into the state coffers were recorded as "additional revenues." Ordinary income for the fiscal year 1938–39 amounted to some 17 billion reichsmarks. Receipts from the Jewish emigration tax and other anti-Jewish discrimination measures can be conservatively calculated at more than 500 million reichsmarks. In sum, then, at least 9 percent of the operating revenues in the Nazis' final prewar state budget—almost 1.5 billion reichsmarks—came from the proceeds of Aryanization. Compulsory exchanges of currency and Jewish-owned stocks for state bonds, which never appeared on the Finance Ministry's books, added to the total. The emigration tax alone brought in around one billion marks between 1933 and 1945—the highest annual amount being 342,621,000 marks in the fiscal year 1938–39, the year in which state-sponsored pogroms led the greatest number of German Jews to flee the country.[41]

Considering what a state today could do with a 9 percent increase in revenue that did not involve increasing the tax burden on its "native" citizenry, we can imagine what a relief the atonement payment and the other discriminatory financial measures against Jewish Germans must have been for the Third Reich's bookkeepers. The measures also seem to have gone down well with ordinary taxpayers. The *Deutsche Steuer-Zeitung*, a leading tax periodical, reported: "The revenues of the excise tax levied on Jews are going exclusively to the Reich, which will devote them to its general tasks and, in that sense, to the benefit of the German people."[42] The Security Service, perhaps overstating things, noted that, in contrast to the pogroms, the "atonement payment met with approval throughout the populace."[43]

After the war, Schwerin von Krosigk would write in his memoirs: "I personally signed off on the atonement payment. But that was where I drew the line."[44] The untruth of that statement is evident in the fact that once the war had begun, Schwerin von Krosigk himself signed a second decree raising the level of personal assets affluent Jews were required to hand over to the state from 20 to 25 percent. The additional 5 percent was payable within four weeks and brought the revenue from the atonement payment to 1,126,612,495 reichsmarks. (Other sources put the total figure at approximately 1.2 billion.)[45]* The exact percentage of the atonement payment was kept flexible to ensure that Göring's financial goals were met. In the summer of 1951, a civil servant in the Federal Republic Finance Ministry testified to the American occupation forces: "As a matter of principle, the percentage of contributions was supposed to be elevated until the full amount of the contribution reached one billion marks. If *the individual Jew* falsely reported his assets or refused to pay all or any part of his contribution, the burden was not transferred to the German people but was left *to the Jews among themselves.*"[46]

GERMANY'S MAJOR commercial banks played a crucial role in helping the government master its dire financial straits and maintain the programs that had made it so popular. On November 14, 1938, the credit division of the Economics Ministry invited the boards of directors of the five biggest Berlin banks—Deutsche Bank, Dresdner Bank, Commerzbank, Reichskredit Gesellschaft, and Berliner Handelsgesellschaft—to a meeting. According to the protocol, the participants discussed Göring's decision "to transfer the entirety of Jewish property and material assets from Jewish hands to state and later, perhaps, private ownership."

---

*In *The Wages of Destruction*, which was published as this book went to press, economic historian Adam Tooze objects that for the fiscal year 1938–39 additional revenues from the dispossession of Jews represented only 5 percent—and not, as I assert, 9 percent—of the total budget. Tooze deems my calculations "obscure" because the billion reichsmarks raised by the atonement payment were paid only gradually (*Wages*, p. 279, n. 133); as discussed above, the payments were made in four quarterly installments. Yet at the same time, citing my book as his source, Tooze acknowledges that the Reich finance minister borrowed a billion marks from a consortium of large banks as an advance on the atonement payment. The finance minister thus immediately had the total amount at his disposal. This is why I have assigned the sum of one billion reichsmarks to the fiscal year 1938–39 (see Tooze, *Wages*, pp. 278–79, notes 127, 133). For further discussion, see "A Note on Calculations" on page 327.

The participants agreed that the state could raise an additional 5 billion reichsmarks, depending on market conditions, from the atonement payment and other anti-Semitic measures to be taken in the future. But the bankers also foresaw a short-term problem. Banks were no longer issuing credit to German Jews because in the wake of political discrimination they had become "bad risks." Thus, Jews would be forced to sell stocks, jewelry, and property to raise their shares of the mandatory payment, and that made the bankers nervous since "the headlong rush to sell off " 1.5 billion reichsmarks' worth of stocks could well cause a "crash in the securities market." To head off the problem, the bankers argued that groups of stocks should be sold off slowly and cautiously. "To avoid unnecessary effort and to benefit the Reich," they proposed "freezing the accumulating securities at the institutions of deposit, then selling them off gradually and in methodical fashion, according to the state of the capital market and in the interests of the Reich's financial administration."

The Third Reich, however, was broke. To ease that situation, the banks offered "to provide the Reich financial administration with a line of credit secured by Jewish securities to be acquired in the future; the terms could be agreed upon easily."[47] Their offer was eagerly accepted. After the meeting, the government required that all Jewish-owned securities be placed into a "safekeeping" account and thus be frozen.[48] This guaranteed that stock values would be protected and that bonds issued by the Third Reich would be kept off the market.

The bank directors were not the ones doing the actual plundering here, but they acted as accessories, helping maximize the efficiency of the dispossession campaign. They were, in effect, fencing stolen goods by turning them into available cash. They were also acting in their self-interest. Deutsche Bank, for example, charged its Jewish customers a service commission of .5 percent, plus an administration fee, on all transactions. In the polite language of banking, the terms of contract read: "For services rendered in conjunction with the payments of contributions, we hereby present our clients, in this case Jewish holders of safekeeping accounts, with a bill for 1/2% of the total sum involved and no less than 1 reichsmark per entry."[49] The secondary exchange of temporarily nationalized securities meant more business, and the bank possessed a first-purchase option. Most of the proceeds from such transactions, however, benefited the state's coffers and reduced the burdens that would otherwise have had to be borne by German taxpayers. The same was true for private life insurance policies, the overwhelming majority of which the Finance Ministry cashed in at the precontracted rates.

The bank, acting as a financial custodian with a mandate from the state, managed the securities in the interests of the Reich and to the disadvantage of its former customers. Periodically, it passed the assets on to the Prussian State Bank or the Reichsbank, which sold them off. Those two financial institutions reported the proceeds of such sales on a form entitled "Trade-In of Securities for the Levy on Jewish Assets," which was submitted to the senior government adviser within the Finance Ministry. The ministry then transferred the corresponding sum of money into an advance receipts account, "Jewish Assets Tax, Security Division," maintained by the Main Accounting Office. This procedure was adhered to up until the final days of Nazi rule.[50] With the stock market rising until autumn 1941, revenues for the Reich also rose—at one point by more than 200 percent.[51] In addition, the Reichsbank later sold off securities on stock markets in occupied countries such as France.[52]

Tax Breaks for the Masses

The confiscation of the assets both of Jews in Germany and, during the war, of foreign nationals was necessary because the Nazi leadership desperately wanted to avoid any broad-based tax hikes—the usual means for financing massive military activity. In late 1937 an assistant to Göring outlined a series of tax increases that would be required in the event of war: income and payroll taxes would rise by 50 percent and corporate income tax by 66⅔ percent, while other forms of earned income would be subjected to an 8 percent hike. Rates for additional income would increase by 30 to 100 percent, and the wealth tax would jump 200 percent.[53] Economists who had been studying the issue since 1936 concluded that "a greater involvement of the working classes via a 50 percent hike in wage taxes would be reasonable," since "all segments of the populace would be burdened in proportion to their incomes."[54]

In the spring of 1939, the financial preparations for war took concrete form. On May 30, a variety of suggestions were put forward, and the Finance Ministry promised to work them up into a coherent set of proposals within ten days. One state secretary, whose authority extended to general economic affairs, had an intriguing idea. He suggested using "anticipated postwar revenues as a way of financing wartime expenditures." An accompanying position paper explained that doing so would make it unnecessary to cover the national debt during wartime. The Finance Ministry proposed levying an additional 25 percent tax on all "natural" persons and all profits earned by corporate entities. That would increase revenues from wage and income taxes by 5 billion and corporate tax revenues by 1.7 billion reichsmarks. The Reichsbank endorsed the proposal.[55] But as of late May, the political leadership had already come to favor an alternate course, the one that would eventually prevail: "In order to cover the costs of the Wehrmacht, we must enlist the economic potential of the Protectorate of Bohemia and Moravia and those territories to be conquered in the course of the offensive."[56]

One Reich strategy, then, was to shift responsibility for funding the Nazi war machine to the citizens of conquered lands—while continuing to spare the majority of its own populace any increased tax burden. Repeatedly over the course of the spring and summer of 1939, civil servants tried to raise tax rates, only to find themselves undercut by the Nazi leadership, which intervened to protect lower- and middle-income Germans. This procedural give-and-take is evident in the work of the Ministerial Council for the Defense of the Reich, which was formed on August 30, 1939, to draw up a blueprint for wartime taxation. Five days later it published a draft of the Wartime Economy Ordinance (*Kriegswirtschaftsordnung*, or KWVO).[57] Paragraph 22 of the ordinance imposed an additional wartime tax of 50 percent on all wages, but it also promptly excluded all but the wealthiest Germans, those with annual incomes over 2,400 reichsmarks. In practice that exempted 70 percent of the German population. An additional 26 percent—those earning between 2,400 and 6,000 marks annually, incurred only minor additional charges.[58] In the end only 4 percent of the population paid the full 50 percent surcharge.[59]

Significantly, the KWVO rejected the proposed across-the-board surcharge of 50, and later 25, percent on general income tax.[60] Broadly targeted taxes were discarded in favor of a system that placed major burdens only on Germany's highest earners, while moderately affecting the next wealthiest 25 percent of society. The shift in policy conformed to Hitler's 1935 directive that "upper-level incomes should be limited during war . . . either through the compulsory purchase of war bonds or a progressively graduated tax on profits."[61]

Nazi propaganda promoted the KWVO as ensuring that "the burden of war was justly distributed and spending power held in check."[62] The German leadership created and maintained a kind of wartime socialism aimed at attracting the loyalty of ordinary citizens. "We have to prevent individuals from profiting," wrote economist Jens Jessen, "while others are sacrificing their lives."[63] Hitler formulated the matter in similar terms: "When the soldier is fighting on the front, no one should be profiting from war. When the soldier is dying on the front, no one at home should be shirking his duty."[64]

Because the KWVO temporarily suspended extra pay for overtime and for night, Sunday, and holiday labor, the take-home income of working-class Germans decreased at the onset of the war.[65] But employers were not the ones who profited: they were required to pay an equivalent sum to the state. Through this regulation, the state took the relatively insignificant total sum of 270 million reichsmarks from the pockets of the working classes.[66] Even a 20 percent hike in taxes on tobacco, spirits, beer, and sparkling wine, which was put in place on September 4, 1939, did not represent a significant burden.[67] These indirect war taxes—the only consumer tax increases imposed by the Nazis—were raised to 50 percent in November 1941.[68] But even then the regime was careful to formulate its regulations so as not to breed popular discontent. For example, in the beer-loving "southern German consumer regions," the tax was kept at 50 reichsmarks per 100 liters, while it was raised to 70 reichsmarks elsewhere. In 1940, the surcharge on a liter of beer (that "mood enhancer," as Goebbels called it) was

14 reichspfennigs in Hamburg and Dresden, compared with only 10 in Munich and Vienna—30 percent less. A tax on wine was never instituted for fear that it would "directly hurt winemakers, whose general economic situation is unfavorable."[69]

Many workers found the loss of overtime compensation a hardship, and the Reich Defense Council reinstated it on November 15, 1939, for work in excess of ten hours a day. Night, Sunday, and holiday pay was also restored.[70] The general prohibition on vacations was revoked, while the ban on extra pay for nine- and ten-hour workdays remained in place. Extra pay did not count toward the wartime surcharge's personal exemption and was taxed at the normal income tax rate.[71]

Many bureaucrats were upset at the loss of income. Economists at the council proposed lowering the annual deductible for the wartime surcharge from 2,400 to 1,800 reichsmarks. Their aim was to restrict consumer spending, but the proposal was rejected by the party hierarchy "on political grounds."[72] The financial experts argued "that the only truly effective means of redirecting spending power lies in increased appropriation of private income for political consumption, i.e., higher taxation." Schwerin von Krosigk voiced his support: "There will be grumbling, but the people will understand."[73] That enraged Goebbels, who railed against the "sterile bureaucrats" in the Finance Ministry for lacking the stuff of "creative statesmen." He dubbed their efforts to strike "at the very subsistence" of the German people "truly pathetic!"[74]

By June 1940, the general consensus among economists was that there was "no chance whatsoever" of getting "any tax measures past Field Marshal Göring or the Führer."[75] On the contrary, bucking all wartime financial logic, the political leadership reinstituted overtime pay for nine- and ten-hour workdays in August 1940. This was a purely populist move taken without any outside pressure. In addition, in December 1940, Armaments Minister Fritz Todt succeeded in declaring income derived from overtime, night, Sunday, and holiday labor exempt from tax and social benefits contributions.[76] As a result, take-home pay rose significantly. Moreover, just in time for the holidays, Christmas bonuses were also declared exempt from the war tax.

The top officials in the Finance Ministry were normally too realistic to approve such handouts. But in the wake of Germany's triumph over France, they convinced themselves that they could afford to be generous, "provided," as Deputy Finance Minister Fritz Reinhardt wrote to his colleagues, "the war ends in 1940." Reinhardt continued: "It will surely make a strong public impression in Germany and abroad if we can do without war taxes in a gigantic war such as this."[77]

The government treated the interests of German farmers with similar benevolence. For Reichsbank director Bernhard Benning, agriculture represented "a special tax oasis," the only branch of the economy that throughout the war "has been given special favors in price-control and tax policies." Agricultural tax revenues remained constant at 700 to 800 million reichsmarks during the war years, "while the state," according to Benning, "simultaneously handed out billions in price subsidies to farmers." Indeed, the prices producers were paid for milk and potatoes were raised by 25 to 35 percent in the course of the war.[78] In 1943, German farmers possessed more than 10 billion reichsmarks in liquid assets held by banks and an even larger amount of ready cash. Their financial security resulted from the preferential treatment given farmers in the KWVO. As early as December 1939, a high-ranking financial administrator complained that the privileging of farmers "is in many cases so grotesque that it can scarcely be kept secret from the rest of the populace, segments of which are being called on to make real sacrifices. To put the matter mildly, it infuriates other people."[79]

In 1941, for reasons similar to the ones motivating tax breaks for farmers, the government raised pensions. The increase was intended both to compensate for the slight inflation during the war and to make up for some of the emergency pension cutbacks imposed from 1930 to 1932. The biggest beneficiaries were small-time pensioners, who received a lump sum rather than a percentage-based hike. Retirees enjoyed an additional 6 reichsmarks per month, while pensioners' widows were given 5, and their orphaned children 4. That represented an average increase of 15 percent. The new pension law also relaxed standards for eligibility. Recipients no longer had to prove, for example, that they or their spouse or parent had paid in contributions during the economic chaos that followed World War I. The pension reform produced, at least in the short term, "visible satisfaction and great joy" among retirees. Three months' worth of arrears were paid out in a single installment, increasing support for the Führer among a group of Germans who frequently held "the opinion that National Socialism had no time for the elderly and physically weak and wanted them to die off quickly."[80]

The 1941 pension reform also introduced mandatory health insurance, the lack of which had been considered a "persistent societal shortcoming threatening the welfare of pensioners." Monthly contributions were set at one reichsmark with exemptions for widows and orphans.[81] Previously, retirees had had to apply for state relief assistance or take out private insurance, which few of them did. The new regulations took effect in August and November 1941.

But not all efforts to expand social programs met with equal success. A further pension reform suggested by the Labor Ministry, for example, which would have gone much further than that of 1941, was blocked by opposition from the finance minister. The proposition by Goebbels in 1944 to raise benefits and lower bureaucratic costs by generally paying lump-sum pensions also ran into resistance.[82] In 1940, the German Labor Front failed to push through a radical reform that would have doubled pension levels overnight and pegged them to the cost of living. The front had hoped to rein in consumer spending and increase its own popularity by providing prosperous retirements for all. But because the reform would have required substantial increases in contributions, the Nazi leadership feared that it would unduly burden average income earners. The finance minister added that wartime sacrifices should not be tied to "promises that no one knows whether we can keep." "The people," he argued, "would view them as a 'populist ploy' rather than a serious pledge for the future."[83]

Significantly, the will to achieve social reform was strongest among those leaders within the Nazi Party who were also the most actively involved in pushing forward the agenda of ethnic genocide. The idea of a huge pension increase in 1944 was budgetary insanity. Yet some within the Nazi hierarchy supported it for the "psychological dividends it would pay among our working ethnic comrades [*Volksgenossen*]." They called for "blue- and white-collar workers to be put on equal footing" to give them a preliminary taste of the harmonious future to come, which would be achieved through a "generous reform of the social welfare state in the interest of working people." The finance minister objected, as did the economics minister, the Reich Chancellery minister, and the Reich's plenipotentiary for the employment of labor. But they had powerful opponents: Martin Bormann, Albert Speer, Heinrich Himmler, and Food and Agriculture Minister Herbert Backe voted in favor of the budget-busting proposal.[84] (Goebbels, Göring, Hitler, and the gauleiters never got involved in the debate.)

On the other hand, the German Labor Front was able to shoot down a planned third hike in tobacco taxes, noting with satisfaction that it had previously prevented further increases in beer, mineral water, and coal taxes.[85] In spring 1943, the finance minister failed to push through a proposed 25 percent tax surcharge on lower-income workers, who thanks to the Nazis' wealth redistribution policies were now comparatively well-off. Göring dismissed the surcharge proposal categorically, and Hitler declined to intervene, citing "demands placed on my time by urgent military matters."[86]

In an internal memo on March 3, 1943, Martin Bormann, the head of the Party Chancellery, noted: "The Führer emphasized that (1) it would be best to do without tax increases during the war and instead to impose levies on wartime profits afterward, (2) if taxes must be raised during the war, then only *income tax*, maintaining a deductible of 6,000 marks, (3) limiting spending power: the Führer repeatedly stressed that wealthy people's income has little effect on purchasing power. The only prices that rise are those on art objects and the like, and that is completely harmless. The spending power of the broad masses is what's important! It is directed toward procuring everyday necessities: food, clothing, etc."[87] Two weeks later, the writer Fritz Nonnenbruch wrote a lead article in the main Nazi newspaper, the *Völkischer Beobachter*, opposing the tax hike planned by the Finance Ministry on the grounds that "doubts have to be raised,

particularly from a National Socialist standpoint, about increasing taxation on incomes under 5,000 to 6,000 reichsmarks."

The policies of socially equitable, progressive taxation achieved the desired results. "The economic situation of the populace is positive," wrote one
leading Frankfurt court official in March 1943. "People meet their financial
obligations, mortgages are paid off, and court-ordered repossessions are on
the decline. The civil divisions of municipal courts are increasingly involved
in cases between tenants and landlords and in support claims. Bailiffs are
mostly involved in estimating the value of household effects."[88] The author
of the report also described how the household belongings of deported
Jews were used to supplement compensation payments to those who had
lost their homes in Allied bombing raids—and suggested that the value of
personal effects destroyed in the aerial bombardments, and not just the
homes themselves, should be included in rough loss estimates.

By 1943, a resigned Bernhard Benning was forced to acknowledge
that in planning a war economy "no energetic measures can be taken in
the lower-income brackets, which would be of particular interest to exploit [as revenue sources]."[89] Reich economists wanted to tax working-
class Germans to curb excess consumer spending and inflation and to
decelerate the pace at which war-related state debt was growing. In the
later phase of the war, Schwerin von Krosigk sarcastically characterized
his own suggested tax hikes, motivated by financial realism, as "tax Bolshevism."[90] He was repeatedly told by intimates of Hitler's and by the
Führer himself that "unfortunately it was too late" for that. Had he initiated such measures "immediately after the war began or just after France
was defeated," his rivals hypocritically informed him, "everything would
have been fine—but the auspicious moment has now passed for good."[91]

By contrast, in May 1943, Joseph Goebbels noted with satisfaction that
new tax regulations had been postponed indefinitely.[92] Nonetheless, he
took the precaution of insisting a short time later that "the Führer [to-
gether with the head of the German Labor Front, Robert Ley] be kept
apprised of the mass psychological implications of taxation plans." The
people, he wrote, "cannot now accept a new burden (Stalingrad—Tunis—
reduction in meat rations—aerial attacks—evacuation)." Under pressure

from the party leadership, Deputy Finance Minister Reinhardt turned against von Krosigk, his superior, demanding that discussion of tax increases had to cease "since it is causing unrest among the populace." In light of "the current ebb in the public mood," Reinhardt wrote, all measures "that could further worsen morale" were to be avoided.[93]

With the fall of Mussolini in the summer of 1943 and the Italian government's declaration of war on Nazi Germany that October, Goebbels called for urgent measures to prevent the German populace from rising up against the regime. "National Socialism," he wrote, "must undergo renewal. We have to bind ourselves more socialistically than ever before to the people. The people must be convinced that we are their fair and generous administrators."[94] That effort was already being made. In late September, the chief of the Reich Chancellery, Hans Lammers, informed the finance minister that Hitler and Göring believed a tax increase "would be best avoided given the current situation."[95] By the end of the year, von Krosigk commented dryly: "One can always find reasons tax increases aren't right. In the spring or after a triumph, the argument is made that we shouldn't jeopardize the upsurge in public sentiment that has arisen from the season or from delight at victory. In fall or after military setbacks, it's that the public mood shouldn't be depressed any further than it already is, with winter approaching or the bad news arriving from the front."[96] At a 1944 conference of finance experts, Benning exclaimed in frustration: "Let me remind you that since the beginning of the war incomes below 3,000 reichsmarks have never even been officially recorded."

In mid-1944, the finance minister believed he had persuaded Hitler to approve a number of indirect tax measures that had been in the planning stages for about a year and a half. They included higher duties on tobacco products and spirits as well as new taxes on movie and rail tickets. Everyday necessities were explicitly declared off-limits.[97] Lammers called on the minister to present a proposal for increasing tax revenues by an additional 3.4 billion reichsmarks. But Hitler put off making a decision for several weeks, only to inform the Finance Ministry that such measures were unworkable in light of the military situation. Although the financial state of the Third Reich drastically deteriorated in the latter half of 1944,

Goebbels continued to threaten the Finance Ministry with a supplementary increase in state pensions. Von Krosigk's suggestion that such an increase could be funded by levying a "general solidarity contribution," which could be justified by the need to take care of wounded war veterans, met with a cool rejection from the propaganda minister.[98]

In February 1945, after military defeats had sealed off nearly all of Germany's foreign sources of revenue, von Krosigk made one final attempt at increasing taxes. Even Goebbels seemed receptive, writing in his diary, "We need to get our feet back on the ground on the money issue." But he later changed his mind. With the Red Army crossing the Oder River and American troops advancing on Würzburg, Goebbels expressed the collective unwillingness of the Nazi leadership to risk alienating the German people. "Krosigk has again submitted his plan for tax reform," he wrote. "His draft is too inequitable for me. It's based mainly on excise taxes. Income taxes, on the other hand, aren't given any consideration. But excise taxes almost exclusively affect the broad masses and for that reason are very unpopular. They represent a grave injustice that we cannot afford at the present juncture."[99]

Tax Rigor for the Bourgeoisie

The extreme populism of Nazi Germany's wartime tax policies is underscored by the government's readiness to tax business and the country's wealthy. Under the requirements of the KWVO, German companies were compelled as of September 1939 to hand over all additional war-related profits to the state. Various loopholes, though, basically rendered these statutes ineffective until 1941, as evidenced by the fact that most companies did not need to apply for loans to finance war-related expansions of their production capacity. The Nazi leadership realized it had to act quickly if it hoped to collect the lost revenues.

On January 1, 1941, responsibility for enforcing the KWVO's provisions on corporate taxation was shifted from the Price Control Commissioner's Office to the Finance Ministry. Administrators there drastically reduced the exemptions that companies were allowed to claim in calculating their profits. The goal was to achieve "more thorough taxation of so-called anonymous capital [a pejorative term for investment funds] and of the tremendously increased income occasioned by the war." The change had its desired effect—the number of companies applying for credit shot up in 1942.

The economics division of the Reichsbank noticed the growing demand for loans and traced it to the "increasing appropriation of wartime profits." In another blow to businesses, the Wehrmacht reduced its advance payments for armaments and increasingly took its time settling its bills.[100] The effect was gradual. Wartime profits, which had reached 750 million reichsmarks in the fiscal year 1941–42 and 1.3 billion in 1942–43, declined only a few percentage points the following year.[101] In response to isolated complaints from manufacturers about overtaxation, the government set a cap for individual companies of 8 percent of total corporate income in 1943.[102]

Businesses suffered more serious effects from the wartime surcharge on corporate taxes instituted in mid-1941. Applying to all corporations with annual returns of more than 50,000 reichsmarks, the surcharge effectively raised the tax on profits, which had already been hiked to 40 percent before the war, to 50 percent.[103] On January 1, 1942, the corporate tax on businesses earning more than 500,000 reichsmarks was raised again, to 55 percent,[104] resulting immediately in a "drastic reduction in business incomes."[105] Thanks to the hikes in corporate taxes, the Reich increased its revenues in the three fiscal years between 1941and 1944 by more than 4 billion marks.[106]

Many business leaders had had enough. The owner of J. F. Lehmann, a medium-sized publishing house specializing in medical textbooks and treatises on German imperialism and race politics, complained in 1942: "Doing more business is a double-edged sword. Ultimately it decreases your earnings since all profits in excess of peacetime levels have to be appropriated and the warehouses gradually become empty."[107] In 1942, a Berlin hotel owner and wine wholesaler named Lorenz Adlon was paying taxes equivalent to 40 percent not of his firm's profits but of its annual turnover of 5.7 million reichsmarks.[108]

Between September 1939 and March 1942, the Reich recorded some 12 billion marks in revenue from war taxes of various kinds. Only the additional duties on tobacco, spirits, and beer, which earned the state 2.5 billion marks, affected the wallets of the majority of Germans. A further quarter of a billion marks came from the temporary suspension of overtime and other labor pay. The remaining 9.25 billion reichsmarks—or 75 percent of the increased domestic revenue—were provided by businesses and high-income earners. Göring's financial adviser Otto Donner commented: "The rapid progression in income taxes, in conjunction with the corporate tax, [ensures] a proportionally large contribution from high incomes to the needs of state."[109] Meanwhile, price and rent increases remained strictly forbidden.

The trend toward soaking businesses and the wealthy gained further momentum in the fiscal year 1942–43. The disproportionately large increase in domestic tax revenues that year can be traced to the state's imposing the so-called real estate inflation tax (*Hauszinssteuer*). Instituted in 1926, it was designed to spread the burden of inflation to otherwise unaffected property owners. Revenues, which averaged around 850 million reichsmarks annually in the first three years of the tax, went to cover a "substantial proportion" of the costs of state-backed construction of new houses and apartment buildings during the Weimar Republic. For that reason, only already standing structures were affected by the levy, which, in keeping with its aim of public utility, was called the Construction Debt Relief Tax.[110] Revenues from the assessment were allocated directly to local authorities.

To stabilize state finances during the Depression, an emergency decree had been issued on December 8, 1931, ordering property owners to pay the questionable tax in advance. In return, the Weimar government promised that it would be lifted in the future—a promise the Nazis legally abrogated on December 1, 1936.[111] The 1942 levy required property owners to pay ten years of the tax in advance in a single lump sum. Because property owners were prohibited from raising rents, they alone bore the burden. In addition, the Reich appropriated other revenues that had previously belonged to local authorities. All told the state collected the considerable sum of 8.1 billion reichsmarks (in today's currency the equivalent of around 100 billion dollars) in additional revenue in 1942–43. The financial newspaper *Bankwirtschaft* hailed the windfall as "a satisfactory result in terms of both limiting consumer spending power and improving the state budget."[112]

The fact that those affected by the real estate inflation tax had paid 4.5 billion reichsmarks of the levy in cash temporarily throttled the circulation of hard currency.[113] Representatives of property owners' associations agreed to the measure because the state again promised to get rid of the tax once and for all. Nevertheless, many property owners feared they would be "fleeced" by government rent controls, compulsory reserve funds, or increases in the basic real estate tax.[114] Indeed, a few months later, Economics Minister Walther Funk announced: "So-called real value assets [*Substanzwerte*] will represent an especially lucrative source of state tax revenue after the war." And in early 1944, Reich economists began discussing new ways "to better exploit property ownership to cover state debts."[115] Polemics against landlords continued to appear in party organs such as *Das schwarze Korps*, the official newspaper of the SS. Citing one such article from November 12, 1942, the president of the higher regional court in Kassel called for "the introduction of protection, under penalty of law, for upstanding tenants against willful harassment" by landlords who had forgotten their sense of social responsibility. The situation, he added, "was crying out for resolution."[116]

The decision to call in (that is, require advance payment of) the real estate inflation tax had been preceded by a lively debate within the Nazi Party leadership on how best to extract revenues from property owners. Since the start of the war, landlords had been legally prevented from renovating their properties. Nevertheless, rents still included tenant contributions toward rebuilding work. Renovation funds held in escrow provided a tempting target. Several gauleiters proposed an across-the-board reduction in rents and set about popularizing the idea in the press. But the finance minister blocked the proposal, arguing that such a move would create excess demand and thus inflation. In the end, it was decided instead to levy the special tax on property owners.[117]

The spirited negotiations over how much the state should demand in advance payments illustrate the emphasis segments of the Nazi state placed on social policies that appeared just and equitable. Initially, in December 1941, officials at the Finance Ministry suggested that the advance payment should be five times the normal annual property tax assessment. That would have raised about 4 billion reichsmarks. But at a subsequent interministerial conference, Interior Ministry representatives pleaded for a "somewhat" higher rate. The Prussian Finance Ministry proposed raising the rate to eight times the normal annual sum, prompting the Reich commissioner for price controls to complain of "a massive handout to property owners." Representatives of the Labor Ministry and the Wehrmacht, on the other hand, warned against making the burden too great. In January 1942, Finance Ministry officials said they would agree to a contribution of seven times the annual norm, but the representative of the German Labor Front, Paul Fleischmann, insisted on nothing less than a ninefold levy. The discussions dragged on through the winter, with representatives from Hitler's Party Chancellery continuing to warn against "giving too much away to property owners." At the end of March, Prussian finance minister Johannes Popitz, secretly a member of the anti-Hitler resistance, proposed bumping up the contribution to twelve times the annual norm. The Party Chancellery let it be known that Martin Bormann "would be in agreement with a tenfold contribution," whereupon Schwerin von Krosigk put the matter to rest: "The proposal is adopted."[118] The additional money taken in from property owners amounted to 18 percent of domestic war-tax revenues in the fiscal year 1942–43.

The process of deciding this matter is a good example of what the historian Hans Mommsen calls the cumulative radicalization of the Nazi state. Mommsen sees the character of the Third Reich as being shaped by competition among officials in various government bureaucracies. Civil servants, in effect, pushed one another to become more radical. The Nazi leadership exploited this dynamic by defining only what they did *not* want and putting pressure on their subordinates to achieve maximum results in the shortest possible time. Civil servants were encouraged to use their administrative imagination—they neither needed nor were given concrete instructions. In the case at hand, the Nazi leadership at no point even considered legislation that would have placed a comparable burden on working people. On the contrary, discussions of the property tax were framed by the general principle that materially better-off Germans were to bear a considerably larger share of the burden of war than poor ones. In this, the decision makers were following the lead of Göring, who as early as November 1938 had suggested financing the arms buildup with the help "of a one-time contribution from the wealth" of affluent German citizens. [119]

A SIMILAR hostility toward the wealthy can be seen in the Nazis' stance on stock market profits. As of January 1, 1941, earnings from stock transactions were subject to a windfall profits tax.[120] A short time later annual dividends, together with all other forms of payments to shareholders, were limited to 6 percent. The limit was adopted, above all, for its "propagandistic significance."[121] Stock values had appreciated on average by around 50 percent during the first two years of the war, with some performing far better. Decision makers within the Nazi Party, including the Führer, had voiced repeated opposition to this form of "effortless" income.[122] On December 4, 1941, the economics minister was empowered to require investors to report any stocks they owned. He was also given authority to issue regulations restricting sales of stocks and the reinvestment of profits from such sales. The immediate purpose of this measure was to force Aryan, as well as Jewish, investors to exchange their stocks for government bonds, which in the short term could not be traded. The long-term goal was to prevent a possible decline of investor confidence in the state and party leadership from becoming visible and depressing the securities market.

An official decree followed promptly on January 2, 1942. Investors were required to report all stocks, as well as shares in mining companies and colonial enterprises, purchased after September 1, 1939, to their local tax offices by April 30. The decree also applied to all stocks that had been transferred to relatives, fiancés, in-laws, business associates, and employees in the preceding six months, the period in which the regulation was being discussed and prepared. The aim was clearly to soak the rich and "neutralize big spenders."[123] Investments valued at less than 100,000 reichsmarks were exempt. Lastly, the Reich Credit Monitoring Commission set limits, varying from bank to bank, on the total value of stocks that individual financial institutions were allowed to keep on deposit.

The Nazi leadership acted again on June 9, 1942. A second implementation decree prohibited transactions with the reported stocks and allowed the economics minister to order compulsory sell-offs. A consortium of the Reichsbank and the Prussian State Bank was empowered to purchase the assets, and within a few weeks it took in stocks valued at 150 million reichsmarks. (The total value of reported securities was around one billion reichsmarks.) State intervention was only partial, aimed at disciplining, not dispossessing, individual investors. The Finance Ministry wanted to retain the possibility of "extracting further concessions to put the brakes on" future stock runs.[124] (An additional regulation requiring local communities to keep 75 percent of their reserve funds in various forms of government bonds also served to chill the securities market.)[125]

Over the course of 1943, a further 140 million reichsmarks in stocks were handed over to the state. But since the consortium was bound to pay the price at which stocks were listed on December 31, 1941, when share values were at their peak, many securities were considered overvalued, making their purchase impractical. Economists at the Reichsbank and the Finance and Economics Ministries reacted by declaring the (lower) original purchase price valid for compulsory stock sales.[126] In late 1943, records indicate a flurry of forced sales, with the government "compensating" gentile investors, like their Jewish counterparts before them, with nonnegotiable government bonds.

The government initially conceived of these mandatory controls as temporary, but they were repeatedly extended as the war dragged on. In early 1943, the Economics Ministry halved the exemption for stocks acquired since 1939 to a total value of 50,000 reichsmarks. The change was intended to hit large-scale investors and speculators who, with good reason, wanted as few war bonds as possible in their portfolios. Economics Minister Funk lamented a "growing obsession with material assets," which he deemed "psychologically dangerous." His goal was "to keep stock values in check, to force investment-oriented money off the stock exchange, and to divert it into treasury bills." The growth in the number of tradable stocks on the market therefore had to be stopped. Stocks acquired by the government as a result of compulsory sales served as "funds for intervening in and protecting market values," which could be introduced to prevent bull markets. "Jewish securities," which were still being held by the state, were explicitly allocated to this fund. In the Protectorate of Bohemia and Moravia, they were confiscated specifically "for the purpose of regulating values on the [German] stock market and being transferred to the Prussian State Bank."[127]

Companies, of course, spent considerable energy trying to obtain exemptions allowing them to sell state bonds they had unwillingly acquired, but most of their efforts were in vain.[128] Nonetheless, state intervention could only temporarily slow stock market growth, not prevent it in the long term. The means with which Germany financed the war created excess demand that inevitably pushed its way onto the market. The Reichsbank was under no illusions that, aside from certain cosmetic measures, it had the power to "eradicate the causes for this growing trend."[129]

Unquestionably, hopes for a quick German victory in the war had fueled early rises in stock values. That optimism was over by the fall of 1941. On the surface, the change in mood had no effect. Investors' appetites for stocks continued unabated. But their motivations had changed. People were now buying stocks to avoid investing their money in the increasingly dubious alternative of war bonds. Skepticism toward Germany's political leadership led investors to hang on to their stocks—observers spoke of "a shortage of inventory on the market"—while demand for securities grew daily. The reason was that, although stock values were increasing, few investors wanted to cash in their profits.[130] Despite the risk posed by war, industrial stocks and bonds appeared to be a vastly more secure option than state-issued securities.

Germans held on tightly to real estate as well. In 1941, the Security Service issued a report entitled "Unfortunate Conditions in the Real Estate Market," which noted that investors were seeking refuge in material assets and warned that there was "no supply worth mentioning" to serve the growing demand for developed and undeveloped real estate.[131] In April of that year, Reinhardt acted to prevent investors from acquiring tangible assets and to channel cash into state bonds by freezing the sale of properties that had been confiscated from Jews.[132]

The Reich followed up in early 1943 by capping stock prices, after markets generally failed to react to "repeated warnings."[133] The stock market remained open, but it no longer served its true purpose. "In the absence of anything else on offer," stock brokers were now "concentrating on government securities."[134]

In 1943, guided by Hitler's tax priorities, the finance minister targeted the uppermost 4 percent of earners for a rate hike. He ran into immediate opposition. In his commentary on the draft legislation, the economics minister objected that the new regulations would humiliate the wealthy and lead to "untenable hostility, considering the proportional burden [already placed] on this segment of the populace versus the rest of the country."[135] Economist Günter Schmölders retorted that the new rate would promote "social equity." But even he acknowledged that the drastic curtailing of profit opportunities might "reward entrepreneurial lethargy, while punishing rationalization, cost cutting, and success."[136]

Having significantly reduced corporate revenues with a battery of business taxes and increasingly lagging behind in paying its debts to private companies, the state levied a 65 percent tax on whatever profits remained. One company was compelled in 1942–43 to exchange the stocks it had acquired since 1939 for nonnegotiable government bonds. That year, it earned nominal profits of 120,000 reichsmarks. Its liability amounted to "55 percent corporate tax plus 30 percent commercial-profit tax and 13 percent excise tax," which added up to 98 percent of total profits.[137] By 1945, the regime was also planning a drastic increase in the wealth tax, which would have been retroactive to 1943.[138]

Industrialists complained that some 80 to 90 percent of business profits were being siphoned off by the state.[139] This figure is clearly exaggerated, but it speaks volumes about the Nazi government's basic tax-policy orientation.

Horn of Plenty for the Home Front

During World War I, the German government scandalously neglected the welfare of soldiers' families. Indeed, civil servants in Wilhelmine Germany seemed intent on reducing them to poverty. Millions of working-class women and children who had been scraping by on their own suddenly faced deprivation when their breadwinners were called to the front. While the men were shedding their blood on the front lines, their dependents were forced to do without basic necessities at home. The state provided just enough to live on, but not a scrap more. The existing legislation to provide for support for soldiers' families during wartime dated back to 1888, and although it had been amended many times, it utterly failed to meet the requirements of modern mass warfare.[140]

The obliviousness of the Wilhelmine government to the needs of military families was a sign of its inability to empathize with the economic situation of the working classes. Decision makers under Kaiser Wilhelm II had sufficient funds at their disposal, but they lacked the social and political imagination to allocate them properly. The idea that mass warfare, for psychological reasons, required equity in the distribution of resources was alien to Wilhelmine elites. As a result, an outmoded system of class rule condemned itself to extinction, squandering what remained of its popular support through indifference—if not actual malice—toward the welfare of the population at large. It was not until September 1918, far too late, that the press secretary to the Reich chancellor finally realized that "homelessness, lack of clothing, and above all starvation cannot be overcome with indoctrination."[141]

The experience of 1914 to 1918 still resonated among the majority of Germans twenty-one years later. When the Nazi leadership drafted the Compensation for Military Deployment Law on August 28, 1939, one key paragraph stipulated: "Previous standards of living and peacetime income levels are to be taken into account when calculating degrees of family support for members of the Wehrmacht." The law aimed at "maintaining [families'] level of personal assets" and "prior economic standing," pledging to help recipients "fulfill existing obligations." Those included newspaper subscriptions, life insurance policies, payments on goods bought on the installment plan, and mortgages.[142] In general, the state supplements strove "to maintain fighting spirit and will and to secure home-front morale."

The vast majority of Germans were much better off than they had been in World War I. The paternal state no longer demeaned ordinary people. It distributed material goods that improved the popular mood. The political leadership unambiguously directed civil servants "to act, in light of their special responsibility toward all the people, with corresponding understanding of the concerns and needs of family members of frontline soldiers."[143] "The greatest possible speed and facility in the delivery of mandatory family support payments" was to be treated as a "duty and point of honor for every branch of the civil service."[144] In disputed cases, decisions were to be made to the benefit of claimants. Without exception, the administrative directives that followed the outbreak of military hostilities strengthened the rights of beneficiaries.[145] In October 1939, German newspapers reported that, at Göring's behest, family support measures had been expanded: "The National Socialist state leadership has freed the frontline German soldier from all worries about the maintenance of his family." From then on, rents were paid in full, and extra benefits of all kinds were handed out.[146] The goal of these generous initiatives was to win over "the heart of the soldier" through demonstrations of "abiding concern."[147]

The immediate response was overwhelmingly positive, and in the euphoria following Germany's victory over France, the state combined the various individual benefit payments under the Law on Deployed Family Maintenance, or EFUG (*Einsatz-Familienunterhaltsgesetz*).[148] Significantly, at the same time, tax exemptions for overtime, night, Sunday, and holiday wages were being introduced. According to EFUG, family maintenance was not considered a kind of welfare payment but rather "an honor-bound duty of the ethnic community [*Volksgemeinschaft*] carried out by the state." There was no suggestion that state supplements and subsidies should be paid back, nor was there any means of testing for eligibility. A major difference for millions of Germans was that, in contrast to normal wages, family maintenance payments were exempt from garnishment to settle unpaid debts. This regulation cost the state nothing; the burden was transferred to creditors.

Supplemental benefit payments for rent, insurance, coal, potatoes, and other daily needs were paid out with minimal bureaucratic delay. The state offered household assistance to families with large numbers of children. It also provided money for special expenditures such as dental bills or children's education costs. In daily practice, civil servants did their best "to compensate for special circumstances and treat [recipients] as individuals."[149] As a matter of course, family maintenance payments were tax-free, and recipients were exempt from consultation charges under their health insurance.[150] As a result of these handouts, working-class women could suddenly afford to give up their factory jobs.

In fact, the government soon had to impose a cap to prevent maintenance payments from exceeding the prewar net income levels of family breadwinners called to fight at the front.[151] The limit was set at 15 percent less than what a soldier had earned, after taxes, on his last monthly paycheck, but the cap meant that most women still received 85 percent of their normal household income. For the first time, many of them were able to keep house without being subjected to the moods and whims of their husbands. Thus, although average household income levels were somewhat lower than in peacetime, stable prices, a freeze on rents, and an exemption from asset seizure made it possible to live in material comfort.[152] If one factors into the equation soldiers' wages and their food rations, many German families actually had more disposable income in war than in peacetime.[153]

An academic study of the family maintenance program conducted in 1943 defined its purpose as "shoring up the popular mood and, in particular, the morale among the broad masses."[154] The program's generosity sometimes worked against its aims, however, by creating envy among neighbors, an appetite for additional benefits, and the desire to take the state for whatever one could get. Some recipients expressed frustration at the increasing scarcity of goods available for purchase. Nonetheless, by and large, the program achieved its goal of neutralizing potential political opposition on the home front, which consisted primarily of women.

In total, the Third Reich spent 27.5 billion marks, an astonishing sum for the time, on family maintenance benefits during World War II.[155] On average, family members of German soldiers had 72.8 percent of peacetime household income at their disposal. That is nearly double what families of American (36.7) and British soldiers (38.1) received.[156]

As part of this massive handout, the government increased subsidies to families under the rubric "population policy measures" from 250 to 500 million reichsmarks between 1939 and 1941. In 1942, the turning point of the war, the total doubled again, and by the end of the war, it still hovered around one billion marks annually. These figures reflect increases in child support and family household subsidies of 25 percent in 1939, 28 percent in 1940, 56 percent in 1941, and 96 percent in 1942.[157] The basis for domestic stability in Hitler's *Volksstaat* was its continual bribery of the populace via the social welfare system.

In 1943, determined to bolster the Third Reich's war chest, Nazi economics minister Walther Funk suggested that "the current tax exemption for family maintenance payments and other such compensation payments should be abolished." His proposal was shot down by the triumvirate of Hitler, Göring, and Goebbels, who saw themselves, together with the party gauleiters, as the ultimate guarantors of popular morale on the home front. "We've been too lavish in our wartime budgeting," Funk remarked dryly in a letter to a colleague. "It will be difficult to break out of the spiral."[158]

Part II

SUBJUGATION AND EXPLOITATION

CHAPTER 3

With Unwavering Efficiency

Foreign Contributions to Germany

A basic problem for the wartime Nazi *Volksstaat* was the balance between supply and demand. In the years before the war, the arms buildup, together with zero unemployment, had led to a dramatic rise in both wages and business profits. The Reich's tax revenues rose to unprecedented levels, but so did private citizens' spending power. Once the war began, despite price and wage controls, both profits and spending power increased further still because of overtime labor and expansion of the workforce. In addition, as we have seen, the sums allocated to soldiers and their families in lieu of regular wages were anything but stingy.

With production increasingly geared to the needs of the military, however, the supply of goods for the civilian populace decreased. At first the drop was moderate, but it became ever more dramatic, opening a gap between consumer spending power and available goods that created not only discontent but black markets, inflationary pressure, and a tendency among investors to seek refuge in tangible assets. By the fall of 1939, the first signs of an economy of scarcity were already evident, and people began to buy up whatever they could get their hands on. Sales figures for linens and bedclothes increased by 45 percent over the previous year, while sales of furniture rose by 30 percent and porcelain and glassware by 35 percent.[1] With the supply of durable consumer items soon exhausted, excess domestic spending power could no longer be converted into goods or services.

Broadly targeted taxes were ruled out on political grounds, although personal incomes rose by 21 percent between 1939 and 1941, largely because of extended workdays. Disposable income more than doubled as a result, rising from 14 to 31 billion reichsmarks.[2] Germany's primary solution to the impasse—a way of both curbing excess spending power and increasing state revenues—was to exploit foreign countries. "If there has to be inflation, better there than here in Germany," said one member of the Finance Ministry, whose sentiments were shared by civil servants in the Reichsbank, the Foreign Office, and the Economics Ministry and by the Führer himself.[3]

Exploiting foreign economies was not just a way of keeping German consumers well supplied. It also brought huge sums of money into Germany's war chest. Both the political leadership and the civil service were constantly upbraiding German administrators who tried to stabilize or treat occupied countries with a modicum of fairness. "You are aware of our fundamental standpoint," read one reprimand, "that the costs of occupying a given area are to be borne by the area itself."[4] The need to ensure that payments would be met led the Reich to intervene in the running of occupied countries' economies. In Serbia, a close intimate of Göring's expressed his gratitude "that the Reichsbank has put such excellent experts at my disposal."[5] In their first few weeks of work, these experts established a new Serbian national bank and issued a new currency, the Serbian dinar.[6] By simply banning most currency exchanges, they succeeded in funneling money held by Serbian citizens to the banks, where it was booked in the new currency. In this way the experts could temporarily put the brakes on the circulation of money and keep the danger of inflation under control so that Serbia would be able to fulfill its obligations to the Reich.

As in every other nation defeated by Germany, the General Government of occupied Poland was forced to pay what was euphemistically termed a "contribution for military protection."[7] The amount was raised annually. In 1942, displeased with the revenues taken in the previous year, Schwerin von Krosigk retroactively increased the compulsory tribute from 150 to 500 million zlotys and set a target of 1.3 billion for the rest of the year. In 1943, the finance minister demanded 3 billion.[8] His deputy, Fritz Reinhardt, attempted to rally civil servants frustrated by the General Government's stalling tactics, exhorting them: "We can't let up the pressure!"[9] On top of the contribution, the Wehrmacht also presented occupied Poland with a monthly bill of around 100 million zlotys for the services of 400,000 soldiers—although only 80,000 were still stationed in the country.[10] The fivefold surplus was used "to cover soldiers' needs for foodstuffs and other goods," with the result that the local populace endured acute shortages of grain, potatoes, meat, and other necessities.[11] In its financial ledgers, the Reich duly credited the General Government for some of its payments. But the balance was credited in name only, and one leading figure at the Reichsbank remarked nonchalantly: "The final settling of accounts with the General Government can be postponed until the conclusion of the war."[12]

OVER THE course of World War II, Germany mandated unprecedented contributions, along with compulsory loans and population-based "quotas," on the defeated countries of Europe. These financial tributes soon exceeded the total peacetime budgets of the countries in question, usually by more than 100 percent and in the second half of the war by more than 200 percent. In January 1943, for example, the finance minister demanded that "two-thirds of the General Government's budget be transferred to the Reich." German administrators in occupied Poland promptly protested, complaining that tributes on such a scale "would render any progress, even in more orderly times, completely impossible." The Finance Ministry remained firm, insisting that the level of contribution to the Wehrmacht was "completely appropriate for the time being."[13] In spring 1944, as the Allies stepped up their bombardment of German factories, occupied Poland was forced to bear the entire cost of transferring military production facilities there. The finance minister was unwilling to give up his "previous guiding principle" that "all the costs incurred by the GG must be covered there."[14] German financial experts duly took note of "the increasing financial-economic yields" from the occupied countries "in the wake of local economic stimulation and the application of new tax-policy methods."[15]

Procurements by German arms suppliers and food importers consumed a quarter of the money the Reich was supposedly spending on the occupation of France. In June 1943 the governing military intendant of Paris estimated that private purchases by soldiers made up a further quarter. Among the techniques used to drive up putative costs were a host of petty regulations—for instance, a decree by the general intendant of the Wehrmacht that occupied countries bear the costs of dental work (including gold crowns and bridges) for German members of the armed forces.[16] All in all, such measures yielded considerable sums of money. The German occupiers also manipulated France's currency, paid for aerial attacks on Britain wherever possible in francs, and used French money to build submarine ports and gigantic bunkers on the Atlantic coast. These expenditures were unrelated to the actual military control of France, as indeed were 75 percent of the so-called occupation costs.[17] In late 1941, the chief French negotiator complained, in vain, to the occupation authorities: "The sums paid under the agreement concerning occupation costs are very frequently used to cover expenditures that have nothing to do with maintenance of the troops."[18]

The situation was similar in Denmark. For the first six months of 1944, occupation costs there were calculated at some 86 million reichsmarks—more than three times what they had been in 1941.[19] A quarter of this sum was earmarked for personnel costs, while the rest went toward material expenditures, especially "construction projects and food procurement in that country."[20] Denmark was the base from which the Wehrmacht supplied food for its soldiers in Norway as well as in parts of Germany itself. In 1942, some 22,000 cows, 17,500 pigs, 2,870 tons of butter, 500 tons of marmalade, 80,000 eggs, and 3,000 tons of fruit and vegetables were delivered to army headquarters in Norway. According to operational reports from the occupation authority in Denmark, in addition to "provisions for German troops stationed in the country, significant quantities of livestock (cows, pigs), butter, cheese, eggs, and saltwater fish" were also "transferred to Germany."[21]

As was surely the case elsewhere as well, occupied Denmark had to use funds from its own operating budget to pay support for children born to German soldiers and local women.[22] Between 1940 and 1941, the Dutch government was also required to meet the Third Reich's obligations under the German-Soviet economic pact to provide the Soviet Union with finished goods in return for raw materials. The total value of those commitments was 60 million reichsmarks, in return for which Germany received 350,000 tons of grain from Ukraine. Because the costs were paid from the operating budget of occupied Holland, the finance minister was able to shift an extra 60 million reichsmarks into the war budget. The money could be used to buy new tanks, artillery, and planes.[23]

The central bank in occupied Poland was required to transfer all its available gold to the Reichsbank in Berlin in return for a pro forma credit. All outstanding debts owed to the Polish government were likewise handed over.[24] To cover its payments to the Reich, the occupying authority in Cracow increased the real estate tax, introduced a head tax, raised the income tax rate, and sold off material assets confiscated from Jews and Poles who had been declared enemies of the state. The tax hikes applied only to Poles. Germans residing in Poland paid no taxes at all on annual incomes of up to 8,400 zlotys.[25] From a tax perspective, it was more advantageous for a German to live in Poland than within the Reich.

THE HAGUE Conventions of 1899 and 1907, to which Germany was a signatory, allowed victorious nations to recover occupation costs from their defeated enemies. But the level of contributions sought by Nazi Germany was completely out of proportion to the principles laid out in article 52 of the Conventions, which Berlin rejected as "too restrictive and outdated."[26] Contributions from occupied enemies were supplemented by subsidies from Germany's allies, the "war-cost contributions" paid by Bulgaria, Slovakia, and Romania. Budget officials in the Third Reich did not hesitate to record these revenues as "occupation costs."[27] By 1943 the majority of the Reich's additional war-related revenues came from abroad, from foreign slave laborers in Germany, and from the dispossession of Jews and "enemies of the state." These sources of income underwrote a significant portion of Germany's military efforts. As noted above, until the summer of 1944 the Reich was able to cover 50 percent of its running war costs from its current budget, whereas in World War I Germany had been forced to borrow 87 percent of those outlays. German financial administrators achieved this "substantial improvement in balance of payments" at other people's expense.

Bernhard Benning of the Reichsbank attached considerable importance to revenues raised to compensate Germany for its putative occupation costs. In 1944, he cited income from conquered states as the "truly dynamic factor" in Germany's financing of the war. "In addition to tax revenues," Benning enthused, "ever increasing and ever more significant amounts are coming in from so-called other revenues." Although "no running annual figures" were kept, Benning added, "the missing numbers can be estimated." Certainly "the latest figure of 26 billion reichsmarks," which had been communicated to him by Deputy Finance Minister Reinhardt, was "sensational."

Benning also specified the types of revenue that had been included under the category "other":

(a) so-called administrative revenues [*Verwaltungseinnahmen*], which Reinhardt puts at 5 billion reichsmarks for 1942 and which come from a variety of sources, including the national railroad, the postal service, the Reichsbank, repayment on old loans, and revenues from the Worker Mobilization Fund (previously unemployment insurance); (b) . . . the war contribution of local communities, which, according to the initial estimate, brought in approximately 1.5 billion marks but which can be currently assessed at 2.5 to 3 billion marks. The vast majority of the remainder (i.e., 18 billion marks) comes in from abroad: defense contributions from the General Government, the population-based contribution from the Protectorate [of Bohemia and Moravia], and especially [payments toward] occupation costs from the conquered countries. The individual totals are not known, but an interesting figure has been communicated for France. In 1943, France had obligations of around 190 billion francs, which converts to 9.5 billion reichsmarks. (One can see that via occupation and the transference of obligations we've succeeded to a large extent in tying the French economy to our own.)[28]

Although the costs of war increased dramatically in 1943, *Bankwirtschaft* magazine summed up with satisfaction at the beginning of the following year: "Thanks to the major increase in 'other' revenues, the proportion of credit financing within total Reich expenditures has not risen. We've been able to keep it, again and again, under the target of 50 percent."[29]

From the very beginning, a major element in Germany's successful exploitation of occupied countries was the manipulation of official exchange rates. In France, German occupiers lowered the exchange rate for 100 francs from 6.6 to 5 reichsmarks—a devaluation of just under 25 percent. This automatically raised soldiers' salaries, which were paid in francs but calculated in reichsmarks. (The franc would, of course, have inevitably become softer under German occupation, but even in late 1942 the exchange rate in Zurich was 16 percent higher than the one set by German occupiers.) Similar action was taken with the establishment of the Protectorate of Bohemia and Moravia. The Czech crown remained the official currency but was devalued by a third.[30] In 1939 the Reich also intervened in Poland and in 1943 in Nazi-occupied northern Italy, where the exchange rate between the lira and the mark was lowered from 100 to 13.1 to 100 to 10. But even that is dwarfed by the 470 percent devaluation of the Russian ruble in 1941.[31] Those responsible for the new exchange rates knew exactly what they were doing. Privately, they acknowledged that the reichsmark was "greatly overvalued in comparison with [other] European currencies."[32]

Currency manipulation benefited both the German economy and individual Wehrmacht soldiers in their role as consumers in the occupied countries. At the same time, exports from Germany, which these countries had often come to rely on as a result of the war, became more expensive, while imports to Germany were made cheaper. Because Germany was forced to import increasing amounts of both raw materials and finished products in the course of the war, balance of trade became a problem—but only theoretically. A significant portion of the goods occupied countries were required to export to Germany were paid for, in direct contravention of the Hague Conventions, out of those countries' own budgets for occupation costs. The remainder were purchased with notes of credit drawn on a state "clearing account"—in other words, they weren't purchased at all.

Clearing accounts were central bank accounts set up by states in the 1930s for clearing their balances of imports and exports. Under the system, exporters received payment in their native currencies from a state bank, while purchasers paid in their own currency to a state institution in their home country. Such transactions, usually between private exporters and importers, were then entered into clearing accounts, which were settled at regular intervals between the states in question. In World War II, the German government exploited this established system to acquire billions in interest-free loans from creditor nations. Financial experts at the time described the transactions matter-of-factly as "coerced one-sided loans" to Germany's advantage.[33]

According to a declaration by the Reich Credit Bank (Reichkreditkasse) on July 10, 1944, Germany had amassed almost 29 billion marks in debts to occupied, allied, friendly, and neutral states as of June 30 of that year. Of this amount, 14 billion marks were owed to France, Belgium, and Denmark alone. Holland, the General Government of Poland, and the Protectorate of Bohemia and Moravia had been forced to buy German war bonds worth almost 13 billion marks. The declaration also addressed the scope of other revenues:

According to estimates from the "Research Group for Military Economics," which [Reichsbank] vice president Pohl discussed in greater detail at the meeting on July 10, 1944, the total contribution of goods and services from the occupied territories during the first four years of the war amounted to some 70 to 80 billion reichsmarks. The amount for the first five years of the war can therefore be set at between 90 and 100 billion. Contributions brought in via clearing transactions account for almost a third of the total. It is plain from this how important it is in the final phase of the war for us to preserve, as best we can, the willingness of the occupied countries to make contributions.

By that point, Germany was no longer in a military position to loot the Soviet Union to repay its war debts, as a plan drawn up in 1941 had envisioned. So the directors of the Reichsbank set out to devise ways to foist Germany's foreign debts onto its creditors. To this end, they drew up a list of "substantial, still unfulfilled demands" that the Reich would present "to the occupied territories" upon the signing of peace treaties, for occupation costs Germany claimed to have paid in advance.[34] The Finance Ministry's proposals for eradicating Germany's foreign debt ran along similar lines. According to Finance Ministry documents, war costs that Germany had incurred, such as "wages, family support payments, and expenditures for train cars, vehicles, uniforms, weapons, etc.," were to be "reckoned up" with the defeated nations of Europe.[35] In an effort to placate his creditors, Reichsbank president Funk characterized Germany's exorbitant foreign debts as "an investment that will retain its value."[36]

GERMAN SOLDIERS were paid in the currency of the country where they were stationed, and they were instructed to spend their wages there to reduce inflationary pressure at home. For the same reason, soldiers' families were encouraged to send or wire them money to buy available goods, many of which were then sent back to Germany. What was available for purchase varied from country to country.

Many units on the Russian front had limited opportunities to spend their paychecks. They transferred the surplus back to the Reich, much to the dismay of the top administrators at the Reichsbank, who condemned the practice in the strongest terms. "When such monies are transferred home," wrote one administrator, "the unused spending power of soldiers in the East manifests itself as increased consumer spending power in the Reich."[37]

But civil servants responsible for war finances soon came up with a remedy. Under the pretense that war-weary troops needed rest and relaxation, soldiers on the Eastern Front were assigned at regular intervals to Western Europe, especially to France. There, the troops were given the opportunity "to live somewhat more luxuriously in compensation for the hardships they had endured."[38] Military paymasters ensured that the soldiers were able to exchange surplus rubles for Western currencies. A high-ranking medical officer reported from France in the fall of 1942 that the troops arriving from the East, as well as members of the navy, "have spent an unimaginable amount of money frequenting bordellos and streetwalkers." A second Wehrmacht medical officer remarked somewhat more prudishly in January 1943 that "the copious savings" that the eastern divisions had at their disposal were leading to "the frequent introduction of harlots from the immediate and general vicinity into the [soldiers'] accommodations area."[39] In this way, the surplus spending power of soldiers in Eastern Europe was diverted not to Germany but to France. German war financiers also manipulated the exchange of rubles into francs so that France ultimately paid for German soldiers' bordello visits, while the exchanged rubles flowed into the Reich's war chest.

Novel Means of Payment

As a rule when German troops occupied a country, they initially procured what they needed with Reich Credit Bank (RKK) certificates, switching over only later to the invaded country's native currency. RKK certificates looked like paper money and were issued in denominations ranging from 50 reichspfennigs to 50 reichsmarks. Thanks to this military-issued surrogate money, German troops did not have to directly confiscate goods from citizens of occupied countries and spared themselves the time-consuming task of issuing requisition receipts, as required by the Hague Convention. This arrangement offered several advantages: German troops remained mobile, and the profit motive was preserved among the population. It also avoided the "humiliating and emasculating effects of requisition [upon subjugated peoples]."[40] RKK certificates were issued and printed by the Reichsbank, but they were not legal tender in Germany.[41] They were, as Reichsbank vice president Emil Puhl put it, "requisition receipts disguised as money."[42] This may have been true for the Germans, but for the recipients they functioned as currency. Therein lay their greatest advantage.

Occupied France was a case in point. Businesses and private citizens had no objection to accepting RKK certificates because a decree had been issued compelling French banks to exchange them for francs.[43] Individual banks swapped the certificates for hard currency from the Banque de France. That institution was then required to turn them over to the Reich Credit Bank in Paris, the hastily established German financial center in occupied France. But since the French national bank received nothing in return, it had no op-

TABLEAU

des

Monnaies Allemandes

ayant cours

20 Reichsmark = 400 Francs

50 Reichspfennig = 10 Francs

AVIS
à la Population

L'autorité allemande fait connaître que, seuls, les billets allemands libellés en **Reichsmarks** émis par la **Reichskreditkassen**, dont les modèles sont reproduits ci-contre en agrandissement, doivent être acceptés en paiement, tant par les particuliers que par les caisses publiques.

Tous les autres billets allemands doivent être à l'avenir, strictement refusés.

Il est rappelé que le taux du change est fixé comme suit :

1 Reichsmark = 20 Francs

2 Reichsmark = 40 Francs

20 Reichsmark . . . . . . =	**400**	francs français
5 Reichsmark . . . . . . =	**100**	francs français
2 Reichsmark . . . . . . =	**40**	francs français
1 Reichsmark . . . . . . =	**20**	francs français
0,50 Reichsmark = 50 Reichspfennig =	**10**	francs français
0,10 Reichsmark = 10 Reichspfennig =	**2**	francs français
0,05 Reichsmark = 5 Reichspfennig =	**1**	franc français

5 Reichsmark = 100 Francs

Cette affiche est en vente chez les Concierges de l'Hotel-de-Ville. et des Mairies de Paris au prix de 0 fr. 50 l'exemplaire.

Public announcement of the introduction of RKK certificates in France, May 1940 (Archive de la Banque de France): "Henceforth, only RKK certificates will be accepted as legal tender."

tion but to print more francs or join with the French financial administration to procure funds elsewhere. The RKK certificates allowed Germany to plunder occupied Europe—and set in motion a succession of problems associated with Germany's conscious decision to export wartime inflation. After passing through the Banque de France, the RKK certificates returned to the paymasters of the Wehrmacht and could be used to procure more goods and services for occupying troops. They were continually in circulation but left no paper trail, in contrast to traditional requisition receipts for confiscated goods.[44]

The beauty of this procedure, from the Reich's point of view, was that it meant minimal bureaucracy for German military administrators. French citizens, from whom the Wehrmacht requisitioned horses, foodstuffs, and fuel, received a form of currency they trusted as soon as they turned in the certificates. As a result, they suffered no direct personal losses, since the wartime dispossession of individuals was coupled to the general circulation of money. The currency strategists in the Reichsbank thereby achieved their goal of distributing the burden of requisitions "to the general public by introducing Reich Credit Bank certificates into the circulation of money within the country."[45] German bayonets forced the defeated enemy to accept ultimately worthless pieces of paper as a de facto equivalent of their own currency. The damage to the French economy was scarcely noticeable at first, while the German economy earned a tidy profit.

Normally, German occupation authorities took RKK certificates out of circulation shortly after the formal cessation of hostilities. This was true, for example, in Denmark, where once peace had been declared the occupied country's own currency became the sole legal tender again. But the Reich chose a different strategy in France, in defiance of "the understandable wish" of the Banque de France that "the Reich Credit Banks, which operate like central banks with their own currencies, be dissolved in the none-too-distant future."[46] The explanation for this exception was the German desire to purchase the great variety of French consumer products.

In practice, Reich occupation authorities responsible for obtaining supplementary food, weaponry, raw materials, or other important resources could "initiate procurements in France" without having to draw funds from their official accounts. All they had to do was acquire RKK certificates and spend them discreetly. But there were limits to this tactic. In July 1943, the intendant director to the commander of the German forces in France called for "the uncontrolled introduction of RKK certificates to be halted," arguing that the practice was undermining efforts "to regulate the economy and allocate occupation funds."[47] The Wehrmacht directorate complained "that the vast majority of members of the Wehrmacht stationed in France are trying, by every means imaginable, to import RKK certificates into France." In early December 1943, the certificates were largely withdrawn from circulation under pressure from French and German economists, who sought to stabilize the franc.[48]

In a 1939 monograph, economist Georg Holzhauer sketched out what would soon become standard practice in the heretofore "almost unknown field" of financing military occupations. "Cash payments," Holzhauer wrote, "are the best means not only for improving record keeping and procurement, as well as the economic utilization of existing supplies, but for the balanced spreading of burdens caused by the occupying army." By dispersing such burdens, Holzhauer argued, occupying forces could "easily confiscate many times" what they could by arbitrarily seizing property from individuals. Equally important in maximizing confiscation was "the strict avoidance of payments in kind." It was crucial to ensure "that [the occupiers] can at all times obtain legal-tender currency for goods and services necessary for the running of war." Holzhauer recommended that suitable means of payment be introduced to "increase revenues and, with them, surpluses from the occupied territory."[49]

In fact, according to one researcher writing in 1941, the introduction of RKK certificates repeatedly elicited "a feeling of satisfaction" in the occupied countries. "The knowledge that equivalent return value is being preserved," he wrote, allowed subjugated peoples to overlook "the fact that the purchaser is the enemy." The author of this study, a graduate student named Helmut Karsten, was supervised by the renowned economist Jens Jessen, who would later join the anti-Hitler resistance. Karsten continued: "Requisitions, on the other hand, which in the absence of visible return value are always perceived as acts of plunder, strengthen feelings of national hatred and resentment at economic exploitation and lead to open and covert attempts to strike back at the enemy. The reactions of a populace disadvantaged and enraged by requisitions range from acts of sabotage to guerrilla fighting and open insurgency."

Individual economic self-interest and the prospect of profits were effective at neutralizing rebellious sentiments. Citing the experiences of German occupiers in France beginning in the summer of 1940, Karsten concluded: "Thanks to the prospects of further commerce and profits they offer, cash purchases are the best means of stimulating production and procuring replacements for exhausted supplies. The latter advantage depends on the transport of goods from distant regions, thereby opening up supply lines that would have been beyond the troops' immediate reach. The same is true of concealed supplies, which are suddenly uncovered when people are given the prospect of profitably exploiting them."[50]

Collective Impoverishment

The practice of occupation forces paying in cash for military goods and services can be traced back to the Union Army in the American Civil War. German and Russian troops had used it as well, in the Franco-Prussian War of 1870–71 and the Balkan wars of 1877–78, respectively.[51] During World War I, German forces achieved "optimal results" by purchasing supplies in local currencies.[52] Cash payments were in keeping with Article 52 of the Hague Conventions, which allowed occupation forces to requisition goods and services without immediate compensation only in emergency situations. But German efforts to impose a cash-payment system during World War I were erratic and uneven. The chief obstacle was the absence of a reliable exchange-rate mechanism, which produced what Karsten called "currency confusion" in occupied countries. The state, hampered by the lack of a "strictly managed bank apparatus" also failed to devise a "unified plan" for the purchase of goods abroad.[53] The exception was in occupied Belgium, where German currency and contribution policies can be seen, in hindsight, as a forerunner of the strategies Germany pursued more comprehensively and systematically in World War II.[54]

But there was also a major difference. In World War I, the imperial army had introduced German marks and Reichsbank-owned foreign currencies into occupied countries. By contrast, RKK certificates, although issued by the Reichsbank, were based on foreign currencies, whose exchange rates against the mark were set by Germany to its own advantage. In theory the Reich could have eliminated RKK certificates once the occupying forces had established themselves and defeated countries were forced to pay occupation contributions in their own currencies. Yet German field intendants saw the certificates as a secondary currency that could be used at any time to bring pressure on occupied countries' financial policies. People living under occupation referred to the Reich Credit Banks in their countries as simply "soldiers' banks."[55]

RKK certificates had been stored at the Reichsbank in Berlin since the beginning of the war. Originally, they were intended for domestic use so that the regime could, in case of war, withdraw silver, copper, and nickel coins as quickly as possible from circulation and use those metals for wartime production. The idea of using the certificates abroad was apparently arrived at spontaneously after Germany's quick defeat of Poland, and it proved a success. In this way, as many scholars have concluded, the Reichsbank developed "a carefully considered instrument of wartime financing, capable of meeting every challenge, from what had been an ad hoc decision."[56]

The term "Reich credit bank" was spurious. It was used solely because the words had already been printed on the paper RKK certificates held at the Reichsbank.[57] In September 1939, the first "Reich Credit Bank" was established in Poland.[58] The board of directors consisted of representatives from the Reichsbank, the Ministries of Economics and Finance, and the Wehrmacht. They were empowered by law to regulate payment and credit systems in occupied regions; in so doing they usurped the de facto rights and duties of central banks. Untroubled by the scruples that normally constrain central bankers, one Reichsbank director, Max Kretzschmann, lauded the RKK certificates as "German currency assistance in occupied regions" and as a means of "reestablishing the possibility of normal life there."[59]

Between the summer of 1940 and June 1941, the main administration of the RKK, led by another Reichsbank director, Ernst Scholz, was located in

Brussels. Afterward, when the focus of its activities shifted to Eastern Europe, it moved to Berlin.[60] Heading up the administrative board was Emil Puhl. He and Kretzschmann, assisted by a highly qualified staff of Reichsbank managers, ran the business affairs of the RKK until 1945. Meanwhile, the Reichsbank assigned experienced civil servants to monitor the central banks of the occupied countries. They were chosen for their ability "to work well" with their colleagues at the Reich Credit Banks.[61] In dual capacities, then, the Reichsbank determined currency policies throughout occupied Europe.

For the system to work, Reich officials had "to diligently monitor the central bank in a given occupied territory." Their goal was to establish a relationship of "trusting cooperation," exploiting the local knowledge possessed by national banks to prevent "occupation authorities unfamiliar with the country" from making otherwise "unavoidable" mistakes. As part of their subtle but thorough supervision of the banking sector, Reich analysts closely monitored the entire range of activities.[62] It quickly became apparent to monitors that the use of local currencies was more advantageous than that of RKK certificates. "All psychological aversion disappears," wrote Holzhauer, "when the means of payment are familiar. In most cases, there's no mistrust at all."[63]

But the novel ways in which German administrators used the money of occupied countries fundamentally altered its essential character. What had been independent currencies that traded on foreign exchanges—and whose relative values could be supported by national banks and economics ministries—soon degenerated into mere means of payment with no international legitimacy. They had no function, Holzhauer wrote, "particularly at the international level, beyond their own respective economies." The currency regulations introduced by German bank commissioners expressly prohibited the national banks of occupied countries from exporting their currency into Germany or any other occupied or allied country.[64]

WITH GERMANY's victories over France, Holland, Luxembourg, and Belgium, the Reich Credit Banks gained the right to hold and manage securities and other valuables.[65] Immediately after the cessation of hostilities with those countries, the Currency Protection Command (Devisenschutzkommando, or DSK) in France issued a binding communiqué to banks, requiring them to report all reserves of currency, gold, gemstones, precious metals, and foreign and domestic bonds denominated in foreign currencies. These resources were to be "taken out of circulation for the time being." To ensure that they were, occupation authorities froze the safety deposit boxes of all bank customers, which could be opened only in the presence of a DSK official.[66] Currency protection officials were usually German customs employees, who were subject to the authority of the Reich financial administration.

Acting on their own initiative, DSK authorities confiscated the contents of safety deposit boxes owned by "enemies of the Reich." By August 1940, according to figures from the Reich Credit Bank in Paris, currency protection officials had taken in a half billion reichsmarks' worth of gold, currency, stocks and bonds, and outstanding claims. The booty included a ton of gold, as well as 389,000 Swiss francs, 850,000 U.S. dollars, and 800,000 stock and bond certificates. One list from the DSK in Bordeaux, which featured names such as Lichtenstern, Leibowitz, Gutwerth, Leibl, and Beck, suggests that the victims were mainly Jewish. (Often the owners of the confiscated goods were simply noted as "unknown.") The assets were then handed over to the Reich Credit Bank in Paris.[67] According to a "progress report" made by the DSK in France, the value of confiscated asserts had multiplied by April 30, 1941. The report states that 2.4 tons of gold had been "secured and confiscated," along with large amounts of gold coins and diamonds, for a total value estimated at 2.85 billion reichsmarks.[68] That sum didn't include substantial caches of foreign stocks and bonds. Ultimately, the Currency Protection Commands succeeded in seizing 53.6 tons of gold in Belgium, France, and Holland alone. The gold was then "transferred by various local DSKs to Berlin."[69]

Reich Credit Banks also managed assets expropriated from individual Jews at the local level. In 1942, for example, the Reichskommissariat Ostland (RKO), the administrative authority for the Baltic States, issued a guideline for the "transport of valuables from the noncommercial liquid assets of Jews, enemies of the state, and unknown owners." They were to be transferred to the Reich Credit Bank in Riga, where they were held on behalf of the RKO's finance division.[70] Entries from the record book in the gold vaults of the Reichsbank concerning transfers from the Reich Credit Banks in Brussels, Antwerp, and Stanisławów tell a similar story.[71]

The costs of transporting Jews from Germany to the death camps in Eastern Europe, which included food for the journey and return tickets for the train crews, were not paid in precious reichsmarks. A teletype message confirming the departure of 941 Jews from Düsseldorf to eastern Poland contains the following passage: "The transport personnel were given a total of 4,703 reichsmarks in RKK certificates to make necessary payments."[72] The Third Reich thus transferred expenses of this kind to the occupied countries.

By August 1941, the Reich mint had printed RKK certificates with a total value of 5.4 billion marks.[73] It is impossible to determine how many certificates were printed in the years that followed. But the system was successful enough that Max Kretzschmann briefed a delegation from Japan in October 1941 on the ins and outs of the German financing system. A short time later, Japanese soldiers were paid in "military yen modeled after the RKK certificates." In Tokyo, the Bank for the Development of Southern Territories was established to regulate currency matters in occupied China, Korea, Indochina, and the Philippines and "to initiate [those areas'] economic integration."[74] A few weeks after the Japanese delegation's visit, a group from India inquired about a similar briefing "because they hoped this flexible currency instrument might be useful in their preparations for liberating India and creating an independent Indian sphere of influence."[75]

In the spring of 1941, Reichsbank vice president Puhl praised the Reich Credit Banks, characterizing them as his institution's "rapid-response team."[76] In 1942, excited by "the experiences we've had in the past year," he announced the following guideline: "The issuance of RKK certificates forces an occupied territory to finance the monetary needs of German troops as soon as they have invaded. In addition, the Reich Credit Banks facilitate the financing of clearing transactions between the Reich and the occupied country. In this manner, pressure from both sides is applied to the country's national bank until it submits and prioritizes the monetary needs of German troops and the advance payments on clearing transactions above its own currency. If a national bank refuses or is unable to do this, a new central bank is founded to take over its tasks." This was the case in Poland and Belgium, where civil servants had fled the country, transferred gold reserves abroad, sabotaged currency printing presses, and otherwise refused to cooperate.[77]

Puhl's summary continued: "By transferring the financing responsibilities described above to the occupied countries, Reich Credit Banks allow us to cover our financial needs without burdening the reichsmark and thus to strengthen the German currency. The covert fiduciary means and methods by which the RKKs penetrate a country and render it useful for our wartime finances have proved very effective in practice."[78] Statement such as this belie Puhl's postwar claim to have been nothing more than an apolitical civil servant who had done his best to prevent the worst abuses.[79]

RKK certificates were the means by which military "victory could be exploited economically." The Reichsbank's leadership praised the RKKs themselves as currency instruments "whose unwavering efficiency and limitless flexibility have never before been witnessed in wartime."[80] The Reichsbank directors had succeeded in developing a method of payment that made possible the gradual impoverishment of conquered lands. It also guaranteed the stability of the reichsmark by softening the national currencies of occupied Europe.

French experts quickly recognized that the procedures introduced by the country's German occupiers would lead "to the exhaustion of our economic foundation and the ruin of our currency."[81] And in July 1940, former Leipzig mayor Carl Friedrich Goerdeler, by now a leading critic of Hitler, analyzed the effects of RKK certificates and concluded: "This system of unrestrained exploitation via unrestrained financial practices will lead inexorably to privation and starvation—first in Germany's European neighbors, then in Germany itself." He warned his countrymen that they would "one day bitterly regret, and be forced to pay for, their gullibility." The following year, Goerdeler complained about the heedless "economic depletion" of European states allied with or occupied by Germany, whose economies, "perhaps with the exception of Denmark," had already been completely ruined. Goerdeler also wrote about the motivations behind Nazi policies of rampant exploitation: "The voracious insistence on maintaining power and fooling the people into thinking that war can be profitable has apparently drowned out all reasonable considerations. There are no longer any brakes such as might be applied by moral principles or a sense of ordinary responsibility."[82]

CHAPTER 4

Profits for the People

Hitler's Satisfied Thieves

On September 3, 1939, Heinrich Böll—then a soldier in the Wehrmacht—wrote his family in Cologne that he couldn't imagine what he was going to do with his "fantastic wage of 25 marks." Sometime later, Böll reported that he was able to purchase a half pound of coffee, back then a luxury item, in Rotterdam for "all of fifty pfennigs." He sent the coffee home, expressing his regret that as a common soldier he was "allowed only one 500-gram package per week." "I'm not very optimistic about Mother's hopes for more coffee," he went on to write from the northern French coast. "But please send me whatever money you have. Perhaps I'll be able to step up my efforts on the coffee front. It can be German money. I'll just exchange it in the canteen."[1]

At that point in the war, German soldiers were allowed to receive up to 50 marks per month—their families transferred the money via army postal service, and it was paid out in the native currency of the countries where soldiers were stationed. Soon the allowance was raised to 100, and before Christmas 1939 it went up to 200 marks, "so that soldiers at least have the opportunity to buy the customary presents."[2] The increase drew a word of caution from the Wehrmacht intendant in charge of Belgium: "I cannot help but mention that, thanks to this measure, the country's shelves are in danger of being stripped completely bare."[3] Soldiers in the

Netherlands were allowed to receive the massive monthly sum of 1,000 marks (around $12,000 today) for shopping purposes. The German bank commissioner complained that "the largest sums" of German money were flowing into Holland from relatives of Wehrmacht soldiers and that the influx would necessarily lead to "damaging effects in currency matters." German economists overseeing Belgium's finances were astonished to find that, in the first year of occupation, relatives of Wehrmacht soldiers had transferred some 34 million marks—and that figure did not include the members of the Fifteenth and Sixteenth Armies—via the army postal service. They warned of "untenable consequences" if they were to have to pay out those transfers from their budget for occupying Belgium. The Finance Ministry, however, turned a deaf ear to their complaints.[4]

And despite the official regulations, soldiers were allowed to take as much money with them as they wanted when entering or leaving Germany during their frequent leaves. In the fall of 1940, the Reichsbank board of directors expressed concern about the situation at the currency exchange office in the Herzogenrath train station near Germany's western border. The office was "under extraordinary pressure from Wehrmacht soldiers in transit," noted one board member, yet employees in Herzogenrath had been "instructed to exchange any and all sums."[5] Starting in January 1941, German customs officials gave up the sporadic "checks for currency" they had been performing on soldiers. Such checks, it was concluded, only caused delays at the border and "irritated" the soldiers.[6]

In 1941, the amount of money soldiers entering Belgium could legally exchange was raised to 300 reichsmarks—considerably more than the average monthly wage of a German worker. Occupation authorities pleaded for the exchange limit to be capped at 50 marks per person, arguing that they needed "to protect the [Belgian] currency" and "curb the inflationary increase in hard currency."[7] The quartermaster general objected, "pointing out that troops from the Eastern Front" on leave in Belgium "were especially in need of relief."[8] The Wehrmacht High Command refused the request "on general grounds of troop support."[9] The army field postmaster general reported regularly about the "huge numbers of packages in his territory being sent back from the field to Germany."[10]

German soldiers stationed in France traveling home, December 1940 (Bundesarchiv)

German soldier on home leave, December 1941 (Bundesarchiv)

German soldiers literally emptied the shelves of Europe. They sent millions of packages back home from the front. The recipients were mainly women. When one asks the now elderly witnesses about this period in history, their eyes still gleam at the memory of the shoes from North Africa, the velvet, silk, liqueurs, and coffee from France, the tobacco from Greece, the honey and bacon from Russia, and the tons of herring from Norway— not to mention the various gifts that poured in from Germany's allies Romania, Hungary, and Italy.[11]

An open letter, published in 2003, from this author to older readers of the weekly newspaper *Die Zeit* asked them to share their recollections. Many respondents reported that what they received depended on whether they were lucky enough to have generous relatives. "I remember a number of nice things," one woman wrote, "that friends and relatives would proudly unpack from parcels received from 'abroad.' . . . People had more respect for the sender and compared him favorably with those who hadn't sent anything back." People who received such luxuries "boasted and bragged to others who had gotten only letters."[12] Interestingly, while female respondents offered accurate descriptions of the period, the men, without exception, denied ever having sent a single package home.

ON OCTOBER 1, 1940, the customs border between Germany and the Protectorate of Bohemia and Moravia was abolished, prompting the Reich protector, the Nazi leader in those territories, to complain about the uninhibited "purchasing frenzy" among German soldiers. "The luggage nets of the express trains," wrote another German official, "are packed to the roof with heavy suitcases, bulky packages, and stuffed bags." Even officers and high-ranking bureaucrats, he continued, were cramming their luggage with "the most extraordinary consumer goods—furs, watches, medicines, shoes—in nearly unimaginable quantities."[13]

Wolf Goette, a young actor at the German theater in Prague who would later have a successful career in East Germany, wrote back home: "Please write and tell me if there's anything I can bring back. I'll do my very best." He added: "Yesterday we bought a wonderful desk. We're always being accosted by a colleague named Wiesner. He's become a true antiques dealer. Yesterday he purchased a marvelous Empire-era etching. Today it was a Gothic Madonna from Spain. It's not the worst idea in the world to invest your money in such tangible assets." In another letter to his family, he wrote: "I've noted your various requests. Yesterday I purchased four kilos of cocoa for you (7 reichsmarks per kilo)." For a relative or acquaintance nicknamed Rolli, Goette procured "a supply of perfume and eau de cologne as well as some light-colored leather gloves for Donna." For a certain Jürgen Müller, who had sent him money, Goette obtained "a portable electric cooking stove together with a pot and a pan." He continued to take orders for goods from his family: "How many sheets of Japanese paper should I get hold of? A sheet costs fifty reichspfennigs. Has the package with the seeds arrived yet? Today I sent off the fifth package of books you requested. I'll send the rest later with the final transport."[14]

In an open letter written for but then censored by the daily newspaper in Worms, Fritz Boas, a junior officer stationed in France, reported the following: "The first thing one does is to 'storm' the shops. . . . Everyone has something to buy for his nearest and dearest back home. Today a letter from 'Mama' arrived requesting some material, if possible thin-striped brown, to make a formal dress, some chamois, and—if manageable—a couple of bars of fine soap and some whole-bean coffee. That's all for now, darling, she says. I'll write soon to tell you what else I'd like. Wait, I almost forgot. Do you still have almonds and white elastic bands?"[15]

"I'm going to pack the butter and the soap (four big bars)," wrote Heinrich Böll, "so that I can send them with the noon mail." He then issued his regular, although officially forbidden, request to his family for more money ("best concealed in a cake") for purchases. A few days later, Böll was again keeping accounts: "I sent another pound of butter yesterday. That makes four in all that are currently en route, as well as a package with a giant 400-gram bar of soap for Mother in honor of her name day. I'm 40 marks in debt, but I'm waiting for your package full of surprises." He didn't have to wait long. A short time later, he reported back home: "I've received the book 'Barbara Naderer' with what was inserted in it. That makes 60 marks (10 from you and 50 from my parents). . . . If you can ensure that things continue this way, I won't have to pass on all the splendid things on the 'black market.' . . . I'd be genuinely happy if I could send you something."[16]

On one occasion it was "a nice engraving from Paris." On others it was cosmetics, three pounds of onions for his mother, a pair of ladies' shoes, and nail scissors. At one point, Böll announced he was undertaking "an exhausting shopping spree" the following day, hoping "to stumble across something" for himself and his wife, Annemarie.[17] A few weeks later, he reported to his mother: "After mess, I returned to my quarters and sweated over the task of packing. No fewer than 11 packages in all: 2 for a comrade, one for the staff sergeant, and 8 for me: 2 for you, one with butter and one with writing paper, 2 for [his brother] Alois's family, and 4 for my family. I'll put the eggs in a package this week because I didn't have enough to send two. You'll be able to get some at home." No sooner had these orders been filled than the young soldier was back in shopper's heaven: "In Paris, I should be able to find some nice things, definitely some shoes for you and some material."[18]

The French nicknamed the tens of thousands of German soldiers like Boas and Böll "potato beetles" (*doryphores*). Of them, historian Henri Michel has written: "Loaded down with heavy packages, German soldiers departed from the Gare de l'Est for home leave. Their luggage was crammed with lingerie, specialties from Paris, and luxury goods of every description. They had been acquired in countless petty transactions, but they did significant damage to the French national economy, playing a significant role in the development of the black market and inflation. They were the reason it was increasingly difficult for everyday French people to procure the basic necessities."[19]

Liselotte S., whose father worked as a medical orderly in France, recalled in 2003:

I know that my mother sent my father money every month. He used it to buy things we lacked at home: coffee, cocoa, cheese, chocolate in various forms, shoes for my mother, for me, and our apprentices, fur-lined and plain leather gloves, once even a pair of motorcycle gloves. . . . Every day packages from France arrived in the mail. My mother also sent money to my father's buddies whose wives didn't have access to the maximum amounts allowed. One time two fur coats arrived—I was only twelve and had to grow into mine. My father used to get around the limits on the amounts he could send by taking packages to other Wehrmacht units stationed nearby. As a driver for the chief medical officer, he had plenty of opportunities, and once the mail delivered ten packages tied together. Whatever we couldn't use in our two-person household, we would swap for other good and services. Workmen who repaired the house and kept up the garden profited from them.[20]

The story was much the same in all the other countries Germany occupied, although the desired goods were often more difficult to come by than in France. A German customs investigation, for instance, cited the following passages from a letter written home to his wife by a soldier stationed in Poland: "The packages for you, my father, and Frieda went out the day before yesterday. Be on the lookout for them when they arrive. . . . The shoes are on their way. . . . I got some material for a couple of pairs of pants for Otto." Anticipating his home leave, he announced: "Ilse won't have to worry about a lack of Easter surprises. I'm well supplied, and I'll be bringing everything home for Easter. Nice things that you probably can't get anymore in Germany. I try to think of everything and get everything I can for you, and you show your gratitude by not writing. Do you think that's fair? You don't need to save the coffee I sent—I'll bring more at Easter. You can give Ida some of the cocoa you've got at home. I've got enough of that as well for you."[21]

In the Baltic States, Reich Commissioner Hinrich Lohse determined that substantial amounts of money were being imported from Germany and exchanged. He reported that soldiers were buying up whatever was available and "then shipping the purchased wares out of the territory."[22] These purchases for export were made possible by extremely high exchange rates, which quadrupled the value of the mark against the ruble. The rate had been set to the advantage of German soldiers with the aim of facilitating plunder. Unlike in the conquered nations of Western Europe, cash could be imported into, then exchanged and spent in, the occupied parts of the Soviet Union with a minimum of "bureaucratic nonsense." Soldiers were allowed to take 1,100 marks worth of RKK certificates, rubles, and German currency with them, as well as 600 zlotys (around 300 reichsmarks) for travel expenses through the General Government of Poland. The only objection raised at the Economics Ministry meeting during which those limits were set came from senior government counsel Hoffmann of the Eastern Economics Staff, who pointed out that they would cause "what amounts to a total clearance sale in the East."[23] The introduction of German currency was only restricted much later—after an urgent request by occupation authorities.[24]

In a letter published in 1954, Otto Bräutigam, a former department head at the Nazi ministry in charge of occupied territories in the East, recalled: "Because of the low prices, the Baltic States were a true El Dorado for German soldiers and the civilians who followed them. There was a gigantic shopping spree." Bräutigam knew whereof he spoke. On August 6, 1941, the first day after his arrival in Riga, he wrote of "buying some things in the 'Wehrmacht department store.'" "There wasn't a lot available," he complained, but then added: "My driver has gotten hold of 25 kilos of butter, which we split in the spirit of fairness."[25]

A soldier's daughter who was born in 1934 reported: "Among the bright spots were the packages my father sent us from the East: tin cans with excellent butter and delicious black tea from his company's stopover in Riga. I can particularly remember the clunky and at first far too large blue shoes and boots, which served me well and kept my feet dry until after the war. I was proud of the satchel of Russian leather I used as a school knapsack. My father 'organized,' as people used to say back then, various leather articles for me. A thick green woolen blanket always accompanied us whenever we children were evacuated to the countryside, as well as a dark-blue knitted sweater with a blue-and-white collar."[26]

In October 1943, when Heinrich Böll was transferred from France to the Crimea, he made one last shipment of butter home, "as a tribute from 'douce France.'" In the heavy fighting of early December, he suffered a minor head wound that probably saved his life. He landed in a military hospital in Odessa, where he wrote: "You can buy anything you want at the bazaar here." He was then sent to convalesce in Stanisławów, Poland, in what is now Ukraine, where he immediately sent one package of chocolate and one bar of soap back home. Shortly before returning to Germany on leave, he wrote: "I'm constantly asking myself if there's anything nice here I can bring you. I've given up on my dream of getting you a pair of these lovely, warm Polish booties. The price is simply too high."[27]

Even in the depths of winter in 1943, while the Wehrmacht was suffering catastrophic defeats on the battlefield, the soldiers of the Eighteenth Army near Leningrad managed, according to statistics from the military post office, to send more than 3 million packages home. They were filled with items that had been plundered, bought at bargain prices, or left over from food rations. To the disappointment of the soldiers, probably because of state restrictions the packages traveling in the other direction were markedly fewer. By then the government was seeking to conceal the extent to which Germans were enriching themselves at the cost of others. According to accounts by the military postmaster general, Karl Ziegler, his department was required "to burn all records of total statistics compiled for the military postal service."[28]

In Norway, occupying German soldiers also did their level best to empty the country's shelves, even though the Norwegians depended on imported food for their survival. While the number of packages shipped from Norway was restricted, occupation authority staff members were allowed to send 2.5 kilos of goods home per month.[29] The packages mainly contained fish, and there was a lively trade in fox fur.[30] For Christmas 1942, the Wehrmacht High Command relaxed the restrictions and even set up a "herring transfer station" to transport "barrels of herring privately purchased by vacationers" via sealed express freight trains to the northern German city of Güstrow. From there, the herring was distributed throughout the Reich.[31]

Only in 1944, when military defeat seemed probable and dissatisfaction among the Norwegian population had reached a critical level, did Reich Commissioner Josef Terboven try to limit the plundering of Norwegian herring to between 7 and 8 kilos annually per soldier. In April 1944, the chief intendant reported that he was doing his best to get the limit raised to between 10 and 12 kilos, although he added that his efforts had "regrettably not yet yielded a final result."[32]

Considering that normal weekly meat and fish rations in Germany at this point were 350 grams (less than a pound), the herring imports represented a nutritional increase of around 50 percent for German housewives. Moreover, that figure includes only officially permitted imports—it doesn't take into account vacationers' prohibited but tolerated practice of bringing fish back with them on passenger trains. In summer 1944, officers finally began disciplining a handful of German soldiers for "illegal herring exports."[33] A few months earlier, in December 1943, the Wehrmacht chief intendant in Norway had noted dryly, "Request rejected," after learning of the Reich commissioner's plans to stop the illegal smuggling.[34] Meanwhile authorities in charge of the German occupation troops had noted as early as summer 1942 that Norwegians were "considerably undernourished."[35]

Even in areas where the military situation was hopeless, officers responsible for troop welfare continued to pander to what had quickly become the habitual greed of German soldiers. In April 1943, encircled army divisions in the Kuban region along the Black Sea ordered one million small-package stamps with the inscription "one small package/front–homeland."[36] In the winter of 1944–45, the commander of 6,000 soldiers trapped by British troops on the island of Rhodes distributed some 25,000 such stamps.[37] In October 1944, the Wehrmacht High Command approved a measure allowing Germans entering occupied Italy to exchange 100 reichsmarks in RKK certificates for lire and to spend the money there. The Finance Ministry protested that the practice would further destabilize the currency and endanger the supply of basic necessities in Italy, and the decision was reversed six weeks later.[38]

Private purchases in the month of August 1943 in occupied France totaled 125 million reichsmarks. Even allowing for the devaluation of the franc, the equivalent would be hundreds of millions of dollars today.[39] Private purchases drove up inflation, disrupted occupation authorities' attempts to control the market, and undermined all forms of economic stability. Stability, however, was precisely what was required to ensure the long-term exploitation of the resources of an occupied country. The functionaries responsible for running occupied economies repeatedly tried to restrict the number of packages sent through the military postal service and to subject German soldiers to customs and currency checks. But customs officials described such checks as "truly precarious" situations that often led to "unfortunate confrontations" and "rebellion and insults."[40] The few occasions when customs officials actually did confiscate goods or currency inevitably "called forth a general mood of bitterness among the troops."[41]

As early as October 1940, to maintain troop morale, Göring had completely abolished the already liberal limits on what soldiers could purchase, dismissing "worries raised from various quarters that stores in the occupied territories would soon be stripped bare" as "negligible."[42] In the same breath he condemned "the measures instituted to enforce restrictions on purchases and shipments" as "psychologically intolerable." Instead he ordered that German soldiers in hostile countries be allowed to buy everything they could afford, with no greater restrictions than applied to native citizens. Existing "prohibitions on the purchases of furs, jewelry, carpets, silks, and luxury items" were to be "immediately" lifted. Also to be abolished were restrictions on the numbers of packages soldiers were allowed to send back home through the military postal service. (Limits on packages in the other direction were retained.)

Göring used the occasion to formulate what became known as the "Schlep Decree" (*Schlepperlass*): "The basic restrictions on the transport of purchased items by soldiers on leave, etc., are to be lifted. Soldiers should be allowed to take with them whatever they can carry so long as it is intended for their own personal use or that of their dependents."[43] Göring also ordered the free shipment through the military postal service of packages weighing up to 1,000 grams (with 200-gram leeway) "in unlimited numbers." On July 14, 1942, customs officials quietly lifted the regulations governing packages whose weight exceeded that limit.[44]

Taking the same view as most of his soldiers, Hitler praised the Wehrmacht as "the most natural middleman available to a soldier who wants to send something to his wife or children." In the summer of 1942, he admonished Admiral Erich Raeder: "When soldiers bring something home from the

Eastern Front," it is "a bonus that benefits the homeland."[45] On occasions in which individual officers and customs officials tried to put a stop to uninhibited plundering, the Führer vented his rage on behalf of the troops: "To put it bluntly: What can I take with me from the East? Treasures of art? They don't exist. All that's left is food to stuff your mouth. Nothing better can happen to it than that it be given to a soldier's family here at home."[46] Around the same time, Hitler remarked that a soldier on home leave "should be considered the ideal and simplest means of transport and should be given as much food as he can physically carry."[47]

The chief of the Wehrmacht High Command, Field Marshal Wilhelm Keitel, quickly translated these statements into a personal decree of the Führer's. The edict read: "Food, intoxicants, and tobacco brought back from occupied territories to the Reich by members of the Wehrmacht on home leave or official business, insofar as they are carried by hand, are to be made immediately exempt from all forms of control and confiscation."[48] In early August 1942, at a high-level meeting devoted to the topic of food supplies, Göring returned to the issue. According to the minutes of the meeting, Göring interjected: "Is the finance minister in attendance?" The deputy minister replied: "Yes, sir! Reinhardt here!" Göring then continued: "Mr. Reinhardt, desist with your customs checks. I'm no longer interested in them. . . . I'd rather have unlimited amounts of goods smuggled in than have custom duties paid on nothing at all."

At the same meeting, Göring issued even more drastic statements. Angered by occupation authorities who were trying to stabilize France's currency to facilitate its long-term exploitation, Göring thundered: "It has been said that we need to restrict soldiers' access to their pay, or it will cause inflation in France. But inflation is what I want to see more than anything else. . . . The franc should be worth nothing more than a sheet of a certain type of paper used for a specific purpose. That will hit France exactly the way we want to hit France."[49]

In her autobiography, a librarian who worked in Hamburg during the Third Reich described the consequences of this attitude: "We didn't suffer any privations. . . . Our food, clothing, and shoe vouchers were honored. Our men were still bringing back meat, wine, textiles, and tobacco from the occupied territories." When the same eyewitness traveled to Cologne in the summer of 1943, after her parents' home was hit by an Allied bomb, she found the train station crammed with soldiers on leave from the Eastern Front whose homes had also been destroyed: "There they stood, having traveled day and night, laden down with knapsacks and packages." Even as late as Christmas 1944, the author's brother, who had been given last-minute leave, was able to produce "a whole goose, half a suckling pig, and a large slab of bacon from his luggage." He also brought home, apparently from his Wehrmacht rations, "coffee, tea, schnapps, and cigarettes."[50]

The effects of Hitler's order, as transmitted by Keitel, to suspend all customs checks are described in an urgent communication from customs officials in the city of Kiel, near the German-Danish border: "There is no doubt that the majority of goods imported by members of the Wehrmacht into German territory under the guise of 'comrades' luggage' are to be sold at dramatically inflated prices. It is equally beyond doubt that members of the Wehrmacht, especially of the navy and the Luftwaffe, are engaged to a considerable extent in such black market activities—for the purpose of personal profit."[51] Deputy Finance Minister Reinhardt intervened to end the quarrels and complaints on Germany's northern and eastern borders by invoking Hitler's decree: "It is the Führer's will that as many foodstuffs as possible be brought back home from the occupied eastern territories and that customs authorities take a hands-off approach."[52]

By sweeping aside restrictions maintained by Wehrmacht intendants, Hitler and Göring encouraged Germans in their spirited, organized, and extremely popular drive to loot the shelves of occupied Europe. At the beginning of the war, the Wehrmacht had decreed that products scarce in Germany could be imported duty-free into the Reich in "amounts of up to 5 kilos in weight"—a relatively modest allotment.[53] The limit was initially maintained despite constant reports from various authorities that it was being exceeded. But by summer 1940, political pressure had forced the Wehrmacht High Command to double the amount.[54]

Göring's Schlep Decree, which legalized the near-unlimited transport of goods from occupied Europe to Germany, was politically motivated. Measured against figures from September 1940, the number of packages sent via military post from France to Germany immediately quintupled and settled at an average of 3.1 million a month.[55] On November 1, 1940, soldiers' pay was increased by 50 percent in Poland, Norway, and Holland, by 20 percent in France and Denmark, and by 25 percent in Belgium. The pay raises were intended to "enable members of the Wehrmacht to satisfy their consumer needs to a greater extent."[56] On behalf of the Wehrmacht leadership, Quartermaster General Eduard Wagner, Field Marshal Walther von Brauchitsch, and Lieutenant General Hermann Reinecke endorsed the decree.

As Böll's letters home make clear, soldiers were quickly corrupted by their new and improved abilities to acquire goods. Prior to the Schlep Decree he noted with a modicum of criticism: "The store shelves will of course now be emptied by soldiers. . . . I have reservations about joining in the stockpiling; although everything is paid for, it reminds me of robbing a corpse. The only thing in particular that I have my eyes on is coffee." In the end, he also bought a polo shirt for 2 marks and a bath towel for 80 pfennigs, but he kept his desires in check, remarking that his comrades' search for bargains "was gradually degenerating into plain and simple hoarding." On another occasion he reflected on his own indomitable desire to buy things: "The devil of temptation is truly a devil. He's everywhere!" Böll was not long in succumbing. Before returning to Cologne on leave he announced to his family: "I've got half a suckling pig for you." Later he looked back with a heavy heart on such happy times: "Alas, I would like so much to bring back a suckling pig or something like that."[57]

In his "Letter to a Young Catholic," composed in 1958, Böll offered a number of recollections from his time in France. He described, for instance, the schoolmaster's wife who had allowed herself to be photographed on a porch in order to show the officers' wives the lovely blouse she had had made from French silk. Böll also described, in tones of disgust, how members of his unit stole sheets, blankets, and toys from deserted houses, packing them up in bundles and shipping them home. He spent *his* time, in his retrospective account, visiting cathedrals and debating ways to practice Catholicism. All he acquired was a book, bought in

Paris, by a Germanophobe whose tirades he juxtaposed with his family's nightly fear in their bomb shelter in Cologne.[58]

In the wake of the Schlep Decree, a debate arose within the bureaucracy over how to define "anything a soldier can carry." According to the Wehrmacht High Command's official interpretation, soldiers were allowed to take with them only "as much baggage as they can carry in both hands without the help of straps or other means of assistance."[59] Soldiers were also required to salute while carrying their baggage. These restrictions raised objections from customs officials in the Finance Ministry, who argued that "limits on the amount of permissible goods should not be set according to the physical strength of entering persons." The officials called for a "generally applicable standard independent of how much a given individual can carry." When the debate found its way into the official customs trade publication, the political leadership ran out of patience.[60]

In August 1942, Göring condemned as "nonsense" the military rule that soldiers were allowed to carry only as much as would not hinder them from delivering mandatory military salutes. That regulation, Göring raged, ran contrary to his "repeatedly" expressed will: "Soldiers can buy as much as they want, whatever they want, and whatever they can carry." Göring's position was summed up by his associate Fritz Klare, who oversaw German food supplies under the Four-Year Plan. Every Wehrmacht soldier, Klare decreed, should be "allowed to import as much food and as many basic commodities as he as an individual can afford and carry. Potential inflationary consequences in the occupied territories need not be taken into consideration." Furthermore, "encumbering" customs regulations were to be lifted.[61] A short time later, Berlin customs officials raided the home of a Luftwaffe colonel and discovered substantial amounts of fine cognac and spirits on which no alcohol duties had been paid. The raid also drew Göring's ire: "The acquisition of limited quantities of wine, cognac, and similar commodities—even those subject to requisition certificates—is not only allowed but encouraged by my express wish. It does not amount to smuggling."[62]

It would take another two months and a further explosion of rage by Hitler for Deputy Finance Minister Reinhardt to issue the following edict—in direct contravention of existing regulations—to the Reich customs authorities: "Members of the Wehrmacht are indeed allowed to use straps and other means of assistance to carry belongings. They are not required to assume 'a military posture' when crossing the border." Soldiers and baggage belonging to them should be treated "as liberally as possible," and customs officials were to "refrain from all confiscations of packages of food that soldiers carry with them." "Heads of finance departments," Reinhardt added threateningly, "will run the risk of being held personally accountable by the Führer, if any of their subordinates transgress this prohibition." Reinhardt justified the edict with reference to paragraph 1 of the Tax Revision Law of 1934, which directed taxation economists in the Finance Ministry to "take into account changing circumstances and popular sentiment." It also bound them to "interpret" every article of law "according to the National Socialist worldview."[63]

At the end of 1943, the Nazi leadership allowed the occupation authorities in France—in the face of the acute danger of inflation—to stop the technically illegal but tacitly encouraged import of hundreds of millions of marks in RKK certificates. But Göring quickly issued a qualification: "I ask you to ensure that the measures to be taken do not lessen the existing legal purchasing capacity of troops transferred west, especially from the Eastern Front."[64] Only when the war began to turn against Germany did Göring feel compelled to stop encouraging private plunder. On May 15, 1944, he gave in to pressure from the Finance and Food Ministries and prohibited "the import of flour, shortening, and meat from the occupied territories." But the edict was never carried out for fear of popular disapproval. In October, the Finance Ministry noted that because of the worsening military situation "the implementation measures for the prohibition edict were not yet in force."[65]

Reading between the lines of Böll's letters home from the field, one senses a tension between his desire to behave with reasonable restraint and the urge, encouraged by Hitler and Göring, to fall upon the defeated enemy like a plague of locusts. Böll, too, exploited the possibilities offered by RKK certificates, writing to his family: "It would nice be if you could smuggle a few credit certificates in a letter so that I can pay my debts." On another occasion, he instructed his wife: "Tell them at home to collect credit certificates. I've got a lot of money to exchange from comrades and for me as well." Occasionally, although not often, the attempts to smuggle money or procure bargains went awry. "That was really bad luck with the credit certificates," Böll wrote once, without elaborating further. "I could have sent a sizeable amount of chocolate or soap." In general, though, soldiers like Böll enjoyed the benevolent protection of Göring and Hitler and could go about their shopping purposefully and happily, sending home whatever they acquired. On one occasion, immediately after returning from home leave, Böll wrote: "Please just send me money in your letters so that I can bring back something of the treasures of this country. So that we, too, can have a small party. Every day will be a celebration."

The zeal of whole divisions of bargain hunters, family providers, and insatiable opportunists considerably alleviated the hardships of war. It fostered a sense of material connection between the battlefield and the home front. The calculated policy of allowing soldiers to personally enrich themselves at the expense of foreign peoples gave rise to the feeling that their interests were being watched over from above and that small oases of pleasure were possible within the larger war. "Do you know," Böll wrote to his wife, "how happy it makes me to be able to send you something?" On another occasion, he rhapsodized: "It was the source of truly indescribable joy for me to supply you with butter."[66] This was one reason for the pervasive—though in Böll's case passive—loyalty felt by Germans toward the Nazis. And it was all the dictatorship required to keep functioning politically. The Bölls—a Catholic family disinclined to sympathize with Nazism—were basically satisfied with their lot. Their money wasn't sitting around uselessly. It was being transformed in France, albeit at ever increasing prices, into practical necessities and luxury items.

The Reich's Flea Market

Individual acts of plunder by buying up goods in foreign countries soon gave rise to more organized forms of criminality. Smuggling and black marketeering were occasionally pursued in the sheer spirit of adventure, but more often than not they were directly motivated by the desire for profit. Between 1940 and 1941, trains in the Alsatian city of Metz were requisitioned by civil servants who then drove on to Paris, where they used tens of thousands of RKK certificates to buy "scarce commodities such as coffee, tea, cocoa, chocolate, cognac, champagne, wine, liqueurs, clothing, nylons, etc." These goods were then brought back by train to Metz, "where postal workers from Nuremberg took possession of them, smuggled them back home, and sold them—mostly, according to one customs document, to other postal workers."[67]

On a small scale, soldiers "misused the military mail" to send home packages containing as many as eight hundred cigarettes from Romania, Bulgaria, or Greece. On a grander scale, they stuffed whole wagonloads of contraband onto Wehrmacht trains returning to the Reich. In one instance, soldiers packed more than fourteen tons of oranges onto a military freight train bound for the southern German city of Rosenheim, where they were delivered to family members as "tokens of affection." A dentist who worked at Auschwitz was apprehended in the Protectorate of Bohemia and Moravia with a heavy lump of gold. Citing a vow of secrecy he had sworn, he refused to provide authorities with any information about where the gold came from.

The head of the Cologne Finance Department resigned himself to the fact that rampant corruption was a consequence of war, one that could not be effectively combated. "With people under considerable physical and mental stress," he wrote, "it is understandable that they should develop a strong desire for intoxicants that, except for tobacco, cannot be satisfied in modest proportions. . . . Our ethnic comrades from humble circumstances are especially willing to pay any price for the wares they want." The Frankfurt customs bureau recorded the case of a Luftwaffe soldier who sold French spirits in Frankfurt to a barkeeper in Kassel; another sent 170 kilos of food from Ukraine, along with carpets and oil paintings, to his wife. Upon being caught, he was sentenced to three weeks' house arrest. In Baden-Baden, "large quantities" of French perfume were traded at inflated prices. Unscrupulous companies mislabeled goods destined for private consumption as "vital wartime supplies"; soldiers passed them off as "Wehrmacht freight." Within the Reich, a Luftwaffe inspector was found with 16,000 marks' worth of RKK certificates intended for a shopping spree in France, while across the border a soldier was caught trying to smuggle jewelry valued at 155,800 marks into Germany.[68]

In the face of ever more brazen acts of criminality, the German military administration in Belgium called for special courts to combat pandemic corruption. The request failed because it was submitted to, of all people, Göring. The military administration's final report from Belgium stated that "repeated requests" for a special court to try soldiers who had been caught black-marketeering had "never received a positive response." The special court had been deemed necessary "because courts within individual parts of the Wehrmacht were inclined to dismiss or even endorse violations of rules by their own members. This was particularly the case in the Luftwaffe."[69] Göring was, of course, the commander in chief of that branch of the German military.

One document in particular sheds light on the topic of organized criminality and therefore merits extensive quotation. It originated in the postal censor's office (*Abwehrstelle Briefpost*, or ABP) in Ukraine, where civil servants examined thousands of letters sent by Germans between the Reich and the occupied territory. The censors' analysis offers precise insight into the ever expanding scope of activities pursued by German men and women from a variety of professions and walks of life. The document bears the rather baroque title "Report A on the Conditions in Ukraine Based on an Examination by the 'German Service Post,' Ukraine, of the Private Correspondence between the Reich and Ukraine of German Companies Deployed to the Reich Commission [*Reichskommissariat*] and Their Employees." The Service Post was responsible for delivering correspondence to and from employees of the German civilian administration in the Reich Commission in Ukraine, as well as to and from employees of companies engaged in the "exploitation of the economic expansion territory of Ukraine." The document is undated, but judging from references in one section to "the crisis at the start of the year" and "doubts and disheartenment," it was probably written after the battle of Stalingrad, most likely in the summer of 1943. All emphases are in the original.

The report reads:

Over the past six months the ABP has examined thousands of letters from Germans assigned to Ukraine. They show, on the one hand, that a large number of Germans in Ukraine have contributed diligently and enthusiastically to the enormous tasks, and [their efforts] reflect the gigantic work being done to build up the European East. The letters also reveal, however, serious and unsettling *signs of corruption*. Criticism and negative sentiments jump out at the reader, and the damage done to Ukraine may appear more significant than it is. But the content of the letters leaves no doubt that the damage is real and that it runs gravely counter to the interests of the Reich and undermines the great efforts undertaken to build up Ukraine.

First and foremost among the signs of corruption in Ukraine is *black marketeering*. The majority of letters from Ukraine are about barter. Conducting business transactions is the only thing about Ukraine that interests the majority of the authors. Everything imaginable and unimaginable is traded for native Ukrainian products (eggs, oils, bacon, ham, etc.). The commodities mentioned in the letters include, among other things, salt, matches, flints, yeast, old clothing, household goods, women's lingerie, handbags, graters, cucumber peelers, suspenders, saccharin, face cream, baking soda, fingernail polish, baking powder, lipstick, and toothbrushes. The letters give the impression, as many of their authors themselves write, that Ukraine has become "the Reich's flea market" and that Germany is unloading its entire surplus of junk wares onto Ukraine. As one letter puts it: Here you can "hawk" everything. The cheapest fake jewelry, medallions, and chains are fobbed off on Ukrainian peasant women. There's apparently a huge market for old and unfashionable clothing in garish colors. In one case, a letter writer asks for the "cheapest glass jewelry," promising to return the crate full of 2,000 eggs. The whole thing, writes one observer in Ukraine, is reminiscent of the "trade" with Negro tribes and the "exchange" of glass pearls for ivory.

The thread running through the letters home from Ukraine is: Scrape together everything you can get your hands on. "Buy up everything"—or something similar—is what the letters say. "Money is

no object." "Don't worry about money—buy whatever you can." Housewives are told to collect all the junk they have lying around at home.
One housewife is even instructed not to give anything to the clothing
drive: "I need everything here for myself." Recipients are told to "hit up
relatives and friends for old clothes," dresses, used household goods,
etc. . . . Money is borrowed for the necessary purchases. Shopping
groups are formed. Whole branches of families come together to organize shipments of exchangeable goods to Ukraine. Friends and relatives
pool their unused points on clothing ration cards from 1942. "I know
our relatives won't give up the points for nothing. You don't have to ask
them to do that." Considerable sums of "reward money" are offered for
help in procuring exchangeable goods. Chains of barter and swap are
organized. Grandfather, as one particularly crass letter puts it, should
send his new boots to Ukraine. In return he'll get eight liters of oil that
he can swap for a new coat, which "we can probably hawk as well."
In another case, the letter writer offers to trade oil for out-of-fashion
women's shoes, with the idea of "cranking up business." That's how the
exchange business is organized in Ukraine and in the Reich.

All scales and sorts of barter are in evidence. Some people have
pounds of salt sent to them and ship their families a dietary supplement
of 5 to 10 eggs every fortnight. Others send home 10, 20, 30, 40 packages
in rapid succession. Others still go so far as to have 10 tons of salt (!)
transferred to Ukraine. (A ton of salt in Ukraine has an exchange value
of 1,000 marks; for a pound of salt you can acquire a chicken, for 10
pounds a sheep.) Shipments of anywhere from 2,000 to 3,000 eggs to individual families in Germany are not a rarity. One letter writer reports
with pride that he sent his wife one and a half tons of goods for Christmas. Another writer mentions that an employee of a trade company in
Ukraine distributes more butter for the purpose of bribes than the entire
yearly ration in the Reich. The following deliveries have also been mentioned: "a crate of alcoholic spirits, karakul [lamb] skins, and 2,300 eggs
(one shipment); a crate of spirits and two barrels of honey (one shipment); package no. 1: two chickens and honey; nos. 3–4: chickens; no. 5:
eggs; no. 6: noodles; no. 7: semolina; no. 8: peas; no. 9: groats; no. 10: bacon; nos. 11–12: beans; nos. 15–16: meat and bacon; nos. 17–19: eggs,

bacon, and flour; nos. 20–22: eggs, sugar, and butter; no. 23: sausage and cakes." (The 23 packages were sent in the space of two consecutive days!)

The trade is not restricted to simple barter. There are also large-scale business transactions, which are possible only with the help of *bribery, corruption, and gross violations of regulations.* Such "large shipments" are smuggled in via official transports. Whole train cars are rerouted to the Reich with the assistance of transport companies and corrupt railroad workers. Train personnel are coveted "contacts" and are "greased" with hefty rewards. (The letters speak openly of this.) Large amounts of goods are transferred by plane—in part with the aid of flight crews. Black marketeers are organizing a parallel postal service. A great many letters and packages are carried by those on home leave or visiting Germany. It has been reported that a "golden pheasant," i.e., a man in a brown uniform, took "a whole sack of letters" back with him on his leave. It is therefore likely that our unit here never got wind of many cases of corruption. The "tradable goods" and the deliveries back to the Reich are often the result of embezzlement. There are descriptions of the "help" of an acquaintance in the "card department" [the department for food ration cards], and the head of a meat company reports in blasé fashion that he has far too little turnover "to put much aside." Deliveries from the Reich earmarked to supply the German administration in Ukraine (fixtures, wine, etc.) are being redirected back to Germany, where they are sold on the black market. Irreparable damage has been done to the economic foundations of Ukraine. It has been reported that irreplaceable karakul lambs needed for breeding have been slaughtered and their skins shipped to the Reich.

The illegal trade is not just aimed at acquiring personal family necessities. It is becoming a *"business,"* carried out on a commercial basis. People are investing and earning money. The letters promise that money grows on trees in Ukraine and that people can get rich there quickly. "Here, you can become a rich woman overnight." Ordinary people are in a position to write home that they have already "earned" thousands. Others want to convert profits made in Ukraine into cars and property in the Reich. In nouveau riche fashion, jewels and expensive furs are purchased for housewives. The letter writers tell of gigantic profits in Ukraine.

Glass jewelry is sold at a 1,000 percent markup. Matches fetch 6 "meters" (=marks), as they're known here, and old suits can be sold for 600 marks. The letters are often written in revolting black market slang. People assure the recipients that they're "good at organizing." They brag about having "pulled off a thing" and praise the "brains" that carried out all these dirty deals. In one such letter, the situation is described as follows:

"Everyone seems to think that their most basic task is to make their own lives as comfortable as possible by hoarding as much food as they can and sending it back home. In any case, superhuman feats have been achieved in this area. Illegal trading and black marketeering are in full bloom. What the Jews used to do is now being carried out in much more highly perfected form by 'Aryans.' "

Corruption is also seeping from Ukraine into the Reich. The deliveries of goods from Ukraine serve as the basis for the new black market in Germany. As is reported in numerous letters, shipments of eggs that often greatly exceed what a family can consume are swapped for rationed or otherwise scarce commodities. Recipients take trips to the countryside to conceal oil smuggled in from Ukraine. People are purchasing material for suits from Ukraine with goods obtained illegally. And the treasures are even used as payoffs. In the case of one shipment of 500 eggs, the female recipient, who is apparently eligible to be drafted into wartime service, is instructed to give 100 to a person working at an employment office.

All of this supports the harsh conclusion that is often drawn in the letters: Ukraine is a black market paradise. People often refer to Germans working in business and civilian administration in Ukraine as 'East hyenas.' "[70]

The details of this report reflect the colonialist mentality of the Führer. In his table talks, Hitler sketched out how he wanted the "natives" in Eastern Europe to be dealt with: "We'll give the Ukranians head scarves, glass jewelry, and everything else colonized peoples like."[71] Meeting with a representative from Germany's ally Croatia, Hitler alluded to the prospect of opening Soviet territories as a market for industrially produced junk. The people there, according to Hitler, "didn't even own the simplest tableware or cooking utensils."[72] In the summer of 1942, Hitler laid out a vision of the future that mirrored what his subjects were already eagerly practicing for their own private gain: "At harvest time, we'll set up shop in every larger market town in every larger spot where we can bring our cheapest products. At the market, grain and fruit will be sold too. Once you've sold something, you can buy something else. . . . The cheapest and brightest calico is wonderful here."[73] After a conversation with Hitler, the Reich commissioner for Ukraine, Gauleiter Erich Koch, declared: "The most ordinary kitsch is good enough for this populace."[74] Hitler was like the boss of the band of thieves. With every such utterance, he supported and encouraged the barely concealed greed of his corrupt soldiers and functionaries.

Nonbureaucratic Emergency Assistance

In the late summer of 1941, while people in the East were dreaming of a black market El Dorado, civilians in Germany's northwestern cities were increasingly feeling the effects of British bombing. Within the space of weeks, the need for rapid assistance for those whose property had been damaged in air raids became one of the Nazi regime's most important domestic issues. The gauleiter of Hamburg, Karl Kaufmann, reported that after heavy raids in September he "personally approached the Führer requesting to have the Jews evacuated so that at least some of those who had been hit by the bombs could be given new apartments."

Such arguments helped persuade Hitler that fall to begin deporting Jews during the war instead of waiting for a decisive victory, as had been previously envisioned. "The Führer reacted immediately to my suggestion," Kaufmann recalled, "and issued the relevant orders to have the Jews transported away."[75] At the Wannsee Conference on January 20, 1942, Reinhard Heydrich underscored the importance of the "question of apartments and other social-political necessities" in the decision to commence with deportations.

On November 4, 1941, the head of the Finance Department in Cologne reported that in his district the "evacuation of the Jews began on October 21 . . . for the purpose of freeing up apartments for those who suffered air raid damage in the cities of Cologne and Trier." The process was "progressing steadily."[76] In fact, where Jews resided largely determined when they would be deported in the massive sweeps of late 1941. The first transports were filled with people who lived in northern and western German cities targeted by the RAF. That October, 8,000 Jews were forcibly resettled to the Lodz ghetto from the cities of Berlin, Cologne, Frankfurt am Main, Hamburg, and Düsseldorf. Ten days later an additional 13,000 people were deported, mostly from cities such as Bremen, Hamburg, Berlin, Bielefeld, Münster, Hanover, Kassel, and Frankfurt am Main, which had already been damaged by or were likely targets of air raids. The deportees were sent to ghettos in Riga, Kovno, and Minsk.[77]

Immediately after the initial wave of deportations, the head of the Cologne Finance Department ordered not only apartments and houses "but also household effects, especially textiles and furnishings, put into the deserving hands of victims of bombing raids, newly married couples, widows of fallen soldiers, etc."[78] The head of the Westphalian Finance Department, who was located in heavily damaged Münster, also instructed his subordinates to ensure "that goods, especially linens and household furnishings, get to the right recipients—air raid victims, newly married couples, war widows, etc."[79] At the express wish of Joseph Goebbels in his capacity as gauleiter of Berlin, district authorities in the German capital hoarded the belongings of deportees "for the purpose of supplying [our] ethnic comrades who suffered damage in bombing raids and as a reserve supply for possible future damage."[80]

In early November 1941, when the Reich finance minister ordered the immediate sale of "Jewish assets" at the best available prices, his first priority was raising quick, easy cash for the Reich. He barely mentioned the destruction wrought by aerial warfare. By summer 1942 that had changed. From then on, "sufferers from bombing damage" were to be taken into account "in the disposal of the household effects" of deported Jews. Mayors were instructed to store confiscated belongings for future eventualities and to transfer the artificially low revenues of the sales to Berlin.[81] A variety of institutions competed with air raid sufferers for a share of the loot. For the modest sum of 1,850.50 reichsmarks, the Cologne city orphanage bought furniture from the Jewish Children's Home; an old-age home, a hospital, the music academy, and the public library also got in on the act. Private citizens, depending on their class and therefore needs, could acquire volumes of Rilke's poetry and sheet music to Mozart's *Requiem*, or simply a pair of shoes, a school knapsack, or a set of bed linens.[82]

In December 1941, Nazi Party ideologue Alfred Rosenberg suggested confiscating the household effects of those Jews "who had fled or were in the process of fleeing" Paris and "all other occupied territories of Western Europe." His sights were set on the personal belongings of Jews in France, Belgium, Holland, and Luxembourg. Confiscated furnishings were earmarked for German civil servants recently assigned to the eastern territories, whose "terrible living conditions" might thus be raised to the levels of comfort to which they were accustomed. Rosenberg advanced the idea of stealing Jews' possessions in his dual function as the Reich minister for the occupied eastern territory and as the head of his own task force (Einsatzstab). The latter body was responsible for the theft of artworks in occupied Europe and routinely inspected the homes of Jews who had fled or been taken into custody "for the purpose of securing Jewish cultural property."

Hitler signed off on Rosenberg's idea several weeks later, with the caveat, presumably after consultation with the finance minister, that "confiscated objects were to become property of the Reich." He also redirected the new confiscations. Because military transports took precedence, making it impossible to transfer seized belongings to German civil servants in the occupied Soviet Union, they were to be used "for the Reich" itself.[83] He envisioned a program of streamlined emergency assistance for German air raid victims. With the RAF stepping up aerial bombardments, seizures from deported German Jews alone would soon no longer suffice to cover the supplies needed.

On January 14, 1942, Rosenberg repeated his order to appropriate "in their entirety the household effects of Jews who have fled or are in the process of fleeing the occupied western territories." To coordinate these seizures, he appointed the head of the German Red Cross, Kurt von Behr, who had previously been responsible for the theft of artworks. Von Behr later boasted that he himself—and not Rosenberg—had devised the "furniture operation," which the Führer then approved.[84] Regardless of who first thought of stealing the household effects of refugees and deportees, there is no doubt that it was the Army High Command that issued the orders that paved the way. The Finance Ministry later determined that Hitler had merely "approved the message," while the Army High Command "ordered it," belying the still common notion that the German military had nothing to do with the Final Solution.[85]

Von Behr was soon presiding over the distribution of scarce commodities such as bed, table, and personal linens, porcelain, dishes, silverware, and household appliances. In the first phase of the operation, replacement household effects were directed to the bomb-damaged cities of Oberhausen, Bottrop, Recklinghausen, Münster, Düsseldorf, Cologne, Osnabrück, Hamburg, Lübeck, and Karlsruhe.[86] The operation was an immediate success, and von Behr was quickly freed from his other duties as "director of the Louvre task force," where he served as Rosenberg's chief looter of art. Thereafter, the Red Cross official dedicated all his energies to the "securing of Jewish household effects for the victims of air raids."[87]

Germany's ambassador to France advised his superiors not to inform the French government in advance about the confiscation of furnishings, since there was ultimately "no formal legal justification for the operation." In a pinch, he added, one could argue for its "immediate historical necessity" as part of a common European battle Germany was waging against Bolshevism.[88] Some of those who participated in the operation may have used that pretense—that the furniture was being requisitioned for the joint German-French struggle against Soviet Communism—to disguise an act of simple theft that violated international law. Göring, however, was not bothered by such scruples. He took it as a matter of course that "household effects from the occupied territories should be placed at the disposal of air raid victims in the Reich."[89] The Vichy government repeatedly demanded "compensation" for "home furnishings transferred to Russia," including the effects of dispossessed Jews, which constituted part of "the French people's collective assets."[90] Vichy collaborators, however, were asking not for those effects to be returned but rather for their value to written off the occupation costs France was forced to pay.

On November 17, 1943, Rosenberg reported personally to Hitler on the progress of the furniture operation. He noted: "With the Führer's

Lightbulbs, children's toys, bed and table linens, furniture, and household effects of all varieties are sorted through by Jewish forced laborers in Paris, then collected and prepared for transport to German cities bombed by the Allies. Paris, September 1943. (Bundesarchiv)

permission, [goods from] some 250,000 Jewish households have been confiscated. Of those, 47,000 have been delivered to the Reich and been placed by regional leaders at the disposal of those who suffered losses from bombing raids. Transport to the Reich is continuing, as are further confiscations in France."[91] Within two months, Hitler's willing and unwilling assistants—French transport companies and Jewish forced laborers—had shipped property from a further 10,000 households to Germany. (The forced laborers received the truly "minimal wage of five francs a day"—the equivalent today of $3.)[92] By the end of 1943, the theft included almost a million cubic meters of furniture, for whose transport more than 24,000 freight cars had been required. (Precise figures for the substantial amount of furniture transported by sea and river are not available.)

A dispute between the president of the Cologne Finance Department and his subordinate in the Finance Office in nearby Trier illustrates how smoothly the supply was flowing. Citing the continual bombardment of his city, the Cologne official demanded the transfer of furniture confiscated from deported Jews in Trier, Cologne's relatively untouched provincial neighbor. His subordinate in Trier countered by saying the furniture was needed locally. After a period of four weeks, the Cologne official relented "because of the plentiful deliveries of household goods from abroad."[93] (Even the transport costs were paid by others.) On May 30–31, 1942, the Allies launched what became known as the "thousand bomber attack" against Cologne. In his final report, the city gauleiter, Josef Grohé, declared somewhat vaguely: "With the help of military commanders in Belgium and northern France, it has been possible to transport large quantities of rationing-exempt textiles to Cologne. Appropriate measures have been taken with respect to providing the populace with furniture, household effects, and basic commodities."[94]

In Belgium, von Behr and his subordinates confiscated the furnishings of 3,868 apartments owned or rented by Jews. Some of the booty went directly to the military, but the vast majority was sent to air raid survivors in Düsseldorf, Mainz, Holzminden, Oberhausen, Cologne, Münster, Wanne-Eickel, Königs Wusterhausen, Berlin, Recklinghausen, Gelsenkirchen, Gladbeck, Bottrop, Aachen, Bremen, Hamburg, Soltau,

Uelzen, Winsen, and Celle. A total of twenty-eight vehicles full of furniture arrived in Aachen within three weeks during the summer of 1943. "Household goods and linens formerly owned by foreign Jews" were distributed to bombed-out German families and "gratefully received." Also among the recipients were large families and wounded veterans, whose claims had long been acknowledged but theretofore unaddressed.

A government document from the summer of 1944 records that the cities receiving the largest shipments were Karlsruhe with 481 freight cars full of furniture taken from West European Jews, Mannheim with 508, Berlin with 528, Düsseldorf with 488, Essen with 518, Duisburg with 693, Oberhausen with 605, Hamburg with 2,699, Cologne with 1,269, Rostock with 703, Oldenburg with 884, Osnabrück with 1,269, Wilhelmshaven with 441, Delmenhorst with 3,260, Münster with 523, Bochum with 555, and Kleve with 310. At the same time the contents of 8,191 freight cars were directed to central depots, where furniture could be promptly transferred to bombed-out civilians. The contents of 1,576 of these freight cars went to families of rail workers living in company settlements, who were, because of their proximity to train stations, particularly at risk of bombardment. The SS claimed the contents of some 500 others.[95]

The goods were also used as rewards, enabling recipients to maintain or renovate their homes in style. The addressees of one freight shipment included a "Obersturmführer Tychsen (Recipient of the Knight's Cross with Oak Leaves)," "Captain Ninnemann," "Captain Adamy," "Sturmführer Brehmer (Recipient of the Knight's Cross)," and "Reich Post Office (Postal Check Office) Director, Berlin, Guilleaume." In another instance of personal profiteering, a party comrade von Ingram, "together with other bearers of the Knight's Cross," received "proceeds" from the furniture operation.[96] Special recognition was paid to "veterans and party members with especially distinguished service records," who were given homes and businesses "previously owned by Jews" in order to "support them in the establishment of an economically secure existence."[97]

Those responsible for carting off Jews' furniture closely coordinated their activities with the offices that organized the deportations. Nevertheless, the Security Police occasionally had to intervene to prevent the looters from arriving at residences before they had been vacated and causing resistance among the Jews scheduled to be relocated. In late 1943, von Behr complained that the Security Service in the Belgian city of Liège had all but stopped taking Jews into custody. "Because of the major bombing damage recently in the Reich," von Behr wrote, "the demands upon my office have substantially increased. I would urge that the Jewish operation in Liège resume at the earliest possible opportunity so that the securing of Jewish furniture and its transport to Reich can proceed." Six months later, on June 13, 1944, after nothing had been done, von Behr once again prodded the Security Police on behalf of his ethnic comrades. "In the interest of bombed-out Germans," he demanded the arrests of the sixty remaining Jewish families living in Liège.[98]

THE FURNITURE operation also involved confiscating shipping containers full of the belongings of Jews who had emigrated. Great numbers of these containers, known as "lift vans" or simply "lifts," had been stranded in the ports of Antwerp, Rotterdam, and Marseilles at the start of the war. In the wake of one heavy aerial bombardment of Cologne in summer 1942, the Reich Finance Ministry, which considered these effects to be German state property, transferred a thousand such lifts from Antwerp to the Cologne city administration.[99] Containers from Rotterdam arrived simultaneously at Cologne's port, and from there some of their contents were transported on to Münster, Mannheim, and Lübeck. Goods not immediately needed were stored, by arrangement with the Finance Ministry, as an "emergency reserve."[100] Berlin was the primary recipient of containers confiscated in occupied Trieste and Genoa after the official Italian government had turned against Germany and realigned itself with the Allies.[101] The contents of many of the containers that had been stored in Hamburg in the spring of 1941 were auctioned off, with the lion's share being bought by the Social Services Administration. The goods were then distributed to various warehouses throughout the city as a "handy reserve in case of catastrophe."[102] The practice of confiscating emigrants' belongings stuck in transit was typical throughout Germany.[103]

The officials responsible for dispersing the property stolen by the state were the heads of local finance departments. The process always followed the same pattern: local officials would compensate bombed-out citizens with money and vouchers for lost household effects, clothing, and so forth in the name of the central Reich government. Applicants would also receive identification cards allowing them to buy replacement furnishings directly or at auction. The proceeds were then handed back to the Reich. In budgetary terms, it was a break-even proposition for the state and its citizens at the expense of dispossessed owners, many of whom had been murdered. An official government notice in the Oldenburg city paper on July 24, 1943, gives an idea of how such sales and auctions proceeded: "Cash sale of porcelain, enamelware, beds, and linens on Sunday, July 25, 1943, at the Strangmann Restaurant in Hatterwüsting. Begins at 4:00 P.M. for noncompensated victims of bombings, at 4:30 P.M. for large families and newlyweds, and at 5:00 P.M. for the general public." The announcement was signed by the mayor. Between 1942 and 1944, the city of Oldenburg took in exactly 466,617.39 reichsmarks from such sales. The city treasurer transferred the money to the Reich's coffers. It was entered in the books under the heading "general administrative revenues."[104]

Because most of the supplies dispatched to northwestern Germany came from the homes of Jews in Holland, the residents of Oldenburg referred to these goods as "Dutch furniture." By summer 1944, German relief workers—with the help of the Dutch delivery company A. Puls—had transported the inventory of 29,000 residences to the Reich. The furniture operation in the Netherlands had commenced with a formal ordinance from the Central Office for Jewish Emigration, which had been set up by the Security Service. The announcement of that ordinance in the *Joodsche Weekblad* (Jewish Weekly) on March 20, 1942, read: "Any Jew who lives in a residence he owns, rents, or otherwise uses is required, by paragraph 3 of the Ordinance of the General Commissioner for Security Affairs of September 15, 1941, to obtain written permission from the Jewish Council in Amsterdam before removing any furniture, furnishings, household objects, or other possessions." Violators were threatened with serious consequences.[105]

In the summer of 1943, shipments of furniture from Prague were arriving in the Ruhr Valley, while used clothing and linens from Prague were turning up in Cologne. In a richly illustrated report, the head of the Trust Office (Treuhandstelle) in Prague, which took goods from the homes of thousands of deported Jews, bragged about how diligently the items had been collected, repaired, and stored. The report was titled "From Jewish Wealth to Collective Property." By late February 1943, the leftovers from the Aryanization of Prague had been piled up and cataloged in city warehouses: 4,817 bedroom sets, 3,907 kitchen sets, 18,267 armoires, 25,640 armchairs, 1,321,741 household and kitchen items, 778,195 books, 34,568 pairs of shoes, 1,264,999 items of linen and clothing, and so on. To the Trust Office employees, these stocks represented an "irreplaceable" wartime reserve.[106]

Deported German Jews were allowed to take fifty kilograms of personal effects with them. Understandably, deportees usually favored items of value and warm clothes. But in many cases, the suitcases and packages containing these belongings remained behind, after their owners were deported. On June 24, 1942, the freight cars of the train that took Jews from Königsberg to their deaths in the Maly Trostinec extermination camp near Minsk were uncoupled and never left the station. A similar scene played itself out on April 22, 1942, in Düsseldorf. Five days later, after the deportees' belongings—which included everything from hot-water bottles and woolen socks to nylons, overcoats, suits, and shoes—had been sorted through, they were handed over to the local Nazi welfare office. Other items among the luggage of the deported Jews—gauze and bandages, soap powder, hard and liquid soap, razor blades, shaving lotion, shampoo, hair oil, ethanol, matches, eau de cologne, salves, shoe polish, sewing sets, toothbrushes, smoking and chewing tobacco, cigarettes, cigars, tea, coffee, cocoa, sweets, sausages, oranges, lemons, and other food—were delivered to the district office of the German Red Cross, a veterans' home, a reserve military hospital, and the military canteen at Düsseldorf's main train station.[107]

Hamburg, which because of its size and its proximity to Britain was hit especially often and hard by RAF raids, represents a case to itself. In February 1941, at the behest of the local gauleiter, the Gestapo confiscated 3,000 to 4,000 lifts in Hamburg's duty-free port and ordered the contents immediately sold off by a Hamburg auction house. The auctions

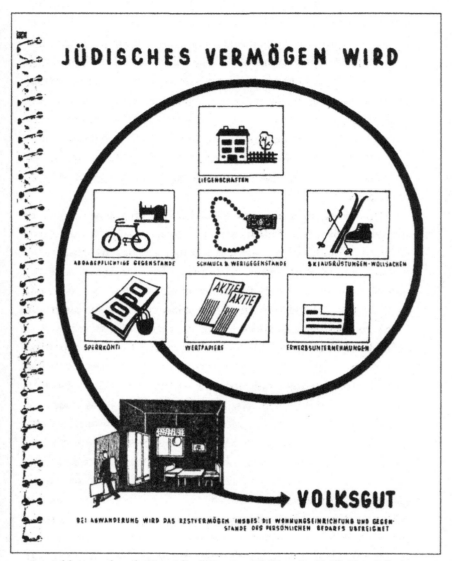

Cover of the report from the Trust Office in Prague, 1942. "From Jewish Wealth to Collective Property: After emigration, remaining assets—especially domestic furnishings and personal effects—are transferred." (Landesarchiv, Berlin)

The poster reads: "1,362,945 books have already been seized. That's enough to fully equip 2,600 local libraries." The private libraries of Czech Jews were utilized for the improvement of German public education. (Landesarchiv, Berlin)

proceeded according to the same criteria of need as in Oldenburg or Aachen, but Hamburg enjoyed a uniquely steady flow of supplies. In addition to the previously mentioned 2,699 freight cars of furniture from West European Jews, forty-five ships transported 27,227 tons of "Jewish commodities" from Belgium and Holland to the city. A total of 100,000 bidders from Hamburg and the surrounding area—most of them women whose husbands were serving in the war—acquired items from these deliveries of stolen property. Around 100,000 households in and around Hamburg thus profited from the sale of furniture, clothing, and thousands of everyday household items and amenities that had previously belonged to some 30,000 Jewish families.[108]

After the war, librarian Gertrud Seydelmann recalled the auctions in Hamburg's working-class districts:

> Ordinary housewives suddenly wore fur coats, traded coffee and jewelry, and had imported antique furniture and rugs from Holland and France. . . . Some of our regular readers were always telling me to go down to the harbor if I wanted to get hold of rugs, carpets, furniture, jewelry, and furs. It was property stolen from Dutch Jews who, as I learned after the war, had been taken away to the death camps. I wanted nothing to do with this. But in refusing, I had to be careful around those greedy people, especially the women, who were busily enriching themselves. I couldn't let my true feelings show. The only ones upon whom I could exercise a cautious influence were those whose husbands I knew had been committed Social Democrats. I explained to them where these shipments of excellent household wares came from and cited the old maxim "Ill-gotten gains seldom prosper." And they acted accordingly.[109]

By conservative estimates, some 100 million reichsmarks' worth of goods (the equivalent of $700 million today) was stolen from France alone in the first year of the furniture operation. The total booty in furniture stolen from Holland reached similar proportions.[110] The actual amount of money taken in, however, was far less since prices for buyers in Germany were lower than the goods' actual market value. The operation was not primarily intended to bring money into the state's coffers. In one report, organizers bragged: "The furniture operation of the Western Office [of the Reich Ministry for the Occupied Eastern Territories] is devoted entirely to providing for the most seriously hit victims of the bombings and offers considerable price relief on the German furniture market. There is no underestimating the psychological effect of the swift provision of household furnishings on the ethnic comrades affected. To take what has become a real-life scenario: if, after large attacks, hard-hit families can be transferred in a matter of hours to fully furnished apartments, it must be seen as a significant factor in maintaining war morale."

Thank-you notes written by recipients "from all social classes" to the offices responsible for collecting and distributing the goods attest to the psychological effectiveness of the emergency relief program. If relief volunteers are to be believed, the Western Office achieved "enormous popularity among all segments of the population." Its activities soon came to be seen not only as "important to the war effort" but also "important for victory among our comrades suffering from privation." Despite increasing transport difficulties, freight trains and barges full of looted household effects took "top priority" when space and time on rails and waterways were allocated.[111]

PARALLEL TO the furniture operation, the Nazi political leadership attempted to placate residents of burned-out cities with extra allocations of food. Together with Goebbels and the Reich commissioner for Ukraine, Erich Koch, Rosenberg and Göring organized "the special delivery of food by train into the Reich for extraordinary circumstances." The supplies came from Ukraine to the detriment of that country's urban population. This relief operation was officially described as a "donation of food from the East."[112]

At the same time, Lieutenant Colonel Fritz Hencke, a personal friend of Göring's, was setting up the Western Exterior Office, which purchased clothing and issued contracts to Dutch, Belgian, and French textile manufacturers. In the fall of 1942, the military commander in these regions appropriated around 8 million reichsmarks per month from the operational budget for the occupation to buy textiles on the black market in France. The goods were earmarked for "the especially needy segment of the German population, in particular those who suffered from air raids."[113] The delivery of ready-to-wear clothing, bought up in large lots or seized from the households of deported Jews, "proceeded under the auspices of the Western Exterior Office using freight trucks driven directly to the affected cities." Those in charge of the operation decreed that convoys of trucks had to be kept permanently ready "so that in the event of an air raid they can be deployed without delay." In addition to clothing and material, the trucks also carried "means of personal fortification such as wine and cognac."[114]

Meanwhile, in the summer of 1942, Göring was also busy planning his "Christmas operation," the purchase of gifts and toys in occupied Western Europe for Germans to put under their trees. As late as December 20, Göring was still ordering that "cosmetics, toys, and general gift items" be acquired in France. This bounty was then transported in 2,306 freight cars and several barges, "primarily to bomb-damaged regions." Shipments were also directed to cities and regions where war morale was threatening to decline: Vienna, Bratislava, Königsberg, and the industrial regions of Silesia.[115] To the same end, Göring spent 176 million reichsmarks in Holland.[116]

The sums of money used for the handout started out high and kept growing. Despite repeated efforts by occupation authorities to reduce nonessential expenditures, by June 1942 the Wehrmacht High Command had already set aside 200 million reichsmarks' worth of French francs for such purchases. A further allotment of 100 million reichsmarks followed in August, while a supplemental 200 million was demanded on September 9 and again in October. On November 20, the Wehrmacht High Command ordained that "244,500,000 reichsmarks in French francs" were to be made available so that, as Göring had ordered, "the procurements on the black market do not lose momentum."[117] All told, in the latter half of 1942, 18.5 billion francs of High Command money were spent on the Christmas operation. The finance minister himself approved the "black market operations" and reported them with a clear conscience to the General Auditor's Office.[118] According to Reichsbank figures, "some 3 billion marks in occupation costs" were used in France in 1942 for the purpose of "importing scarce commodities into Germany," more than a fifth of which were for the Christmas operation.[119]

Göring announced his plans for the Christmas operation to the Reich leadership on August 6, 1942. In the assembly hall named after himself in the Aviation Ministry, he called on the assembled ministers and leaders of occupied territories "to extract the maximum so that the German people can live their lives." After complaining that looting was no longer considered a matter of course in war, he declared: "I intend to loot anyway, and to loot thoroughly, insofar as I am sending a series of purchasers, equipped with special dispensation, first to Holland and Belgium, then to France. They will have until Christmas to buy up more or less everything available in the best stores and warehouses. I will then hang these things in shopwindows here at Christmas so that the German people can buy them." Göring envisioned shoppers' being able to snap up "clothing, shoes— whatever's available."[120]

By early November 1942, food rationing offices were already issuing supplemental Christmas vouchers. The public responded with gratitude. The Security Service reported: "The announcement of an allowance for wine and liquor for those working long hours or doing heavy manual labor was particularly welcomed. . . . All in all, the special Christmas allocations have allowed many ethnic comrades to forget their pressing everyday concerns."[121]

The windfall of goods wasn't truly cheap. Procurement of gifts was funded as usual from the occupation budgets, and Germans enjoying these privileges paid for them as well, bringing more money into the state coffers. Nonetheless, people had enough income at their disposal to spend on gifts, wine, schnapps, coffee, butter, and sugar. And when they did so, the Christmas operation had the additional, calculated benefits of lowering inflation by curbing excess domestic spending power and bringing new revenues into the treasury.

On Christmas Eve 1942, Goebbels reflected with satisfaction on the Nazi policy of full stomachs and happy hearts: "The special allocations of foodstuffs have paid off again. My gifts of something extra for old people and large families have worked wonders."[122] That same day, as it became clear that celebrations planned for January 30 to commemorate the tenth anniversary of the Nazis' assumption of power would coincide with the no longer concealable news of German defeat at the battle of Stalingrad, Hitler found himself longing for the next public relations miracle. Martin Bormann noted: "The Führer repeatedly emphasized that we could achieve the maximum effect if we announced to the German people that day another increase in food rations and other allowances." Hitler wanted to keep the German people eating from his hand. (This was "no longer possible," however, after the overblown Christmas operation.)[123] Nonetheless, Hitler insisted on the "maintenance" of rations "at their current level by increasing the contributions of the occupied territories."[124]

In the summer of 1943, plans began for the next Christmas operation. Jews had been systematically stripped of their property, and the currencies in occupied countries had been ruined. In light of the situation, Göring decided to fall back on the assets of "enemies of the state" to raise the means to "purchase coffee and other items on the black market in France and Belgium."[125] He had shied away from such a step in the past to avoid German assets abroad being confiscated in retaliation. But by summer 1943, his scruples toward ethnic comrades who owned foreign assets had disappeared. The material welfare of the masses had greater priority.

CHAPTER 5

The Mainstay: Western Europe

Shopping Sprees in Belgium

In the fall of 1941, Heinrich Böll was temporarily transferred from France back to the Cologne area. His task there was to guard Soviet prisoners. The sight of these men—shattered by the harrowing war on the Eastern Front and weakened by captivity—left him depressed. For him the fate of the prisoners reflected the tedium of his own existence, both in his lowly soldier's duties and as a member of the Wehrmacht. Böll began daydreaming about Belgium, a country he had come to know during the German invasion and occupation of May 1940: "My one great worry right now is whether I can get to Antwerp or not. All the nice things that I want to bring back—coffee, cigars, and cloth, ah, if only it could be." Böll got to make his trip, and his fiancée, Annemarie Czech, received "a short sleeveless sweater."[1]

During the spring of 1943, to ensure that soldiers' wives and girlfriends were kept supplied with such amenities, Hermann Göring ordered that "the visual appearance of retail stores in Belgium, as well as other spots where people enjoy themselves, be maintained in conditions almost like those of peacetime."[2] By decree, "gourmet establishments, bars, and other enjoyment spots" in occupied Europe were to be kept open, "if they were or could be frequented by German soldiers for the purposes of rest and relaxation." Stores where "nonessential goods" were sold were also to remain in business "so that German soldiers can buy whatever their hearts desire, as long as there are wares on the shelves. Prices have to be kept at an appropriate level." Against Göring's will, shops and other establishments in the Netherlands deemed "nonessential to the war" had been closed. They were to be "reopened as inconspicuously as possible."[3] In such establishments German soldiers were able to spend Dutch and Belgian money freely.

But where was the Reich getting the money to fund its soldiers' extravagance? The answer is, from the occupied countries themselves, through a range of methods that varied from state to state but everywhere attempted to preserve the appearance of legality. Shortly after the invasion, the Wehrmacht intendant responsible for Belgium summarized how the German occupiers set the contribution to be paid to the Reich: "For political reasons, the finances and economy of the Belgian state have to be kept largely intact. It has been agreed to demand of the Belgian state, as a partial payment toward occupation costs, a sum of money that it can just barely, with the greatest of sacrifice, raise."[4] In addition to the official contribution, both France and Belgium were compelled to make further payments for "accommodation services" (Quartierdienste).[5] The monthly sum was initially set at more than double the state's normal monthly tax revenues.[6] It was raised from an initial 80 million reichsmarks to 120 million in the first quarter of 1941.[7] To maintain currency stability, the German occupiers subsequently capped the official contribution at 80 million reichsmarks a month, but the Wehrmacht consistently demanded an additional 20 to 30 million for the quartering of troops.[8] By September 1941 the level of actual monthly payments had settled at 120 million.

This burden was borne by a country with a population of only 8.3 million. The total Belgian state budget had been around 11 billion francs in 1938, with the government borrowing some 3 billion francs to stimulate an economy badly hit by the Depression. Now German occupiers were demanding an additional 18 billion or more annually.[9] An anonymously circulated Resistance flyer from 1941 put the statistics in more or less accurate context: "If revenues from taxes and duties were raised from

11 to 16 billion [francs], as Germany is demanding, we'd still have to borrow 25.5 billion to fulfill the conditions dictated by Germany. From whom are we going to borrow? Add to these figures the reserves of raw materials and food that the Germans have taken from us, and you get a very clear picture of the policies of plunder and starvation that the Third Reich is pursuing against our country. Indeed, Germany is sacrificing our entire state to advance its imperialistic aims. It is treating us as a population of slaves who exist only for the benefit of the Reich."[10] In the summer of 1941, many German units stationed in Belgium were redeployed to the Eastern Front, but there was no reduction in occupation costs. The Wehrmacht commander in Belgium decided to appropriate funds to construct a number of airfields and gigantic bunkers along the Atlantic coast. For him it was a given "that everything we need to wage war here against England must come from here as well."[11]

In late October 1941, German bank commissioner Hans von Becker warned of the instability of the Belgian currency. The chief intendant of the Reichsbank also advised that "occupation costs need to be adjusted to the capacities of the country." He complained that "Belgium had been burdened with exceptionally high war-related costs" and was being "plundered from all sides without regard to the maintenance of its currency."[12] By August 1942, before the invasion of "purchasers" (led first by Göring, then by Albert Speer), the Reich Credit Bank in Brussels protested that about a third of the total occupation costs were being allocated for private and war-related "deliveries outside Belgium."[13]

According to a survey commissioned by the military commander in Belgium, Germans "purchased"—with Belgian money—18,500 motor vehicles in 1941 alone. The German railway system acquired 1,086 locomotives and 22,120 freight cars there in the same period, as well as huge amounts of coal, cement, rolled steel, scrap metal, copper, lead, textiles, and industrial products of almost every variety. Between the start of the occupation in late 1940 and February 28, 1942, Belgium contributed a total of 2.6 billion marks to the Reich. Military administrators bragged with sadistic pride of how efficiently they had driven Belgium "to the brink of exhausting its reserves." Considering Belgium's relatively small population, they boasted of achieving far better results than their colleagues in France or Holland.[14]

And that was just the beginning. As the tide of war turned against Germany in 1942, the demands placed on occupied countries knew no limits. In the first six months of 1942, the monthly burden on Belgium included 8 million reichsmarks for accommodation, 120 million in occupation costs, and 72 million in clearing advances for exports to Germany.[15] The total amounted to 2.4 billion reichsmarks annually. In 1943, clearing payments exceeded even occupation costs.[16]

Purchasers hired by individuals, private German companies, and German government agencies made uninhibited use of the Belgian market. For 1942, the military administration estimated that black market transactions accounted for 30 percent of the total value of purchases made by Germans on Belgian soil in the local currency. These transactions were technically illicit, but some were actually approved by military agencies. The Surveillance Office of the Military High Command frequently granted entities claiming to have special needs permission to make purchases on the black market. Among them was the "Schmidt Task Force," whose only purpose was "the acquisition of wares of all sorts." The Armaments Ministry, the SS, the Motor Vehicles Division of the Central Western Army, and the Army Medical Station also exercised these privileges.[17]

In addition to extorting heavy contributions, Germany stole Belgian gold. In 1941, the Vichy regime in France agreed to transport from Dakar to Marseille forty-one tons of gold that the legitimate Belgium government had succeeded in shipping to French colonies in West Africa. In Marseille it was handed over to a representative of the Reichsbank.[18] Under international law, however, Germany could not simply confiscate gold reserves belonging to another nation. In February 1941, after consultation with Göring's state secretary, Erich Neumann, occupation authorities invented the pretense of "external occupation costs" incurred by Belgium. The concocted expenses were to be paid out of the Belgian treasury. "Open seizure," Reich bureaucrats maintained, "is better than covert confiscation."[19] On July 3, 1941, the administrative council of the Reich Credit Bank in Belgium reached the following decision: "As an advance payment

The following illustrations come from a secret report by the German military administration in Belgium entitled "Belgium's Contributions to the German War Economy," March 1, 1942. (Bundesarchiv-Militärarchiv, Freiburg in Breisgau)

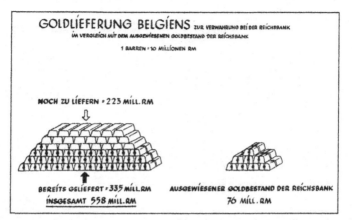

The text reads: "Shipments of gold from Belgium for holding at the Reichsbank, compared with the Reichsbank's known gold reserves. To be delivered, 223 million reichsmarks. Already delivered, 335 million reichsmarks. Total, 558 million reichsmarks. Known gold reserves at the Reichsbank, 76 million reichsmarks."

"Values of assets from enemies and Jews that are controlled within Germany's area of command and have at least mortgage value, compared with the capital stock of I. G. Farben. Ca. 700 million reichsmarks: assets from enemies and Jews. Ca. 800 million reichsmarks: capital stock of I. G. Farben."

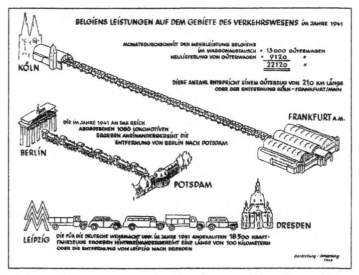

"Belgium's contribution in 1941 to German transportation. Monthly average in used freight cars, 13,000; new deliveries, 9,120; total, 22,120. This number is the equivalent of a 210-kilometer-long freight train, or the distance between Cologne and Frankfurt am Main. Lined up in a row, the 1,086 locomotives delivered to the Reich in 1941 would stretch from Berlin to Potsdam. Lined up in a row, the 18,500 motor vehicles purchased by the Wehrmacht in 1941 would stretch 100 kilometers in length, or the distance between Leipzig and Dresden."

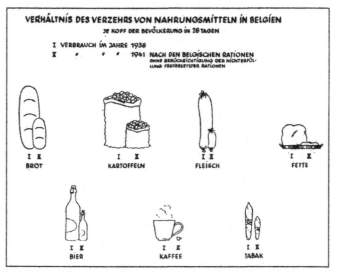

"Per capita food consumption in Belgium, every 28 days. I. Consumption in 1938. II. Consumption in 1941 (unfulfilled rations not taken into account). Bread. Potatoes. Meat. Shortening. Beer. Coffee. Tobacco."

for external occupation expenses, Belgium is to transfer ownership of those gold reserves currently held in Berlin. This demand, however, will be made known to Belgians only at a later date."[20] The forty-one tons of gold were worth more than a half billion reichsmarks, but their practical value for the German war economy was far greater since gold was the only means of payment the Reich could use to purchase scarce resources in noncombatant countries like Spain, Portugal (tungsten), Sweden (steel, ball bearings), Switzerland (weapons, transport vehicles), and Turkey (chrome).

The following year, the Reichsbank protested the planned announcement of the transfer of ownership, citing currency concerns, specifically the need to pretend that the Belgian franc was still covered by gold reserves. The Foreign Office, on the other hand, wanted to publicize the act of theft, on the assumption that with the end of the war all occupied countries would be presented with a bill for external occupation costs, which would include weapons production in Germany and the maintenance of soldiers' families.[21] In Belgium's case, those debts would be balanced against the gold reserves and debts from German clearing "balances."[22] In the end, no such complicated declaration was formulated. Instead, on October 9, 1942, the head of the finance department in Berlin and Brandenburg simply appropriated the gold that had been stolen from Belgium, with French help, in the name of the German Reich. The ostensible legal basis was the Reich Contribution Law (*Reichsleistungsgesetz*) of September 1939, which ordered the mandatory exchange of gold, as well as stock and bond certificates, for reichsmarks. In accordance with this legislation, the Reichsbank compensated the national bank of Belgium with a half billion reichsmarks, which were deposited, however, in a frozen account accessible only to the German state.[23] The trade division of the Foreign Office reported to State Secretary Ernst von Weizsäcker and Foreign Minister Joachim von Ribbentrop: "With that, thanks to the efforts of the Foreign Office and in particular envoy [Hans-Richard] Hemmen, gold valued at 550 million reichsmarks has been officially transferred to the possession of the Reich."[24]

Meanwhile, France was taking care to protect its own gold reserves.

The Banque de France repeatedly transferred parts of those reserves to banks in Switzerland to keep them from falling into German hands.[25] Göring's associates in Berlin who were responsible for keeping tabs on foreign gold took a relaxed attitude toward France's activities. "In an emergency," one of them remarked, the Swiss holdings "could be relatively easily commandeered to serve the Reich's interests."[26]

According to German calculations, the Belgian state spent 83.3 billion Belgian francs on the needs of its civilian population during the four years of German occupation. In the same period, German occupiers expropriated 133.6 billion francs in currency and goods, including clearing advances. And that sum does not include the theft of Belgian gold reserves, the confiscated assets of Belgian Jews, and other forms of plunder that are difficult to quantify. When they were driven out by the Allies in 1944, the Germans left behind a country that was economically shattered.[27]

Holland without Borders

With its 8.8 million inhabitants, Holland was slightly larger in population than Belgium. Occupation costs imposed there between 1940 and 1942 officially amounted to 100 million guilders per month (the equivalent today of more than $1.5 billion), which were transferred to the Wehrmacht High Command. In addition, 3 million guilders were to be paid monthly to the Reich commissioner, whose small staff oversaw the administration of the Netherlands.[28] The exchange rate between the guilder and the reichsmark was set at 1 to 1.33. But the Wehrmacht often exceeded the official limit on occupation costs by more than 20 percent.[29] The demands were devastating in a country whose total state expenditures in 1939 had amounted to only 1.4 billion guilders.[30] By the end of 1941, the Netherlands had already amassed 4.46 billion guilders in debt.[31] A year later that figure was up to 8 billion.[32]

Since invading Holland in May 1940, the Germans had pursued the idea of creating an economic union that would benefit the Reich, or, in the Nazi euphemism, "effecting an economic merger with Germany." By April 1, 1941, preparations had been completed, and the economic border between the two countries was abolished. In one stroke, occupation and finance authorities opened up the Dutch market to German purchasing power. But the economy was in no condition to cope with added strain. So much money had been spent in the first six months of the occupation that "a national loan of 500 million Dutch guilders" (665 million reichsmarks) had to be issued "to relieve pressure on" the national bank of the Netherlands.[33] Dutch bankers had no choice but to grant the loan, having been forced by their occupiers to redeem "huge sums of reichsmarks" exchanged by German purchasers.

Administrators responsible for keeping the economy of the Netherlands functioning tried to halt the practice of making the Dutch state pay for German purchases that emptied Dutch shelves. They had no success. "It is well known," the German finance chief in The Hague wrote, "that previously ample reserves" were being bought up "to an enormous extent with RKK certificates." The goods purchased then "passed across the German border by the usual means under the guard of uniformed German personnel."[34] Instead of compensating the Netherlands for such hoarding, German economists balanced their accounts with Holland in spring 1941 by inventing fictional occupation costs. The Dutch Finance Department had to write off 400 million reichsmarks in German debt and deliver gold valued at a further 100 million reichsmarks.[35] It was only in 1944, to stave off the complete collapse of the guilder, that the currency border was reestablished.[36]

In March 1944, the Economics Ministry calculated that the Netherlands had paid a total of some 8.3 billion reichsmarks in occupation costs.[37] Since German civilians, government agencies, and businesses had purchased goods valued at 4.5 billion reichsmarks, three-fifths of all the putative occupation costs in Holland were directly aimed at enriching Germans.[38]

To help the Netherlands raise that money, occupation administrators increasingly adapted Dutch business, corporate, and wealth taxes to fit the German model of soaking businesses. In the first few days of the occupation, they imposed a war-profits tax of 10 percent on Dutch businesses, raising it in two increments to 35 percent of net profits within three months.[39] According to one Dutch newspaper, this tax and others would allow the Dutch state (and ultimately Nazi Germany) to claim as much as "83⅓ percent of all profits."[40] Unlike in Germany, the wage tax in the Netherlands was raised across the board by 10 percent on July 1, 1942. Occupation authorities also planned to raise the sales tax to fund the Dutch contribution to a vaguely conceived "anti-Bolshevist campaign." During the spring of 1942, in the interests of social equity, Reich economists discussed "a class-sensitive levy on assets, especially large-scale assets (industry, 'plutocrats')." Such a measure, wrote Dutch anti-Semite Rost van Tonningen, "would certainly be very popular" within the Dutch Nazi movement.[41] Once the new taxes had taken effect, the Dutch newspaper *Nieuwe Rotterdamsche Courant* calculated, some businesses would be paying 112 percent of their profits.[42]

On February 9, 1942, General Commissioner for Finance and Economic Affairs Hans Fischböck, the official in charge of the economic exploitation of Holland, proposed to the Finance Ministry a "plan to demand from the Netherlands, in addition to their contributions thus far, a running payment for 'external occupation costs,' dated retroactively to July 1, 1941, and amounting to 50 million reichsmarks per month, 10 million of which are to be paid in gold." Fischböck had already discussed the suggestion in detail with van Tonningen, whom the Nazis had put in charge of the Dutch National Bank. According to Fischböck's proposal, the Netherlands would pay a "solidarity contribution to the joint struggle" against Bolshevism. Germany's finance minister concurred enthusiastically, offering "no substantial objections." On May 2, 1942, Reich Commissioner Arthur Seyss-Inquart asked van Tonningen to transfer the money to the Reich treasury and the gold to the Reichsbank's Berlin depository. That move earned the finance minister Göring's "special gratitude for the alleviation of our gold and currency concerns."[43]

Heavily Burdened in France

After defeating France in June 1940, German occupiers divided the country into five zones. Alsace-Lorraine was informally incorporated into the

Reich, though never officially annexed. The two northern departments fell under the control of a military commander who also oversaw the administration of Belgium. Italy was allowed to administer a small stretch of territory along the French-Italian border. The main portion of the country was divided into occupied and unoccupied zones (the latter being subsequently occupied in November 1942). Unoccupied France was ruled by the Vichy regime, which collaborated with Germany. In occupied Paris, the Reich installed an administrative staff to assist the military commander. The staff consisted of an administrative and an economics division, the former directed by Werner Best, a senior SS and Gestapo officer, until mid-1942.[44]

The economics division, whose responsibilities included all financial matters, was headed throughout the occupation by Elmar Michel, a career civil servant from the Economics Ministry.[45] In the fall of 1940, he was also given leadership posts in the German Commission on Foreign Trade and the German Currency Commission. His mandate covered all of French national territory.[46] Within Michel's division, Reichsbank director Leopold Scheffler headed the unit devoted to overseeing "currency, credit, and insurance." He was responsible for monitoring the French Finance Ministry, as well as French banks and insurance companies.[47] Carl Schaefer, the former president of the Reichsbank in Danzig and one of the founders of the Reich Credit Bank in occupied Poland, was given responsibility over the Banque de France.

The military administration of occupied France was only part of an elaborate system of governance that expanded as the war progressed— and as the Reich's appetite for foreign assets increased. The German city of Wiesbaden, headquarters of the Armistice Commission set up by Germany following its invasion of France, became a crucial second power center. Hans-Richard Hemmen, whose services would later prove invaluable in the seizure of Belgian gold, headed the commission. Its primary task was to negotiate with the Vichy regime on matters concerning the whole of France. The Reichsbank maintained an office in Wiesbaden, led by another of its directors, Heinrich Hartlieb.

One final locus of authority was the German embassy in Paris, whose presence in the capital was intended to signal the Reich's (insincere) acknowledgment of French sovereignty. Embassy staff, who often acted as Hitler's negotiators on the ground in occupied France, also provided a kind of early-warning system for Berlin. But their influence in setting policies remained limited.

The armistice treaty required France to pay a daily tribute of 20 million reichsmarks—an unprecedented sum—to its occupier. Nonetheless, the Reich Finance Ministry complained that the sum was too modest and lobbied to have it increased. High-ranking ministry officials justified their demands with innocuous-sounding arguments: care, they said, should be taken to avoid "unnecessarily burdening" a later peace treaty "with obligations pertaining to financial matters and money-transfer policies."[48] By January and February 1943, the daily demands of the Wehrmacht, not including the purchasing sprees ordered by Göring and Speer, had reached 29 million reichsmarks. As the administrative council of the Reich Credit Bank ascertained, the total expenditures created "a need for French currency of approximately 35 million reichsmarks a day, or around one billion marks per month."[49]

The rampant greed of the occupiers meant a drastic increase in the amount of money in circulation in France. State expenditures for civilian needs in all of France totaled some 130 billion francs per year between 1941 and 1943. Initially, occupation costs amounted to roughly the same, essentially doubling the state's budget. But in the final two years of the occupation, those costs shot up rapidly. The huge jump in 1943 was a direct result of German military defeats in Eastern Europe and increases in arms production. A similar phenomenon can be observed in all the countries occupied by Germany. At a meeting of Nazi leaders in Berchtesgaden on April 28, 1943, Göring complained that "the financial contributions from France are insufficient." There was a need, he said, for "a serviceable taxation apparatus to take in direct taxes." Changing the system, Göring suggested, should be a major priority.[50]

In addition to daily payments toward occupation costs, France was soon forced to provide hefty clearing advances to finance the export of goods to Germany. Between 1941 and 1943 advances were increased from

20 to 45 billion francs, and budgetary estimates for 1944 reached nearly 90 billion. France was also required to pay for the quartering of German occupiers as well as Italian troops in the southeast of the country. The Wehrmacht raised money by imposing collective fines on individual cities. Nantes, for example, was required to pay an extra 10 million francs in the first nine months of the occupation. In Cherbourg and Bordeaux, the figures were 6 million and 2 million francs, respectively.[51] These sums do not include the value of property requisitioned by the Wehrmacht during its surprisingly swift march through the country.

In response to German pressure, French tax revenues increased significantly between 1941 and 1943—from 68.2 to 101 billion francs. But the budget deficit grew just as fast, increasing from 160 to 220 billion francs. The shortfall for 1944 was projected to be 317 billion. As a result of German greed, state expenditures were more than triple normal state revenues.[52]

How much did France end up handing over to Germany in the course of the occupation? Estimates vary but a fairly accurate picture can be gleaned from the figures provided by several different agencies. According to an official Reichsbank report in the spring of 1944, total occupation costs paid to the Reich by France amounted to 680 billion francs. In addition, 120 billion francs in goods and services were exported to Germany—about half of which had been financed on credit.[53] Since the occupation continued for another four months, another 10 percent can be added to this total. After the liberation of France, new finance minister Aimé Lepercq would claim that Germany had bled the country for the equivalent of 900 billion francs.[54] The French national debt had risen during the occupation by more than a trillion francs.[55] The Bank for International Settlements calculated the occupation costs demanded from France in 1944 to have been 35.25 billion reichsmarks, or 705 billion francs, not including clearing debts. These sums do not include contributions paid by Alsace-Lorraine, which was more or less treated as a part of Germany, or southeastern France, where the money went to Italy.

Taken together, these estimates support the conclusion that direct German revenues from France exceeded 800 billion francs, or 40 billion reichsmarks. In the unsentimental estimation of Reichsbank director

Hartlieb, the plundering provided "effective relief for the Reich budget and ultimately spared Germany from having to take out credit from the national bank, while also greatly burdening France's budget and currency."[56] In 1959, Pierre Arnoult, a historian of the occupation, summarized the German technique of maintaining the appearance of fairness by paying for needed goods and services in the local currency. "They didn't take anything away from us by force, " he wrote. "They purchased everything correctly—but with money they took from us."[57]

The French finance minister was required to transfer payments for ongoing occupation costs to the account of the Reich Credit Bank in Paris. Just as individual Germans essentially stole French goods by purchasing them with worthless RKK certificates, the Reich continually raided this occupation fund for expenses that had nothing to do with France. For example, of the 6.5 billion reichsmarks (21.3 million per day) of contributions France paid between January and October 1942, the Reich used 720 million marks to procure "horses, food, and amenities for the eastern troops"—that is, German armies fighting in the Soviet Union. A further 840 million marks were officially allocated for "black market purchases, stocks and bonds, and works of art."[58]

The fiduciary basis was laid in the first few weeks after Germany's invasion. A bank account designated "Occupation Costs France B" was set up to receive funds for the ongoing, considerably inflated expenditures of the Wehrmacht and its soldiers. A parallel account, "Occupation Costs France A," was established for money that was then "loaned" to finance German attempts at self-enrichment. In the first six months of the occupation, a number of large sums of money were, to use the official lingo, "diverted." They included 536 million reichsmarks for the families of "French workers deployed in Germany"; 250 million for the Economics Ministry "for raw materials and the acquisition of partial stock holdings"; 9 million for the Food Ministry "for the purchase of livestock"; and 5 million for the Transport Ministry for the acquisition of a large portfolio, deposited in France, of stocks in the International Sleeper Carriage Company of Brussels.[59] The policy division of the Finance Ministry deposited revenues earned in France into Account A for the explicit "use of the Finance Ministry."[60]

The Reich used various means to conceal its campaign of plunder and theft. For example, the exchange rate between the franc and the mark, which had been set to benefit German buyers, was selectively manipulated: the official rate was one reichsmark to 20 francs, which represented a 25 percent devaluation of the prewar French currency, but for outstanding German accounts receivable, the prewar exchange rate was used. To take another example, the Finance Ministry pocketed around 5 million reichsmarks in savings left behind by French people expelled from Alsace and Lorraine. And if all else failed, funds could simply be transferred from Account B when Account A ran out of money: on March 3 and October 9, 1941, transfers of 600 and 900 million francs, respectively, were made at the behest of the Finance Ministry.[61]

"Private" companies and purchases were also used to conceal monies that were in fact going to the Reich. In the short interval between May 16 and October 14, 1942, a Nazi-owned company called Roges, ostensibly founded to trade in raw materials, received transfers of 700 million francs for acquisitions in France. The funds came not via Account A but directly from Account B, which was supposed to be devoted exclusively to costs arising from the occupation.[62] Meanwhile, private citizens and officials alike redeemed a total of 2.5 billion reichsmarks in RKK certificates (1.3 billion of them in 1943), which were never recorded from Account A.[63] RKK certificates were not handed out for free. They first had to be paid for in reichsmarks, creating revenues for the German treasury.

In September 1943, Nazi armaments minister Albert Speer began to buy French machinery for German factories through a newly founded company called Primetex, for which 300 million francs in start-up money had been secretly siphoned off from the occupation costs budget.[64] Primetex operated alongside Roges.[65] Its CEO was ministerial director Wilhelm Bender of the Finance Ministry. Its stated mission was "the acquisition and commercial exploitation of confiscated goods in all occupied areas as well as the purchase, storage, and resale of raw materials essential to the war effort."[66]

The balance sheets for the Occupation Costs France A account are today held at the French National Archive in Paris. A glance at the accounts for the period 1940 to 1943 reveals a common thread. In all recorded transactions, government offices, companies, and private individuals from Germany paid reichsmark equivalents for major purchases they had made in francs. The Finance Ministry was at pains to conceal that it simply kept these sums of reichsmarks, while paying for French goods with francs siphoned from the occupation costs budget. Transactions were handled through an intermediary institution in Berlin, essentially a front, called the General Retailing Corporation. (The Nazi regime used similar letterbox companies, such as the Berlin office of the Central Economic Bank of Ukraine, to exploit Eastern Europe.) Monies transferred to the General Retailing Corporation were forwarded to the Reich treasury, "where they were recorded as budget revenues in Expected Revenues and Expenditures XVII, part XV of the extraordinary [wartime] budget." Likewise, German investors, firms, and banks that bought French stocks paid the going rate in reichsmarks, which ended up in the German treasury, while French vendors were paid in francs from the budget set aside for occupation costs.[67]

The Reich also forced the French government to pay out francs for purchases made by private German companies in France, while Berlin retained the reichsmark equivalents the companies had paid into a state institution called the German Settlement Bank. On November 9 and 13, 1940, the AEG company in Berlin was allocated the equivalent of 4.3 million reichsmarks in francs for an acquisition spree in France. That same month the Deutsche Bank procured 20.25 million reichsmarks' worth of francs. On October 23 the Cautio Trust Company in Berlin requested 3 million reichsmarks' worth of francs, followed by an additional million on November 20, 1.5 million on December 5, and 2 million on December 27. The Dresdner Bank got into the "French business" on December 11 with 2 million reichsmarks' worth of francs, with a second sum of 3 million following on January 23. The Berliner Handelsgesellschaft, a major private bank in the German capital, followed suit with 1.3 million on January 20, 1941, and a further million on February 11.

Large corporations and individual trading companies had a vested interest not only in covering their ongoing supply needs but also in buying up foreign stocks available on the French market. Banks and trust companies acquired securities on behalf of anonymous clients. To that end, they did business with the Westminster Foreign Bank in Paris, which had been put under receivership, as well as the Banque de Paris et des Pays Bas, the Crédit Lyonnais, and Lloyds & National Provincial Foreign Bank.[68] (The Westminster Foreign Bank remained, at least initially, their preferred address.) The Prussian State Bank spent a considerable sum of money transferring shares of the Mines de Bor corporation into German hands.[69] Stock offerings were passed along for review to the German commissioner of the Westminster Foreign Bank via the German commissioner of the Banque de France. Both the French Currency Protection Command and the economics division of the Military High Command approved such transactions, noting that the stocks that were sold "came from French, and partly Jewish, hands."[70]

Like private companies, German government agencies wasted no time tapping into the funds extorted from the French state. On December 5, 1940, the Army High Command drew 20 million reichsmarks from Occupation Costs Account A to purchase general necessities. Shortly before Christmas that year, senior officials in the Propaganda Ministry went on a shopping spree for the equivalent of 750,000 marks, and a Berlin-based association of German goldsmiths helped itself to 500,000 marks.[71] On December 17, 1940, the mayors of the cities of Düsseldorf, Essen, and Wupperthal began to make purchases in France. They were followed by the mayor of Frankfurt and the president of the Rhine region on January 20 and 21, respectively. On February 21, 1941, the mayor of Berlin sent an acquisition team, outfitted with 701,000 marks, to France.[72] The gourmet food wholesaler Riensch & Held and another food company, Emil Köster AG, bought up delicacies to take the sting out of the privations of wartime. On October 17, 1940, Karl Haberstock, Hitler's personal art buyer, received 1.5 million francs from Account A. Shortly before that, the Economics Ministry had transferred a sum equivalent to 75,000 marks to the Reich treasury via the bogus General Retailing Corporation.[73]

Present-day military historians such as Hans Umbreit obscure what really transpired when they write of transactions being "paid for" with the help of "credit taken out against the costs of occupation."[74] Credit is a means of financing purchases, not paying for them, and even though the borrowers repaid the loans, the Finance Ministry didn't transfer any of the money to France. This practice went on for the entire duration of the occupation and was not subject to negotiation.

The economic consequences for France were severe. As the delegate to the Armistice Commission who was responsible for French finances remarked: "To the extent that products were imported to Germany from France and the purchasing price flowed back into the German Settlement Bank and thereby into the Reichsbank, the French Finance Ministry was forced to take out the equivalent amount in francs in state loans to pay off French creditors. The positive effects this had on the value of the reichsmark were mirrored in the negative effects it had on the value of the French franc."[75]

The German Settlement Bank had the same address and telephone number as the Reichsbank, and the two institutions used identical forms, strongly suggesting that the former was a division of the latter. And in fact, the *Handbook for Civil Servants*, published by the Reichsbank in 1941, explicitly stated as much.

Italy: Unpaid Bills

When German troops seized control of the northern half of Italy in September 1943, the German Foreign Office immediately issued a memorandum spelling out the relationship between occupation costs and the settling of clearing accounts. The diplomats apparently knew only too well that their plans violated international law and stipulated that the memo "under no circumstances be forwarded in the original." The document read: "The military situation compels us to transfer or import such large amounts of finished products and raw materials that it would be practically impossible for us to settle accounts via the clearing process. These materials will have to be paid for with money placed at our disposal by the Italian government as a contribution toward war costs. The resumption of clearing activities will become a parallel economic system of compensation and concealment." By creating the illusion that Germany intended to repay its debts, "the resumption of the clearing system," which had been abandoned after the overthrow of Mussolini, served "to counteract the suggestion, advanced within Italy and abroad by enemy propaganda, that Germany was 'plundering' Italy."

To convince major Italian companies to continue delivering products to Germany, prior debts from the period of the German-Italian alliance had to be paid. The unsettled accounts revealed "a significant deficit to the advantage of the Italians." Clearing that debt, the Foreign Office concluded, meant that a "fixed monthly sum of around 100 million liras," or 13.2 million reichsmarks, would have to be diverted from the Italian contribution to German occupation costs. That sum could also be increased "if circumstances warranted." So it was that average Italians paid the debts run up by German contractors to Italian vendors in the years preceding 1943. The authors of the Foreign Office memorandum also trained their sights on the savings that Italian forced laborers and prisoners of war had cobbled together for their families. In addition, since northern Italy was still officially allied with Germany, it would be required to pay a "monthly contribution of between 200 to 250 million liras" for forced laborers as part of its general "contribution toward the costs of war."[76]

The total worth of what Germany confiscated from occupied Italy was far greater—the equivalent of around 10 billion reichsmarks. Although Allied troops liberated Italy piece by piece in the eighteen months that followed, the wealthy north remained under German control until near the end of the war. Once Mussolini had been freed from prison and reinstalled as the head of the puppet Repubblica Sociale Italiana, northern Italy was not officially required to pay occupation costs per se, but it was still responsible for what was euphemistically called a "contribution" of 7 billion liras a month to the war effort.[77]

As they did elsewhere, the Germans calculated the contributions based not on the actual costs of stationing their troops in the country but on their own budgetary requirements. The projected need for 1942–43 was around 81 billion liras.[78] The previous budgetary estimate had anticipated significant revenues that Fascist Italy was supposed to extract from the territories it had occupied up until August 1943. It also included income from parts of Italy that the Allies were gradually conquering. Yet despite Fascist Italy's obvious inability to raise those revenues, the German occupiers continued to use the old budget as the basis for calculating its war contribution.

In March 1944, the chief financial expert for the German agent general in occupied Italy prepared a detailed breakdown of the economic situation. According to his calculations, the populace under German control had a total annual income of 130 billion liras. Out of this, they were expected to contribute 84 billion liras per year, leaving only 46 billion to pay for all public and private expenditures. And that was only part of the story. "In addition to the war contribution," the author wrote, "Italy also has to pay advances on soldiers' accommodation, requisitions, damage to Wehrmacht property, and war-related harm to the German people, as well as advances on settlement transactions. We also have to consider Italy's own wartime obligations (war damage, military pensions, etc.)."[79]

The treaty dictated by Nazi Germany to the remnants of Fascist Italy on October 23, 1943, removed all obstacles to the continual upward spiral of payments demanded by Berlin. In one of the central passages of that agreement, Italy was required "to provide" the greater German Reich "with a war-costs contribution that meets the economic needs of German organizations." Whereas in 1940 the German occupiers in France still took the trouble of setting up two separate accounts, to maintain at least the appearance of distinguishing between occupation and nonoccupation costs, the Finance Ministry now declared that what Germany did with Italian money was "our concern alone." "Insofar as liras can be used for necessary purchases outside Italy and [we can save] the equivalent in reichsmarks," a ministry report concluded, "this represents a contribution to our external occupation costs."[80] Not surprisingly, the Reich Food Ministry and the Roges company, as well as Göring and the commissioner of the Armaments Ministry under Albert Speer, all availed themselves of considerable sums of liras to make purchases in northern Italy. In the end, a third of occupied

Italy's contributions went toward German arms. The rest was spent on wages for soldiers and military personnel, miscellaneous purchases, and the building of fortifications.[81]

Germany's fiscal policies in occupied Italy led to inflation, shortages, and privation. Together with the Allies' military triumphs, these conditions led more and more Italians to join the partisans or engage in acts of civic protest. In June 1944, for instance, 70,000 workers in Milan and 50,000 workers in Turin went out on strike. Finance Ministry envoy Hubert Schmidt had a ready answer: "A solution to this problem will probably be found only in the form of sending larger numbers of striking workers to German concentration camps." But on the question of Italian indebtedness, he was at a loss. "The Italian state deficit is in a period of unstoppable growth," he concluded in August 1944. "Regular revenues for the budgetary year 1943–44 have dropped by around 30 percent over the preceding year and now cover just 14 percent of expenditures."[82]

CHAPTER 6

Room for Expansion: Eastern Europe

Slave Labor for the Reich

No one knows exactly how many forced laborers worked in the Third Reich, but estimates usually range from 8 to 12 million. Most of these people came from Eastern Europe and toiled under dangerous and inhumane conditions, often in the German arms industry. To preserve appearances abroad and avoid stirring up resistance in occupied countries, German companies paid forced laborers for their work, though the wages were 15 to 40 percent lower than those for German workers. Meanwhile the Finance Ministry tried to get its hands on as much of these workers' pay as possible, developing a range of schemes for confiscation.

Conditions were somewhat better for people from Western Europe but they, too, were exploited both physically and financially. From 1940 on, the Reich Finance Ministry used every available pretext to divert part of the wages paid to involuntary foreign laborers in Germany to the state treasury. For example, reichsmarks paid by German firms to compensate the families of some 250,000 Belgian workers ended up in a general account kept by the German state. The money was then transferred to the main treasury, while dependents of the Belgian workers received Belgian francs paid from the budget for occupation costs. In other words, German companies paid full wages, only for the treasury to collect—in addition to wage taxes—the portion of their paychecks that workers sent back home. In the end, it was Belgium's own economy that was paying to support the workers' families.[1]

The same practice was applied to laborers from Holland, France, Croatia, Serbia, Bohemia and Moravia, Slovakia, and, later, occupied Italy. Whether people worked voluntarily or involuntarily made no difference. The transactions involved—and similar ones—represented a major source of income for the German treasury. As in the cases described earlier, the Reich's accountants recorded the receipts under the nebulous heading "General Administrative Revenues." Writing in 1944, renowned jurist Raphael Lemkin identified the core of what was essentially a gigantic swindle: "The occupied countries not only finance exports to Germany but also pay their own people working in Germany."[2] In the first six months after the French capitulation, for example, more than half a billion reichsmarks owed to families of French workers "employed" in Germany were confiscated by the treasury and paid out in francs from the occupation budget.[3] Revenues to Germany soon fell, however, because the number of French citizens working there, voluntarily or involuntarily, significantly declined with the signing of an armistice treaty between the two countries and the return home of French POWs. In the case of Belgium, as with Germany's allies, money confiscated from foreign workers' wages was credited to Brussels in the two countries' clearing account. That made no difference, though, since Germany had little intention of settling its debts.[4]

When German troops occupied the north of Italy, its former ally, in September 1943, more than a half million POWs were taken back to the Reich as forced laborers. Once again, the state confiscated part of their wages, using what was by then the established system of diverting money from occupation budgets to pay foreign workers' families. German companies using forced labor were required to transfer wages to an account at the Deutsche Bank. From there the money was sent on to the "wage savings account" at the German Settlement Bank. These sums, of course, never found their way back to Italy. Instead, the economics minister ordered: "They are to be held in Berlin, where they will be kept at the disposal of the Italian government. How to use these sums of reichsmarks is a decision that will be made at a later point in time." In reality, these assets were secretly converted into German treasury bonds, which would have been used to pay concocted external occupation costs had Germany won the war. The records of monetary transfers to the general account at the Deutsche Bank for individual Italian workers determined the payments made by the Banca del Lavoro in Italy to those workers' families. To raise money for those payments, the Italian finance minister was required to provide the bank "with adequate credit."[5]

THE PROCEDURES governing forced laborers from Poland and the Soviet Union were far harsher. An order issued in 1942 described what German soldiers were to do with the meager belongings of male and female workers taken prisoner in rural Ukraine: "Possessions left behind as well as any cash" were to be handed over to the village elder, who was in turn to sell the material assets. "Animal inventory (horses, cows, pigs, sheep, chickens, geese, etc.) as well as hay, straw, and field crops" were to be "immediately" offered up for sale to the economics command of the local Wehrmacht division. The village elder was required to transfer the revenues from such sales, together with any confiscated money, to a sham account at the German treasury. The treasury would then, theoretically, refund the money when rural workers returned home so that they could use it to "reacquire livestock and seed materials." No one knows what would have actually happened to Soviet forced laborers in the event of a German victory. As it was, their assets were converted into cash that flowed directly into the Reich treasury.[6]

Once they arrived in Germany, forced laborers were assigned to German companies, which were required to pay their new workers wages at the low end of the scale. On August 5, 1940, the Reich Defense Council issued a decree requiring Polish workers in Germany to pay a "supplemental social compensation fee in addition to the normal income tax." (The draft version of this edict dated back to 1936, when the Finance Ministry considered levying a special "performance compensation fee" on wages earned by German Jews.)[7] The revenues from the special fee on Polish laborers went directly to the Reich. Meanwhile, the Finance Ministry secured permission to extend the levy to other particularly disadvantaged groups. Before long, Jews and Gypsies were also compelled to pay it.[8]

According to the first implementation decree that followed, the levy applied to all Poles living within Germany, even those who were voluntarily employed, as well as those Poles who lived in parts of Poland annexed by the Reich. An exception was made for Poles who worked in agriculture since the wages negotiated for them were, in comparison with the German standard, particularly meager: room and board plus pocket money of between 8.50 and 26.50 reichsmarks per month.[9] The supplemental social compensation fee was set at 15 percent of workers' gross wages. The official justification for the levy was that Polish workers did neither social nor military service, nor did they pay contributions to the German Labor Front or make compulsory donations to the main Nazi charity, the German Winter Relief Fund.[10]

In addition, voluntary and involuntary Polish workers were automatically assigned, without exception, to the top income tax brackets (categories I and II). Categories III and IV, which had been introduced to benefit poor German families, "were ruled out as a matter of principle." This discriminatory tax rule had been imposed on Jews on February 17, 1939, one year after the German finance minister had stripped them of eligibility for tax deductions for children.[11] Jews were automatically assigned to category I. (The rules governing Soviet workers were repeatedly modified, but never to the benefit of German employers or the laborers themselves.)

In practice the tax policy operated as follows: a Jewish man with a wife and one child who performed forced labor at Daimler-Benz in 1942 received a monthly wage of 234 reichsmarks. He was required to pay 108 marks in taxes and contributions to social welfare programs to which he and his family were theoretically entitled. Non-Jewish colleagues who received the same wages had to pay only 9.62 marks in taxes and 20.59 marks in contributions.[12] The amounts deducted from the wages of Jews—as well as of Gypsies and forced laborers from Eastern Europe—were thus more than triple those demanded of German workers. The Reich was able to double its wage tax revenues during the latter half of World War II on the backs of involuntary workers assigned to German industry and voluntary laborers in the annexed parts of Poland. A portion of the remaining wage packet was earmarked to be sent home to workers' families. The German employer would pay an equivalent sum into the general bank account set up by the Finance Ministry for worker remittances. The General Government of Poland was then required to pay out the earnings to the families in Poland. In this way the Reich compelled the Polish people to pay for labor performed on German territory.

But there were limits to how much money Berlin could swindle from Poles this way. As early as the fall of 1940, the measure had drawn complaints from the occupation administrators, who sought to stabilize conditions in Poland, if only for Germany's benefit. The German general governor in Poland, Hans Frank, vehemently protested that the Finance Ministry was "cutting the wages" of Polish workers in the Reich and that "the treasury was hoarding the surplus, if indeed there is a surplus, entirely for itself in the form of social benefits contributions." The result, Frank complained, was that the General Government "had to use state funds for the maintenance of families whose providers were working within the Reich."

According to Frank, Hitler himself was "quite astonished at this development." In Frank's account, the Führer warned: "If the financial administration of the Reich is indeed not transferring the wages earned by Polish workers in the Reich to the General Government but is instead using them covertly within the Reich, that is an absolutely unacceptable situation."[13] Individual German companies and the gauleiters in East Prussia also objected that Polish workers were being too harshly exploited. The system, they complained, removed all incentives to work harder and more conscientiously.[14] In 1943, the Reich Central Security Office demanded that "all instances of discrimination against Poles be avoided for the time being" in the face of "the increased intractability of the Polish resistance movement."[15]

Yet on top of all the taxes and social benefits contributions, Polish and Soviet forced workers' wages were docked a further 1.50 reichsmarks per day for room and board in the labor camps. According to one economist's estimate, only around 10 reichsmarks were left of a Russian or Polish worker's weekly wage of 40 marks, once taxes, contributions, and room and board had been deducted. The economist warned, however, that "given the shortages of consumer goods in the Reich, [we should prevent the workers] from spending the entire sum."[16]

To combat this potential problem, the Economics Ministry developed an Eastern Workers' Savings program, which "utilized the simplest possible form of savings bonds." Under the system, the payroll departments of German companies were issued special savings bonds "with relief printing and denominations in Arabic numerals." The companies were then required to pay the equivalent amount to the Reich treasury. In theory, forced laborers would have been able to redeem their savings, with 2 percent interest, when they returned home. But the wording of the relevant legislation was vague: "the amount saved" was to be made available "to the saver or a member of his family, subject to the specific regulations of the Reich minister for the occupied eastern territories or the Wehrmacht High Command."[17]

The bank that had ostensibly issued the savings bonds, which were given to all the forced laborers from the Soviet Union, was the Central Economic Bank of Ukraine.[18] The funds paid by German companies were transferred to that institution's purely fictitious Berlin office. There, they were recorded as a single lump sum rather than deposited into individual accounts. The hypothetical paying out of this money was "to proceed in the native currency of each particular country." The funds could not be withdrawn by workers while they remained in Germany, only once they had returned home.

The Berlin office of the Central Economic Bank of Ukraine was one of many fronts for the Reich treasury. When one considers how Germany dealt with "ethnic aliens" and how its Eastern European forced laborers were often worked to death in conditions of virtual slavery, the Eastern Workers' Savings program emerges as just another way for the Reich to appropriate other people's money. As historian Manfred Oertel writes: "Ultimately, all the taxes, contributions, and 'savings' of Polish and Soviet workers from their forced labor in Germany were a specific form of tribute" designated for the war chest of the Third Reich.[19] So, too, was the income Western European workers sent back to their home countries.

THE BUDGETARY advantages of using forced labor are obvious. It allowed the state treasury maximum access to workers' wages, thereby stabilizing wartime finances, transferring burdens from German taxpayers, and—as a welcome bonus—protecting the tight market of available consumer goods from additional spending power. Had the Reich relied instead on the increased labor output of German women or on lengthened working hours, several additional billions of reichsmarks would have come into circulation. But there would not have been anything more to buy in stores. That would have put a strain on the reichsmark and possibly had a negative effect on popular opinion.

An examination of domestic wage taxes between 1941 and 1945 reveals that a considerable portion of revenues came from foreign laborers. The benefit to companies like Daimler-Benz and Krupp was hardly negligible, considering that foreign workers were paid 15 to 40 percent less than their German colleagues. But the benefit to the German people, the *Volksgemeinschaft*, as embodied by the Nazi state, was far greater. In practice, the Reich appropriated 60 to 70 percent of the wages paid by those firms.

Wage tax revenues from foreign labor for the period in question totaled 6.5 billion reichsmarks. (In the case of agriculture, Berlin kept wages artificially low, creating, as noted above, an indirect subsidy for farmers to the tune of at least 3.5 billion marks.) An average of 500 million marks came into the state annually through the confiscation of foreign worker remittances. That amounts to a total of an additional 2.5 billion marks, which the Reich recorded as "general administrative revenues."[20] Assuming that the Eastern Workers' Savings program brought in a further 500 million, then the state earned at least 13 billion marks—in today's terms, $150 billion—from forced labor. The size of this figure belies the traditional historical assumption that it was companies that profited most from forced labor. Instead the exploitation was perpetrated on a far grander scale, by the whole of society itself. The billions in state revenues from forced labor took a significant load off ordinary German taxpayers.

And this was only one of the advantages that individual "ethnic comrades" derived from their acceptance of a government campaign not only to wage war against others but to dispossess them of everything they had.

Few documents have survived in the German federal archive about the theft of wages and benefits from forced laborers and the benefits derived by the German populace. But one significant indicator of both is the level of subsidies paid out of the Reich's general budget to social welfare agencies, which were perennially strapped for cash during the war.*

Table 1: State Subsidies to Social Welfare Programs, 1938-43

	Subsidies (in millions of reichsmarks)	Index Points	Percent Change
1938	640.4	100	
1939	748.6	116	16
1940	940.4	146	26
1941	1,395.3	217	48
1942	963.1	150	-31
1943	1,119.2	174	16

In table 1, the drastic decline in 1942 stands out. The obvious explanation is that the establishment of a forced-labor economy reduced the need for expenditures to keep the social welfare system afloat. The table shows that within the space of only three budgetary years the subsidies needed by Germany's social welfare system had more than doubled. If that increase had continued unabated, state subsidies would have reached 2.14 billion marks by 1944, and 2.35 billion by April 1945.

This linear calculation of potential increases in subsidies is based on an average annual increase in index points of 37.5. (The corresponding numbers for 1942, 1943, 1944, and 1945 would have been 250, 287.5, 325, and 362.5, respectively.) If one takes into account the actual decrease to 150 in 1942 but continues to use this rate of growth, subsidies would have reached 187.5 index points in 1943, 225 in 1944, and 262.5 in 1945. Extrapolating from these figures, one sees that the Reich "saved" approximately 2.2 billion

---

*The author is indebted to Albert Müller for his assistance with these calculations.

reichsmarks between 1942 and May 1945. Those savings can be traced back to the denial of social benefits to forced laborers and the mass murder of Jewish claimants.

Not surprisingly, the huge influx of forced laborers in 1942 is also reflected in the wage tax revenues taken in by the Reich.

Table 2: Wage Tax Revenues, 1938–43

	Revenues (in millions of reichsmarks)	Index Points	Percent Increase
1938	2,090.8	100	
1939	2,645.7	126	26
1940	2,979.3	142	11
1941	4,223.4	209	42
1942	4,539.2	217	7
1943	5,001.2	239	10

The figures in table 2 show that wage tax revenues more than doubled between 1938 and 1943. There are two major jumps: 26 percent from 1938 to 1939 and 42 percent between 1940 and 1941. The first increase reflects the incorporation of Austria and Sudeten Czechoslovakia into the Reich, as well as lengthened working hours after the start of the war.

The second can be traced to the massive use of forced laborers in German industry. Without that influx, revenues after 1940 could hardly have increased by any more than 5 percent annually and would have diminished as Germany's wartime fortunes began to fail. In monetary terms, without forced labor, projected tax revenues between 1940 and the first quarter of 1945 would have totaled around 17.3 billion reichsmarks. The actual proceeds were, of course, far higher since forced labor was used more intensively in the final stages of the war. Assuming a further 10 percent increase in wage tax revenues in 1944 and the first quarter of 1945 (to reflect the increased reliance on forced labor), actual proceeds probably totaled 23.8 billion reichsmarks from 1940 through early 1945. The difference between the two figures—6.5 billion marks—reflects a conservative estimate of the amount by which German taxpayers benefited from revenues generated by taxes on forced labor.

New Central Banks

Except for the chaotic weeks of German retreat in the final phase of World War II, the Wehrmacht "paid" for practically all its needs in Northern, Western, and Southern Europe in RKK certificates or local currencies. Consequently, the extent of the larceny can be roughly measured in Wehrmacht expenditures. The same, however, was not true for the German-occupied parts of the Soviet Union. There, the Wehrmacht seldom used money or certificates to make acquisitions. A significant portion of what it needed was simply requisitioned through obscure "receipts" or without any paperwork at all. According to an order from the Wehrmacht directorate, "all nonmilitary or private property up to a value of 1,000 reichsmarks is to be paid for in cash." For larger acquisitions, preprinted acknowledgments of receipt were to be filled out. These expenses included food, which was "under no circumstances to be paid for in cash."[21] But the question arises: what did private property mean in a system where most everything had been collectivized? Unlike other occupied countries, the Soviet Union was plundered in ways that cannot be measured in officially recorded transactions.[22]

On June 9, 1941, Reichsbank director Max Kretzschmann gave the administrative council of the Reich Credit Banks a top-secret briefing on the short-term tasks they would soon face. Reichsbank officials had already organized six mobile credit banks to serve the immediate needs of the troops.[23] On June 12, 1941, the order came through, "in light of planned military operations in the East," to increase the number of pre-ordered RKK certificates "by 1 billion to 1½ billion reichsmarks." This was to be carried out with "maximum speed."[24] Ten days later, Operation Barbarossa began. As the pace of the German advance into the Soviet Union slowed in late July, the Reich treasury printed some 10 billion counterfeit rubles. These, however, were never used.[25] No sooner had German units moved through a given area than RKK employees had Russian coins melted down "in line with the European mobilization of metals."[26]

The administrative council had already met on June 9 to discuss how "a new bank of issue—the Moscow Reserve Bank—could be grafted onto the Russian banking system." The launch of the new bank, it was envisioned, would take about three months and would enable the Reich to print rubles that were legal tender. Even before the German invasion of the Soviet Union, Kretzschmann had weighed the option of initially introducing various forms of currency. "Should the occupied part of Russia be divided up into governmentally distinct districts," he wrote, "it would require the establishment of several banks of issue."[27]

One day later, on June 10, 1941, another top-secret meeting took place in the Finance Ministry. The subject was "the imminent eastern deployment." The participants discussed issuing credit to those German firms that would be responsible for restoring industrial and agricultural production after the invasion—a major concern for German troops. According to the minutes of the meeting, Finance Ministry administrators assumed that most production facilities "would be destroyed before falling into German hands." Participants debated how to raise the collateral for loans to repair damaged industrial infrastructure. Reserves of natural resources were ill suited to this purpose, the officials agreed, "since petroleum and mining and agricultural products were, as per orders, to be transported back to Germany." To solve the problem, the directors of the future Reich Credit Banks in the Soviet Union were instructed to forgo demands for collateral and issue unsecured loans. It was the only way, the Finance Ministry concluded, "to extract the maximum amount possible."[28] As the invasion and occupation progressed, Reich Credit Banks would issue tens of millions of marks in loans to firms involved in the occupied Soviet Union.

But the central bank that issued the ruble was in Moscow, which was not under German control. Hence, the administrative council of the Reich Credit Banks came out in the late fall of 1941 in favor of issuing a new currency, "the eastern crown, with a value of two crowns to the mark." A member of the Reichsbank board of directors, Maximilian Bernhuber, was chosen to oversee the founding of the new central bank. But the project stalled. Leading German civilian administrators in the Baltic States lobbied against the idea, saying it would upset the local populace. And as time passed the military objective of securing the front lines took top priority.[29]

But another Reichsbank plan to introduce a new currency, the karbowanez, for Ukraine, was a success. The law creating the Central Currency Bank of Ukraine (ZNU) came into force on June 1, 1942. The bank was modeled on the central bank the Nazi regime had set up for the Polish General Government. The influence of German occupiers on currency policies was "ensured by the fact that the two directors of the Currency Bank were to be appointed by the Reichsbank."[30] As in the case of other regional currency programs, the finance minister demanded that rubles exchanged in Ukraine for the new banknotes "be transferred without compensation to the main administration of the Reich Credit Bank, so as to serve the interests of the Reich."

The exploitation of compulsorily exchanged currency was common practice in German-occupied Europe. The Finance Ministry had used the same procedure to confiscate French francs in Alsace-Lorraine and rubles in East Galicia after that province was taken from the Soviet Union and added to the Polish General Government in 1941.[31] From the latter annexation, the Reich had taken in some 340 million rubles, which the new bank of issue in Cracow handed over for "utilization."[32] Moreover, when the Reich itself annexed parts of Poland in 1940, German state bankers had kept some 660 million zlotys that Poles had been forced to exchange for reichsmarks. That money was "appropriated in its entirety via the Reich Credit Banks in Poland and the bank of issue in Poland." A Reichsbank representative boasted: "A sum equaling more than 300 million marks was extracted for the Reich. Although the Reich was required to use it to redeem Polish banknotes in the annexed eastern territories, thereby recording a loss, we were still able to transform it into a kind of contribution to the war costs from the rest of Polish territory."[33] In April 1940, after handing over daily business operations to the bank of issue in Cracow, the Reich Credit Banks kept 306 million zlotys, the equivalent of 153 million reichsmarks, which had remained unspent. Schwerin von Krosigk commented dryly: "I do not overlook the fact that the realization of zloty assets I have approved contributes, in a relatively imperceptible form recognizable only to experts, to the burdens on the Polish economy."[34] Representatives of the German Reich used these sums of money in the remaining franc, ruble, and zloty zones to buy up goods that would otherwise have had to be paid for with funds set aside for occupation costs.

The new Ukrainian currency increased the number of banknotes in circulation in the occupied Soviet Union without the Reich's having to resort to forgery. It also led to an immediate devaluation of rubles that had been hoarded in Ukraine. In Germany's financial press, the new money was praised as contributing to a "healthy price and currency ratio."[35] Yet Ukraine did not suffer from money hoarding, as German officials had suggested it would in justifying the new currency; it suffered from the greed of its occupiers. The new banknotes offered numerous opportunities for Germans to exploit Ukraine and exacerbated the very problems they were nominally meant to combat. When Ukrainians tried to exchange large-denomination ruble notes for karbowanez, the branches of the ZNU did not pay out in cash. Rather they credited the amount to frozen bank accounts, which account holders were not allowed to access.

The official rationale for this policy was "to curb excess spending power among the native populace."[36] In reality, the sums confiscated were transferred via the Reich Credit Banks and the Wehrmacht directorates to German soldiers and black marketeers in those parts of the occupied Soviet Union where the ruble was still legal tender. The money was used to buy up massive amounts of food. (Only a small portion of it was shipped back to Germany between 1942 and 1943—most was exported to the Wehrmacht's other theaters of operation.) The Ministry for Occupied Eastern European Territories, concerned about maintaining a functioning economy in Ukraine, implored the Finance Ministry to pay for these supplies, but that appeal fell on deaf ears.[37]

The result of the German spending spree was that occupied Ukraine was constantly having to print more money. In February 1943, the new currency was barely seven months old, but the financial division of the Reichskommissariat Ukraine was already describing the situation as "extremely critical." The amount of money in circulation had risen by 80 percent within the space of a few months. The currency, which was becoming worthless, had flowed from "the pockets of the Wehrmacht and its employees" into the hands of "the local populace."[38] In 1942, one bank official reported, "up to 90 percent of occupation costs had to be covered with treasury bonds from the ZNU"—in other words, by printing more money.[39]

Ordinary German Consumers

Germany was unable in either the First or the Second World War to produce enough food to meet its own needs. With the utmost effort, the Nazi leadership succeeded in producing 83 percent of what it required domestically, but imports—especially of cooking oils and feed for livestock—remained necessary in order to keep the populace well nourished. Germany's dependence on foreign trade meant that the British fleet could easily put pressure on the Reich with blockades, and the collateral effects of war brought decreased harvests and further hindered efforts toward self-sufficiency. The needs of the munitions industry led to unavoidable shortages in artificial fertilizer, which required the same chemicals needed for the production of gunpowder. There were also shortages of agricultural manpower, as well as of horses, tractors, machinery, and fuel. It was more difficult to ensure the timely delivery of seeds to maximize harvest yields. To combat one of these problems, the Nazi leadership decided shortly after the beginning of the war to use Polish labor in German agriculture.

The Reich Food Ministry had gotten a head start in dealing with the anticipated shortfalls. As early as 1936, ministry officials saw to the stockpiling of reserves of grain and the building of new silos and warehouses, using subsidies and tax breaks as incentives to get private industry involved.[40] Göring viewed such facilities as "an indirect form of armament." In the summer of 1938, to accelerate preparations, he appointed the highly efficient state secretary of the Food Ministry, Herbert Backe, to oversee the expansion of grain-storage facilities.[41] By June 30, 1939, Germany had 5.5 million tons of grain reserves, and the figure remained constant a year later. But by June 30, 1941, the reserves had dwindled to 2 million tons; a year later they were down to a meager 670,000. In response, officials at an emergency meeting called by Göring in August 1942 decided to step up Germany's extraction of food from occupied countries. As a result, Backe was able to get grain reserves back up to 1.2 million tons in 1943 and 1.7 million in 1944.[42]

Unlike in World War I, the Food Ministry instituted a complex rationing system in the first phase of German mobilization. In late August 1939, a few days before German soldiers marched into Poland, food ration cards were already being distributed. Commenting overoptimistically on what she saw as Germany's poor prospects for military success, Simone de Beauvoir wrote on August 28, 1939: "No one begins a war by handing out cards for bread rations."[43] But de Beauvoir was mistaken. When Germany invaded Poland in September 1939, it had a cleverly devised and well-planned food distribution system in place that would continue functioning until the final days of the conflict.

As early as 1939, Backe's subordinates and advisers decided to reduce the relatively cost-intensive production of meat and eggs to the minimum that they thought the populace would tolerate. Because roughly five kilograms of grain were required to produce one kilogram of meat, the move allowed Germany to exploit its agricultural resources better. Initially, generous allowances for other kinds of food were combined with price controls, and draconian punishments were meted out to people caught dealing on the black market. The public viewed the rationing system as fair, especially since it gave preference to selected categories of recipients such as physical laborers, pregnant women and breastfeeding mothers, children, and the ill. The rationing procedure also took account of regional differences in eating habits.

Even with food rationing and wartime changes in people's eating habits, shortfalls occurred. But as it had not done in World War I, the German leadership transferred the burdens of those shortages to people in occupied countries, to disadvantaged minorities, and to Soviet prisoners. The result was famine in Poland, Greece, and especially the Soviet Union; in psychiatric hospitals, ghettos, concentration camps, and POW camps, people starved to death. Summing up the government's attitude, Göring proclaimed: "If someone has to go hungry, let it be someone other than a German."[44]

This sentiment was reflected in a document laying out the central guidelines for German rule in the Soviet Union: "Under no circumstances should the status quo be maintained; rather, it must be consciously departed from by incorporating Russia's food economy into the European framework. This will necessarily lead to the extinction of both the [native agriculture] industry and large segments of the population." Another passage reads: "Tens of millions of people in these areas will become superfluous and either die or have to move to Siberia." The plan was to have them march there on foot.[45]

The same cruelty also informed the official policy toward Soviet prisoners of war. As late as November 13, 1941, Quartermaster General Eduard Wagner proclaimed that "prisoners who don't work in the camps will be left to starve." In December, the political leadership changed course. From then on, camp commanders were to try "to preserve as many POWs as possible and make them capable of working." The reason for the shift was a German military defeat outside Moscow, which forced German military and economic strategists to plan for a longer, more uncertain war. POWs were now to be employed as forced laborers. Yet that change in policy took some time to take effect and came too late for the many captured Soviets who had already been weakened by malnutrition.

The new directive did not affect the general policy of allowing Ukraine's urban population to go hungry. Wagner prohibited soldiers from giving away "any provisions allocated for troop maintenance to the populace of the occupied territories." To prevent food shortages back in Germany, the 3-million-strong army was to feed itself "from the soil." The officers in charge of troop maintenance were instructed to be ruthless in keeping supply requisitions to a minimum. The urgency was compounded when the Reich was forced to order a temporary stoppage of food deliveries from the agrarian south of the Soviet Union to northern regions and urban centers. Along the route taken by the German invaders, whole stretches of land were left stripped of anything edible. In December 1942, officials within the German agrarian administration in southern Russia spoke of "an 800-to-1,000-kilometer-wide swath" in which all available foodstuffs were to be confiscated and eaten.[46]

The German invader saw little reason to provide for civilians. "For economic reasons," the Nazi leadership quickly decided, "taking large cities is undesirable. It's more advantageous to place them under siege." On September 20, 1941, the Wehrmacht's food and nutrition expert, Professor Wilhelm Ziegelmayer, noted in his diary: "In the future we will be burdened by demands that Leningrad be allowed to capitulate. It will have to be destroyed in accordance with a scientifically based method." On November 27, Hamburg mayor Carl Vincent Krogmann jotted down an account one of his administrators had given of an official trip to the front near Leningrad: "It is assumed that the majority of the people in Leningrad, around 5.5 million, will starve to death." The Nazi minister for the occupied eastern territories spoke of "a bitter necessity that is beyond all sentiment."[47] Around the same time Göring foresaw "the greatest incidence of death since the Thirty Years War."

Eduard Wagner announced that "Leningrad, in particular, will have to starve to death." Two months earlier, in a letter to his wife, he had written: "For the time being we're letting them stew in St. Petersburg." One couldn't, Wagner wrote, take on the care of several million people by burdening "the wallet that pays for our subsistence. Sentimentality has no place here."[48] At least a million people in Leningrad starved to death during the two-and-a-half-year German siege of the city.

The commander in charge of the Ukrainian city of Kharkiv received instructions that "the German Wehrmacht has no interest in maintaining Kharkiv's urban population." Kharkiv was occupied by the Sixth Army under Field Marshal Walther von Reichenau. On the question of how "troops in the East should behave," he concluded: "Maintaining local residents is like giving away cigarettes and bread—an example of misdirected compassion." At about the same time, reports came in from the occupied Crimean town of Kerch that "the pace of the liquidation of Jews has been accelerated because of the precarious food situation in the city."[49]

Meanwhile, in May 1942, the Army High Command issued an order aimed at ensuring that cupboards in Germany were full. It allowed soldiers on the Eastern Front to send back home, in addition to the usual small packages, one of up to twenty kilograms. The official justification for the directive was the need "to free troops from unnecessary baggage." Nonetheless, the High Command stressed the importance "of preventing customs officials from checking the contents of these packages at recipients' homes."[50] If the typical "laundry package" were to be examined, Hamburg's chief financial officer wrote, officials would discover that the contents consisted "exclusively of smoked pork."[51] In December 1942, Göring granted the Wehrmacht permission to organize an "additional package operation for all frontline soldiers on home leave" from Africa, from submarines, and from the Eastern Front.[52] In Ukraine, food worth 37 million reichsmarks was purchased expressly for this purpose.[53]

In a meeting with Reich commissioners and military commanders on August 6, 1942, Göring demanded a dramatic increase in the amount of goods extracted from occupied territories. "It is of no concern," Göring thundered, "if they say that their people are dropping dead of starvation. Let them drop dead so long as not a single German does."[54] The relatively small state of Serbia, which had already lost its most fertile regions to German occupation, was required to deliver an additional 100,000 tons of wheat and corn.[55] Similar demands were placed on France and Belgium for contributions to the "anti-Bolshevist" struggle, in which Germans were putatively shedding their blood on Europe's behalf. Food exports from France to Germany rose 50 percent between 1942 and late 1943.[56] In August 1942, after a conversation with Hitler, the Reich commissioner for Ukraine, Erich Koch, laid out a set of guidelines for food policies. The summary protocol read: "Ukraine is required to provide everything Germany lacks. This requirement is to be fulfilled without regard to casualties. . . . The increase in bread rations is a political necessity crucial to our ability to pursue the war to its victorious conclusion. The grain we lack must be extracted from Ukraine. In light of this task, feeding the civilian population there is utterly insignificant."[57]

As historian Christian Gerlach has shown in his 1999 study of Belarus, the difficulties the Nazi government encountered in keeping Germans well fed accelerated the pace of the mass murder of European Jews. In the summer of 1942, State Secretary Backe ordered huge quotas of grain and meat delivered to Germany from the General Government, previously a recipient of food from the Reich. This action drew energetic protests from the director of the food department in Poland, Karl Naumann, who pointed out that the Poles were undernourished. Backe responded: "The 3.5 million Jews remaining in the General Government of Poland will have to be cleansed this year."[58] That number was either a drastic exaggeration or a typo—the actual population of Jews was much smaller—but the intention is clear. During a meeting of the General Government on August 24, 1942, Naumann told administrative heads: "The maintenance of the estimated 1.5 million Jews in the population has been abandoned, with the exception of 300,000 Jews who are useful to the Reich because of artisan or other work skills. . . . The other 1.2 million Jews will no longer be given food."[59] And in fact, by the end of 1942, well over a million Jews had been murdered in the gas chambers of the General Government.[60]

Gerlach has also demonstrated that the German leadership took equally drastic measures earlier, in September 1941, when they radicalized their food policies toward Soviet prisoners. By that point, it had become clear to senior officials that Germany was not going to be able to conquer Russia before the onset of winter. On September 4, Backe refused a request by the Wehrmacht for 2.1 million tons of grain and 652,000 tons of meat, saying that the troops would have to feed themselves from resources available in occupied territories and at the front. With explicit reference to the strikes of 1918, when Germans had revolted in response to food shortages at the end of World War I, Göring ruled out reducing food rations on the home front and issued an order dated September 16, 1941: "As a general principle for occupied territories, only those who work for us should be assured of receiving the food they need." He also decreed that "ruthless conservation measures" be undertaken to ensure food imports to Germany. A short time later, after a conversation with Backe about the situation of captured Red Army soldiers in detention camps, Goebbels noted: "The catastrophic starvation there exceeds all description." In the officers' mess in Riga, Wehrmacht soldiers were quoted as discussing their "assignment to let Russian POWs starve and freeze to death."[61]

By February 1, 1942, 2 million of the 3.3 million Red Army prisoners—60 percent—had died either in German detention camps or in transit. Excluding the first three weeks of the war, when captured soldiers were generally in good physical condition, an average of ten thousand Soviet prisoners died per day. In World War I, the German home front had suffered from food shortages, but only 5.4 percent of the 1.4 million Russian POWs died in German detention. Considering that most of those POWs were either wounded or physically depleted, it's clear that the German leadership under Kaiser Wilhelm II closely followed the guidelines of the Hague Conventions.

On October 4, 1942, with the rigid policy of starvation in place toward Soviet POWs, Jews, and the populations of Soviet cities, Göring gave a Sunday address in Berlin's Sportpalast to mark the end of the harvest season. He told his audience that "we are feeding our entire army from the occupied territories." He also announced that food rations would be increased in the months to come, especially in areas susceptible to aerial bombardment. In addition, a "special allocation" would be made available at Christmas. As for the parts of Eastern Europe that Germany had conquered, Göring proclaimed: "From this day on things will continue to get better since we now possess huge stretches of fertile land. There are stocks of eggs, butter, and flour there that you cannot even imagine." A few days previously, in a speech to mark the start of the Winter Relief Fund, Hitler had stoked listeners' hopes that the "opening up of space in the East" would soon allow for a return to "near-peacetime conditions." The Eastern Front, Hitler promised, would allow Germany "to pursue the war to its successful conclusion without major privations."

With Hitler having laid the groundwork, Göring's address encouraged the German populace to have faith in their regime. The Security Service reported an overwhelmingly positive public reaction to Göring's speech. "Göring spoke to the heart and the stomach," read one report. "The detailed description of the continually improving food situation in the Reich," another stated, has strengthened "the belief that we have put the worst behind us." The working classes, in particular, saw Göring's promises as "something concrete." Moreover, throughout the country, people "were no longer as worried about the military situation—for example, the duration of the fighting in Stalingrad." The author of a Security Service report on October 12, 1942, wrote "that the mood among women has improved considerably since, with good reason, the promise of an increasingly better food and subsistence situation is particularly important to them." Goebbels, too, noted "a veritable surge in the mood of the German people."[62]

THE SHEER amount of key agricultural products the Wehrmacht diverted from the Soviet Union can partly—but only partly—be gauged by the figures the Reich Office of Statistics kept for the years 1941–42 and 1942–43.[63]

Table 3: Soviet Food Transfers to the Reich, 1941–43, by Recipient

	Wehrmacht (in tons)	Home Front (in tons)	Total (in tons)
Grain	3,385,021	988,318	4,373,339
Meat	435,058	60,585	495,643
Oils and Margarine	90,732	632,618	723,350
Potatoes	1,880,240	15,535	1,895,775

Recent statisticians have pointed out that these numbers do not include foods "directly produced or seized by the troops themselves." The amounts, writes one researcher, "while lower, would still be large: for grain alone, for example, hundreds of thousands of tons. One should also keep in mind the maintenance requirements of Reich citizens who worked in Eastern Europe (civil servants, employees of companies involved in the East)." Furthermore, the official statistics do not include the personal shopping sprees millions of German soldiers went on during the two years in question. Even the Reich's own statisticians concluded that the amounts of unrecorded "food extractions" were "quite considerable, even if less than the recorded amounts." One can thus add a conservative estimate of 15 percent to the official Wehrmacht statistics to reflect the minimum amount of food consumption. In reality, that percentage was probably much higher.

Comparing these totals with statistics for the amounts of agricultural goods produced within Germany shows that the exploitation of Soviet territory increased the Reich's grain supplies by 10 percent, its stocks of oils and margarine by more than 60 percent, and meat by around 12 percent.[64] It's easy to grasp how theft on this scale led to mass starvation in the Soviet Union.

A minimum allowance of 2.5 grain units (GU) per year is needed to keep a person alive. One GU is the equivalent of 100 kilos of grain and varying amounts of other foods. In the early 1940s, Backe's academic advisers, the renowned agronomists Emil Woermann and Georg Blum, developed a conversion table used by the Reich Food Ministry.* Based on the amount of energy that could be derived from various types of nutrition, it served as the scientific foundation for calculating wartime food rations. (Today, the system is used to distribute humanitarian aid efficiently in areas of catastrophe.)

The GU scale illustrates the devastating impact of German seizures of agricultural products in Eastern Europe. Again, the figures come from the Reich Office of Statistics.

Table 4: Nutritional Value of Soviet Food Transfers to the Reich, 1941–43, by Recipient

	Wehrmacht (in GUs)	Home Front (in GUs)
Grain	33,850,210	9,883,180
Meat	21,752,900	3,029,250
Oils and Margarine	3,084,890	21,509,010
Potatoes	3,760,480	31,070
Subtotals	62,448,480	34,452,510 .
plus 15%	9,367,272	
	71,815,752	
Total		106,268,262

*Potatoes, for example, were multiplied by a factor of 0.2, legumes by 1, a cow by 5.7, a pig by 4.2, eggs by 4.2, margarine by 3.4. The category of meat in table 4 has been assigned a value of 5, the median between beef and pork.

Since table 4 covers two years, if the total is divided by five (2.5×2), the resulting figure represents the number of people whose nutritional basis for survival was removed. Before the war, the Soviet Union produced 101 percent of the food its population needed. That percentage would have declined, owing to wartime disruptions in production, even without German plundering.[65] The seizure of food for the Reich meant that approximately 21.2 million Soviet citizens saw the nutritional basis for their survival eliminated.

The reality of Soviet suffering was almost certainly worse than the calculations indicate. A statement from a conference of German state secretaries held on May 21, 1941, asserted: "The war can be continued only if in the third year of the conflict the entire Wehrmacht is fed on Russian supplies. It will undoubtedly entail starvation for many millions of people, when we extract what we need from their land."[66]

A letter written from the Ukrainian city of Kirovgrad in the summer of 1942 gives a clear sense of the spirit with which Germans went about plundering food in Eastern Europe. The author was an employee of a firm whose task it was "to register and secure all production facilities, agricultural as well as industrial, and to secure the southern part of the Eastern Front, with all its wealth of food and amenities." After opening with an anti-Semitic remark ("Jews? Forget about them!"), the author characterizes his primary job as relieving "the home front as much as possible from the need to send supplies." Anything left over that "the Wehrmacht couldn't find a use for" was to be sent back to Germany. "Huge amounts of wheat, sunflower seeds, sunflower oil, and eggs are being transported for distribution to the Reich. If, as my wife wrote me, the few weeks of food production should see the successful delivery of sunflower oil, I can say with pride that I was directly involved in this operation."[67]

Food extracted from occupied countries was primarily allocated to German soldiers, who then sent a not inconsiderable portion back home. Beginning in 1942, an increasing amount of food was also shipped directly back to the Reich for workers engaged in hard physical labor, pregnant women, and Aryan senior citizens and infants. But supplies also went to ordinary German consumers—those who possessed standard food ration cards that didn't allow for any special allocations. They, too, were to be kept happy and content.

The level of the rations and the relative equity with which food was distributed strengthened Germans' faith in their political leadership. It was not until February 1945 that complaints were heard from women with children in Berlin that they were not "regularly receiving whole milk."[68] Decades after 1945, German women still recalled: "During the war we didn't go hungry. Back then everything worked. It was only after the war that things turned bad."

Then there were cities like Leningrad, where in January 1942 between 3,500 and 4,000 people died every day. One survivor recalls: "It was nearly impossible to get hold of a coffin. Hundreds of bodies were simply left lying around, wrapped only in cloth, in cemeteries or the surrounding areas. The authorities buried the bodies in mass graves, which were dug by civil defense troops with the help of explosives. We didn't have the strength to dig normal graves in the frozen ground."[69]

Part III

THE DISPOSSESSION OF THE JEWS

CHAPTER 7

Larceny as a State Principle

Inflation and Aryanization

In the standard historical view, German businessmen and bank directors were the ones who profited most from the Aryanization of Jewish-owned property. This widespread but mistaken impression has been strengthened by studies of firms' activities during the Nazi years that a number of European states and large corporations commissioned professional historians to undertake in the 1990s. More nuanced academic treatments have shown that Nazi functionaries at all levels of the bureaucracy also benefited from the Aryanization process. The most recent research has focused on ordinary Germans, as well as Poles, Czechs, and Hungarians, who were often paid for services performed for the Reich in money or goods seized from Jews. Yet studies that focus exclusively on individual, private profiteers fail to get to the heart of the question: what ultimately happened to the property of Jews who were first dispossessed and then murdered?

The answer requires an understanding of how Germans financed World War II. Almost everywhere in Europe where Aryanization took place, the liquidation of Jewish assets was carried out by state or occupation authorities. Corruption, embezzlement, and self-enrichment accompanied this process, as it does with every revolutionary redistribution of assets. But as a rule, private citizens who acquired expropriated stocks, real estate, furniture, or clothing paid for them—even if the prices they paid were lower than the assets' inflationary wartime market value. Moreover, without exception, Jewish-owned assets were first nationalized, then privatized. In the lingo of German financial administrators, Jewish property "fell" to the state.

Although much of what was confiscated was sold off at bargain prices, state treasuries earned significant revenues from the transactions. The expropriation and sale of Jewish assets in 1938 was not just a one-time emergency measure the Reich took to close gaps in state finances. The procedure served as a model for use in the countries and regions Germany conquered during World War II. Aryanization was essentially a gigantic, trans-European trafficking operation in stolen goods. It may have taken different forms in different countries, but the ultimate destination of the revenues generated was always the German war chest. These funds enabled the Reich to defray its main financial burdens. Exact figures on the magnitude of the theft are difficult to come by, however, since in many places the nationalization of Jewish assets coincided with the blanket dispossession of other groups of people.

THE NAZI-CONTROLLED General Government of Poland provides a vivid illustration of how expropriation worked. In 1939, Poland had a Jewish population of around 2 million. Shortly after invading the country, the German occupiers froze all bank accounts, safety deposit boxes, and security accounts registered in Jewish names. By decree, the owners of these assets were required to keep them all at one bank. Deposits of more than 2,000 zlotys—around $12,000 today—had to be paid into accounts from which the owners could withdraw no more than 250 zlotys a week to cover their costs of living. In cases where state-appointed trustees were already overseeing Jewish assets, they were required to follow the new rules.[1] In November 1939, the Trust Office of the General Government of Poland was founded. It was responsible for securing what had been Polish national assets, confiscating property that had become ownerless because of the war, and dispossessing Jews and "enemies" of the Reich.[2] The revenues were ostensibly to be directed, as the government's financial division in

Cracow never tired of stressing, to the "main account of the General Government" itself.[3]

The Trust Office took over some 3,600 businesses, most of which had been owned by Jews. Of those businesses, around a thousand were considered "major." Jewish real estate assets in Warsaw included some 50,000 pieces of property with a value of at least 2 billion zlotys. They were to be sold off "as soon as humanly possible." To facilitate the sale of massive amounts of personal property, the trust administrator, Oskar Friedrich Plodeck, formed the Trust Utilization Company (Treuhand-Verwertungs GmbH). This corporation sold off the household effects and clothing of Jews who had been deported to ghettos and of Polish Christians who had fled the country or been declared enemies of the state. By the time the company, which was organized as a private firm, finished its work in 1942, Plodeck could report that it had taken in property worth some 50 million zlotys.[4]

Strict rules prevented local officials from pocketing significant amounts of this money, even if occasional abuses did occur. As a rule, the surplus revenues from "trustee"-managed property, capital, and businesses were diligently transferred to the main account of the General Government. Initially, trustees issued meager support payments to the previous owners of these assets, and an official of the Trust Office even proclaimed that "the right to own property remains for the time being unchanged." It was only after Jews had been deported and murdered that their belongings, which had been managed in the interest of the state and which had, in effect, already been confiscated, legally became "abandoned assets" and "property of the General Government."[5]

But the governments of countries conquered by Germany were required to pay the proceeds of such windfalls back to the Reich in the form of occupation fees. According to figures from the Reich Finance Ministry in October 1941, the occupation costs for Belgium represented 125 percent of that country's regular state revenues. In the Netherlands the figure was 131 percent; in Serbia, 100 percent.[6] A Reichsbank study that used a different methodology estimated the cost for the first year of the occupation of

France at 211 percent of regular state revenues. For Belgium, it arrived at a total of 200 percent, and for Holland 180 percent, of normal state income. Norway's costs were calculated at 242 percent.[7] And by late 1942, "Wehrmacht requisitions of approximately 240 million Norwegian crowns" represented "339 percent of tax revenues and 95 percent of the gross national product."[8]

Occupation authorities and collaborating governments were willing to accept some inflation but would not allow it to spiral out of control. Berlin was also anxious to avoid hyperinflation, which made it difficult, as in the case of occupied Greece, to exploit the resources of a country and establish a cooperative relationship between occupation authorities and the Reich. Occupied countries' currencies had to retain their function as a means of payment. When inflation began to emerge as a problem, the Reich resorted to the seizure of Jewish wealth. The procedure was kept top secret.

The selling off of Jewish assets was one of several ways of slowing down inflation in occupied Europe and countries allied with Germany. The German government funneled the proceeds from the sale of those assets into individual state treasuries. From there they were transferred to the budgets for occupation costs. The precise system differed from country to country and depended on local political conditions.

Expropriation procedures were shrouded in extraordinary secrecy, which makes them difficult to reconstruct. A case in point is Belgium, where Jews had to be dispossessed directly by the German military commander, after local administrators refused to cooperate. The Nazi ordinances were almost certainly decreed on May 16, 1941, at a meeting in Brussels involving leading occupation officers; Göring's deputy, Erich Neumann; and high-ranking civil servants from the Reich Finance Ministry. According to the minutes, the sole subject discussed was "the question of occupation costs," which had to be kept down "because of concerns about currency stability."[9] A fortnight later, the German military commander in Belgium ordered Jews to report their assets. There is reason to believe that at the May 16 meeting the Finance Ministry officials demanded the establishment of a special office for expropriation. The minutes include the following notation: "In addition, we request that a specially authorized agent be assigned. (Deputy Neumann interrupts: 'That doesn't require any discussion.')"[10] The appointment of such agents in German-occupied countries was common practice. In November 1944, confronted with resistance in the German-occupied north of Italy, the German commissioner at the Banca d'Italia wrote that from then on, in Venice and Friuli, "instructions concerning the consolidation of confiscated bank assets of individual Jews are to be forwarded directly to the responsible bank." To carry out the seizures, German bank commissioner Maximilian Bernhuber sought the aid of the commanding officers of the Security Police and the Security Service.[11]

The dispossession of citizens of a foreign country for the benefit of the German war chest was planned in conversations involving small groups of senior officials. Under no circumstances was there to be a paper trail. The German civil servants who carried out the orders from above apparently tried to treat the seizures, which violated international law, as discrete measures undertaken by the various occupied countries and territories themselves. Historian Gerhard Aalders has recently concluded that this approach was used in Holland. According to Aalders, German occupational authorities were continually "entering" funds in the books, then "transferring" them to general accounts, realizing "a high degree of success in concealing their actual aims."[12]

Financial Aid for Serbia

Serbia is the only country in which enough documentation has survived to make it possible to reconstruct with a fair degree of clarity the decision-making process regarding Jewish assets. Serbian Jews were murdered with extreme rapidity. A scant year after the German invasion, in mid-April 1942, the head of the Wehrmacht military administration summed up the situation: "Months ago I had all the Jewish men we could round up here shot and had the Jewish women and children interned in camps. With the help of the Security Service, I've procured a 'delousing vehicle' with which the clearing of the camp will be completed for good in around 14 days to 4 weeks." (The author was referring, of course, to a truck in which women, children, and the elderly would be suffocated by exhaust fumes.) A few weeks later, most of Serbia's approximately 22,000 Jews were dead. On May 23, the head of the Jewish division in the Foreign Ministry proclaimed: "The Jewish question in Serbia is no longer acute. The only matters left to be settled are legal ones concerning assets."[13]

The unit designated to confiscate the assets was Department 17 (later changed to Department 12) of the General Plenipotentiary for the Economy in Serbia; it was headed by a Reichsbank administrator named Hans Gurski. No sooner had units of the Wehrmacht and the SS exterminated Serbia's Jews than members of the occupational authority and administrators of Göring's Four-Year Plan began discussing how to utilize the material assets left behind.[14] According to a memo dated May 23, 1942, the Foreign Office assumed that these assets, once claims by Germany had been settled, would be put "in a kind of fund to be managed by the Reich."[15] Representatives of the Administrative Commission for Jewish Real Estate and Property also anticipated "the possibility that Jewish assets in Serbia will later fall to the Reich."[16] The majority of administrators saw the revenues to be earned from Aryanization as an advance payment on the as yet unspecified "wartime reparations" Serbia would be forced to make to the aggressor, Germany.

Four-Year Plan administrators had begun lobbying for "exploitation [of assets] for the benefit of the Reich" on March 21, 1942.[17] But the Finance Ministry opposed the idea. In May 1942, the ministry's representative, Christian Breyhan, proposed that "for the sake of order" the revenues "should flow into the Serbian [occupation] budget." It would then be up to the German military commander in Serbia "to determine what the money would be used for and to transfer it accordingly to the Serbian administration."[18] A month later, a conference was called to debate the issue. The representative from the Foreign Ministry reported: "At a meeting held on June 19 in the Office of the Four-Year Plan in Berlin concerning the liquidation of Serbian Jewish assets, the following was decided. The wealth of Serbian Jews is to be seized for the benefit of Serbia. The seizure is to be made for the benefit of Serbia because a seizure benefiting the Reich would [visibly] violate the Hague Conventions. We Germans will, however, indirectly profit from the revenues."[19] Article 46 of the Hague Conventions prohibited the confiscation of private property in wartime, but that stricture applied only to the occupiers, not the national administration of the occupied country.

A few days after the Berlin meeting, Göring endorsed the objections of the financial administrators and ordered Jewish assets in Serbia confiscated on behalf of Serbia, with an eye toward "providing financial assistance for the Serbian budget, which has been greatly burdened by occupation costs."[20] He also instructed the General Plenipotentiary for the Economy "to hasten the transfer of all managed assets south of the Danube so that Serbia can begin as soon as possible to exploit them." (North of the Danube, in the region of Bachka, or Bačka, local ethnic Germans had already taken matters into their own hands.) It was also decreed that "the Serbian government must pass a regulation, in the interests of the Serbian state, concerning all assets belonging to Jews who held Serbian citizenship on April 15, 1941."[21] (The Serbian Ministerial Council issued such a ruling on August 26, 1942.) Along with strengthening the Serbian dinar and maintaining the appearance of following the Hague Conventions, the occupational authority sought to stabilize the collaborationist government of Milan Nedic "by freeing up Jewish assets for the benefit of Serbia."[22]

Indeed, in the latter half of 1942, Serbia was on the brink of financial collapse. "The burdens of war amounted to more than double the regular expenditures in the Serbian budget," one official reported, "which were themselves partly deficit financed." From the German perspective, such a state of affairs represented "an extremely serious threat to the currency."[23] Up to that point, monthly occupation costs had run at around 500 million dinars. Serbian Jewish assets amounted to between 3 and 4 billion dinars.[24] That was enough to cover occupation costs for six months or to slow inflationary pressure on the Serbian currency for even longer.[25] The effect was dramatic. In September 1942, shortly after the Berlin conference, the Foreign Ministry representative was able to report that the issue of "limiting occupational costs" did not "need further exploration at the moment."[26]

Cursory pronouncements such as this offer no hint of the top-secret methods Germany used to seize Jewish assets in occupied Europe. Across the continent, German occupiers—and later the collaborating financial administrations and national banks of the occupied countries themselves—thoroughly destroyed any paper trail. Usually through laws passed by the puppet governments, the occupiers turned national institutions into dealers in stolen property. As a result, Jewish assets flowed into national budgets, where the Reich could appropriate the revenues at will. The sinister, secret origins of this source of wealth had simply been erased.

Hungarian Demands

Adolf Hitler and the regent of Hungary, Admiral Miklós Horthy, had a famously contentious relationship, but Germany and Hungary maintained an increasingly close-knit alliance between 1938 and 1941. Germany needed Hungary for its geostrategic position in southeastern Europe. Hungary needed Germany in order to regain territories it had been forced to cede under the 1920 Treaty of Trianon. In 1938, in what was called the First Vienna Award, Hungary reacquired parts of Slovakia and, a few months later, land in Transcarpathia, a territory in present-day Ukraine. The Second Vienna Award, in 1940, gave Hungary the Romanian region of North Transylvania. In 1941, Hungary acquired the Yugoslav regions of Bachka, Baranya, and Prekmurje. Together with Slovakia and Romania, which were also allied with Germany, Hungary declared war on the Soviet Union in 1941.

From 1943 onward, the Hungarian government sought to steer the country, which was surrounded by German troops, out of the war and reach a separate peace agreement with the Western Allies. As a result, the Wehrmacht occupied Hungary on March 19, 1944, installing a Reich special envoy and a cooperative Hungarian government with limited autonomy. In the meantime, the Red Army had advanced to within striking distance of Hungary's eastern border, and it was only a matter of weeks before the fighting would reach Carpathia. Although Hungary was under German occupation, there was broad consensus among the country's reactionary-conservative leaders that it had to be defended against the "stampede from the steppe." Compared with the prospect of Soviet domination, occupation by Nazi Germany seemed the far lesser of two evils.[27]

Since 1938, the Hungarian government had passed laws discriminating against and partially dispossessing Hungarian Jews. A crucial move in Hungary's financing of World War II was a law in July 1942 annulling all loans taken out by the government from Jews in World War I. The law gave the government financial room to maneuver in what had become the drawn-out conflict with the Soviet Union. Ostensibly, the annulment was carried out on behalf of a "Fund for Jewish Emigration."[28] In fact, it was an act of expropriation to bolster wartime finances, comparable to similar measures taken in the Protectorate of Bohemia and Moravia, Slovakia, and Germany itself.

In return, the Reich paid off a small portion of its clearing debts for 1943–44 by "repatriating" some 100 million reichsmarks in Hungarian stocks and bonds—something Budapest had vehemently demanded.[29] Most of those securities came from bank accounts of dispossessed Jews. In September 1941, for example, securities owned by Julius Zwicker, a Jew from Brno, were confiscated. Among them were Hungarian bonds, issued at 7 percent interest and with a face value of 96,000 dollars. In February 1944, the German treasury paid 182,898.75 reichsmarks into the "Emigration Fund of Prague," which was supposedly established to help Jews leave the country. This sum was then invested in long-term Reich war bonds. Since the original owner had long since been murdered or had fled abroad, the German treasury could rest assured that it would never have to pay off those war bonds. In reality, the transaction amounted to nothing more than a transfer of funds within the German war chest. The Reich was using assets like those that had belonged to Zwicker to cover its mounting debts to Hungary for petroleum and food.[30] (Hungary was, after Romania, the second-largest oil producer in Germany's sphere of influence.)

On March 20, 1944, one day after German troops invaded Hungary, the Wehrmacht leadership assembled at the garrison town of Jüterbog, just south of Berlin, to sign a treaty of friendship with senior representatives from the Hungarian military. According to the agreement, Germany was to bear the costs of occupying Hungary.[31] The German rationale was obvious. Because of the precarious military situation, the Reich wanted to keep expenditures of men and material to an absolute minimum in the newly occupied country. For that, it needed the active cooperation of Hungarian generals and reactionary-conservative forces. Assuming its own costs would allow the Reich to counter opposition from Hungarian nationalist elements. After a few days, Hungary was given partial sovereignty, and both the new Hungarian government and the Hungarian army were treated as allies.

The Jüterbog agreement provoked the immediate ire of Schwerin von Krosigk, who cited his responsibility to see "that state debt does not increase unnecessarily and that the Reich does not incur obligations that it will later be unable to fulfill." Moreover, von Krosigk argued, the burdens and sacrifices "in the broad European struggle" had to be evenly distributed. "Having Hungary assume the costs" was the best way of ensuring its "offsetting the expenditures connected with the occupation by implementing other financial-political measures, thereby energetically countering unavoidable wartime inflation—in the interests of both Hungary itself and the Reich."[32] One of those "measures" was the selling off of Jewish assets. Thus, instead of following the original course of moderation, the Finance Ministry's representative in Hungary made the usual heavy demands for compensation for occupation costs.

In April and May 1944, the new Hungarian government confiscated the assets of Hungarian Jews. Their deportation was organized by Adolf Eichmann with the help of the Hungarian police. The disposition of their assets fell to Leopold Scheffler of the Reichsbank, one of the first German administrators to arrive in Budapest after the invasion. Scheffler had been responsible for overseeing the financial administration of France and, after a short apprenticeship in occupied Poland, had helped found the Central Currency Bank of Ukraine. Now he was assigned to Budapest. On April 23, he promptly fired the sitting president of the Hungarian National Bank and appointed the more compliant István Belatiny in his stead. ("He's always worked well with us," Scheffler assured his superiors.) On April 26, Belatiny ordered all Jewish-owned assets and securities stored in safety deposit boxes turned over to the Hungarian National Bank. On April 28, Scheffler was already inquiring about gold and currency reserves, as well as what reports and expertise he could expect—especially from the bank's economics division.[33]

Transferring responsibility for occupation costs to Hungary was a significant success for the Reich. At a meeting called on May 23, 1944, to discuss affairs in Hungary, satisfied civil servants in the Economics Min-, istry were able to conclude: "The Hungarian Jewish legislation has been expanded. The Hungarian government expects that the great financial exertions necessary for the war effort can be offset by continuing to expropriate Jewish assets. These assets are thought to account for at least one-third of the total wealth of the country. We can assume that we will have numerous opportunities to liquidate Jewish wealth."[34] The Hungarian representative who recorded the minutes and reported back on the meeting commented in June that "the radical solution to the Jewish question" was continuing apace. Jews "forfeit their Hungarian citizenship upon leaving Hungarian territory, and their assets fall to the Hungarian state." As a result, "we have been able to meet the increased financial demands upon the Hungarian state with confiscated Jewish funds." The amount of currency in circulation "did not have to be dramatically increased," and short-term inflation had been avoided. Nevertheless, the Hungarian representative added, the inflationary situation was precarious "due to the extensive purchases made by the German Wehrmacht."[35]

The civil servant responsible for the dispossession of Hungarian Jews, Albert Túrvölgyi, also directed the state monopoly on alcohol. The monopoly was established in 1941, and taxes on alcohol were continually increased to raise funds for Hungarian troops fighting alongside their German allies against the Soviet Union. The double responsibility, which he assumed in 1944, meant that the drive to "Magyarize" Jewish assets and to bankroll the war in Hungary came together in one person.

As the war drew to its conclusion, the Hungarian government's policies of confiscation proved harder and harder to put into practice. In early October 1944, Göring's economic adviser Otto Donner reported on the financial situation in Budapest. He predicted that Jewish assets could be utilized to the benefit of Hungary's wartime budget. But he also cautioned that because "only the most liquid assets" could be sold to help balance the budget, the effect would be at best short term.[36] Nonetheless, the sums in question over the duration of the occupation amounted to several hundred million reichsmarks. The money was raised by Hungarians selling off Jewish assets to other Hungarians. But the sums taken in on paper by the Hungarian treasury were transferred directly into the budget for the German occupation and were paid out to German soldiers. They also went to buy food, oil, and essential raw materials, such as bauxite, for export to Germany.

Emil and Henny Uhlmann

With the atonement payment of 1938–39, the Nazi government appropriated around a quarter of all the tangible wealth of German and Austrian Jews. The rest of their assets—for example, rental properties—were put under the administration of trustees and thus remained, for the time being, untouched. But it was not uncommon for the state to sell off those assets and reinvest the money—ostensibly for the benefit of the previous owners—in government treasury bills. The transformation of personal assets into government bonds took considerable pressure off public finances in wartime Germany. While there are no exact figures for the total amount of money extracted by what amounted to compulsory loans, the transactions were numerous enough that the state media watchdog ordered journalists on August 28, 1941, "not to mention the exchange of stocks held by Jews for $3\frac{1}{2}$ percent treasury bills."[37] The practice, also used in occupied countries like Holland and France, of trustees discreetly liquidating property, stocks, gold, silver, and other assets and directing the proceeds into government bonds amounts to nothing less than an outright confiscation without a formal act of law. The leadership reasoned that either appropriation legislation would be passed at a later date or the assets would disappear when the Reich went bankrupt. To the civil servants responsible for wartime finances, it mattered little whether they merely controlled Jewish wealth or legally appropriated it.

But sometimes legislation was passed. Nazi officials and senior civil servants met throughout 1941 to formulate a law authorizing the seizure of assets from Jews. Foreign Office employees released a draft on March 15 that described confiscation as meeting "the demands of Jewish emigration." The innocuous language aimed to avoid the impression that the confiscation of assets was "a measure for financing the war."[38] On November 21, 1941, the government formally issued the eleventh ordinance of the Reich Citizenship Law. In one stroke, the assets of German Jews, many of which had already been converted into government bonds, were officially expropriated. Outstanding government debts to Jewish institutions or individuals were simply erased. The Nazi leadership instructed civil servants to leave as few traces as possible of what they had done. Debt cancelations were to be entered "without recording the name of the individual Jew who had given the securities in payment."[39]

Wiping out old debts without compensation was ideal for a budgetary policy guided by the idea, unusual for its day, that no more than 50 percent of what was needed for the war should be acquired on credit. Now new lines of credit could be opened. Revenues in Germany alone from this form of larceny can be conservatively estimated at 2 billion reichsmarks.

In special cases, the Reich opted to transfer seized Jewish assets directly to local communities. In May 1941, Hitler declared that this option would apply especially to "wealth and assets" that were "by their very nature useful for the fulfillment of obligations of local, autonomous public entities." Hitler's target was real estate that could be used for expanding or constructing streets, "for public squares, parks, and sporting facilities," or for similar public amenities. A document accompanying Hitler's directive suggested that suitable properties could be used, "for example, to house local civic offices, schools, Hitler Youth clubs, children's and old-age homes, and Red Cross facilities." Later in the war, vacant properties would become sites "for the construction of residential facilities for the victims of aerial bombardment." In Hammer am See, in Bohemia, for instance, "properties owned by the Jewess Ginzky" were to be transformed into a "recuperative facility for those suffering aftereffects of the war." Assets such as furnishings and household necessities could also be removed if they were needed by "government offices, institutions, asylums, hospitals, etc."[40]

On September 16, 1942, Walther Bayrhoffer, the Finance Ministry's representative on the Reichsbank board of directors, called on local finance offices to "transfer immediately" all formerly Jewish-owned securities, or the proceeds earned from their sale, "to the Reich treasury in Berlin." A similar order was issued for property. The prelude to Bayrhoffer's move came in May 1942, when the Finance Ministry concluded that "an enormous amount of Jewish real estate has fallen to the Reich" because of paragraph 3 of the eleventh ordinance.[41] These acquisitions were noted under the heading "Individual Measures XVII" of the Supplementary Budget, which had been created to take account of "extraordinary revenues and expenditures of war." The revenues resulting from the liquidation of Jewish assets were recorded there under chapter 7, part 1. They included stocks and bonds from Jewish households. (Part 2 of the same chapter was to be used for securities "that have fallen to the Reich for other reasons." Part 3 was for general "revenues from administration and liquidation.")[42] In early 1944, Schwerin von Krosigk ordered the "seized goods in the possession of the Reich treasury" liquidated in order to balance the Reich's budget.[43]

In 1942 Reichsbank president Walther Funk and Heinrich Himmler agreed that any gold, gemstones, and cash taken along to the death camps by European Jews would be handed over to the Reichsbank. The Reichsbank paid the prevailing market rate for gold, gold coins, and foreign currencies into a special treasury account that was cynically assigned a fictional owner named Max Heiliger ("Max Holyman"). This was how the state appropriated the remaining belongings of those exterminated at Belzec, Sobibor, Treblinka, Majdanek, and Auschwitz, including gold fillings removed from corpses' mouths. According to a memorandum of September 22, 1942, on the "Liquidation of Property Related to the Resettlement and Evacuation of Jews," cash was to be paid into the account of the SS camp management at the Berlin-Schöneberg branch of the Reichsbank. Foreign currency, precious metals, jewelry, gemstones, pearls, and dental and scrap gold were to be collected, and the concentration camp management in Berlin was "put in charge of the immediate transfer of these valuables to the Reichsbank." Watches, pocket knives, fountain pens, wallets, and similar items were to be sold at military commissaries for predetermined prices. "All proceeds," read one memo, "are to be turned over to the Reich." Ethnic German settlers in Eastern Europe were allowed to buy clothing and shoes that were in good condition, but here, too, the proceeds were to be turned over without exception to the Reich.[44]

At the International Military Tribunal of 1946, Albert Thoms, a civil servant employed by the Reichsbank, testified about the direct deliveries of gold, gemstones, dental gold, and securities. Thoms said that in the summer of 1942 he had been informed by Reichsbank vice president Emil Puhl that the SS would immediately start shipping these items to bank headquarters. Between then and late 1944, an SS man named Bruno Melmer dropped off such goods by the crate, for which Thoms issued him receipts. Thoms then distributed the goods "to the relevant departments of the Reichsbank for processing. Stocks, securities, and bonds were transferred to the securities department. I kept coins and gold in the precious metals department." Gemstones were handed over to the Berlin *Pfandhaus*, or pawnshop—in Germany pawnshops were run by local governments—"with the request that they be sold for as much as possible." The proceeds were deposited into the account of "Max Heiliger." From there, the monies were transferred "from time to time" into the war budget, where they were recorded as proceeds from "individual measures."[45]

Personal effects delivered to the Main Trustee Office East (Haupttreuhandstelle Ost) were handled in much the same way. The items came from Jews in the part of Poland annexed by Germany as well as from Poles who had been declared enemies of the state or had been forcibly resettled.[46] By and large the transfer and disposal of Jewish valuables proceeded efficiently. On October 4, 1943, Himmler remarked—accurately—that "the riches" of Jews had "as a matter of course been immediately handed over to the Reich."

The exceptions—the isolated cases in which individuals lined their pockets and the extermination machine engaged in unauthorized self-financing—prove the rule. For example, following the eradication of the Warsaw ghetto, the Finance Ministry was eager to know what had happened to any belongings that had been left behind. Although the SS insisted that everything had been transferred to the treasury in line with procedure, no "valuables identified as coming from Warsaw" could be located.[47] But that was unusual. Far more typical was the bureaucratic diligence with which authorities disposed of property belonging to Jews killed in Simferopol, Crimea. In February 1942, the head of the Security Police there reported to army headquarters that "all timepieces confiscated as part of the Jewish operation have been handed over as per order to the treasury in Berlin."[48]

The techniques for selling off Jewish belongings and assets had their roots in Göring's Jurisdiction Regulations for Jewish Assets of January 1939. The directive required German Jews to offer gold, gemstones, platinum, and pearls "for sale" to the government. As a result, the Economics Ministry became the center for the acquisition of gemstones and objects made of precious metals. It enlisted the help of the Berlin city government, specifically Department III of the municipal loan office, to convert these valuables into cash. To offset its administrative expenses, Berlin received a commission of 10 percent of the price. It was paid by those who were being forced to sell their belongings. Department III's explicit mandate was "to seize gemstones and objects made of gold, platinum, and silver from Jewish owners and, by selling them off, to help procure the necessary currency and gold reserves to maintain state finances and wage war."

Gold watches were mainly sold domestically and jewelry made of low-grade precious metals was melted down, but particularly valuable jewelry, gemstones, and pearls were sold abroad in order to bring in hard currency for the war effort. Diamanten-Kontor, a company based in Berlin, and Idar-Oberstein were responsible for prying gemstones from their settings and, if necessary, recutting them. In 1941, the finance minister offered several justifications for this procedure, including the creation of jobs: "The work is also necessary and important because it ensures that gemstone cutters will be able to employ a fixed number of qualified personnel." After the stones had been recut, Diamanten-Kontor delivered them, arranged according to size and value, in "ready-for-sale lots," each accompanied by an estimate of its monetary value.

The preferred market for gemstones was Switzerland. But the reluctance of people there to purchase gemstones of such dubious origin meant that "only a small percentage of the diamonds and pearls handed over to the central office" could "be exchanged abroad for hard currency." Jews who surrendered valuables between 1939 and late 1941 received 10 percent of the items' domestic value, with 10 percent of that amount deducted for administrative costs.[49] An edict of Göring's in the summer of 1943 expressed the urgency the Reich attached to this method of raising money. Göring ordered the confiscation of stamp collections owned by "enemies" and Jews, with the goal of "acquiring as much money as possible through their sale." "The currency situation," he wrote, "requires us to use all the means at our disposal to acquire currency, even when the individual proceeds don't dramatically improve the books."[50] Finance Ministry officials occasionally protested at having to be involved in such transactions, but in the end their expertise was viewed as crucial. For example, in March 1941, Göring ordered Schwerin von Krosigk to take possession of two crates of gold and jewels seized from the Rothschild family in Paris. Von Krosigk did so unwillingly—especially as the proceeds from the sale of the valuables were to go not to his ministry but to a "special fund." Göring replied that the Finance Ministry had the most "experience in the optimal liquidation of Jewish jewelry," that is, how to sell off seized valuables at the best possible price.[51]

Along with Department III of the municipal pawnshop in Berlin, a number of local pawnshops also engaged in selling off Jewish-owned jewelry. The director of the municipal pawnshops in Dortmund reported in August 1941: "Jews can't make complaints of any kind about the prices we pay. They have to take what we offer them." On the subject of his own place in national history, he added: "If in future years a researcher who only knows of Jews by word of mouth should come and go through the files in the Dortmund city archive, he will conclude that the municipal pawnshops of Dortmund did their small part in finding a solution to the Jewish question."[52] The Dortmund pawnshop was the central point of sale for jewelry owned by Jews in Westphalia.

THE WORK of historians Gisela Möllenhoff and Rita Schlautmann-Overmeyer offers a detailed picture of how Jewish assets were confiscated by the state. Using the example of one wealthy Jewish couple, Emil and Henny Uhlmann, they show how the emigration tax (*Reichsfluchtsteuer*), the levy on Jewish wealth (*Judenvermögensabgabe*), and the mandatory registration of assets combined to fill the German treasury:

> The value of their securities and bank assets totaled 12,500 reichsmarks. Their house and property were assessed at 34,700 reichsmarks. After the emigration tax and the atonement payment, 21,350 reichsmarks of the original 47,200 remained. When they fled to Luxembourg in April 1940, they were allowed to take along only 10 reichsmarks each. A state-appointed trustee managed their assets after their departure and seized the money that came in from the rental of their property. As a result, the couple became dependent on a relative's financial support. Their house was officially transferred to the Reich and appears on a list of municipal property from February 18, 1941. Remaining assets were confiscated when the emigrants were stripped of German citizenship and when those who remained behind (relatives) had been deported under the eleventh ordinance of the Reich Citizenship Law of November 21, 1941.[53]

In this case, the German people saved themselves 47,180 reichsmarks in taxes. That sum allowed the state to avoid tax increases—equivalent to a 50 percent hike for eight hundred workers with two children each—that would otherwise have been necessary because of the financial situation. At the same time, the state was able to absorb some excess spending power in the middle of the war by selling off the Uhlmanns' possessions to the highest bidder or at preset prices.

A few weeks after the Uhlmanns escaped to Luxembourg in April

1940, German soldiers conquered that country. In October 1941, they were deported to the Lodz ghetto. Emil Uhlmann died there of exhaustion on November 7, 1942. Seven weeks earlier, on September 17, 1942, Henny Uhlmann had been taken to the Chelmo extermination camp. There, that same day, she was murdered in one of the camp's mobile gas chambers.[54]

CHAPTER 8

Laundering Money for the Wehrmacht

Collaborators and Constitutions

The Wehrmacht invaded Norway on April 9, 1940. Two years later, Reich commissioner Josef Terboven installed Norwegian fascist leader Vidkun Quisling as the country's prime minister. Inevitably, the Reich looked to Norway for funds to aid its war effort. Norway's Jews numbered just over 2,100, but like their counterparts throughout Europe they were forced to turn in all their possessions.

In late October 1942, a few days after the Norwegian cabinet moved to "Aryanize" the country, Quisling issued a two-part secret decree: "1. Pocket and wristwatches confiscated during the seizure of Jewish assets according to the law of October 26, 1942, are to be handed over immediately to the Wehrmacht for use in the war and to the German Security Police. 2. Confiscated gold, silver, and jewelry are to be used to help meet the costs of war and are to be put, via the Security Police, at the immediate disposal of the German government."[1] (The letter containing this decree was the basis for Instruction no. 2 of the Liquidation Office for Confiscated Jewish Assets.) In total, Quisling's office sold off the possessions of 2,173 Norwegian Jews, with an estimated value of 23 million Norwegian crowns, or some 11 million reichsmarks. Securities and similar assets were sold for the benefit of the Norwegian treasury.[2]

Although the sums in question were comparatively small, the money found its way into the Norwegian budget. From there it passed into the account for occupation costs and finally directly into the pockets of German soldiers, the budgets of procurement officers, and the wage packets of Norwegian workers employed to build military fortifications.[3]

In November 1943, accountants from the Reich General Auditor's Office checked up on "gold and silver items" stored at the German civilian administration in Oslo. (These items consisted mainly of valuables handed over by the Liquidation Office.) The previous Christmas, in 1942, 337 gold and other timepieces had been given free of charge to Alois Windisch-Graetz, Eduard Dietl, and Ferdinand Schoerner, the commanding generals of German units stationed in Norway. Subordinates who had been of particular service found the timepieces under their Christmas trees as tokens of their superiors' appreciation.[4] Later instructions directed that concert and upright pianos be handed over for the entertainment of German troops.[5] Moreover, after paying in devalued Norwegian crowns for all the textile articles the Liquidation Office had collected, the Reich shipped them back to Germany.[6]

THE SITUATION was entirely different in Belgium, which had been invaded in May 1940. As elsewhere, a collaborationist government was installed, but in Belgium, the anti-Jewish campaign was carried out exclusively by the German military administration—not by Belgian authorities. On October 28, 1940, a few months into the occupation, the German military commander ordered that Jews be subjected to "such measures as are deemed absolutely necessary to maintain security." Among them was the registration of all Jewish residents of the country and all businesses in which Jews had influence. In addition, the Wehrmacht introduced regulations requiring advance military approval for every ordinance concerning Jewish businesses and properties. They also ordered "the removal of Jews from all public offices and positions."

Three weeks later, German military leaders took their next step. On November 16, the commander in chief of the army, Field Marshal Walther von Brauchitsch, decreed that "the highest priority should be given to accelerating the removal of Jews from the economy; existing stocks from Jewish businesses should be liquidated for the benefit of the troops or the Reich." But the Belgians proved reluctant partners, and the plan "to de-Jewify the economy, as in France, through legislation passed by the occupied country" was a failure. The Belgian cabinet secretaries who had remained behind after the government went into exile refused to cooperate, citing "constitutional conflicts."[7] This example of noncompliance stands in stark contrast to the collaboration that was the rule almost everywhere else in Europe.

The contrast with Belgium highlights the vested interest the Norwegian government had in the "de-Jewification" of the country. It also shows that German expropriation policies faltered when they could not exploit the anti-Semitism of civil servants in the occupied country itself. While confiscation and liquidation institutions in Oslo ran with maximum efficiency, German generals in Brussels complained about highly obstructionist "circles within the Belgian judiciary." The Belgian Chief state prosecutor, for example, explicitly forbade his notaries to certify contracts concerning the liquidation of Jewish assets. The occupation authorities—who were members of the Wehrmacht, not the SS—forced du Roi to step down. "His instructions, however, remained in force" because no one in the Belgian judiciary was prepared to annul them.

Consequently, on December 21, 1943, the German military commander was compelled to issue an order allowing German notaries to certify Belgian contracts. Even then, occupation authorities had difficulty finding customers for confiscated assets, either because Belgians sympathized with the victims of Nazi persecution or because they took note of Germany's declining military fortunes. In any case, Belgian courts of chancery pursued a similar course of obstructionism. Throughout the occupation, they adamantly refused to strike from their records the 6,057 Jewish businesses that Germans had liquidated in the country. The Belgian Ministry of Justice was ordered to carry out this task, but it, too, declined to do so.[8]

Earlier in the occupation, on May 31, 1941, the German military administration had issued an "Ordinance on Economic Measures against the Jews." The edict mandated the registration of all Jewish-owned real estate, ordered Jews to place securities in escrow, and required them to deposit whatever cash they possessed in bank accounts. In total, Belgian Jews reported ownership of 7,700 businesses, 3,000 parcels of commercial real estate, and 17,400 private savings and investment portfolios.[9] By February 1942, the German military commander in Belgium could claim that "Jewish wealth has been documented."[10] But many Belgian Jews were able to avoid reporting their liquid assets, safety deposit boxes, bank accounts, and stock holdings because Belgian bank directors and employees made no efforts to find out which of their customers were Jewish. Even accounts easily recognizable as Jewish-owned were left untouched. The only accounts that were reported were those whose owners, fearing the consequences of disobedience, had "spontaneously" identified themselves.[11]

Deeply concerned about the efforts of Belgian citizens and public officials to obstruct the seizure of Jewish assets, the Nazi administration tried a different tack. Following the invasion in 1940, the German occupiers had set up a shell corporation called the Brüsseler Treuhandgesellschaft (Brussels Trust Company) to administer the seizure and disposal of property belonging to Jews and other "enemies" of the Reich. Though registered as a legitimate business entity, the company was nothing more than a front for the Wehrmacht; German military employees served in its senior executive posts and eventually dominated its board of directors. "This close connection," wrote one official, "ensured that the central importance of the military administration in the Brussels Trust Company was respected. The board of directors, which was set up later, consisted likewise mainly of employees of the military administration, including the director of the economics division, who was the board's chairman."

On April 2, 1942, the German military commander in Belgium issued an ordinance entitled "The Forfeiture of Jewish Wealth for the Benefit of the Reich." The decree empowered the Brussels Trust Company to act as the Reich's agent for the dispossession of Belgium's Jews, while maintaining the facade of legitimacy before the Belgian public. The company promptly took over the disposal of "cash, diamonds, and jewelry" that had been seized from Jews being held at a deportation center inside military barracks in Mecheln, near Antwerp. (A company operative was assigned to the barracks.) Stocks, bonds, and bank deposits, as well as the proceeds from the sale of Aryanized assets, were transferred to the Société Française de Banque et de Dépôts in Brussels, which had been already put under the company's control.[12]

In the winter of 1944–45, after German troops had retreated from Belgium, Reich military officials filed their final report on currency and finances. The report contained a number of omissions, one of which is significant in the present context. In addition to the funds officially transferred to cover occupation costs, "further sums of Belgian francs" flowed "to the occupying authorities as administrative receipts." The money was "mostly fines, . . . monetary punishments, proceeds from the sale of confiscated contraband and black market wares and the like." But the writer of the report noted that records had been kept only for the period between October 1, 1943, and March 31, 1944. During that period, such proceeds amounted to merely a few million reichsmarks; nevertheless, he pointed out, they "did have the practical effect of lowering real occupation costs."[13]

Concealed under the heading "Administrative Revenues," which the final report downplayed, were the seized assets of Belgian Jews. It is impossible to say how much money was involved. The sum couldn't have been very large, given the relatively scant wealth of Belgium's Jews. Deposits were made periodically, in amounts ranging from 3 million to 12 million reichsmarks.[14] In the autumn of 1944, a civil servant in the Reich Finance Ministry listed the following items under the heading "Remaining Tasks of the Reich Commissioner, Belgium": "The Trust Company (Because of Jewish Wealth)"; "Enemy and Jewish Wealth (Transferred Securities)"; "Demands on the Eastern Ministry by the Reich for the Transport of Jewish Furniture"; "Artworks Taken Away by the Rosenberg Task Force."[15] The civil servant apparently felt the need to follow up on these matters because they concerned monies that were either to be secured or recovered for the military budget. It is unclear from the documents which, if any, of these tasks were ever carried out.

Dispossession without a Dispossession Act

In Holland, also invaded by the Wehrmacht in May 1940, the German military established a small civilian supervisory administration. Unlike in Belgium or Norway, there was neither a German nor a local law formally dispossessing Dutch Jews. Yet the revenues the Reich would ultimately collect from the Netherlands were surprisingly large. On October 22, 1940, the Reich commissioner announced that certain businesses would be subject to registration requirements. On March 21, 1941, a follow-up order was issued, called the Ordinance on the Treatment of Businesses Required to Register. As neutral as that title may have sounded, its final paragraph was crystal clear: "This ordinance takes effect immediately upon being made public. It will be known as the 'Ordinance on the Removal of Jews from the Economy.'"

On January 10, 1941, the standard "atonement" payment had been levied on Dutch Jews. It was followed on March 26 by mandatory controls on currency and gold transactions. On May 27, Jews were ordered to register all properties used for agricultural purposes. On August 8, stocks and bonds became subject to registration, as, three days later, did all remaining Jewish-owned property.

But the ordinance of August 8 did not mention dispossession or forfeiture of assets by Jews for the benefit of the German or Dutch treasuries. Instead, the wording dealt more generally with "the handling of Jewish wealth." A Security Service document spoke of the "amassing of all Jewish assets" for use at a later date to pay for forced Jewish emigration. A hollow phrase about "establishing an emigration fund" concealed the fact that these assets were being directly used to finance the war.[16]

German authorities in Holland went to great lengths to conceal the ultimate destination of the stolen property. All cash and checks from Jews were deposited into an account of the Lippmann, Rosenthal & Co. Bank, which had quietly been turned into a financial center for the Aryanization process. Securities were to be either kept there or held in escrow at other banks. "Collections of all kinds, art objects, objects made of gold, platinum, or silver, as well as cut and uncut gemstones, semiprecious stones, and pearls," also had to be "handed over."[17] In addition, as of May 21, 1942, Jews had to report all outstanding private debts and remaining payments owed to them.[18] Despite the Jewish-sounding name of the bank, it was run by German directors for the purpose of disposing of Jewish property.[19]

Dutch brokers at the Amsterdam stock exchange helped the Reich sell off around 80 percent of the stocks previously owned by Jews. Dutch institutions also assisted in the liquidation of other types of assets, such as jewelry in bank safety deposit boxes. This procedure was intended to assuage Dutch concerns that a direct seizure of valuables would violate the Hague Conventions' prohibition on occupiers confiscating native assets. On the surface, the process looked legitimate since the assets were not being formally seized, merely transferred. The proceeds from liquidation sales were initially invested in state and industrial bonds—but a short time later the funds were converted exclusively into Dutch government securities. In a feature unique to the Netherlands, part of the revenues from Jewish assets were converted directly into German treasury obligations, but that made no real difference since Dutch treasury obligations, too, went exclusively toward covering the monetary needs of the occupiers. Both the Dutch treasury and the German Reich made regular interest payments to the Lippmann, Rosenthal & Co. Bank. These were immediately reinvested in state bonds. Thus, they flowed back into the Dutch state's coffers, where they were then transferred to the occupation budget. The fact that the transactions were carried out via a collective account, so that the value of individuals' property could only have been estimated, shows that no effort was being made to manage individuals' assets in their own interest.

This procedure was doubly advantageous from the German perspective because it made Dutch financial administrators accessories and allowed the Reich to claim, however disingenuously, that it was not confiscating the assets of Dutch Jews. The system used in Holland did not require a formal act of dispossession because, formally, the assets seized were only being reinvested, not confiscated. (If Reich officials had felt the need for legislation, it could have been retroactively instituted five, ten, or even fifteen years later.) The Reich commissioner for Holland simply collected the proceeds from Jewish assets that had been converted into state securities and transferred the money to the specially created Administrative Office for Property and Pensions in The Hague. That was the end of the paper trail. If no one appeared to claim ownership when the state bonds and the accrued interest came due, the debts did not have to be repaid—and the claims of the putative owners simply disappeared.[20]

The assets of "enemy aliens" and Dutch citizens who had fled the country were placed under compulsory receivership—a perfectly legitimate practice under international law and one that existed in Britain and the United States. Yet in 1942 and 1943, the German Enemy Assets Administration liquidated all assets belonging to Jews and deposited the proceeds into a newly opened account at the German Audit and Trust Company in Amsterdam. There the money was converted, in the names of its owners, into Dutch government bonds. In this way, the funds went in their entirety toward financing the German war effort.[21]

As soon as the transfer of assets had been concluded in 1942, the commander of the SS in The Hague, who also served as the city's police chief, reported: "On October 15, open season will be declared on Dutch Jewry. A massive police operation will commence, which will involve not only German and Dutch police organs but also the labor division and membership of the Nazi Party, the National Socialist movement in the Netherlands, . . . the Wehrmacht, etc. At the same time, I will begin to publish [regulations] allowing the seizure of assets of Aryans who harbor Jews, who help them flee across the border, or who provide them with false identification. The culprits will be transferred to a concentration camp. This is all intended to stem the massive flight of Jews that has occurred."[22]

Official estimates of liquid assets stolen from Jews totaled around 150 million guilders. Aryanized businesses yielded "far in excess of 200 million," Jewish property and real estate approximately 150 million. The total of all assets, according to Dutch estimates, was "a round sum of more than a half billion guilders," or, as the German occupiers put it, "a sum that has to be of concern for Dutch economic life."[23] In late 1943, German economists used the operating figure of 600 to 700 million guilders. In addition, German Jews living in the Netherlands paid a lump sum of 10 percent of the value of their assets to the Reich Finance Ministry.[24]

According to postwar Dutch figures, however, Jews in the Netherlands were robbed of some 1.1 to 1.5 billion guilders—or 1.4 to 2 billion reichsmarks. Part of the discrepancy may arise from the fact that German authorities did not take into account the effect of corruption in decreasing the sales value of some Jewish assets. Moreover, certain appropriated assets recorded as belonging to enemy aliens may have actually belonged to Jews. Conservatively estimated, the German occupiers—in cooperation with the Dutch State Bank—converted at least 1.5 billion reichsmarks' worth of Jewish assets into Dutch government bonds. During the course of the occupation, Germans extracted 14.5 billion reichsmarks' worth of goods and services from Holland. The portion of those costs borne by Holland's tiny population of 140,000 Jews amounts to around 10 percent.[25]

Thick as Thieves in France

In occupied France, the Reich set up an elaborate and highly secretive system to Aryanize Jewish assets. Jewish-owned property was sold off and the proceeds invested in French government bonds, which put the funds within reach of the occupation budget. The German occupiers used other, more transparent means to gain access to "enemy" assets. Article 46 of the Hague Conventions regulated the general administration of businesses, property, and securities seized from citizens of occupied states.

These rules applied equally to both the Axis and the Allies. But the Reich interpreted enemy assets to include not only the property of citizens of hostile states but also those material assets left behind by French people who had fled the country, as well as the belongings of citizens of neutral states who resided in hostile nations. (A Swiss citizen who owned a factory in France and lived in England, for example, was classified as a "resident enemy" [*Aufenthaltsfeind*].)

Nazi Germany's official policy during the war was to "act as a trustee on behalf of the legitimate owners to maintain" enemy assets and the profits derived from them.[26] On the surface, the German trust commissioner took great care to follow the letter of the law. In reality, however, he transferred large amounts of this wealth into accounts that helped finance the war. This was possible because individual trustees were granted full power of attorney "to take certain administrative measures in the interests of the security and preservation" of assets.

In France, the Reich trained its sights on assets worth approximately 2.5 billion reichsmarks.[27] But the individual "administrative measures" taken were determined both by the Nazi leadership's insistence on the option of confiscating those assets at a later date and by the temporary need, for appearances' sake, "to preserve" them.[28] Enemy assets were also subject to the full range of currency regulations. Gold, currency, and foreign securities were to be offered up for sale to the Reich Credit Bank in Paris. That institution purchased the assets and transferred their equivalent value in francs to the Trust Office, taking the money from the occupation account. A similar procedure was used for motor vehicles subject to mandatory sale.[29] For all these transactions, the trustee received nominal compensation in the form of French treasury bonds. Germany doubly profited from these transactions. First, they gained gold, hard currency, and securities that they could use to make purchases in neutral countries. Second, they could immediately stop the redemption of the treasury bonds handed out in compensation, thereby helping to stabilize the franc. Liquid assets from enemy-owned businesses were subject to similar treatment. They "were transferred to the Trust Office," where they were "invested" in treasury bonds. In the rare case where trustees decided to sell off individual companies, the dividends, profits, and all other forms of capital income from those enterprises were likewise put into bonds.[30]

As in other countries where German occupation had unleashed inflation, the German commissioner at the Banque de France took immediate measures to restrict the flow of currency. One of those measures was a system of cash-free payment agreed to by the main administration of the Reich Credit Banks and the Banque de France in November 1940. Under the agreement, French business owners received payments for goods and services delivered to the occupiers in the form of bank credits issued by the Banque de France on behalf of the Reich Credit Bank in Paris.[31] The occupiers also encouraged payment by check, reduced the number of large-denomination bills in circulation, issued bills of exchange with a nine-month maturity date, and proposed paying out some state subsidies in four-year treasury bonds. All these measures aimed at restricting the volume of money in the wake of massive occupation spending.[32] At the same time, the occupation authority continued its policy of keeping interest rates low, which France as well as Germany had instituted in the fall of 1939 to ease the burden on state finances. Part of this overall fiscal strategy, in France as well as in many other European countries, was the confiscation of Jewish assets.

In November 1941, the German Currency Protection Command in France ordered state obligations that had come due to be paid out only on the express request of the holder of the debts. In the case of government bonds placed in receivership, including all bonds owned by Jews and enemies of the Reich, the securities were frozen.[33] This measure had the immediate effect of relieving pressure on the treasury.

This system of financing the war was in all likelihood the one used by all German commissioners at the central banks of German-occupied countries. Between 1941 and 1942, Germany and allies such as Hungary and Romania officially "collected" (that is, confiscated without compensation) all government bonds voluntarily or involuntarily acquired by Jews. It made little difference whether or not confiscation was accompanied by a piece of legislation. Even when assets were not legally expropriated, the freezing of bonds when they came due still provided considerable financial flexibility for countries waging World War II.

THE WEHRMACHT had another technique for raising money quickly. When the Allies landed in Morocco and Algeria in November 1942, Germany and Italy invaded Vichy France and Tunisia. Within a few weeks, the Wehrmacht demanded payments of 3 billion francs a month "for the protection" of the French colony.[34] The French government did not have nearly enough money to cover this additional expense.

Immediately on landing in Tunisia, the Wehrmacht arrested Moïse Borgel, the leader of Tunisia's Jewish community, and a number of prominent Jewish community members. They were soon released—on the condition that the Jewish community provide forced laborers for the construction of Luftwaffe bases. Tunisia's Jews were also required to pay more than 31 million francs for the upkeep of those laborers. According to historian Michael Laskier, "In order to meet the various German demands, the Jewish leadership was compelled to mortgage real estate and to use the property of affluent Jews as guarantee for bank loans. Thus, the terror organized against the Jews had a significant financial aspect."[35]

The situation was hardly atypical. The practice of forcing Jews to mortgage property or other assets as security for war loans was a common means of theft used by Wehrmacht officials. Few specific details are available about the extent of this practice, but evidence suggests that the intendant director of occupied Belgium discussed instituting similar policies with the official responsible for Jewish affairs in the Reich Finance Ministry. Because the auctioning off of Jewish assets had foundered on the opposition of Belgian financiers and the reluctance of ordinary Belgians "to purchase formerly Jewish-owned property from the military command," the Wehrmacht officer suggested "taking out the highest possible compulsory mortgages in the name of Jewish owners." Sufficient credit was available, the officer argued, and "the monies raised could then be confiscated. In this way, the Reich would quickly be able to realize at least part of the value of this property without having to sell it off below its actual value."[36] In Germany, too, discussions were held about compulsory mortgages on Jewish property "in the interests of financing the war."[37]

As was the case almost everywhere else in occupied Europe, the dispossession of Jews in France evolved in a series of individual measures: the estimation of the value of assets, restrictions on the owners' control over them, and the imposition of trustee administrators, who then liquidated those assets. On October 16, 1940, Walther von Brauchitsch held a meeting in the Ritz Hotel in Paris with the head of the economics division of the Wehrmacht High Command, Elmar Michel; the head of the administrative division, Werner Best; and the former minister of Würtemberg, Jonathan Schmid. The minutes included a summary of the meeting's agenda: "Ministerial Director Michel is to report on the state of the measures we have planned concerning Jewish businesses in occupied French territory in light of the ordinances that have already been prepared." Brauchitsch welcomed "across the board" suggestions on "an acceleration of those measures since it is unclear whether we Germans will be in a position in a couple of months to carry out or forcibly implement those measures we have deemed proper for Jews in France." In response to a question, he "said he actively supported the idea of mostly appointing French citizens as trustees."

In light of the diligence displayed by the Wehrmacht's generals and the occupation authority's leading economist, SS officer Werner Best—who would have normally been responsible for enforcing anti-Semitic ideology—apparently felt it unnecessary to deliver the standard lecture on the Jewish question. (He restricted his remarks to comments on road traffic.)[38] But his silence did not indicate a lack of interest. In a previous conversation with the German ambassador in Paris, Best had sketched out some "inspirations" he had on how to "gauge whether Jewish property in occupied territories can be expropriated."[39]

On October 27, 1940, eleven days after the meeting at the Ritz, the Wehrmacht High Command ordered the mandatory registration and classification of all Jewish-owned businesses in France. The ordinance, which had been proposed by Michel, also applied to businesses that were only partially owned by Jews and included all branches of commerce, banking, trade, and industry. The firms thus identified were to be put as quickly as possible into the hands of provisional custodians. The German military commander in the country wished "to cleanse France of Jewish influence" and place the "existing resources of those businesses" at the disposal "of the German home front, the Wehrmacht, and the French people."

From the outside it looked as though Jewish businesses were being required only to register themselves with the occupation authorities. But those in charge saw themselves as performing an "inventory" and considered the simultaneous naming of custodians a sufficiently elastic legal basis "for quickly carrying out the process of Aryanization."[40] German plans for the ultimate expropriation of Jewish wealth foresaw an active role for French legislative and executive institutions. In the short term, this expectation proved problematic. Only "gradually," with the application of pressure, was the French government "moved to issue its own laws."[41] German officers and officials attached to the Wehrmacht had to push the measures through themselves in the interest of increasing available funds. On several occasions, the military command asked the Security Police to arrest individual Jews to facilitate the seizure of their businesses.[42]

In October 1940, Michel reported: "The elimination of Jews from the French economy is under way in the occupied territories. . . . Superfluous Jewish businesses have been liquidated, and their inventory has been placed at the disposal of other businesses. Economically necessary businesses have been Aryanized by their provisional custodians." The measures had been taken, according to Michel, so as to "serve, first of all, the interests of the French people." The German authorities expected that the Vichy government in nonoccupied France would institute similar measures in the near future.[43] For the most part, French citizens acted as custodians. German administrators had to be appointed only in exceptional cases in order to secure sufficient influence over particular businesses.[44] This tactic conformed to the policy ordered by Göring, who sought to "play up the participation of French businesses."[45]

French collaboration was part of an overarching German political strategy aimed, in the words of the German ambassador in Paris, at "divorcing France from the Jewish world." In so doing, the Reich hoped to sever the French bond with liberalism and Western democracy.[46] Thus, from the very beginning, the proceeds from the Aryanization of Jewish businesses "were to flow into the French treasury," a policy that "alienated" some German occupation officials.[47] As long as the dispossession of Jews was carried out as an internal French affair, Germany could claim to be observing—at least superficially—the rules of the Hague Conventions. As early as August 1940, the judicial division of the Military High Command had cautioned that the planned Aryanization of the French economy would have to appear "to the outside world as if it were a private transfer of assets."[48]

Two examples illustrate the common French and German interest in *Entjudung* ("de-Jewification"). On March 6, 1941, a certain A. Labbé, an unemployed former representative of the Hamburg-Amerika shipping line in the French city of Cherbourg, addressed a letter to Karl-Heinz Gerstner at the German embassy in Paris. Labbé thanked the recipient for his efforts "on behalf of my being used as a provisional custodian or the like" and asked the embassy to intercede with the Military High Command to obtain permission for him "to take over the trusteeship of Jewish or enemy assets." In September 1941, after some further correspondence and with Gerstner's help, Labbé was given custodianship over the Hotel Ayoun Mireille in Boulogne sur Seine.

On August 1941, Gerstner asked the Military High Command whether a Frenchman named Lucien Léontard "could be appointed commissioner of a Jewish business." Gerstner cited Léontard's knowledge of economics, his language abilities, and his positive attitude toward Germany. The would-be collaborator was then considered "recommended by the German embassy."[49]

The German occupiers also used the "atonement" payment demanded of Jews in Paris to stimulate French interest in the theft of Jewish property. On December 14, 1941, the Military High Command levied a collective fine of one billion francs on Parisian Jews.[50] The French state apparatus, which was charged with collecting the money, seized a large portion of that sum from stock holdings left behind by the de Gunzburgs and the Javals, two extraordinarily wealthy families who had fled to America.[51] There was no need for Nazi Germany "to send specialists to help complete the implementation of the ordinance in the case of non-payment," as the Reich Finance Ministry had previously offered French authorities.

To improve German-French relations, the Military High Command wanted to transfer a quarter of the money to the Secours national and other French charity organizations, but the Finance Ministry insisted on the entire sum's being handed over to the Reich. A compromise of 10 percent was eventually reached. Thus, 100 million francs from the atonement payment went to French people, many of whom had suffered as a result of British air raids on Paris. The funds were distributed by the Comité ouvrier du secours immédiat, a committee formed expressly for that purpose.[52]

The German occupation administration in Tunisia pursued similar policies during the brief war in Africa. In December 1942, Rudolf Rahn, special ambassador from the German Foreign Office, sent a telegram describing the chaotic conditions in Tunis, where both the city and the port had been badly damaged by British bombing. Rahn reported that local police units and civilian committees had been formed to provide emergency relief. His telegram continued: "Since international Jewry is responsible for Anglo-American attack in North Africa, a sum of twenty million was raised from Jewish wealth by the Security Police and Security Service and given to a mixed Arab-Italian-French committee for the immediate support of air raid victims. Should enemy bombing of the civilian population continue, further sums will be raised."[53] Three months later, Rahn announced by telegraph that the relief committee formed at his behest had "paid out fifty million francs from fines on Tunisian Jews to families, mainly Muslim, victimized by bombings."[54] In the final days of the war, German occupiers also used confiscated Jewish money to provide emergency relief for air raid victims in Italy and Hungary.[55] In occupied Kryvyy Rih, Ukraine, the local military commander allocated the apartments of murdered Jews to locals on the basis of poverty and need.[56]

It wasn't until 1942 that the German military commander in France ordered a nighttime curfew for Jews and required them to wear yellow stars. But by 1941, when the Vichy government issued a series of anti-Semitic ordinances, he had achieved his main goal in shaping French policy toward Jews. The ordinances included the Jewish Statute, which relegated Jews to second-class citizenship and paved the way for deportations. The Vichy regime also created a special commission, the Commissariat général aux questions juives, to ensure that the ordinances were put into practice. On November 29, 1941, following the German model of the late 1930s, the Vichy regime passed a law requiring Jews to join a newly founded organization, the Union générale des Israélites; at the same time it disbanded all other existing Jewish organizations.[57]

These and other measures allowed Germans to carry out the theft of Jewish assets with a minimum of personnel. The economics division (Wi I/1) of the Military High Command, which was responsible for the Aryanization campaign, consisted of five military administrative counselors, a chief inspector, a secretary, and three staff assistants. Most of these individuals were assigned to a special subdivision called "the Representative of the Military Commander to the General Commission for Jewish Questions."[58] Together with a handful of auditors from other divisions, they were able to oversee the elimination of Jews from the French economy.

Officially, Aryanization was carried out by the Commissariat général. A special unit of it, Section IX (Direction générale de l'Aryanisation économique), was responsible for dispossessing Jews. Seized securities were managed by the French Finance Ministry, assisted by the Caisse centrale de dépôts et de virements de titres (Central Depository for the Custodianship and Transfer of Securities), founded in May 1941. This institution sold off securities wherever possible and put the revenues into French treasury bills and other government bonds. Its mandate was to keep the German machinery of war and plunder well lubricated with cash.

FROM THE perspective of the majority of French Jews, it was French citizens and special French agencies that were responsible for the everyday reality of Aryanization. Germans took direct control only of the assets of Jewish immigrants from Germany and Austria and, as of the fall of 1942, of nonnaturalized Jews from Poland and Bohemia and Moravia, and of Jewish citizens and residents of hostile nations.[59] (These exceptions accounted for 50,000 Jews out of a total Jewish population of 330,000 in France.) To administer the wealth of French Jews, Department Wi I/1 of the Military High Command in France appointed Ferdinand Niedermayer as general administrative commissioner. He sold off Jewish businesses and ensured that the proceeds "were secured in the interest of the Reich."[60] Niedermayer assumed his post in August 1941, serving "on the one hand as general commissioner and on the other as a special representative of the party to involve Germans in viable [Jewish] businesses."[61]

Niedermayer's office letterhead read, "Military Commander in France, Finance Division, German Jews."[62] The Finance Ministry ordered "that revenues generated be transferred to the Reich treasury."[63] Even after France was liberated, Niedermayer was still in a position to transfer securities, jewelry, and stamps valued at 60 million reichsmarks to the Reich treasury.[64]

To utilize enemy wealth, including major assets owned by Jews, the military administration had established the "Trust and Auditing Office of the Military High Command" in December 1940. Lieutenant Hans Kadelbach was charged with organizing this rapidly expanding administrative division. In February 1941, he suggested turning over the entire system of disposing of enemy and Jewish wealth to a private auditing company, Treuverkehr Deutsche Treuhand AG in Berlin. Kadelbach sat on the board of directors of the company, which was also associated with Deutsche Bank.[65] The wholesale transfer of authority to a private company was one of many instances of outsourcing in the Third Reich.

The office where the personnel of the Treuverkehr company worked was never formally established or defined. Those involved considered it "a fiscal construct, . . . a convenient point for collecting money, of a temporary nature" and "without fixed legal form."[66] In fact, it was another shell company. In keeping with orders issued by Michel in May 1942, the office took on the following responsibilities:

> a. maintenance of a card catalog in which lists of Jewish businesses, their custodial administrators, and other units are kept and continually updated
>
> b. collection of Jewish contributions ordered by my deputy at the General Commission for Jewish Questions for the purpose of de-Jewifying the economy; regular reporting on revenues; and regular consulting with the aforementioned deputy about the amount of money that should be taken in
>
> c. participation in approval proceedings in Aryanization cases by means of short assessment reports (so-called file checks) to be delivered to the responsible offices, as designated by me.[67]

The military administration deemed the Treuverkehr company "essential to the war effort," since it "administer[ed] Jewish and enemy assets valued at several billion francs."[68] French administrators headed the General Commission for Jewish Questions, but the Wehrmacht maintained an office at the commission for its own deputy. The deputy was responsible for overseeing the removal of Jews from the French economy and, though he was a German and a Treuverkehr employee, he was also a member of the ostensibly French-run Service du contrôle des administrateurs provisoires (SCAP), an organization that had been created in December 1940.[69] The filing system maintained by Treuverkehr to document the Aryanization of the French economy was housed in rooms 649 and 649a at the Hotel Majestic in Paris and was "constantly tended to by one male and two or three female employees." According to a Treuverkehr report, the catalog contained regularly updated note cards for more than 10,000 companies and more than 1,500 administrators. (In total the Commissariat général estimated "the number of Jewish businesses in occupied France at around 22,000.")

The division of labor among the economics division of the Military High Command, the Treuverkehr company, and the Commissariat général followed set rules. The French side submitted Aryanization projects for approval to the Treuverkehr deputy. He passed them on to be vetted by an officially designated commercial auditor. Finally, the trustee approved the sale of Jewish businesses, often attaching certain conditions.[70] For the military administration it was important "that French authorities operate freely and autonomously in applying German ordinances within their areas of responsibility." For this reason, German auditors stamped Aryanization applications not as "approved" but rather as "in accordance with regulations."[71]

An ordinance dated June 21, 1941, stipulated that Jews were allowed to open their bank safety deposit boxes only with the express permission of the Service du contrôle—in other words, of the German occupation administration. Reichsbank director Leopold Scheffler, whom the military administration had put in charge of overseeing French financial and credit matters, warned: "I will hold bank directors personally responsible should there be evidence of any violations of this ordinance."[72] In contrast to their Belgian counterparts, "the overwhelming majority" of French bank directors "timorously followed German regulations."[73]

ONE MONTH later, on July 22, 1941, the Vichy government issued law no. 3086, "aux enterprises, biens, et valeurs appartenant aux juifs" (regarding all companies, goods, and valuables belonging to Jews).[74] The law came into force on August 26. It closely followed the spurt of dispossession procedures Germany instituted between 1938 and 1941: Jewish assets in all forms were transferred to a trustee (administrateur provisoire), who sold them off and converted the proceeds into government securities. French Jews were never officially dispossessed. Article 1, paragraph 1, defined the law's purpose as to "erase any and all influence by Jews on the national economy." In practice, however, the law was aimed chiefly at using nearly all the assets of French Jews to fill the German war chest. Jews in Vichy France and in France's North African colonies, although those territories were not initially occupied by German forces, also surrendered their property to the French state—and thus ultimately to the German war chest—because they belonged to the overall French fiscal system.

Article 1 of the law exempted all French state securities and bonds issued by local municipalities or state-run companies from compulsory administration. This was logical, since the law, like its German predecessor, was aimed at converting the largest possible percentage of Jewish assets into state bonds. To achieve this aim, which was never explicitly spelled out, article 12 allowed administrators of Jewish businesses to sell off any assets under their control, including those that were subject to third-party claims. Article 18 left no doubt that the main thrust of the legislation was assets liquidation. If an administrator was slow to sell off assets, it was within the jurisdiction of the president of the relevant commercial court to appoint a more compliant liquidator.

The uncompromising clarity of the law's intent seems to contradict the general principle laid out in article 7, according to which the trustee was to manage assets in the spirit of a benevolent father ("*L'administrateur provisoire doit gérer en bon père de famille*"). But this familial responsibility was defined not as maintaining the welfare of Jews but rather as advancing the interests of the French finance minister.

Another crucial issue addressed by law no. 3086 was what to do with the revenues generated by this massive liquidation of assets. The law decreed that all proceeds from the sale of assets subject to compulsory trustee administration were to be paid into the state deposit account (*Caisse des dépôts et consignation*). There they were converted into French government securities, which helped finance the German war effort.

It was hardly a coincidence, then, given the financial impetus behind the law, that the Commission for Jewish Questions was located on the place des Petits-Pères, just fifty yards from the main entrance to the Banque de France. Article 17 decreed that purchasers of Jewish assets were to pay, whenever possible, in cash. (This was also the case for Aryanization transactions in Germany itself and later in Hungary.) The money then had only to be taken the short distance to the Banque de France, where it was converted, perfectly legally, into state securities.[75]

The liquidation of Jewish assets peaked in 1942. As the amount of Jewish property available for sale diminished, proceeds fell by more than half in 1943.[76] Nevertheless, the Treuverkehr company continued to charge hefty fees for its auditing services, in addition to keeping revenues from businesses still in trusteeship and setting its own profit margins.

Profits from assets in trusteeship were also converted into French treasury bills (*bons du trésor*). The German Enemy Assets Administration later characterized the situation this way: "Following guidelines from the military administration, [trustees] deposited the proceeds in medium-term accounts at offices of major enemy banks that were under German administration. At regular intervals, when enough capital had accrued, they then bought French treasury bills."[77] At the insistence of the German commissioner at the Banque de France, who wanted to maintain good relations with his French colleagues, claims of "enemy" creditors were also converted into French, and not German, state bonds.

Nonetheless, these funds, too, ultimately ended up in the German war chest. By and large, the revenues generated by Jewish assets remained in France as long as they were paid into Treuverkehr accounts. The German administrators preferred this procedure so as to reduce French inflation and allow the country to pay the staggering occupation costs Germany had imposed. When, in 1943, some trustee revenues were transferred directly to the Reich treasury in Berlin instead, they amounted to the relatively small sum of 22.5 million reichsmarks.[78]

CHAPTER 9

Subsidies to and from Germany's Allies

Slovakian Equity

The Reich also took in significant revenue from its allies, usually in the form of contributions to help underwrite Germany's military campaign in World War II. The countries in question raised that money, in turn, by dispossessing their Jewish populations. Yet often, German financial demands put the economies of allied countries under such strain that the Reich was forced to intervene with subsidies of its own—paid for with the proceeds from the dispossession of German Jews and Jews in occupied countries. In terms of financial exploitation, however, it ultimately made little difference whether a country was occupied by or allied with Nazi Germany. Where defeated enemies were compelled to pay occupation costs, Germany's allies were forced to make so-called contributions to the German war effort.

A case in point was Slovakia. Slovakia owed its existence as an independent country of 2.65 million inhabitants to Hitler's Germany, which between 1938 and 1939 divided Czechoslovakia into two states. The ideology of the Slovakian People's Party, which dominated the new nation, was a mixture of anti-Semitic and class-warfare propaganda. Alexander Mach, the country's interior minister, who managed to maintain contact with communist functionaries, exemplified this ideology. Shortly after the nation was formed, he declared: "Everywhere else, Jews who possess gold, gemstones, and riches have been swept out, and we will do the same. Slovakia's strength is labor. People here who don't work don't eat. Wealth that has been accumulated by theft will be taken away! That's the practical solution to the Jewish question."[1] The newspaper *Slovenska Politika* echoed these sentiments in July 1940: "The issue here is, above all, the Jewish question. Without a radical solution to this question, we cannot improve basic social conditions."[2]

A Slovakian government ordinance defined who was to be considered a Jew. In general the law barred those who matched the legal description from public employment and partially or completely banned them from certain academic professions.[3] In 1939, in an attempt to improve conditions for the rural poor, the Slovakian government issued a decree requiring Jews to register property used for agriculture or forestry. A few months later, a law was passed that nationalized those properties and stipulated how they were to be divided up and allocated in the interests of social "equity." The legislation subjected 101,423 hectares (250,000 acres) owned by Jews to nationalization—enough land to provide 20,000 landless Slovaks with small farms. (At an average family size of six, that meant that 120,000 people—or almost 5 percent of the total population—stood to benefit.) On April 25, 1940, a law explicitly aimed at creating "a strong Slovakian middle class" ordered the Slovakization of Jewish-owned businesses.[4]

In the summer of 1940, following the passage of laws that had dispossessed Jewish farmers, merchants, and business owners, a plan was conceived to deport Slovakian Jews to Madagascar. The government in Bratislava was the only one among Germany's allies to support the idea, which had originated in Berlin. Slovakia's support of the proposal was largely due to the effort of Dieter Wisliceny, whom Adolf Eichmann had sent to Bratislava in August 1940 as his point man for Jewish affairs. Wisliceny's first priority was to remove Jews from the Slovakian economy, and he served as an occasional consultant on questions of Aryanization. Using the German model, he set about to redraft Slovakian laws, at the same time overseeing the creation of a special bureau to promote Slovakization, the Central Economics Ministry. The ministry was patterned after the special agencies that had been set up for the purposes of confiscation and deportation in Vienna and Prague. Wisliceny also helped establish a fund ostensibly to be used to promote Jewish emigration. The fund, similar to the one set up in Germany, was in reality an account created to receive the massive profits made from selling off Jewish assets. The notion that it was an emigration fund was a transparent pretense, since the Slovakian finance minister was the only one who had access to it. On September 2, 1940, the minister ordered Jews to report their assets to the government for the express purpose of "fixing" their value.

By early 1942, the Slovakian government had sold off 9,987 out of a total of just over 12,000 registered Jewish businesses.[5] A further 1,910 had been Aryanized. The Slovakian middle classes profited not only from this direct redistribution of wealth but also from the disappearance of competition. For their part, Slovakian entrepreneurs derived considerable advantage from the new practice of awarding business contracts along racial lines.[6]

The Slovakian Statistics Office and the Jewish Central Union, an organization created by the Slovakian state, kept tabs on these criminal undertakings. According to statistics compiled by Anton Vasek, the anti-Semitic head of the Jewish division within the Interior Ministry, Jewish assets in Slovakia amounted to some 4.5 billion crowns, or around 387 million reichsmarks. Estimates made by the Statistics Office and the Central Union were lower, ranging from 2.5 to 3 billion crowns.[7] But even the conservative estimates must have represented a huge temptation for the Slovakian finance minister in Bratislava, considering that the entire regular Slovakian national budget in 1941 was just over 3 billion crowns, some 500 million of which went toward military expenditures.[8]

When Slovakia entered the war against the Soviet Union in late July 1941, the government immediately encountered financial problems. Historian Ladislav Lipscher describes how those problems were addressed: "At a meeting on August 25, called by the head of the government and including all major government representatives, serious concerns were raised about deteriorating state finances in the aftermath of Slovakia's entry into the war against the Soviet Union. The finance minister reported that the deficit in the proposed budget would reach almost 600 million crowns by the end of 1941. To curb inflation, it was decided to raise needed revenues—500 million crowns—by introducing a 15 percent levy on Jewish assets."

A few days later, on September 9, 1941, the Slovakian government passed a law instituting the levy. The move raised the compulsory contribution from 15 to 20 percent of Jewish assets and, as Germany had done in 1938–39, made the country's Jewish population collectively responsible for payment. The official justification for the law was that it would have been "grotesquely unfair" to burden Slovakia's non-Jewish citizens with 500 million crowns in expenses since they were in no way responsible for the war. (In previously setting the levy at 15 percent to raise 500 million crowns, the Finance Ministry estimated the value of Jewish assets at 3.3 billion crowns.) According to Lipscher, the levy failed to achieve its desired effect because Slovakian Jews no longer possessed the necessary resources to pay the fine. In the end, however, it was easily paid off by transferring frozen but not yet confiscated Jewish savings accounts, as well as stocks and bonds, to the national treasury.[9]

In his 1942 annual report, the governor of the Slovakian National Bank declared that because of German demands for contributions to the war the amount of money in circulation had dramatically increased, to the detriment of the national economy. But he added that the problem would have been far worse "had the Slovakian National Bank not taken neutralizing measures."[10] Foremost among those measures was the dispossession of Slovakian Jews. The sale of their belongings brought revenues into the treasury, allowing it temporarily to check the skyrocketing amount of currency in circulation.

Because Slovakia suffered from a housing shortage, 11,518 Jews in Bratislava were issued notices of evacuation in the winter of 1941–42. By March 1942, 6,720 people had been forced to leave the city and move to internment camps. On March 26, deportations to Auschwitz and Majdanek commenced. Within the space of thirteen weeks, the Slovakian government deported 53,000 of the country's 89,000 Jews. On May 25, 1942, the state announced a law authorizing such deportations and nationalizing

Jewish assets. The deportations were later discontinued after intervention by the Catholic Church.

Slovakia was required to pay Germany a fee of 500 reichsmarks for every Jew deported, with the total coming to 26.1 million marks. The sum was included in annual German-Slovakian clearing transactions and increased German spending power and credit flexibility. The Finance Ministry placed the money "at the disposal of the Reich SS leader."[11]

According to Slovakian estimates, Germany forcibly extracted some 7 billion crowns in goods and services from its ally during the course of World War II.[12] Almost 40 percent of this sum came from the proceeds of the Aryanization of Jewish assets. To curb inflation caused by the war against the Soviet Union and by demands from Germany, the Slovakian National Bank propped up the crown, at least temporarily, by liquidating those assets. But that wasn't enough.[13] As early as 1942, the Reich had to provide the bank with a million reichsmarks in confiscated gold and currency. By 1944, the subsidy had grown to 10 million reichsmarks. The Reich also "placed gemstones and diamonds," some of which had been seized from Dutch Jews, at the bank's disposal "for absorption purposes."[14]

The Reich proceeded in similar fashion with the independent state of Croatia. On April 10, 1941, as the Wehrmacht occupied Zagreb, the Nazi-supported Ustaše movement proclaimed the birth of the new nation, which included Bosnia-Herzegovina. Four days later, the newly formed Croatian government froze bank accounts and deposits belonging to the country's 30,000 Jews. Sixteen days after that, a special law was issued requiring Croatia's Jewish minority to register their property and compile detailed lists of assets. A mandatory "Jewish contribution to the needs of the state" quickly followed.[15]

Most of Croatia's Jews were sent to concentration camps within the country, where they were killed. A small number went underground or were deported to Auschwitz in the summer of 1942. It was only after that, on October 30, 1942, that the Ustaše government officially confiscated Jewish assets.[16] The 1943 Croatian state budget recorded a deficit of 1.25 billion kuna—or 62.5 million reichsmarks. Most state expenditures, according to a 1943 report in the *Frankfurter Zeitung*, were to be covered by "loans as well as revenues from nationalized Jewish assets, which are estimated at some 1.25 billion."[17] A small deficit remained, since a portion of those revenues was reserved for Germany, which charged a fee of 30 reichsmarks for each person—from a total of 4,927—deported to Auschwitz.[18]

Bulgaria's Wartime Budget

Even before the Axis powers launched their all-out offensive against Greece and Yugoslavia in 1941, German economists were in Bulgaria advising that country's government. From January 23 to February 1, 1941, a top-secret German commission—led by Hitler's special envoy Hermann Neubacher—visited the capital, Sofia, to help prepare the financial ground for the impending war.[19] On the final day of consultations, Germany and Bulgaria signed an agreement under which the Wehrmacht received what was officially described as a loan of 500 million leva, or around 15.6 million reichsmarks. In addition, Bulgaria agreed to build up its armed forces.[20]

By March 3, the Reichsbank was already projecting that the loan would have to be increased to 900 million leva, a move that followed on March 25.[21] In April, with the war under way against Greece and Yugoslavia, the Reich Credit Bank extracted a further 500 million leva from Bulgaria, bringing the total in loans to 1.4 billion leva.[22] The next increase of 500 million came two months later, and this pattern continued until August 1944.[23] As a member of the Axis, Bulgaria annexed parts of Thrace and Macedonia after the Wehrmacht's victory over Greece and Yugoslavia in April and May 1941. As compensation for the Wehrmacht's "assistance," Bulgaria was required to assume responsibility for all past and future costs incurred by German forces within Bulgarian territory.

The Bulgarian government budget for 1940 amounted to 8.4 billion leva, an increase of 10 percent over the previous year. The additional expenditures were financed by a general tax hike, a onetime levy for "national security," and "a significantly higher taxation of upper-income brackets and large capital reserves and sales." In 1941, the budget grew a further 20 percent, reaching 10.1 billion leva. In parliamentary budget debates, Bulgarian finance minister Dobri Bozhilov justified the expenditures as a necessary response to the war in Europe and promised that "the less privileged segment" of the Bulgarian citizenry would not suffer as the government increased its revenues.[24]

The government's actual expenditures in 1941 rose to 17 billion leva because of the annexation of Yugoslav and Greek territories. The 1940 budget had been doubled without anything even approaching a corresponding growth in the Bulgarian economy. The government tried to rein in expenditures for 1942, but its efforts failed and a supplementary budget had to be introduced to meet the various demands coming from Germany. Berlin was now insisting on funds to supply German troops fighting in the newly annexed ("liberated") territories, for the construction of roads and railways between Greece and the Reich for use by the Wehrmacht, and for noncompensated exports to Serbia, which was under German occupation. Applying the same system it had used in occupied countries, Germany reached a deal with the Bulgarian government forcing the national bank in Sofia to deliver, without compensation, all Wehrmacht RKK certificates in circulation to the local Reich Credit Bank. "That practice," one official in Berlin noted, "is established and has proved itself effective in the past."[25]

In addition, Bulgaria was forced to export food and tobacco products to the Reich. In contrast to the procedure in other countries, Germans "paid" for some of these goods—but in a form that was scarcely distinguishable from extortion. Starting in 1941, the Reich settled its clearing debts using war bonds, which were soon to be worthless. The president of the Association of People's Banks in Sofia hypocritically described this form of grand larceny as "the intervention of the reichsmark for the financial solidity of the Bulgarian currency." He proudly added that Bulgaria "was the first European country to make an important contribution to the creation of a single European currency." In fact, the Bulgarian National Bank in Sofia received some 710 million reichsmarks in war bonds in the period before the summer of 1944.[26] That was the nominal equivalent of the 22.4 billion leva Germany extorted from its tiny, economically weak ally.

The career of Dobri Bozhilov illustrates how compliant Bulgarian politicians were in granting the Reich's wishes. In September 1942, the former finance minister became Bulgaria's prime minister, a position he held until May 1944. On an official state visit he made to Hitler's Wolfsschanze field headquarters in the fall of 1943, the Führer dictated a list of loans Bulgaria would have to offer—without any prospect of "comprehensive economic settlement"—to Germany "in the interest of the common struggle that is our fate." As in Finland, Romania, and Hungary, Hitler invoked a vision of prosperity once the war had been won, promising to "give my friends everything they request" at that point.[27] In truth, right up until the bitter final days of the war, the Germans merely took everything they could. Bozhilov's acceding to their demands made things that much easier.

The agreement reached by Germany and Bulgaria prohibited members of the Wehrmacht from buying up goods while in transit through Bulgaria, but this prohibition was of no real significance. It wasn't until January 6, 1944, after the military situation had taken a turn for the worse, that Bulgarian customs officials were allowed to inspect the baggage of German troops and the packages they sent through the military postal service. Bulgarian officials had repeatedly complained about "mass shopping sprees," which had caused "shortages of goods, inflation, and, consequently, bitterness among the Bulgarian population toward German soldiers."[28]

In 1942, the proposed Bulgarian budget included a special tax on Jewish wealth for the first time. It was projected to raise some 1.5 billion leva, in comparison with only 628 million to be taken in from increases in regular taxes.[29] The anti-Semitic Law for the Protection of the Nation had already been introduced a year earlier, on January 21, 1941. With certain exceptions, Jews were henceforth considered foreigners, prohibited from various types of employment and required to register their entire assets with the Bulgarian National Bank. No sooner had registration been completed in June 1941 than the government decreed that "persons of Jewish background" would have to pay a onetime levy to the Bulgarian treasury.

For people with assets of over 200,000 leva (or 6,000 reichsmarks) the rate was 20 percent; for assets of over 3 million leva, it was 25 percent. According to later official estimates, the resulting revenues were projected to top 1.8 billion leva.[30]

The state imposed other measures of economic discrimination against Jews. In the summer of 1941, it introduced the lev as the sole legal tender in the annexed parts of Macedonia and Thrace. The rate for Jewish residents exchanging drachmas or Yugoslavian dinars was set 30 to 50 percent lower than "for all other depositors."[31] While it was issuing such anti-Jewish legislation, Bulgaria also passed laws dispossessing Greeks who lived in the annexed territories.[32]

As it turned out, state revenues from the special tax levied on Bulgarian Jews in 1942 amounted to only 709 million leva, or around half of what was expected. In 1943, the government planned to take in an additional 400 million leva from the tax and more than 1.5 billion "from the sale of properties and other valuables." The German envoy noted in his regular report on Bulgarian finances: "This is no doubt a matter of selling off real estate and securities confiscated from Jewish owners." The assets in question came from Jewish residents of Macedonia and Thrace, who were deported in the spring of 1943.[33] On March 2, 1942, anticipating what was to come, the government had decreed that the assets of emigrating Jews would fall to the state.[34] As in Germany, the proceeds from this governmental larceny were recorded as "additional revenues."

On August 29, 1942, a law came into force entitled A Compilation of Measures for the Regulation of the Jewish Question and Related Matters. This legislation assembled the anti-Jewish laws that had been previously issued into fifty-nine articles and laid the groundwork for a Jewish Commission. The importance of financial considerations was reflected in the fact that representatives from both the Finance Ministry and the national bank were allowed to sit on the commission's administrative council. Article 43 provided for the "confiscation of stocks and other securities" for the benefit of the Bulgarian state. Article 45 required Jews to register other liquid and deferred assets with the national bank, including insurance policies, wills, loan documents, and bonds. Article 47 stipulated that these assets were to be sold off "at public auction." For the sake of appearances, Bulgarian civil servants credited the proceeds from the sales of such assets to their individual Jewish owners. (Only the declared value of the assets was credited, however, not their actual price at auction. Because of rapid wartime inflation, higher sums were often fetched, "with the difference falling to the state.")[35]

In early 1943, Bulgarian Jewish commissioner Aleksandar Belev requested the Reich to begin deporting "economically well-situated Jews" from his country.[36] Fear of stirring up anti-Bulgarian sentiment abroad led the Bulgarian government to cancel the request, saving the Jews in Bulgaria proper from German gas chambers but by no means putting an end to their dispossession.[37] In a diary entry from June 1943, a Wehrmacht economist in Sofia recorded "that the majority of Sofia's Jews have been relocated to the provinces."[38] In total, Belev disposed of Jewish property valued at some 4.5 billion leva.[39] A substantial portion of this money landed in German hands, in the form of subsidies that the Reich constantly extracted from its ally.

On February 22, 1943, Belev met with Eichmann's deputy Theodor Dannecker to confirm a previous agreement to deport Jews "from the new provinces of Thrace and Macedonia to eastern German territories." The final destination for the 11,343 deportees was the Treblinka concentration camp, where they were killed. Bulgarian settlers moved into residences previously occupied by Jews and continued the ethnic cleansing of the two regions.[40] At the same time, Greeks who were expelled from the areas concerned were forced to flee to the German-occupied part of Macedonia. There, they were housed in residences left behind by Jews who had been deported from Salonika and the surrounding area. In this way, just as parts of Macedonia and Thrace were turned over to Bulgaria, the disputed territories in what is today northern Greece were Hellenized.

The Politics of Romanian Gold

The brutal exploitation of allied and occupied countries often put local currencies under extreme pressure. In two cases, the proceeds from the dispossession of local Jews weren't enough to stabilize such currencies. Consequently, the Reich had no choice but to transfer gold from its "own" reserves to prevent monetary collapse. One case was that of occupied Greece. The other was that of Germany's ally Romania.

In December 1940, ostensibly at the request of the Romanian leadership, Hermann Neubacher traveled to Bucharest as a special envoy of the German Foreign Office. His mission was to see "that the Reich put technical advisers at the disposal of the Romanian government." Those advisers included Reichsbank director Louis Wolf, a specialist in export and currency matters, and two government counsels, a Dr. Krebs and Hans Gurski, who would also be given responsibility for the "de-Jewification" of Serbia.[41] But the true reason for Neubacher's visit emerges from the transcript of a conversation from October 1940 involving officials at the Economics and Finance Ministries. "Above all, we want to have influence over the petroleum economy," one speaker asserted. "The Reich marshal [Göring] has indicated that the excess production of 3 million tons (300 million reichsmarks) is to be secured for the Reich. In the short term it is not possible to balance accounts with supplies from our side. The National Bank [of Romania] will have to advance the money. This can have inflationary consequences. To combat these, the Romanian government will be supported by a staff of German advisers." At the end of their consultations, one participant concluded: "Some day they will have to tackle the Jewish question (Aryanization) just as we did."[42]

In the summer of 1940, following the signing of the Hitler-Stalin Pact, Romania had been forced to cede northern Bukovina and Bessarabia to the Soviet Union. A short time later, in response to German and Italian pressure, the country also had to give up northern Transylvania to Hungary and southern Dobruja to Bulgaria. Those territorial losses meant a wave of 260,000 ethnic German refugees who suddenly had to be cared for. Most were sent back to Germany, while 77,000 others were resettled in southern Bukovina and northern Dobruja, which remained parts of Romania. To assist in the resettlement, Romania issued a series of laws between October 1940 and June 1942 dispossessing its Jewish minority. At first, the proceeds generated from the sale of Jewish property were allocated directly to aid for the refugees. Later, once Romania had become actively involved in fighting the Soviet Union, more and more of the money went toward the war effort.

On October 4, 1940, all rural Jewish-owned properties in Romania were officially expropriated. On October 10, the government confiscated all Jewish-owned *Pfandbriefe*, or German-backed bonds, and nationalized Jewish hospitals and public welfare facilities. These confiscations helped reduce short-term government debt. The state, forced to issue credit to refugees to help them rebuild their lives, could take on new obligations without upsetting the budget balance. Romania was also able to underwrite the deliveries of supplies that the Reich demanded. Many of the Jewish community and public welfare facilities that were nationalized at this juncture were converted into centers for refugees.

On November 12, the Romanian government confiscated all Jewish-owned forestland as well as all businesses involved in processing agricultural and timber products. On March 27, 1941, urban properties were expropriated, and on May 2, the Central Office for Romanization was founded. As one Reich official noted, "the material basis" for housing refugees from former parts of the country "was the 260,000 hectares of farmland that became part of the state's domain with the resettlement of ethnic Germans and the dispossession of Jews." Simultaneously, laws were passed barring Jews from certain types of work, therefore creating jobs for ethnic Romanian refugees.[43]

Naturally, the Reich did not just let the new Romanian owners take over abandoned German properties and businesses free of charge. As in other countries where ethnic Germans had been "retrieved" by the Reich, Romania was forced to make a lump-sum payment to the German treasury. Joint Romanian and German committees estimated the value of individual properties. The total came to 7.7 billion lei, or 130 million reichsmarks, a sum that was paid off in installments. Beginning in the summer of 1942, most of the money was allocated to the Wehrmacht's intendant for Romania, who used it to pay for food for German troops, soldiers' wages, and private purchases on the Romanian market.[44]

That money was intended for ethnic Germans who had resettled within the Reich, but instead they received compensation in the form of property confiscated in Poland. To acquire the necessary farmland, Eichmann's troops brutally expelled 62,000 Poles from the Warthegau, the part of Poland annexed by Germany. Those refugees were quartered west of Warsaw on General Government territory, in residences previously occupied by Polish Jews. In the winter of 1940–41, some 72,000 Jews— 10,000 more than the number of Poles driven out—were forced to march on foot to the Warsaw ghetto, which was already suffering from overcrowding and widespread malnutrition.

By the end of 1942, German commissioners under SS leader Heinrich Himmler boasted that they had resettled some 500,000 ethnic Germans. "In the main," wrote one commissioner, "the resettlement of immigrants has been financed by the uncompensated exploitation of wealth previously in the possession of alien races [*fremdvölkisches Vermögen*]—without having to make recourse to the resources of the Reich." The claim wasn't entirely true. In 1941, the Finance Ministry had allocated 300 million reichsmarks for resettlement.[45] Nonetheless, lump-sum compensation payments received for the property of ethnic Germans in Romania, the Soviet Union, Italy, and Croatia bolstered the administrative revenues in the Reich budget and were used to procure goods and services in those countries. No sooner had ethnic Germans from Romania crossed the Danube than Himmler's attaché at the Reichsbank, Hermann Waldhecker, proposed that some of Germany's debts to Romania could be paid off "from the resettlement."[46]

The procedure was called "natural restitution." At the end of the resettlement chain, Jews were always forced to bear the costs, while German soldiers spent the proceeds from the sale of assets left behind by those who were being repatriated. Because resettled ethnic Germans were compensated with property confiscated from Poles, and the Poles in turn by property confiscated from Jews, it was ultimately the Jews in the Warsaw ghetto who were squeezed to pay for what the Wehrmacht consumed in Romania. Many ghetto inhabitants froze or starved to death there. Those who survived until the summer of 1942 were sent to Treblinka and murdered in the gas chambers.[47]

In the summer of 1941, when Romania joined Germany's war against the Soviet Union, the anti-Jewish laws being issued in Bucharest took on an entirely new dimension. In late July, the Romanian finance minister forced the Jewish community of that city to buy 10 billion lei in war bonds. In September, the army confiscated bed frames, mattresses, and linens owned by Jews for use in military hospitals. In October, a law voided all claims on outstanding loans held by Jewish creditors. The state trampled on the rights of Jews in order to increase revenues. Meanwhile, Romanian Jews were forced to hand over gold, silver, jewelry, and other valuables to the state treasury. They were also obliged to pay various fines and a special tax four times as large as the one paid by non-Jews. On January 3, 1942, a decree ordered Jews to surrender their clothing and remaining household linens; on May 16, they were required to raise a collective wartime contribution of 4 billion lei, and in June, Jewish cemeteries were handed over to local governments. The dispossession of Jews generated revenues for the Romanian state and eased the burdens of war for the majority of Romanians. In all, Jews were forced to cover between 25 and 33 percent of all loans taken out by the country to finance the war.[48]

The beginning of the plunder coincided with Hermann Neubacher's arrival in Bucharest, which in turn was accompanied by the arrival of German troops. "There should be no talk," noted one German Finance Ministry official, "of an occupation." Instead, German troops were officially in Romania for "training" purposes.[49] However one wished to describe their mission, the German troops needed money. On December 31, 1941, Reichsbank director Rudolf Sattler flew to Bucharest "at the urgent request of the Foreign Office" to "assist envoy Neubacher in negotiations with the Romanian government about monetary support for the German troops." Sattler lived in Oslo, where he was responsible for overseeing the national banks of Norway and Denmark and for regulating the flow of funds to pay for occupying troops. His job now was to apply "the experience gained in Oslo and Copenhagen" to Romania.[50] The result was apparently a success. A few months later, Romanian head of state Ion Antonescu complained: "How long do they think I can remain in charge of the government, when demands are issued every ten days for a billion lei for the German troops?"[51]

Carl Friedrich Goerdeler, the former mayor of Leipzig, had protested that no sooner had Wehrmacht personnel been stationed in Romania than the country's public finances began to dissolve: "Romania is being burdened with occupation costs that the state cannot shoulder."[52] German economic attaché Carl Clodius also predicted that "the currency will be endangered" since the demands of the Wehrmacht for 7 to 8 billion lei a year (much less than would ultimately be consumed) could scarcely be managed in an annual state budget of "only around 30 billion lei."[53]

At the end of September 1941, at Neubacher's behest, Karl Blessing (later the head of the Central Bank of West Germany) conducted a study on the state of the Romanian currency. He found that both prices and the amount of money in circulation had tripled since 1937. The sole reason was "the issuance of loans for state purposes, especially military and economic purposes." Romania's entry into the war against the Soviet Union had made it necessary "to increasingly tap the national bank." Blessing found that "the German troops present in the country had also required, for professional and personal purposes, sums of lei that had been provided by the Romanian government in return for equivalent credits in the clearing account in Berlin." By September 13, 1941, those credits already amounted to 15.5 billion lei. Blessing calculated that German demands were responsible for 41.4 percent of the Romanian state debt in the first nine months of 1941. Further Werhmacht demands in the period up to February 1942 amounted to "some 16 billion lei." Since the proceeds from the Romanization of Jewish assets were directed into the state's war chest, to slow the accretion of debt, it can be safely assumed that much of this money ultimately landed in German pockets. The levy of 4 billion lei imposed on Romanian Jews in the spring of 1942 allowed the state to fulfill the demands of the Wehrmacht for only one month without having to print more money.

Blessing complained about various deficiencies within the Romanian state apparatus and explicitly blamed "the Jews" as playing a part in the rapid rise in prices. Should the devaluation of the leu continue "virtually unchecked," he warned, Germany and Romania would be faced with a very serious danger "not only of social unrest but of a decline in Romanian production." He suggested raising taxes, creating incentives for Romanians to open savings accounts, and reducing all expenditures not deemed essential to the Romanian war effort.[54]

For its part, the Romanian government tried to get the Reich to scale back its demands. The leadership in Bucharest required Wehrmacht intendants to renegotiate its financial contribution every ten days. Individual military units sometimes found themselves unable to pay their bills, since the Romanian government—with Neubacher's support—had decided that introducing huge amounts of money into circulation would "endanger the currency and lead to inflation." Once German military attachés had been convinced of this danger, Antonescu hoped that, "by refusing to provide lei, we can force the Germans to reduce their troop strength." But Hitler objected, reminding Antonescu that, thanks to the war against the Soviet Union, Romania had not only reacquired northern Bukovina and Bessarabia but been given the right to administer and plunder Ukrainian Transnistria. In August 1941, the two leaders came to an agreement that Jews in Bukovina and Bessarabia were to be immediately dispossessed. A short time later, after a successful joint campaign in Ukraine, the Wehrmacht and the Romanian armed forces concluded a treaty that included the following passage: "Deportation of Jews from Transnistria. Deportation across the Bug River is not feasible at present. Therefore, they will have to be detained in concentration camps and pressed into forced labor until the conclusion of operations, when deportation to the East will be possible."[55]

In the summer of 1941, the number of Wehrmacht personnel who had to be provisioned in Romania averaged between 50,000 and 60,000. Despite official prohibitions, German soldiers repeatedly tried to smuggle surplus Romanian goods out via ship or freight train as "Wehrmacht resources." Those shipments, bound either for Germany itself or for Russia, were not always successful. A member of the German army mission in Romania wrote in his diary: "For days and even weeks, the Romanians hold up individual shipments and whole trainloads of necessities that are supposed to be sent back home, by order of the Army High Command. All attempts to remove obstructions to transport of Wehrmacht resources only lead to individual shipments being let through after weeks of waiting." There was no great mystery as to the cause of the delays. Even the German intendant in Romania admitted that the country suffered from "undeniable shortages of some basic necessities."[56]

To redress the situation in Romania, the Nazi leadership decided to use shipments of gold to stabilize the currency, which had been so seriously undermined by the Reich's own policies. With increasing insistence, the Romanian government had been demanding since July 1941 that Berlin pay at least part of its debts in gold, so that the Romanian National Bank could "show an improvement in its gold reserves." Recognizing the danger "that Germany might have to introduce its own currency into Romania, if currency difficulties aren't checked," several of Hitler's advisers acknowledged the gravity of the problem.[57] Neubacher supported Romania's demands, as well. Large amounts of gold had previously been shipped to the Romanian National Bank to stabilize the leu in June 1940, and in early 1942 the shipments were resumed. Together, the two sets of shipments amounted to some eighteen tons.[58]

Confident of his own position, Antonescu made no effort to fulfill all of the Wehrmacht's demands. On the contrary, his chief negotiators fought with Wehrmacht intendants over every leu. On January 1, 1943, the German general in charge of the Wehrmacht in Romania felt compelled to issue a statement about "the shortage of lei": "Our goal has to be to spare German soldiers in Romania another decrease in pay, to use all means at hand to further reduce material expenditures, and to avoid destabilizing Romania's currency."[59]

At the same time, the reversal of its military fortunes on the Eastern Front meant that Germany had to move more and more units to Romania to establish field hospitals and bases for reinforcements. To this end, a secret agreement was concluded between German foreign minister Joachim von Ribbentrop and his Romanian counterpart, Mihai Antonescu, on January 11, 1943, at Hitler's Wolfsschanze command center. (Economics Minister Walther Funk, president of the Reichsbank, was also

present at the meeting.) The accord provided for the delivery to Romania of thirty tons of gold, with a value of 84 million reichsmarks. In addition, the Reich government promised to pay 43 million Swiss francs to Romania within six months in order "to avoid the sale to Switzerland of Romanian export goods deemed essential to the German war effort." Thanks to these measures, the Romanian government was able to stabilize the country's currency in the short term and to procure Swiss-made weapons and matériel for its own army, which had suffered heavy losses on the Eastern Front and needed to be reequipped.[60]

Antonescu had arrived at the Wolfsschanze accompanied by a large entourage. While he was in transit, the commanding German officer in Bucharest reported to the head of the German army mission, who was traveling with Antonescu's group, about "difficulties in acquiring lei." Simultaneously the Wehrmacht leadership, represented by General Hermann Reinecke, declared that, on the "lei issue, the Romanians should be enlisted in the interest of our joint pursuit of the war." When the members of the Romanian delegation returned home, they made "an impression of being very satisfied" on the German officer who accompanied them.[61]

Antonescu's satisfaction with the deal ebbed quickly once he returned to Bucharest. On February 2, he repeated his earlier refusals to make "Romanian advance payments" toward meeting Wehrmacht demands, asserting: "Only after binding statements have been issued from German officials about the timetable for the delivery of the promised gold, and the first of those deliveries has actually been made, can Romania begin to provide promised monies for German troops." The initial delivery left the Reichsbank's gold depot on February 15, 1943, headed for Bucharest. At the last minute, however, as a revised waybill shows, the value of the gold being shipped had been reduced by about one-third, to 19,998,820.57 reichsmarks. As a result, a month later the Romanian finance minister refused to make payments in full to the Wehrmacht. The Reichsbank delivered the remainder of the gold in three shipments on April 15, April 18, and May 2, 1943.[62]

In the run-up to the negotiations at the Wolfsschanze, Reichsbank vice president Emil Puhl had tried to thwart Romanian claims against the

Reich, which, as he put it, "now, on top of everything else, include demands for payment in gold." Afterward, he remarked indignantly that Antonescu "had succeeded in wringing concessions from the German side." Goebbels also noted that, in the wake of recent military defeats, Romania "was zealously concerned with creating a stable gold reserve."[63]

The Romanian National Bank used the gold to stabilize its shaky currency. Thanks to those resources, and revenues earned from the Romanization of Jewish assets, the finance minister was able to declare in May 1943 that the state "has since October 1, 1942, no longer had to tap the national bank"—in other words, print more money.[64] In return for the gold and the Swiss francs, the Reich received fuel and foodstuffs. The Romanian Finance Ministry also issued leu notes for the wages and upkeep of German soldiers. As spelled out in the transcript of the negotiations, the purpose of these transactions was to stabilize the Romanian currency and to enable "the issuance of additional currency in the German interest." In return, and after consultations with German representatives, Romania pledged to increase its 1943 petroleum exports to Germany and Italy to 4 million tons. In addition, Romania was to provide "at least 15,000 tons of oil cake as well as 90,000 tons of oil seed" for the cooking needs of German housewives and to contribute, retroactively to October 1, 1942, 525 million lei a month to the Wehrmacht to pay for a raise in soldiers' wages.[65]

On February 9, 1944, after a personal order from Hitler, Germany assured Romania that it would pay for future "deliveries of grain with shipments of gold." An official at the Reich Finance Ministry noted of this guarantee: "The Führer must have had political reasons." Accordingly, 10.3 tons of gold were to be transferred to the Romanian National Bank's depository at the Swiss National Bank. Shortly before Romania switched sides in the war in August 1944, however, the government in Bucharest insisted that "equivalent values in currency or gold" be paid, if Germany made any further demands for its many soldiers stationed in the country. The chief German negotiator balked, but in the end he declared his country willing "to transfer a further 20 million Swiss francs of gold to Romania," if that country continued to provide the German populace with grain and legumes (*Hülsenfrüchte*).[66]

Although the gold transactions were kept top secret, regent Miklós Horthy in neighboring Hungary got word of them. When Germany occupied Hungary on March 19, 1944, he complained: "They'll simply cart everything off and they won't be paying in gold, as they do with the Romanians, but with their worthless paper money."[67] That was in fact what happened in Hungary, for the most part. The Germans paid in pengö, not in marks, and, as recounted above, they helped Hungary's financial administrators underwrite some of the occupation costs with proceeds from Jewish assets. The latter tactic drew no objection from Horthy.

CHAPTER 10

The Trail of Gold

Inflation in Greece

At the beginning of 1944, the Wehrmacht made a failed attempt to deport 8,000 Jews from Athens to Auschwitz. Without much assistance from local authorities, the relatively weak units of occupying German soldiers were able to round up only about 1,200 people. By contrast, the occupiers succeeded in deporting nearly all the Jews of Salonika, where Greek officials cooperated with their German occupiers.

For centuries, Salonika had been a mixed Turkish-Bulgarian-Greek-Jewish city. As late as the 1910s, its residents had used Ladino, the language of Sephardic Jews, as their lingua franca. Between 1912 and 1941, Salonika's Jewish community lost tens of thousands of members through emigration prompted by growing Greek nationalism and economic misery. An entry in the 1927 *Jüdisches Lexikon* reads: "When Salonika became part of Greece, moves were made to force Jews out of prominent positions in society. . . . The exchange of refugees with Turkey [1922] also led to the emigration of many Jews, who were compelled to make room for Greek refugees returning from Turkey." In the eyes of local Jews, it seemed that "the new arrivals brought anti-Semitism with them." Even as far back as 1912, the new Greek city government had tried to expropriate Jewish cemeteries in the center of town. Its attempts failed, but the properties were confiscated in 1942 and 1943 under the German occupation. Today, the local university occupies those sites.

To this day, many Greeks continue to suffer from selective memory when it comes to the fate of their Jewish fellow citizens. A documentary volume published in English by the Greek Foreign Ministry in 1998 talks about the philo-Semitism of Eleftherios Venizelos, modern Greece's most influential politician, whose government was the first in Europe to call for an independent Jewish state. But the 1927 *Jüdisches Lexikon* leaves no doubt that Venizelos adopted his position "in an effort to 'de-Jewify' and Hellenize Salonika."[1]

This aspect of the deportation of Salonika's Jews is well known; what is less well known—indeed ignored in the literature of the Holocaust—is the joint German and Greek exploitation of the assets of those Jews. Here, too, there is a connection between the enormous occupation costs the Germans imposed on its defeated enemy and the attempt to stabilize the local currency through the Aryanization of Jewish property. Some twelve tons of gold belonging to Jews from Salonika were sold for this latter purpose. Those involved in the transactions, both German and Greek, maintained absolute silence after the war about what they had done with the stolen gold. It requires painstaking detective work—and a host of footnotes—to reconstruct this historical episode.

IN 1941, the population of Greece numbered more than 7 million. The cost of living had risen steadily between 1930 and 1940, but at a relatively moderate rate of some 5 percent annually.[2] Greece was a poor country, still trying to cope with the effects of the Greek-Turkish war, which included mass deportations and resettlements. Prior to the German invasion, the gross national product totaled 60 billion drachmas, the equivalent of only around 1 billion reichsmarks. On April 27, 1941, after a brief military campaign, German troops occupied Athens. Together with their Italian and Bulgarian allies, they divided the country into three occupation zones. The largest was put under Italian administration, and some northern regions were controlled by the Bulgarians. The Germans occupied other important regions in and around Salonika, Attica, and Crete.[3]

From the time of the invasion until November 1943, career diplomat Günther Altenburg served as Reich envoy in Greece. But the real power rested with Hitler's special deputy for southeastern Europe, Hermann Neubacher. On October 5, 1942, he was given supplementary authority over economics and finance in occupied Greece. His official title was special envoy to the Führer for Greece. The two offices were combined in the fall of 1943, when the diplomat Hans Graevenitz succeeded Altenburg, but Neubacher continued to pull the strings in the background.

The main importance of Greece was strategic, since it could be used as a base for launching attacks on the Royal Navy. German paratroopers had taken Crete in the final days of May 1941, and they had designs on Malta and Cyprus, whose capture would have spelled the end of Britain's naval and air presence in the eastern Mediterranean. The Germans failed in their attempts to gain those two strongholds, but they were able to retain possession of Crete. As the tide of war began to turn against Germany in 1942, enormous sums of Greek drachmas were spent on fortifying the island.

Greek tobacco became more and more important economically and as a means of boosting morale on the home front. By the spring of 1942, 270,000 tons of Greek tobacco had been sent to Germany, and administrators in the Foreign Office announced that they had acquired an additional 600,000 tons. The total amount dramatically exceeded the annual demands of German smokers and promised to yield almost 2.5 billion reichsmarks in tobacco taxes for the Reich treasury.[4] Other major import products included chromium and other metallic ores, olive oil, currants, and silk for the production of parachutes. Transport was organized by the Schenker company, which enjoyed a monopoly in Greece. Schenker's representative in Salonika also served as a spy for the Security Service.[5]

Even during peacetime, Greece had been required to import food, but the war cut off all the country's trade routes. The domestic market was immediately shaken when Bulgaria was given control over fertile regions in the north, while German troops also took whatever they could from the land.[6] In the first few months of the occupation, the Greek currency

began to lose its value—a fact that the Reich Finance Ministry registered with alarm in 1942.

In a ten-page letter to his ministerial colleagues responsible for matters of war, von Krosigk cited Greece as an example of the potential economic perils of military occupation. Von Krosigk entitled his missive "More Efficient Organization of Financial Relations with Non-German Territories in the Interest of Securing an Optimal Wartime Economy." In it, he described the dangerous consequences of rejoicing too long in the success of the blitzkrieg and failing to develop sensible financial and occupation policies. "Inflation," he argued, "means the total disintegration of the economic system. On the one hand, it leads to drastic reductions in productivity. It also leads the populace to hold goods and merchandise off the market, as the Romanian peasants did their grain. It completely undermines any sort of economic planning for the country in question."[7]

In July 1942, Hitler expressed his concern to Mussolini that Greece was "on the verge of a financial—and with it an economic and political—catastrophe."[8] In September, the Finance Ministry repeatedly drew attention to the imminent collapse of the Greek currency. If the situation was allowed to continue, a ministry official warned, "it would not only cause the ruin of the Greek economy" but also deny the occupying powers any "normal opportunity for purchasing goods or utilizing services" in Greece. It had already become "significantly more difficult to carry out tasks essential to the war effort there."[9] A series of strikes by blue-collar workers and white-collar civil servants in Greece led government officials in both Rome and Berlin to conclude that drastic action had to be taken. In light of the "intolerable consequences of the decline in purchasing power" in Greece, Hitler ordered in the first half of September that "efforts be made to combat all major causes of the problem."[10] Hitler's decree left the concrete measures up to the discretion of his economists.

The causes of inflation in Greece included the country's general economic weakness, the lack of a professional financial administration, and the wartime disruption of the country's key source of income, commercial seafaring. But the most important cause by far was the unrestrained plundering of Greece by both German and Italian troops. According to estimates from the Wehrmacht's economics staff in Greece, plundering wiped out "some 40 percent of real Greek income" in 1941. A year later, "occupation costs and state expenditures accounted for around 90 percent of real gross domestic income."[11]

With the continuing devaluation of the drachma, agricultural products began to disappear from shops and farmers' markets, which were subject to price controls, and increasingly popped up on the black market. As a result, agricultural production declined. In the winter of 1941–42, the poorer segments of the Greek population were already suffering from food shortages. Göring commented: "We can't be overly concerned with starving Greeks. That's a misfortune that will befall many other peoples."[12] Göring's flagrant indifference came in the wake of horrific newspaper reports. "Children are dying by the thousands," wrote one witness. "Roadside ditches are becoming their graves, children search through piles of refuse in the street for scraps to eat, and parents keep the deaths of their children secret from the authorities. Mothers toss the bodies of their dead babies over the walls of cemeteries in order to keep the infants' food ration cards."[13]

German politicians could afford to ignore this side of war. But they couldn't ignore the "plight" of their own troops. Wages paid in drachmas soon had hardly any purchasing power at all. Soldiers complained, and many began to exchange military supplies on the black market for daily necessities.[14] In January 1942, a survey of soldiers' correspondence revealed that the authors of "60 percent of all letters" were concerned with getting goods and money "in order to achieve profits from the exchange or sale of merchandise at several times the original purchase price."[15]

It was to combat such an economic collapse that Hitler appointed Neubacher his special emissary in Greece at the beginning of October 1942. Ever optimistic, the German leadership saw the appointment as a short-term expedient "since in 1943 it is assumed there will be a new [i.e., more advantageous] military and political situation in the Mediterranean sphere."[16] Mussolini, for his part, appointed a special emissary for Italy's occupation zone: a man named D'Agostino, who was a diplomatic envoy and a bank director with experience in economic restructuring. After a

preliminary conference in Rome, D'Agostino met with Neubacher on October 24, 1942, in Athens. They agreed "to curtail purchases made by Axis troops on the Greek market, to temporarily suspend all food exports, and to activate transports of food to the country." In addition, they promised "to improve supplies of cooking oil for the population as quickly as possible" and—significantly—to institute a temporary hiatus on payments to occupation troops.[17]

Neubacher pledged to provide the Greek populace "with the basic necessities of life at prices affordable to people of all social classes."[18] To combat inflation, credit was to be restricted, and price controls, which had proved ineffective anyway, were to be lifted in order to bring prices on the free market back to at least a semblance of normality. A Greek law also required joint-stock companies to increase their capitalization by 20 percent (the money that was collected from investors went directly into the state treasury). To stimulate production, a law was also passed requiring all able-bodied Greeks to work.[19]

Neubacher used a variety of sometimes unconventional methods to fulfill his promises. He had food imported from occupied Serbia, as well as from Bulgaria and Romania. He also enlisted the International Red Cross to deliver aid to Greece. This initiative, which was tolerated by Britain and actively supported by Sweden and Switzerland, was a major coup that stabilized the Axis occupation. Soon Swedish ships full of Canadian wheat were regularly calling at Greek ports.[20] Neubacher even arranged for 8 million reichsmarks' worth of sugar and potatoes to be purchased in Germany for Greece, turning over the proceeds in drachmas from this transaction to the Wehrmacht. A short time later, the Finance Ministry raised the sum of money allotted for such purchases by 3.2 million reichsmarks.[21] Schwerin von Krosigk added a further 4.3 million marks for the expansion of economically important roads, breaking with the policy that such construction was to be paid for by the occupied country itself.[22] Neubacher did not cut soldiers' pay, but he forbade them from receiving money from home. Eventually, soldiers were paid half in drachmas and half in so-called canteen money, vouchers that were valid only in German military commissaries.[23]

Neubacher's resolution to supply German troops in Greece "wherever possible from Germany, Italy, or third-party countries" would ultimately become linked to the deportation of Jews from Salonika. In the early phase of the occupation, packed freight trains traveled to Greece and returned empty, except for occasional loads of ore and tobacco. It was these empty freight cars that would transport Greek Jews to death camps in Central Europe.[24]

The Jews of Salonika

Neubacher's interventions helped bring relative stability to the drachma, but his package of measures accelerated the ghettoization, dispossession, and deportation of Jews. Discriminatory policies began immediately after the special emissary's arrival in Greece. Few administrative documents from the German occupation of Greece have been preserved, but the connection between the deportation of Jews and the fight against inflation can be persuasively demonstrated.[25] The travel expenses submitted by legation counselor Eberhard von Thadden, the Foreign Office official responsible for "Jewish questions," provide one piece of corroborating evidence. Immediately after Hitler charged Neubacher with the "special mission of stabilizing economic conditions in Greece," von Thadden visited Athens for "several weeks." The Reichsbank also made it known that a "legation counselor" would be "accompanying emissary Neubacher."[26]

In the following months, von Thadden made frequent flights from Berlin to Athens, Bucharest, Rome, and Vienna. "In the places named," he wrote in claiming his travel expenses, "negotiations were held in conjunction with the operation of the Reich special emissary for Greece, to whom I was assigned."[27] From the start, then, the activities of the special emissary and the officials responsible for policy toward Greek Jews were conceptually linked.

Even more significant were the dates of von Thadden's trips. He left Berlin for Rome on October 18, 1942, and stayed in the city for talks with the Italian foreign minister until October 21. On October 23, he arrived in Athens, where he made his first public announcement the following day. With the exception of a short visit to Rome, he remained in Greece until November 30. On December 11, von Thadden flew from Berlin to Bucharest, where Neubacher was normally located, traveling on to Athens before returning to Berlin on December 22. On February 4, 1943, he made a train trip to "headquarters," Hitler's Wolfsschanze command center, staying until February 8.

The writer Felix Hartlaub was present and made a transcript of the conversations in the daily war registry of the Wehrmacht High Command. The topic of the meeting was the Wehrmacht's need for funds in Greece and the resulting friction between military leaders, on the one hand, and Neubacher and Altenburg, on the other. "To clear up these issues," Hartlaub wrote, "a conference was held on February 5 in restricted zone 1 [where Hitler resided] between representatives of the Foreign Office and the Wehrmacht. It was determined that 20.3 billion drachmas could be secured monthly and that Wehrmacht debts of 18 billion could be covered. Additionally, it was determined that construction projects could also be carried out with these sums."[28]

Neubacher, who also took part in the conference, agreed to pay Wehrmacht expenditures, which he had pressed to be kept at a minimum, in drachmas.[29] A few weeks previously, he had assured the government in occupied Greece that occupation costs would be "suspended." The contradiction between these two positions can be resolved by considering why the Foreign Ministry's point man for Jewish questions would have taken part in such high-level discussions.

The 20 billion drachmas a month that Neubacher had promised the Wehrmacht were equivalent to approximately 140,000 British gold pounds, or sovereigns. All in all, the twelve tons of gold plundered from the Jews of Salonika had a value of some 1.7 million sovereigns. Immediately after Neubacher's arrival in Greece in October 1942, the German occupiers began pressing for Salonika's Jews to be dispossessed. On January 3, 1943, Eichmann's deputy Rolf Günther flew to Salonika, presumably to help set policy toward Jews there. Meanwhile, Foreign Office undersecretary Martin Luther wrote to Altenburg in Athens that "Günther of course would be available to work with him." On January 26, Altenburg officially informed

Greek prime minister Konstantinos Logothetopoulos about the deportation plans. From Logothetopoulos's reaction, the veteran diplomat Altenburg judged that "difficulties" were "not to be expected."[30]

In early January 1943, Eichmann informed his assistant Dieter Wisliceny about an imminent initiative "to solve the Jewish question in Salonika in cooperation with the German military administration in Macedonia." One month later, Wisliceny and Alois Brunner arrived in Salonika as Eichmann's envoys. On February 6, 1943, Wehrmacht officer Max Merten, who was responsible for the local military administration, issued an order requiring all Jews to wear the Star of David and relocate to the city's ghetto. He also issued curfews and restrictions on communication.[31]

On March 1, 1943, Jewish families in and around Salonika were required, ostensibly for statistical purposes, to declare their total assets. Those affected by the rule had to fill out forms in Greek and German with lists of all valuables, including, under category F, "gold, precious metals, currency, and jewelry." On March 8, the Greek government established the "Office for the Management of Jewish Assets" (Yperesia Diacheiriseos Isrilitikis Periousias, or YDIP), headed by a lawyer named Elias Douros. The office was initially under the command of the German military administration; oversight was later transferred to the Greek Finance Ministry.[32] Greeks who purchased Jewish property were required to pay the sale price into account no. 707 at the Salonika branch of the Bank of Greece. German auditor Eberhard Kuhn monitored the account to ensure that "it benefited Greeks who are in some sense positively inclined toward Germans or have rendered various services for them."[33]

The deportations began on March 15, 1943, and were intended to "be concluded in six weeks' time."[34] (The process actually took somewhat longer.) In total, 43,850 Jews were deported from Salonika and a further 2,134 from surrounding areas under German occupation. Several thousand fled to Italian-controlled areas.[35] On March 16, Altenburg directed Wisliceny to provide Logothetopoulos with "an overview of the anti-Jewish measures." According to the German minutes of that meeting, Wisliceny was able to "fully convince [Logothetopoulos] and remove all doubts."[36] Thadden was also present in Greece for the crucial period of March 2 to April 4, further evidence of the close collaboration between officials responsible for Jewish matters and those working on fiscal policy.[37]

Some of the residences and household furnishings left behind by Jews were given to Greeks who had fled from Bulgarian-occupied areas of northern Greece.[38] The ancient Jewish cemetery at the center of Salonika was obliterated as part of the general dispossession of Jewish associations and religious institutions. The site, which encompassed 357,796 square meters, was quickly converted into available real estate, divided into lots, and auctioned off. Even the headstones were sold.[39]

As in other countries occupied by or allied with Nazi Germany, the Wehrmacht's seizure of private property had a single aim. Proceeds transferred into a central account at the national bank relieved inflationary pressure on the local currency, which had been caused by German greed. Such revenues obviated the need to print additional money. The sale of Jewish property helped absorb at least part of the excess consumer spending power that had accrued because of a lack of available goods. In the short term, however, this form of redistribution of wealth didn't greatly benefit either consumers or the national treasury. The expropriation procedure was too slow and cumbersome. Neubacher needed and achieved quick results. The assiduousness of the Wehrmacht in collecting gold in Salonika is obvious and well documented. Neubacher's interventions to stabilize Greek finances were directly linked to the deportations of 46,000 people to Auschwitz.

After the war, the exact workings of the deportation and expropriation process became clearer. In 2000, Heinz Kounio, the president of the Assembly of the Jewish Community of Thessaloniki (as Salonika is now known), explained the role of Max Merten, the Wehrmacht officer responsible for the fates of these people: "Merten was the most powerful man in the city. He told us, 'Bars of gold are the price [of survival].'" Several days before their deportation to Auschwitz, Jews were confined in a temporary concentration camp. "There they were required to hand over everything, including jewelry and all items of gold. From that moment on, the jewelry was gone. Merten and his assistants collected it in sacks."[40] Andreas Sefihas, president of the Jewish Council in Thessaloniki, told a similar story, also in 2000: "I alone had to pay [Merten] 1,000 gold British sterling in hope of winning my father's release from one of those camps."[41]

On October 17, 1942, a week before Hermann Neubacher's arrival in Greece, Merten demanded that the Jewish community hand over 10,000 gold pounds in return for the release of Jewish men from forced labor.[42] On October 21, after pressure from the Greek foreign minister to reduce occupation costs, Neubacher replied that "certain measures have already been undertaken." (Shortly before his arrival in Athens he had made the local Wehrmacht command lower expenditures.[43] He had already discussed the situation with the Wehrmacht High Command.)[44]

It was no accident that the Wehrmacht demanded that payments be made in gold. In July of that year, Merten had selected several thousand Jews for forced labor, employing them in the construction of roads and airstrips, in railroad maintenance, and in mining for ore. Their work was supervised by the Todt Organization, the Nazi public works authority, which often used slave labor. The authority needed forced Jewish labor because inflation had made it impossible to pay Greek workers. But there was no place to house the slave laborers, and most of them, according to one internal document, "had to sleep outside." Food, too, was in short supply, and "a great number of [Jews] developed lung infections and died." This was clearly an inefficient way to carry out construction projects, and so on October 17, 1942, Merten revoked the order forcing Jews to do slave labor. Instead, he demanded ransom in the form of gold. Gold could be stored as a hedge against inflation and could be sold on the gold exchange, its wartime value having appreciated, on the day the wage laborers had to be paid.[45]

In early November, Merten demanded 3.5 billion drachmas from the Jewish community, which were to be paid directly to the Wehrmacht. He later reduced the amount to 2.5 billion but stipulated that it be paid in gold. According to the terms of the agreement Merten dictated to the Jewish community, the gold was to be delivered in installments of 5,000 British pounds by December 15, 1942.

In total, the Wehrmacht squeezed 25,000 gold pounds from Jews in Salonika to meet its operating costs for November and December 1942. According to figures from the German commissioner at the Bank of Greece, Paul Hahn, that was the equivalent of 500,000 reichsmarks.[46] The coins were sold on the gold exchange and thereby converted into paper money, which went to pay the wages of German soldiers and Greek workers performing services for the Wehrmacht. On January 11, 1943, a Todt Organization official, reporting on construction projects, wrote: "As I have already stated, the military commander has promised Salonika-Aegean [divisions] a half billion drachmas, as soon as the sum has been raised by the Jewish community. He was not, however, able to name a precise date."[47] After the war, Merten also openly admitted using proceeds from the sale of Salonika's Jewish cemetery to pay Greeks working for the German occupiers.[48] In 1943, the Reich Economics Ministry stated that in late 1942 wages for road construction and the mining of ore in northern Greece "had been made available from what was then an unknown source. It later emerged that these funds were money that had been raised from Greek Jews."[49]

THE REICH's initial measures in Greece had a haphazard quality; theft on a grand scale commenced with the ghettoization of Jews in March 1943. Using spies and torture, Eichmann's henchmen—Brunner, Wisliceny, and their staff—compelled defenseless people to confess where they had hidden jewelry and money. "Thus," writes historian Michael Molho, "the cellars in Vélissariou Street [in Salonika] were filled with a treasure trove like that of Ali Baba. Atop the tables were neat piles of rings with diamonds and gemstones of all colors and sizes, brooches, medallions, armbands, gold chains, wedding rings, watches of all sorts, coins sorted according to stamp and date, American and Canadian dollars, British pounds, Swiss francs, etc. On the floor were heaps of vases, Chinese porcelain, rare objects, and rugs. Crammed into a relatively confined space was a surfeit of riches that Alexandre Dumas himself, with all his imagination, couldn't have pictured reflected in the eyes of the Count of Monte Cristo."[50]

After the war, the Jewish community of Salonika estimated that some 130 million marks in gold and jewelry had been stolen from them. That would be the equivalent of forty-six tons of gold. A more conservative and thorough estimate was made by the historian Joseph Nehama in 1946. Nehama calculated that the Germans plundered "the impressive amount of more than twelve tons of pure gold" from Greek Jews.[51] That figure corresponds exactly to the "most moderate calculation" made by the World Jewish Congress in 1948 of 1.7 million gold pounds.[52]

Since gold was not the only type of valuable stored in Vélissariou Street, the actual worth of the stolen property would have been far greater. In all likelihood, some of this property was sold to Greeks for more gold. The figure of twelve tons seems about right. According to records from the Bank of Greece in 1944, the occupation costs for June 1942 amounted to 250,000 gold pounds. Taking this figure as the monthly average for the following twelve months, Greece would have had to pay exactly 3 million gold pounds in occupation costs. But the bank's figures show that drachmas with a value of only 1.26 million gold pounds were handed over to the Germans. There was thus a shortfall of 1.74 million gold pounds to cover the Wehrmacht's running costs. That is almost exactly the sum arrived at by the World Jewish Congress in 1948.[53]

So where did the gold end up? It was only on June 15, 1943, several weeks after the deportations, that Merten ordered "the sum total of Jewish assets secured, or to be secured in the near future, in Salonika-Aegean transferred to the Greek state as represented by the governor general of Macedonia."[54] In his testimony before a war-crimes tribunal in 1964, however, Merten said that the gold remained in German hands. Reich emissary Altenburg then ordered it transported to Athens and brought to the German consulate. Statements made by the usually precise Wisliceny also point toward Athens.[55] According to Wisliceny, Mertens "deposited money, jewelry, and similar items at the Bank of Greece." Wisliceny also testified that some 280 million drachmas in cash had been deposited "in a general account at the Bank of Greece," from which the money then went to the German military commander.[56] A statement by an assistant of Eichmann's, Otto Hunsche, corroborates Wisliceny's postwar testimony.

In a dispute over how to pay for the transport of 46,000 people from Salonika to Auschwitz, which cost 1,938,488 reichsmarks, Hunsche insisted that the "confiscated wealth of the Jews" be allocated not to the SS but to "the military commander of the Aegean [military administration] in Salonika."[57]

Nazi Germany may also have sent a small portion of the precious metals plundered from Greece to Vienna. (Shipments may have included platinum, which was desperately needed for industrial purposes, or silver, which was required by the flourishing German film industry.) This author was unable to find any German documents proving that such deliveries took place. But Jacques Stroumsa, who was forced to board a train for Auschwitz with his family in 1943, recalls in his autobiography a stop, "probably at a small train station near Vienna, when the train doors suddenly opened" and Alois Brunner motioned for him and his brother to get out. "When we reached his compartment in a normal train car," Stroumsa wrote, "he commanded us to carry a heavy wooden crate, followed by a second, equally heavy one, over to the main entrance of the station. Immediately thereafter, the train went on."[58]

It remains unclear why most of the gold from Salonika was transferred to Athens. The most likely theory is that it was to stabilize the inflationary drachma—with the cooperation of the Greek Finance Ministry and the Bank of Greece—in the period before November 1943. Three personnel decisions support this hypothesis. First, from October 1942 to February 1943, the beginning of the Nazi intervention in currency policies, the German commissioner at the Banque de France, Carl Schaefer, was assigned to Athens to work with Paul Hahn.[59] Schaefer had gained valuable experience curbing inflation in France. Second, in January 1943, after the governor of the Bank of Greece was forced to resign, he was replaced by a cooperative deputy governor named Hadjikyriakos.[60] And third, Neubacher appointed a new finance minister and minister without portfolio, Hektor Tsironikos, whose "friendliness toward Germany was beyond question." He was soon put in charge of the Social Services, Health, Economics, Labor, and Agriculture Ministries, since he "possessed the complete and utter trust of the special emissary."[61]

It appears that, with cooperation from Hadjikyriakos and Tsironikos, Greek brokers sold off the gold looted from the Jews of Salonika at the exchange in Athens. They accepted payment in huge sums of paper drachmas, with which the Wehrmacht then covered its expenditures. In this way, inflation could be checked or at least slowed for a few months and prices could be kept stable.[62] As a result of such transactions, most of the gold of the murdered Jews of Salonika would have ended up in the hands of Greek gold traders and speculators, while Germans used the drachmas to pay for Greek goods and services and to pay German soldiers' wages. To support this thesis, it's necessary to present a chain of evidence. The first links in this chain are the discussions and decisions that led the Reichsbank to deliver gold to Greece in the latter half of 1943.

Gold on the Athens Exchange

In mid-June 1943, at a "departmental meeting on Greece," ministerial director Friedrich Gramsch, acting as Göring's representative, was quoted as saying that he didn't think the use of gold and currency was "at the time practical for the acquisition of services in Greece." But Neubacher, who also took part in the meeting, insisted on "returning, if necessary, to this question in the course of developments" that could not be determined that day.[63] September saw a rapid deterioration in the currency situation, which had been relatively stable since the preceding December. This prompted Hans Graevenitz to contact Neubacher by telegram with a request for gold. "In order to stage an effective intervention," he wrote, "a temporary allocation of further resources would be advisable."[64] (The word "further" belies claims Graevenitz would make in self-defense after the war that at that point no gold had been appropriated.) As a temporary measure to shore up the drachma, the "military commander, with the support of the special emissary of the Foreign Office for Southeastern Europe," confiscated the entire assets of Athens's 8,000 Jews and transferred them "for administration to the Greek state."[65]

Initially Berlin refused to send any more gold, and inflation continued to rise in Greece, causing morale problems among German soldiers, whose pay was no longer sufficient to purchase all the things they wanted to buy. On November 13, 1943, the Luftwaffe's Southeast High Command sent a telegram to Göring's staff: "The German soldier sees that price gouging is going on with food that he himself cannot afford because he is not being given enough money. Occasional pay raises such as the one on November 11 are viewed as completely pointless. The German soldier would like to be able to purchase food in the area where he is serving, at least at Christmas, in order to send it back home to his family, since those on the home front suffer more from the war than the Greek population. The necessary consequence, since he is not able to purchase it normally, is black market wheeling and dealing of the most odious sort." The general who wrote this communiqué called for "energetic measures" aimed at allowing his men "to send [at least] Christmas gifts back home."[66]

On November 8, a few days before the soldiers' complaints reached Göring's office, the topic had already been discussed at a high-level departmental meeting. Participating along with Neubacher were the economics minister, the finance minister, and the managing director and president of the Reichsbank, as well as Göring's confidant Gramsch. Among a number of further measures they decided on to stabilize the Greek currency was the use of Reich gold reserves, which had been tried out in January 1943 in Romania. Beginning in November, the Reichsbank regularly transferred gold—a total of more than eight tons—to Athens via its Vienna branch. The deliveries were made by courier plane. By strategically selling off that gold, Reich officials responsible for the Greek economy were able to create a measure of stability for the inflationary drachma.[67]

The deliveries began ten days after the November 8 meeting. Previously announced price hikes in Greece were canceled, and Wehrmacht intendants were instructed "to temporarily postpone nonessential purchases."[68] A portion of the money saved went toward giving dissatisfied soldiers a substantial pay raise in December.[69] The curb on spending did not stop but did help slow inflation. Neubacher sanctimoniously promised that, while Greece would have to pay certain top-priority contributions in advance, the money would be debited to the occupiers. (He would later boast that because he had "kept this promise general enough, without specifying a repayment deadline or an interest rate," the Reich had taken on no "inordinate commitments.")[70] By the end of the German occupation of Greece, however, despite the airlift of gold and efforts to rein in spending, inflation was running at no less than 550 million percent.[71]

Yet despite hyperinflation, which caused the drachma to collapse in the summer of 1944, the commissioner in charge of monitoring the Bank of Greece, Reichsbank director Paul Hahn, argued in his final report that he had succeeded in "preserving the drachma's viability as a means of payment for as long as possible." Doing so, Hahn added, had been "a matter of fundamental concern for the German Wehrmacht."[72]

After the war, those who had been responsible for the transfer of gold cited it as evidence of their humanitarian compassion. "In the middle of November [1943]," wrote Neubacher in his memoirs, "I began the gold campaign at the Athens exchange. . . . The Greeks were utterly surprised. No one had thought it possible that Germany would put gold on the market."[73] Hahn described his own activities in similarly glowing terms. The Greeks, he wrote, had viewed the "flow of gold owned by the German occupiers" as a political act that compared favorably "with earlier financial aid measures from foreign countries," such as Britain. The campaign, Hahn boasted, "earned respect and appreciation within Greek economic and financial circles."

Those circles, it must be pointed out, had turned a tidy profit from the gold transactions. Many leading Greek businessmen served as brokers and bought up tranches of gold at exchanges in Athens, Salonika, and, to a lesser extent, Patras. According to Hahn, the Reich turned to trusted Greek brokers to handle the sales. Transactions were carried out "via the Bank of Greece."[74]

Hahn's final report, written in the winter of 1944–45, summed up his three years as German bank commissioner at the Bank of Greece. That report was published, in slightly revised form, in 1957. His account contains an extensive description of the gold campaign. A careful examination of the document (see pp. 262–263), however, reveals that the first deliveries did not date from November 18, 1943, as a number of later apologists and Hahn himself in the text of the report claimed, but rather from February 4, 1943. In addition, Hahn divided gold received into several rubrics. A set of columns at the bottom of the page lists deliveries, most of them after November 1943. They are described as having been "dispatched" from the Reichsbank to Athens. (At this point the Reichsbank was working almost exclusively with looted gold.)

But Hahn's first set of figures records shipments starting on February 4, 1943, and continuing until September 21, 1943. The amounts begin to decline in May. Hahn noted vaguely that the figures corresponded to shipment "lists" in Berlin and Vienna and that the gold had been "received" in Athens. There is no indication, however, as there is in the second set of figures, that the gold had been "dispatched" from Berlin to Athens. Consequently, there is no hint about the gold's original source. In a draft version of Hahn's report, a reader noticed the seeming discrepancy, circling the column of figures from February to September 1943 and writing "1944?" in the margin.[75]

Hahn didn't make that correction. The inconsistency, together with the general secrecy surrounding the sale of gold prior to November 18, 1943, gives rise to the suspicion that the first set of figures refers to gold owned by the Jews of Salonika. The deliveries of gold from the Reichsbank, which only commenced in earnest in November 1943, totaled 324,000 gold pounds and 5,112,570 gold francs. The amounts Hahn recorded between February and September of that year were significantly higher: 455,000 gold pounds and 9,340,290 gold francs.[76] According to Hahn's final report, the Reichsbank dispatched, "all in all, some 24 million" reichsmarks' worth of gold.[77] At the rate of 2.8 million reichsmarks per ton, the total would be equivalent to 8.6 tons. If one uses this standard for the period from February to September, German economists must have allocated at least twelve tons of gold during that period to prop up the drachma. This figure is nearly identical to the amount of gold plundered in Salonika, as estimated by Joseph Nehama. There can be little doubt that the Salonika gold and Hahn's unidentified shipments are one and the same.[78]

Neubacher and Hahn's intervention, using gold plundered from Jewish households, had the immediate effect of stabilizing the Greek currency.

Ausweislich der Bücher des Bankenkommissars, dessen Bu-
chungen mit den listenmässigen Aufgaben der Reichshauptstadt
Berlin und der Reichsbankhauptstelle Wien übereinstimmen, sind
in Athen folgende Goldtransporte eingegangen:

			Goldpfund	Goldfrancs
4.	2.	1943	48.000	1.250.000
28.	2.	"	63.000	---
2.	3.	"	33.000	800.000
3.	3.	"	-	1.700.000
3.	4.	"	50.000	---
13.	4.	"	33.000	480.000
14.	4.	"	33.000	480.000
8.	5.	"	50.000	800.000
9.	6.	"	50.000	700.000
3.	7.	"	50.000	560.000
5.	7.	"	-	640.000
31.	7.	"	45.000	640.000
2.	8.	"	-	510.290
29.	8.	"	-	480.000
21.	9.	"	-	300.000
			455.000	9.340.290

Ferner sind nach Aufgabe der
Reichshauptbank Berlin folgende
Sendungen nach Athen abgegangen,
deren Eingänge im einzelnen man-
gels vorhandener Unterlagen von
der Dienststelle nicht mehr geprüft
werden können

x Von Berlin nur im	5. 2.	1943	4.000		22.570
RM-Betrage v.1Mio.	15.11.	"	6.000		140.000
angegeben	17.11.	"	50.000	x	1.200.000
x1 Von Berlin nur im	2.12.	"	50.000		-
RM-Betrage v.1,4 Mio	9.12.	"	70.000	x1	-
angegeben	29.12.	"	48.000		1.250.000
	3. 1.	1944	48.000		1.250.000
	20. 1.	"	48.000		1.250.000

Mithin sind für die Dienststelle
Athen insgesamt eingegangen: £ 779.000 Fr.14.452.860

Im Ablauf der Aktion sind noch L 5.934 Fr. 11.700
durch Interventionskäufe am
Athener Markt dem Bestand zu-
geführt worden

Excerpt from Paul Hahn's final report about his activities as Reichsbank commissioner in Greece, April 12, 1945. See translation on next page.

According to the records of the bank commissioner, whose entries correspond to task lists from the Reich capital in Berlin and the main office of the Reichsbank in Vienna, the following shipments of gold were received in Athens:

	Gold pounds	Gold francs
4. 2. 1943	48.000	1.250.000
28. 2. "	63.000	---
2. 3. "	33.000	800.000
3. 3. "	-	1.700.000
3. 4. "	50.000	---
13. 4. "	33.000	480.000
14. 4. "	33.000	480.000
8. 5. "	50.000	800.000
9. 6. "	50.000	700.000
3. 7. "	50.000	560.000
5. 7. "	-	640.000
31. 7. "	45.000	640.000
2. 8. "	-	510.290
29. 8. "	-	480.000
21. 9. "	-	300.000
	455.000	9.340.290

Moreover, according to information from the Reichsbank in Berlin, the following shipments were dispatched to Athens. Their arrival could not be confirmed by the office because the relevant documents were missing.

x Listed in Berlin	5. 2. 1943	4.000		22.570
as the equivalent	15.11. "	6.000		140.000
value of 1 million	17.11. "	50.000	x	1.200.000
reichsmarks	2.12. "	50.000		-
x1 Listed in Berlin as	9.12. "	70.000	x1	-
the equivalent value of	29.12. "	48.000		1.250.000
1.4 million reichsmarks	3. 1. 1944	48.000		1.250.000
	20. 1. "	48.000		1.250.000

The office assumes that the following arrived in Athens:	L 779.000	Fr. 14.452.860

In the course of the operation, the following supplementary amounts were introduced to the Athens exchange via interventionary purchases:	L 5.934	Fr. 11.700

The Reichsbank's economists noted with satisfaction: "We were able to basically check the upward trend in prices." On May 19, 1943, a gold pound still cost only 249,000 drachmas, rising to 380,000 as the intervention began. Except for a single short spike, the exchange rate held steady. Only in late August did the value of the gold pound exceed its previous high against the drachma, in October 1942.[79] In the interval, the Wehrmacht intendant for German-occupied Greece was able to report that the economic situation had "largely settled down" and that prices had been drastically reduced relative to those of late 1942. Simultaneously, Neubacher cut the Wehrmacht's budget for expenditures by a third. But from September 21 to November 17, 1943, once the remainder of the gold plundered from Salonika's Jews had been sold off and the proceeds spent by the Wehrmacht, the price of a gold pound rocketed from 474,000 to 1,900,000 drachmas. On November 24, after the first delivery of gold from the Reichsbank, the price went back down to 900,000 drachmas.[80]

The infusions of gold between February and September 1943 were included in Hahn's balance sheet but not in the text of his final report. Neubacher suppressed them entirely from his memoirs and treated that period of his tenure in Greece with the utmost discretion. In late April 1943, Fritz Berger, a ministerial director in the Finance Ministry who apparently had not been informed about what was going on, addressed an urgent letter to the "Wehrmacht Finance Division, Greece." In it, he complained that Neubacher had reduced Greek contributions to the occupation costs by more than 85 percent. That move, Berger objected, "would lead to a dead end" and force the Reich to pick up the extra costs. Three weeks later, the chief intendant to the military commander in southeastern Europe, who was well aware of the true situation, received a telephone call and noted: "The subject of the urgent letter has been rendered obsolete after telephone negotiations by the special emissary with the relevant Berlin offices."[81] Clearly the Finance Ministry had been informed in the meantime about the rationale behind Neubacher's temporary concern for the Greek treasury—and his top-secret strategy for making up the Wehrmacht shortfall with the gold from the Jews of Salonika. It is likely that Nazi officials discussed the strategy only orally. No written record exists. In any case, by July 15, 1943, Berger acknowledged that "all [the Wehrmacht's] major needs have been met by emissary Neubacher, and the complaints registered in this regard were based on false suppositions and are therefore unjustified."[82]

Neubacher met those needs by selling gold on the Athens exchange. In July 1943, an officer of the economics command in Athens observed: "Speculation had driven the price of the [gold] pound up to 540,000 drachmas. The fact alone that emissary Neubacher spent a short time in Athens drove it back down to 400,000. Through the sale of small amounts of gold, the price was later further reduced to 340,000 drachmas."[83] That the price of gold fell with the mere arrival of Hitler's special emissary shows how much influence he had on the Greek gold exchange in July 1943; there had already been nine interventions by that point. In many ways, Neubacher's memoirs echo the story told by Paul Hahn, but with one crucial difference: Neubacher moved the gold transfers forward in time so that they would fall within the period of the official "gold campaign."[84]

German-Greek Silence

So it was that between October 1942 and September 1943 the German occupiers—assisted by the Greek finance minister, the Bank of Greece, and various "trusted brokers"—propped up the drachma using gold they had plundered from the Jews of Salonika. In so doing, they directly financed the German Wehrmacht.[85] "The point of the gold campaign," Neubacher recalled, "was as follows: The hard currency purchased was used to cover occupation costs. Consequently, pressure on the treasury to print more money was relieved." The campaign allowed Neubacher, despite heavy inflation, to maintain the Greek currency as a means of payment.[86] The Greek budget was also indirectly relieved of occupation costs.[87]

The dispossession of the Jews of Salonika was carried out to the direct financial benefit of German troops. As German bank commissioner Hahn concluded, "the main goal of the gold campaign" was to "raise the necessary means of payment for financing the Wehrmacht." Even today, more than sixty years after the war, Germans and Greeks who took part in the campaign refuse to acknowledge that at least three-fifths of it was funded by gold that belonged to Greek Jews. It's hardly surprising that they remain reluctant to discuss a scheme that masked—through innocuous-seeming transactions on the gold exchange—the dispossession of citizens of an occupied country for the welfare of the occupiers.

In an attempt at self-justification, Hahn published his final report of 1944–45 as a monograph in 1957. There he confirmed that international law had been violated but tried to shift the responsibility, noting: "The entire gold campaign was in the hands of the bank commissioner, who also had sole responsibility for administering inventories of gold"—including gold from the Jews of Salonika.[88] According to German military reports, "between two-thirds and three-fourths" of the occupation costs during the gold campaign were "covered by the gold proceeds."[89] That was also true during the first, unofficial phase of the campaign—only in that case the gold in question represented the assets of 46,000 Jews from northern Greece, almost all of whom were murdered in Auschwitz.

The transactions remained so secret that, after the war, there was no need for either Germans or Greeks to deny them. No one asked where the gold had gone. Instead, for decades, the public chose to believe a story told by Max Merten to a fellow prisoner while serving time in a Greek jail in 1957. According to Merten, the gold of the Jews of Salonika—a veritable "hoard of the Nibelungs"—had been lost at sea. This tall tale, which was repeated by Neubacher, Hahn, and Altenburg, convinced even the legendary Nazi hunter Simon Wiesenthal, who in 1971 sued representatives of the Greek government in a Vienna court for 100,000 deutschmarks "for his help in discovering a fortune in gold and platinum that was carried off by the Germans from Greece in World War II." (The representatives successfully argued that "Wiesenthal's information in this matter was worthless.")[90] Even as late as 2000, Merten's story was still taken seriously. That year, professional divers searched the ocean floor near the southwestern tip of the Peloponnesus for a fishing boat containing the "Jewish treasure" of Salonika, which Merten claimed to have intentionally sunk there. A conflict soon arose as to who would claim the treasure, depending on whether it was found in national or international waters. Speculation about the value of this sunken treasure—"more than $2 billion," according to reports by both the BBC and CNN in August 2000—was as baseless as the story itself.[91]

After the war, it must have been common knowledge in Athens financial circles where the gold had gone. It had neither been sunk at sea nor carted off to Germany. Most of it had remained in Greece, where it had changed hands for money. A 1998 volume entitled *Documents on the History of the Greek Jews* draws on the archive of the Greek Foreign Ministry, but it only really begins in 1944; the gap could be filled by publishing the relevant documents from the archives of the Reich Finance Ministry and the Bank of Greece and the papers of the major Greek collaborators. The main decrees leading to the dispossession of Greek Jews between 1942 and 1943 deserve to be carefully documented. Particularly important would be the agreements struck by the Greek government with Hahn, Schaefer, Neubacher, and Altenburg regarding the stabilization of the drachma.

Without a public reckoning of this sort, the reputations of the civil servants involved remain untarnished. On July 18, 1960, the *Frankfurter Allgemeine Zeitung* published a letter to the editor marking Neubacher's death. It was written by the historian Percy Ernst Schramm. The headline read, "Recollections of Dr. Neubacher." Schramm wrote: "The world has become poorer today because a person has taken his leave of us who, while he may have engaged with the Nazis, never sold himself; a person who knew how to survive even under the most terrible circumstances and in the end found an opportunity to show just what he could do."

From Rhodes to Auschwitz

In the summer of 1944, a few weeks before most German troops withdrew from Greece, 1,673 Jews from Rhodes and 94 from the neighboring island of Kos were loaded onto ships and deported via the port city of Piraeus. Their terrible journey began on July 24 and ended on August 16 in Auschwitz-Birkenau. Most standard reference works on the Holocaust—with the notable exception of those by Raul Hilberg—view this particular deportation as evidence of the blind racial hatred of Nazi policies since shipping Jews to the death camps was seemingly given priority over the safety and other interests of the retreating German troops.

"At a point in time," writes historian Hagen Fleischer, "when the Red Army was preparing to topple the Axis states in southeastern Europe like so many dominos, and when Army Group E was making its initial preparations for evacuation, [an act] that would necessitate abandoning valuable military material on the [Greek] peninsula, the waste of precious transport space along the sole, already overburdened line of retreat makes a mockery of any sort of strategic considerations."[92] Lea Rosh and Eberhard Jäckel also speculate that in Greece—the outermost fringe of Germany's sphere of power in July 1944—the "whole insanity of the Nazis" was revealed.[93]

Assertions like these may represent the prevailing wisdom, but they do not correspond either to the reality on the ground or to the military decision-making process. The deportation of 1,767 people, who were first put aboard small cargo ships and then onto a freight train, did not divert resources from the Wehrmacht's other transport needs. In fact, the military had its own interest in the deportations, which will now be described.

RHODES, WHICH sits in the Dodecanese chain of islands, was officially still part of Italy in 1943. Occupied by Germany in September of that year, after Italy switched over to the Allies, the island had 45,000 inhabitants. The local Italian administration remained in place, and the local branch of the Banca d'Italia was made responsible for organizing financial support for the German troops.[94] On May 10, 1944, the head of the Wehrmacht High Command gave the commanding officer of the extremely isolated Sturmdivision Rhodos the inflated title of commander of the eastern Aegean. The promotion order also defined the role of the island's intendant: "He is responsible for Wehrmacht-related administration, especially for supervising the exploitation of the countryside to meet the needs of the three branches of the Wehrmacht, including the acquisition and distribution of monetary resources. The intendant is subordinate to the Wehrmacht intendant of the Military High Command in Greece."[95]

In early June, the commandant of Crete informed Hitler that the heavily fortified island had "four months' worth of supplies" and needed only 1,500 tons of monthly replenishments. But Hitler, who wanted the island to have six months' worth of reserves, ordered that 6,000 tons of supplies be sent every month from Piraeus to Crete.[96] The situation was similar with Rhodes, which was also conceived as a bulwark. Most of the other German forces were being withdrawn from the Aegean Sea in what the German leadership kidded themselves into believing was a temporary retreat.

It was already clear by the second half of June that German troops on Crete and Rhodes—a total of some 70,000 men—would soon be cut off from their supply lines. Their military mission was "to offer the greatest possible resistance to the enemy, even in isolation, to sacrifice themselves to buy time and occupy enemy forces."[97] For several weeks, the Wehrmacht tried to replenish supplies of food, vehicles, weapons, and munitions by sea. Most German supply ships that were able to make the perilous voyage returned to Piraeus with empty holds. Fuel shortages, the superiority of British warplanes and submarines, and heavy air raids on the ports of Piraeus and Salonika increasingly limited the number of journeys that could be made. Short nights under clear, moonlit skies didn't make the undertaking any easier.[98] It made practical sense to use the ships' cargo capacity to maximum effect. On June 8, the Jewish population of Crete—around 300 people—was herded onto a ship bound for Piraeus. They died, along with some 200 other prisoners, when the ship came under enemy fire and was sunk.[99]

In the first weeks of July, the head of sea transport for the Aegean redirected ships from western Greece in order to "bring higher-priority supplies" to the Dodecanese.[100] From mid-June to July 10, German sailors succeeded in shipping 4,000 tons of supplies to Crete and 5,000 tons to Rhodes; subsequent deliveries brought additional supplies to the two outposts.[101]

While the Jews of Rhodes were being deported there was no talk of

German retreat. In fact, on July 31, the chief intendant in Greece, Werner Kersten, ordered an emergency program of repair for "ships indispensable for supplying the islands."[102] In August, 3,626 tons of supplies were received in the Dodecanese, mostly in Rhodes.[103] On September 6, 1944, the freighter *Pelikan* docked off the city of Rhodes with supplies from Piraeus.[104] All the ships involved in these deliveries sailed back to the mainland with empty holds.

In late August, a few days after Romania and Bulgaria changed sides and more than a month after the deportation of Jews from Rhodes, Hitler ordered occupying troops in mainland Greece to withdraw north and secure a line stretching from Corfu, in the northwest, through Ioánnina and Kalabáka, in north-central Greece, south to Olympia in the Peloponnesus.[105] Until then, contrary to Hagen Fleischer's assertion, German troops had few problems transporting weaponry and other material *out* of Greece. The real difficulty was moving supplies south *within* Greece: the fragile network of railways and roads leading south had been continually subjected to partisan attacks and disruptions at key points. The retreat north began after Hitler issued his order, which was forwarded to the various Wehrmacht units in Greece. Only then, a full month after the deportation of the Jews of Rhodes, was a second decree issued: "Use empty trains to transport materials to the north." Even at this late juncture the Wehrmacht had empty trains at its disposal. In his final report, under the heading "Transports toward Germany," the special deputy for Greece wrote that because of the relatively limited volume of cargo, "no difficulties" had arisen.[106] The "overburdened" lines of retreat claimed by many historians simply did not exist.

On August 28, the commanding admiral in the Aegean ordered that supplies continue to be sent to Rhodes and Crete. (The order, as other documents show, was never carried out.) Several days later, Hitler allowed the partial evacuation of the heavily fortified islands. For security reasons, the retreat was carried out via air. The planes carried fresh supplies for the 12,000 troops who were to remain behind on Crete and the 6,300 on Rhodes.[107] Their orders, communicated by telegraph, read: "If pickup impossible, battle to last bullet" to "free troops for operations on the mainland and defense of home front."[108] The evacuation continued into early October.

GERMAN COMMANDERS hadn't decreed any special anti-Jewish measures when they occupied Rhodes in September 1943—for the simple reason that they had no interest in doing so. But by July 13, 1944, the troops needed funds. It was then that Lieutenant General Ulrich Kleemann, the commandant of the eastern Aegean stationed on Rhodes, ordered Jews detained. The arrests were to be carried out within four days.[109] On July 13, the day of the order, three ships set sail from Portolago on the island of Leros, a night's sail from Rhodes, to pick up the detainees. The ships were forced to turn around "because of enemy positions," but they succeeded in making the journey, loaded with fresh supplies, on the night of July 20–21.[110] There were protests from the soldiers on Rhodes against the deportation order of July 13, and although it is not known what form it took, Kleeman found himself compelled to issue a second, explanatory order on July 16, aimed at combating "doubts." He tried to convince his troops of the necessity of a "radical solution to the Jewish question," about which ordinary soldiers were unqualified to pass judgment.[111] Almost all the island's Jews were rounded up within a few days.

Shipping agents in Portolago, where the deportation was organized, filed regular reports. According to one report, 96 Jews from the island of Kos arrived on July 24, followed the next evening by the Jews from Rhodes. The daily log read: "July 25: Wind NW, Speed: 6; Surf 4–5." There was a level 2 alert until "0400 hours, when the Jewish transport from Rhodes on the MS *Störtebeker, Horst,* and *Merkur* made port." The log continued: "Necessary provisions and water supplies for 1,750 Jews immediately provided for scheduled journey." Because of poor weather, the ships could not set sail again until July 28, and when they did the convoy had been expanded by two more ships and given a military escort. The log recorded: "2030 hours MS *Horst, Störtebeker, Merkur, Seeadler,* and *Seestern* embarked for Piraeus. 51 tons scrap, empty commercial containers, and 1,700 Jews."[112] The convoy made a stopover in Samos.

Between July 16 and 31, the period in which the Jews of Rhodes and Kos were taken to Piraeus, the head of the naval transport office on the nearby island of Leros filed a report listing the contents of one shipment. It read: "(1) supplies from the mainland: 1,599 tons, 4 trucks; 14.7 centimeters packages, 2 soldiers; (2) to the mainland: 216 tons, 1,750 Jews."[113] (These figures and the ones that follow show small discrepancies in the number of deportees, which are due to deaths in transit and imprecision in counting.) In his fortnightly review, the head of the central transport office in Piraeus reported the arrival of fourteen motorized boats with the following, extremely light loads: "8 tons currants, 37 tons munitions, 82 tons coal, 37 tons equipment, 14 tons trade supplies, 298 tons empty containers and scrap, 33 soldiers, and 1,733 Jews." On August 1, "1 female Jew" arrived belatedly on the MS *Pelikan*.[114]

The historian Michael Molho describes the journey from the perspective of the deportees:

> On June 24, the detainees are crammed into three transport barges towed by a schooner. After a journey reminiscent of Dante's Inferno, they arrive in Piraeus, where they are handled roughly. Those who in the opinion of the navy watchmen are slow to disembark are brutally mistreated. An elderly woman is beaten so badly with a revolver that her brains splatter the surrounding detainees. Seven deportees have died at sea, twelve more are in the process of dying, and the rest are starved, thirsty, helpless, and exhausted. In Piraeus they are robbed of everything they have on them. Belts and shoe soles are searched, and whatever is concealed there confiscated. The brutish guards go so far as to search the private parts of helpless, horrified women. False teeth, bridges, and crowns are ripped from people's mouths. The booty is collected in four crates usually used for transporting cans of petroleum. The crates, suddenly converted into treasure chests, are filled to the top with jewelry, bars of gold, gold coins, and valuables of all kinds.[115]

Shortly after their arrival in Piraeus, the deportees boarded trains for Auschwitz. According to research carried out by survivors, a total of 1,673 Jews were deported from Rhodes and 94 from Kos. Twenty-one died in transit, 1,145 perished at Auschwitz, and 437 died in labor camps. Only 151 Jews from Rhodes and 12 from Kos survived.[116] In 1947, Rhodes had 60 Jewish inhabitants. Kos had one.[117]

THE DEPORTATION of the Jews of Rhodes seems at first glance to be a crime motivated solely by an insane ideology of racial genocide. Historical materials suggest, however, that the Wehrmacht organized the deportation because it fit in with their military aims and provided an immediate benefit. By the time the Jews of Rhodes arrived in Piraeus, the Wehrmacht was no longer able to make purchases in Italian liras, which were still legal tender on the island. The same was true for the drachma in nearby areas. The desperate financial situation explains the voracious appetite for gold, which led Wehrmacht members to rip it out of people's mouths. Along with exchangeable goods, gold was the only viable means of payment in Greece, as well as on Rhodes. In early July, the commanding admiral of the Aegean had demanded "payment of the balance [of occupation costs] in gold." Without it, he feared "a catastrophic effect on our defensive strength."[118] In October 1944, the Central Office of the Reich Credit Banks concluded that "the Wehrmacht authorities had great success in the period before their retreat [from Greece] by meeting their obligations with gold."[119]

The valuables so viciously stolen by German soldiers on July 31 in Piraeus represented only a small portion of what the Jews of Rhodes had once possessed. The vast majority of their belongings remained on the island. (They were held—or more accurately ignored—by British troops until May 8, 1945.) When the Jews were moved to hastily established ghettos in the city of Rhodes and three villages, Pepo Recanati, a Jewish Greek Security Service collaborator from Salonika, convinced them "to take along a lot of provisions and valuables: jewelry, gold, securities, etc." The Wehrmacht then confiscated those possessions. As for what they left behind, Molho writes: "Accompanied by informants, the Security Police searched the abandoned houses for hidden treasures. Whatever could be transported—household items, linens, furniture, glass, books—was carefully packed."[120] Immediately after the Jews were gone, Ulrich Kleemann formed a "committee for securing Jewish estates."[121]

On July 20, the Jews were taken to the German-Italian military airfield in Rhodes, where a German officer in a white shirt seized their valuables. According to the recollections of one survivor, Violette Fintz, the officer had a translator at his side (probably Recanati) who spoke Ladino. German soldiers filled four sacks with jewelry.[122] The deportees were told that the jewelry and other valuables were being confiscated "to pay for the maintenance of the Jewish population."[123] (There was a parallel instance of theft in Jerba, Tunisia, where some 4,500 Jews lived in two ancient ghettos. Pressured by the worsening military situation, the Wehrmacht commandant there demanded fifty kilograms of gold from the city's head rabbi, threatening to bomb the Jewish quarter if he did not get it. In the end forty-seven kilograms of gold were handed over.)[124]

The decision to dispossess the Jews of Rhodes was not spontaneous. Military officials responsible for war finances had long talked about it as a possibility. On July 31, 1944, with the looted valuables in the possession of the island's German occupiers, chief intendant Werner Kersten summarized their discussions. In a secret report on the Wehrmacht's needs in Greece, he wrote: "The Navy High Command reported in late June 1944 that the delivery of fresh supplies to Crete and the Aegean islands was endangered and called, in the interest of the islands' defense, for the ruthless impounding of gold and currency as well as basic regulation of the currency."[125] Although Kersten doesn't explicitly mention Jews here, the context of his report strongly suggests that he was referring to Jewish assets. The Wehrmacht had already confiscated gold from the Jews of Salonika in 1942–43 to pay its ongoing costs. In the summer of 1944, Wehrmacht officials once again decided to use this proven option.

Faced with accelerating inflation, the Wehrmacht commander for mainland Greece, who was also responsible for Rhodes, suggested using "exchangeable goods from supplies of confiscated property (Jewish assets, etc.)" to supply German troops.[126] At the time of his suggestion, the only significant assets left were those of the Jews of Corfu, Ioánnina, Crete, and Rhodes. Kleemann's secret directive of July 16, cited above, encourages the same conclusion that Jewish assets were sold off to pay the Wehrmacht's operating costs. The deportation of Rhodes's Jews, Kleemann told his soldiers, was justified by "the political and economic conditions in the area of command."[127]

Responsibility for abandoned real estate was transferred to the island's Italian administration, clearly with the goal of converting it into paper money for use by Wehrmacht soldiers.[128] Transportable property remained in German hands. The funds were urgently needed. According to eyewitness testimony from Erwin Lenz, a German soldier who served in a penal battalion on Rhodes, malnutrition began to spread in the fall of 1944, affecting even "the German troops who had remained on the island." Lenz happened to see a secret communiqué from the newly appointed island commandant, Major General Eduard Wagner. "In this communiqué," Lenz testified, "Wagner informed [the unit's Nazi Party head], among other things, that he had ordered Lieutenant Captain Günther to exchange belongings confiscated and secured from Jews, who had been deported several months previously, for food from local merchants." The transactions "would have to be carried out very delicately," however, because Wagner feared encountering difficulties from the International Red Cross, which was sending aid to the island's residents. "In addition," Lenz concluded, Wagner ordered "all participants to maintain strict silence about the source of the goods to be exchanged. Nonetheless, other German soldiers told me that transactions of this sort did indeed take place."[129]

Part IV

CRIMES FOR THE BENEFIT OF THE PEOPLE

CHAPTER 11

The Fruits of Evil

Profitable Genocide

Reich officials often justified their policies toward the Jews with arguments about economic necessity. For example, one German bureaucrat stationed abroad during the war made the reasonable-sounding—if morally abhorrent—assertion that the sale of Jewish assets was "an effective means of price regulation."[1] But the sale of Jewish household effects and the confiscated wares of Jewish businesses by no means eliminated the shortages in supplies caused by the war and by the larcenous greed of the Germans. It could only reduce those shortages for brief periods of time and in certain regions. This was nothing more than a classic instance of the law of supply and demand. There is no evidence to support the propagandistic claim that ghettoization and deportation of Jews put a stop to "contraband and black market trading."

The immediate effect of the complete dispossession of a group of victims was an increase in supplies of consumer goods—especially clothing, furniture, kitchen appliances—that were in great demand. The sudden availability of goods—and not the alleged prevention of black market trading—was what stabilized prices. A second market mechanism also played a role. The removal of a significant number of urban inhabitants reduced the number of consumers, which in turn reduced demand at a time when supplies were increasing.

The fact is that Jews were not the ones who engaged in black market transactions. The real culprits, as the war progressed, were German soldiers and those who purchased supplies for the German military and civilian agencies. By creating unbridled demand for goods wherever they set foot, citizens of the Reich destroyed the price equilibrium everywhere in Europe. They also developed an active self-interest in blaming others for what they themselves did.

THE PRECEDING chapters have discussed the actions taken by officers and civil servants in the German military administration. In many places—Belgium, Salonika, Tunisia, and Rhodes—they directly organized raids for the purpose of plunder. In other occupied territories—Serbia, France, and Italy—they put pressure on local authorities to dispossess Jews for the benefit of the Wehrmacht. Statements by General Ulrich Kleemann, by Max Merten, and by army commander in chief Walther von Brauchitsch, who in 1940 attached "the highest priority . . . to accelerating the removal of Jews from the economy," attest to the Wehrmacht's role in the anti-Semitic campaigns. Everywhere they went, these men acted in accordance with the motto Gold is the price of survival.

Before the victims of Nazi looting could be deported from the occupied territories, German military officers had to agree on and, in most cases, provide the necessary means of transport. They did this without the slightest objection—and not simply because they hated Jews or were willing to sacrifice the last vestiges of their consciences out of a supposedly innate German need for obedience. The officers helped carry out the deportations because the deportations served their own interest.

Historians continue to debate how much responsibility individual German soldiers must bear for the acts of murder committed during the Holocaust. But an equally compelling concern for scholars should be identifying the structural factors—apart from popular racist ideology—that motivated the Wehrmacht to seek the removal of the Jews from the European continent. It is matter of historical record that policies of "ethnic disentanglement" (*ethnische Entflechtung*) and the looting of food and other necessities accelerated the Final Solution. Ceaseless Nazi propaganda alleging that Jews represented an enemy fifth column promoted passivity among Germans in the face of mass murder. Alongside these three rationales, considered standard in the literature of the Holocaust, the current volume proposes a fourth: field officers' interest in extracting the largest possible contributions from occupied countries toward the costs of occupation. The motivation was not personal greed but the professional determination of the military leadership to wage war in such a way that financial shortfalls would not affect military strategy and troop morale.

At first glance, the material resources gained from the "de-Jewification" of Europe appear scant, amounting to no more than 5 percent of the total revenues that flowed into the German war chest between 1939 and 1945. Yet this figure is misleading. The Reich attached great importance to the proceeds from the Aryanization initiatives. In every budgetary debate, whether in a democracy, a corporation, or a dictatorship, one of the most contentious issues is who will bear the greatest burden. Another is how far to stretch finances during times of crisis. German economists insisted that no more than 50 percent of war costs be financed through credit. Every bit of revenue thus counted for double, for both its own value and its value in increasing the self-imposed credit limit. Within this context, even a few percentage points made a big difference. Additional revenue sources eased the ongoing financial crisis and allowed the regime to forgo unpopular measures, such as hikes in beverage taxes or cuts in soldiers' pay.

A second aspect of the asset-seizure campaign is even more important. The main revenues from liquidated Jewish assets fed the German war machine during the decisive period between the beginning of the summer offensive in 1942 and the battle of Kursk in 1943. The offensive of 1942 was originally planned to proceed through the Caucasus to Iraq and cut England off from the Suez Canal. The 1943 campaign was intended to strike a major blow at the Soviet Union and restore German momentum in what had become a dire situation on the Eastern Front. For this, the Third Reich had to mobilize all its resources. A significant portion of the funds needed to finance these campaigns was raised from Jewish assets in Serbia, Greece, France, Holland, Belgium, Poland, and, of course, Germany itself. Using stolen Jewish wealth, Germany succeeded in covering 70 percent of the occupation costs for Greece for a number of months, and the Nazi leadership employed a similar strategy with its allies Slovakia, Croatia, Bulgaria, and Romania between 1941 and 1942. Examined from this perspective, Germany's Aryanization initiatives can be seen as a crucial part of a much larger mobilization.

In the war budget for 1942–43, taxes on German property owners accounted for 18 percent of domestic revenues. Contributions from occupied countries, bolstered by the proceeds from "de-Jewification," accounted for a similar percentage of foreign revenues. Such additional sources of revenue allowed the regime to shift burdens from German taxpayers. They also allowed field commanders to slow the rapacious exploitation of occupied countries, such as Greece, while at the same time financing soldiers' pay, military construction projects, and weapons purchases. At a precarious point in the war, the dispossession of European Jews brought significant resources into the German treasury, enabling the regime to avoid overtaxing its citizens. That encouraged stability within Germany and a willingness among the people of occupied lands to collaborate with the Reich, thereby lessening the fallout from Germany's military defeats.

When German and non-German economists converted Jewish assets into war bonds, they did not formally violate prohibitions against dispossession enunciated in various national constitutions and the Hague Conventions. Ostensibly, they were merely transferring assets, making Jews into creditors of countries that were waging war or had been occupied. But the creditors were murdered in gas chambers. Whatever German financial specialists told themselves about the likely fate of Jews deported "for work details in the East," they must have known that their unwilling creditors would never be seen again. They had a vested interest in genocide since they themselves benefited from the result. Comparing the concrete policies of "de-Jewification" in the various regions of Europe makes clear that dispossession did not necessarily have to go hand in hand with widespread elimination. In France, Romania, and Bulgaria, political considerations, the course of the war, and the willingness of national or local groups—or even individuals—to help those who were being persecuted sufficed to break the logic of genocide.

Historians who have investigated the legal and moral dimensions of the Aryanization campaigns have generally ignored the financial technique, introduced by Nazi Germany in 1936, of funding military aims by forcibly shifting private investments into government bonds. This scholarly blind spot is all too appropriate, as the Nazi regime was at pains to conceal the material benefits of its epic-scale larceny. During the war, reports about the compulsory conversion of Jewish assets into war bonds were forbidden, and concrete figures about the proceeds earned were kept secret. Instead, the persecution of Jews was depicted in Nazi propaganda as a purely ideological issue. The defenseless victims of a mass campaign of murderous thievery were treated as enemies whose lives had no value whatsoever. In 1943 the Wehrmacht High Command prepared a list of nineteen political and military problems that could potentially cause unrest among soldiers. Officers were supposed to be able to respond to these questions with consistent answers. The list contained the query "Have we gone too far with the Jewish question?" The answer read: "Wrong question! Basic principle of National Socialism and its view of the world—no discussion!"[2] But scholars should not confuse Nazi propaganda with historical fact.

AFTER THE WAR, courts throughout Europe took up the matter of the reparations owed by the East and West German states to the victims of Nazi aggression. On numerous occasions, legal representatives of both the Federal Republic and the German Democratic Republic argued that in those lands occupied by the Reich the dispossession of Europe's Jews was the work not of the Nazi authorities but rather of the governments and administrators of the occupied countries themselves.

There is a grain of truth to this argument. As the preceding chapters have shown, most of the material goods stolen from Jews changed hands in the countries and regions where they had been looted. The expropriations themselves were usually carried out by officials of the occupied state. Citing these facts, postwar German reparations courts dismissed tens of thousands of lawsuits originating outside the boundaries of the Third Reich.

The reality, of course, is far more damning. The present volume has demonstrated that the proceeds from the sale of purloined Jewish assets almost always found their way, directly or indirectly, into the German war chest. The Reich and its citizens also benefited from the increased availability of capital, real estate, and goods ranging from precious stones and jewels all the way down to the cheap wares sold at flea markets. The dispossession of the Jews also stabilized the economies and calmed the political atmosphere in occupied countries, greatly simplifying the task of the Wehrmacht. Goods sold off at less than their actual worth provided an indirect subsidy to both German and foreign buyers.

The exploitation of the Jews was attractive to politicians in occupied countries such as Greece, France, and, late in the war, Hungary. The occupation costs demanded by Germany were massive and, ultimately, ruinous. But German occupiers also offered the countries they controlled the possibility of easing their burden by jointly robbing and then eradicating a convenient scapegoat—Jews. The connection here has often been overlooked, both in the recent literature on the Aryanization campaigns and in the detailed reports of national commissions of historians called on to investigate the dispossession of European Jews. It was obvious, however, to observers at the time. On August 3, 1944, the *Neue Zürcher Zeitung* in Switzerland wrote: "With the Aryanization of Jewish businesses [in Hungary], the purchase price set by the government is to be paid immediately in cash. This shows that the operation, as was the case previously in Germany itself, possesses a certain fiscal significance (the easing of wartime finances)."[3]

At present only rough estimates of the total amount of Jewish assets Germany looted and liquidated during World War II are available. The economist Helen B. Junz has developed an extremely useful methodology, which she describes in her book *Where Did All the Money Go? The Pre-Nazi-Era Wealth of European Jewry*. A more exact calculation, using her formula, is still needed. Existing data on Aryanization in some European countries should also be revisited and expanded in light of the results of the present investigation. Until that time, however, it is safe to say that a total of between 15 and 20 billion reichsmarks in assets from the households of European Jews were liquidated, and the money earned was diverted to pay German war costs.

Since sums of money, large and small, from liquidated Jewish assets were used to pay soldiers' wages throughout occupied Europe, any goods acquired by those troops—from butter sent home to Cologne to sleeveless sweaters purchased in Antwerp and even cigarettes—were underwritten to a greater or lesser degree by the estates of dispossessed and murdered Jews. The same is true for official deliveries of food from occupied countries and Germany's allies to the homeland. They, too, were paid for with money extracted from the exploitation of Jewish assets in France, Holland, Romania, Serbia, Poland, and elsewhere. While butter for German families may have come from Switzerland, it was paid for, at least in part, by gold and currency confiscated in the death camps. Adding to these figures was the use of Jewish slave laborers: from 1940 onward 50 percent of their wages flowed into the state treasury, where it made up a small percentage of the funds needed for support payments to German women and children, as well as for arms purchases. The system was arranged to benefit all Germans. Ultimately every member of the master race—not just Nazi Party functionaries but 95 percent of the German populace—profited in the form of money in their pockets or food on their plates that was paid for by looted foreign currency and gold. Victims of bombing raids wore the clothing and slept in the beds of those who had been murdered. The beneficiaries could breathe easier, thankful that they had survived another day, and no doubt thankful also that the state and the party had been so quick to come to their aid.

The Holocaust will never be properly understood until it is seen as the most single-mindedly pursued campaign of murderous larceny in modern history.

War Revenues, 1939-45

The preceding chapters have presented a great number of specific budgetary figures: proceeds from various expropriation campaigns, account balances, percentages, and so on. The current chapter focuses instead on the total sums involved. The following pages sketch out the structure of Germany's wartime revenues with an eye toward answering two questions: First, how did the portion of operating revenues that came from German citizens compare with that extracted from occupied Europe and the Reich's allies? And second, how was the burden of costs borne by Germany itself divided among the various classes of taxpayers?

The table of estimated war contributions from other countries in Europe, below, is based on four documents drawn up relatively late in the war by civil servants in the Reichsbank and the Finance Ministry. These documents provided the most significant figures, which have been expanded with information from other sources and estimates by the author.

Because Germany had no intention of paying off clearing debts owed to occupied (and allied) countries—balancing them, instead, with fictional external occupation costs—Göring's advisers felt no compunction about entering these sums as revenues. This trick produced an accurate accounting only when the Reich immediately spent the clearing "advances" on goods and services in the countries in question. Often it didn't. Moreover, those responsible for the Reich budget made no distinction between contributions from subjugated nations and from allied countries, recording all revenues as payments against (greatly exaggerated) occupation costs.

Wherever there are competing figures, the more conservative one has been used in the tables below. It's important to note that the numbers themselves represent only a part of the wartime damage the Third Reich inflicted on occupied Europe and its own dependent states.[4]

The "Donner Factor" in the second-to-last line of table 5, requires explanation. On closer examination, the figures for the Soviet Union and for "Captured Property" appear much too low. Otto Donner, Göring's financial adviser, thought as much in 1944, and to correct the figures, he

Table 5: Revenues from Occupied Countries and Dependent States, 1939-45 (in Billions of Reichsmarks)

	Occupation Costs (March 31–Aug. 31, 1944)	Clearing Amounts (Aug. 31, 1944)	Estimated Total
Belgium	5.31	4.99	11.00
Bulgaria	.35	0.82	1.17
Croatia	.19	1.05	1.20
Denmark	2.40	1.41	3.50
France	31.60	8.54	40.14
Gen. Gov. (Poland)	1.49	4.12	5.50
Greece	.50	.24	1.00
Hungary	1.00	1.35	2.50
Italy	5.19	.15	10.00
Netherlands	9.29	5.59	14.50
Norway	5.04	.14	7.00
Protectorate (Czech.)	2.31	2.43	5.00
Romania		1.13	3.00
Serbia	.31	.51	1.00
Slovakia	.03	.80	.80
Soviet Union	4.50	.54	5.40
Spain		.11	.11
Switzerland		.65	.65
Captured Property	1.00		1.00
Subtotal			114.47
+Donner Factor			17.16
Total			131.63

suggested adding 9 to 18 percent to the total to cover "amounts that aren't statistically measurable." In light of what has been described in the preceding chapters, a Donner factor of 15 percent has been added for goods and services that cannot be documented in German-dominated Europe. Even this figure may be too low.

The total sum of over 131 billion reichsmarks is about nine times more than what the German Reich received in regular tax revenues in the last year before World War II. But this figure represents only a part, albeit a large one, of the external revenues Germany extracted via plunder between 1939 and 1945. Wage taxes automatically paid by slave laborers, their contributions to the social welfare system, and the de facto subsidies their labor provided to German agriculture should be added to the total. General administrative revenues extracted from the compulsory savings accounts of Eastern European workers and sham remittances of wages to family members drive the final reckoning even higher.[5] These, too, were budgetary resources acquired at the cost of foreign countries.

There are no documents available that break down the exact sources of general administrative revenues. A rough estimate, however, can be made based on a balance sheet drawn up by the statistics office of the Finance Ministry in 1944. This document includes contributions from the General Government of Poland and the Protectorate of Bohemia and Moravia, which have to be subtracted, since they have already been listed in the above table. (Nazi statisticians considered the Polish and Czech territories to be part of the Reich.) Increased profits earned by the Reichspost, the Reichsbahn (German rail), and the Reichsbank, which have to be considered internal sources of revenue, should also be excluded.[6] Nor can wartime contributions paid by local states and towns within Germany be treated as additional sources of wartime revenues. Although these contributions—totaling slightly more than 10 billion reichsmarks—could not be spent on local projects, there is no evidence that the shift of funds to the Reich treasury exerted a negative influence on public opinion.

Subtracting these sums from general administrative revenues yields an amount of money that statisticians within the Finance Ministry recorded under the nebulous category "Remaining Revenues." The question arises as to how much of this money was earned by relatively honest means. Table 6 gives an estimate of general revenues, including a separate figure for those earned by "legitimate" means. This latter sum was arrived at by using figures from the "Remaining Revenues" column in the regular Reich budgets for 1938 and 1939. Because they include the proceeds from the Aryanization campaign, the atonement payments, and the occupation of Austria, Bohemia and Moravia, and parts of Poland by German troops, these figures are relatively high. Nonetheless some 1.5

billion reichsmarks per year came from sources that can be considered legitimate. Assuming the amount remained constant over five and a half years of war, around 8.25 billion reichsmarks of the money entered under the category "General Administrative Revenues/Remaining Revenues" came from regular domestic sources. The rest constitutes external revenues—money earned by plundering the citizens of foreign states. The following estimate for 1944–45 has been kept conservative—possibly too conservative—to reflect Germany's territorial losses in the final phase of World War II.

Table 6: General Administrative Revenues/Remaining Revenues (in Billions of Reichsmarks)

	Regular Budget	Supplemental Budget	Total
1938	2,927.5	——	2,927.5
1939	3,410.7	310.8	3,721.5
1940	2,980.1	1,480.2	4,460.3
1941	3,939.8	1,928.2	5,868.0
1942	4,169.5	2,443.0	6,612.5
1943	4,744.1	3,222.6	7,966.7
1944–45			4,000.0
Total (excluding 1938)			32,629.0
"Legitimate Revenues," 1939–45			-8,250.0
Revenues from Plunder			24,379.0

Based on these calculations, approximately 24.5 billion reichsmarks were acquired by theft from "foreigners." The German finance minister recorded these funds as "general administrative revenues." That figure includes credits for transfers of wages to the families of forced laborers as well as approximately 4 billion reichsmarks robbed from German Jews after 1939. It also takes into account sums paid by the German military commander in Belgium from the proceeds of the Aryanization campaign, purchases made in reichsmarks by German firms in German-dominated Europe, and many other sources of income.

Adding revenues from forced labor and general administrative revenues to Germany's income from mandatory tributes, advances on clearing debts, and war contributions from allied states produces table 7.

Table 7: External War Revenues
(in Billions of Reichsmarks)

Occupation costs plus clearing transactions	131.50
Revenues from forced labor not recorded under general administrative revenues (including social welfare payments and indirect agricultural subsidies)	12.00
General administrative revenues	24.50
Total external war revenues	168.00

This balance sheet of larceny contains several billion marks in double bookings. In certain cases the goods and services procured through state theft were paid for twice: money to procure goods was sometimes diverted from occupation budgets, which then had to be replenished. German businesses that bought foreign raw materials, machinery, or unfinished products to build artillery, warplanes, or transport vehicles enjoyed the same advantage. These sources of income have been included in "external revenues" because they did not in any way disadvantage German buyers. Indeed, buyers profited from such dirty dealing.

On the other hand, several categories of income are not included in the total of Germany's external war revenues. In the absence of reliable data, the final figure does not reflect the amount of business and commercial taxes saved by using forced labor and looted factories, raw materials, and unfinished products. The accuracy of the individual figures and estimates above can be debated. The overall picture, however, remains clear.

By even the most conservative estimates, the Third Reich extracted no less than 170 billion reichsmarks of its ongoing war revenues from "foreign" sources. That figure is ten times what the Reich raised in 1938 and the equivalent today of some 1.7 to 2 trillion euros ($2–2.2 trillion).

The policy of plunder was the cornerstone for the welfare of the German people and a major guarantor of their political loyalty, which was first and foremost based on material considerations. The unshakable alliance between the state and the people was not primarily the result of cleverly conceived party propaganda. It was created by means of theft, with the spoils being redistributed according to egalitarian principles among the members of the ethnically defined *Volk*.

In determining the relation between internal and external sources of revenue, routine expenditures have to be factored out. They are by no means part of additional wartime spending. For the German Reich, those costs, which exclude all war-related spending, can be fixed at around 20 billion reichsmarks annually and include the normal costs of government, basic social services, and the maintenance of a defensive army. With these expenditures factored out, it emerges that the German treasury recorded the remarkably low figure of 77 billion reichsmarks in internal war revenues, earned via direct and indirect taxation during the course of World War II. (That figure excludes wage tax revenues from forced labor, the contributions paid by the General Government and the Protectorate of Bohemia and Moravia, and the portion of general administrative revenues earned through plunder.) Adding "legitimate" general administrative revenues yields the following total:

Table 8: Total War Revenues from within the Reich (in Billions of Reichsmarks)

Excluding wage taxes from forced labor	70.50[7]
"Legitimate" general administrative revenues	13.50
	84.00

These calculations use the lowest available estimates of looted or extracted external resources and the highest credible ones for German war-tax revenues. The German contribution to the ongoing costs of war can therefore be estimated as, at most, one-third—while external sources account for at least two-thirds of wartime revenues.

The upper classes forked over the lion's share of these increased internal revenues. Low- and middle-income Germans (about two-thirds of all taxpayers) paid increased wartime taxes on tobacco, beer, and sparkling wine. These amounted to around 12 billion reichsmarks, or around 16 percent of internal wartime tax revenues. Add to that figure the extension of working hours, which resulted in increased wage-tax revenues beyond those of slave labor. On the other hand, the wage tax burden was lowered for individual earners of paychecks since, as of the fall of 1940, overtime, night, and holiday wages were declared tax-exempt. Simultaneously, revenues from income, business, and windfall profits taxes increased dramatically. In 1939, the Reich took in 2.6 billion marks in wage taxes, while earning 4.4 billion from income taxes on the self-employed. Assuming that the latter figure would have been around 4 billion for 1939 had Germany not gone to war in September, we can calculate that the German war chest earned at least 16 billion reichsmarks from steeper additional taxation of the private revenues of the self-employed between September 1939 and early 1945. Wartime increases in corporate taxes can be estimated at around 12 billion reichsmarks. In addition there were revenues from taxes on war-related profits, which accounted for at least 4 billion reichsmarks, and revenues from property taxes of around 8 billion. That yields a total of 40 billion reichsmarks that relatively affluent Germans contributed to the war effort.[8]

In terms of all wartime revenues, internal and external, low- and middle-income Germans, who together with their families numbered some 60 million, accounted for no more than 10 percent of the total sum. More affluent Germans bore 20 percent of the burden, while foreigners, forced laborers, and Jews were compelled to cover 70 percent of the funds consumed every day by Germany during the war. The middle and working classes derived advantages from the Third Reich's dual emphasis on race and class: "wartime socialism" combined with a sense of racial superiority and imperial adventurism guaranteed solid support for the regime well into the second half of the war. Material self-interest suppressed any acknowledgment of the criminal basis of the Nazi social welfare state among the majority of Germans.

Two clear conclusions emerge from these elaborate calculations. First, at least two-thirds of German war revenues were earned from foreign or "racially foreign" sources.* Second, the remaining third of the costs were distributed extremely unequally between the various economic classes in German society. One-third of taxpayers bore more than two-thirds of the burdens of war, while the vast majority of Germans paid only the small amount left over.

The discrepancy in the tax burdens placed on wage laborers and on businessmen is even more glaring. As described in earlier chapters, the average working-class family in Germany was never forced to pay any direct war taxes, and even the increased duties on beer and tobacco products were balanced out by unusually generous military pay scales and support payments to soldiers' families. On average, the vast and not particularly affluent majority of Germans enjoyed more disposable income during the war than they had before it.

The subject of discussion here has been war-related revenues, which, up until August 1944, covered around half of Germany's wartime expenditures. The rest was financed on credit. The next chapter discusses how the Third Reich raised that credit on German financial markets and how it planned to saddle conquered countries with the repayments on those loans, once Germany had emerged victorious in World War II.

---

*This figure has provoked some controversy. For further discussion see "A Note on Calculations" on p. 327.

CHAPTER 12

Speculative Politics

Silent and Illusory

While the proportion of costs for World War II that Germany was able to defray without credit was far greater than it had been in World War I, the Reich finance minister still had to borrow significant amounts of money. This was done through what finance experts call "silent" or "invisible" loans. The Nazi regime did not try to convince the populace to buy long-term war bonds, as the Wilhelmine government did between 1914 and 1918. Instead, it borrowed money directly from credit institutions, using short-term war bonds—without any legal fanfare and unbeknownst to investors—as collateral.

Starting in 1936, savings banks, building societies, credit unions, and insurance companies underwent a gradual and largely unnoticed transformation into reservoirs of state capital. The same was true of pension funds, which at the time possessed large capital reserves. With no evident resistance, bankers agreed to take state bonds into their portfolios. They were, in effect, making a long-term investment with the mostly short-term savings of their customers. The secret to the success of the "silent loans" was the appearance that the transactions were voluntary. As early as January 1940, the German press was ordered not to mention the possibility of a compulsory wartime freeze on savings accounts.[1] A regulation to this effect was rejected by the Nazi leadership as "completely wrongheaded and politically unviable." The German worker was to be kept "under the impression, at least, that he was not being restricted in his ability to do what he wanted with wage-earned income" and that the state had no intention "of taking anything in any form away from him."[2] Göring's financial adviser Otto Donner praised the system for its closed circulation of capital, which was based on the fact that "the recipient of income takes that income, which he cannot use legally, to the bank. Credit institutions transfer the money to the finance minister in return for promissory notes."[3]

The "silent" transformation of the contents of more than 40 million savings accounts and other forms of investment into state bonds kept a continuous supply of money flowing into the Reich treasury. There the money was spent on the war and thus literally destroyed.[4] Earlier chapters examined how cash was exchanged, primarily by Wehrmacht soldiers, for goods and services in occupied territories. This was a way of partially restoring the equilibrium, which had been disturbed by the war, between available goods and paper money. Yet a significant amount of money remained in private hands, and the regime wanted Germans to save as much as possible. This, in turn, necessitated rigid price and wage controls, and the suppression of domestic black markets.

SILENT LOANS did not affect only Germans with savings accounts. Reich bank commissioners also compelled financial institutions in occupied countries to buy up German bonds to help finance the war. By the end of the war, German bonds accounted for more than 70 percent of the investments of Czech banks.[5] In France, "enemy investments" were converted into bonds that the French government had to issue in order to pay for German occupation costs.[6] Because a significant proportion of the enormous contributions demanded of occupied countries were raised in the form of state bonds, the various national banks and financial administrations of those countries were under constant pressure to subjugate their own national money markets to the interests of German wartime finances. Organizing this complex system was one of the main tasks of the German bank commissioners.

The silent-loan finance economy began on September 12, 1939, with a formal ordinance concerning a supplemental budget for the fiscal year 1939. The ordinance empowered the finance minister to procure "a sum of up to 15 billion reichsmarks through credit for war expenditures."[7] Once begun, the cycle of borrowing was unstoppable. By 1945, the Reich had accumulated 110 billion reichsmarks in debt at commercial German banks, 54 billion at savings and loan institutions, and 25 billion at insurance companies.[8] At the same time, it had 33 billion marks in what were euphemistically listed as clearing obligations. In reality, these were loans that the Reich intended to pass off on occupied and allied nations in the event of a German triumph in World War II. (If Germany lost, it would simply default.) The remaining Reich obligations consisted of what economists call "uncovered debts," a euphemism for obligations paid for by the printing of more money, which the Reich treasury increasingly resorted to late in the war.

The system did indeed function silently—that was its great advantage. But it meant that government finances were always precarious since an ever greater proportion of state revenues consisted of "floating" debts that were not based on long-term credit agreements. The risk, as one financial expert warned in 1944, resided in the fact that "the broad masses of the populace have control over sums in the high billions in short-term notes and even paper money, which they could decide at any minute to withdraw from the market."[9]

In contrast to Germany, both Great Britain and the United States financed the war through long-term war bonds. Their success was due to robust propaganda campaigns, such as the Wings for Victory weeks in Great Britain and the "Now—All Together" poster series in the States. One sold-out war-bond concert held on April 25, 1943, at New York City's Carnegie Hall featured Arturo Toscanini, Vladimir Horowitz, and the NBC Symphony Orchestra and succeeded in raising $11 million in the space of two hours. On the program was Tchaikovsky's First Piano Concerto.

In Britain, 1.7 billion of the 4.6 billion pounds raised through war bonds by late 1942 came from small investors.[10] Relative to the total population, low-income earners in Germany would have had to buy 23.5 billion reichsmarks' worth of long-term war bonds to equal that level of commitment. (And the regime would have had to have sold 61 billion marks' worth in total.) Hitler could only dream of such mass support. It would have been inconceivable for Wilhelm Furtwängler, Edwin Fischer, and the Berlin Philharmonic to have performed Beethoven's Fifth Piano Concerto to convince people to buy war bonds to pay for warplanes, rifles, and heavy artillery.

In the United States and Great Britain, public confidence in the two governments' ability to win the war was based on their success in activating a broad social consensus. This was not the case in Germany. In early 1943, the economist Bernhard Benning asked with dismay: "Why have we in Germany, who take a backseat to no one in matters of propaganda, refrained [in this area]?"[11] Great Britain also instituted regular broad-based tax hikes, which combined with controlled inflation to keep finances solid. Wartime revenues from taxes and duties rose by 336 percent over peacetime receipts in Britain, compared with only 196 percent in Germany.

A significant portion of the Reich's increased revenues came from its annexed territories, from its exploitation of forced labor, and from profit based on dispossession, financial manipulation, and genocide. It is clear, therefore, that the increase in the tax burden in Great Britain was more than double that in Germany. Moreover, in stark contrast to the situation in Germany, 85 percent of the increased revenues from taxes and contributions came from British citizens earning the modest sum of 500 pounds or less a year.[12]

In October 1942, fearing "a hopeless devaluation" of the reichsmark, a high-level civil servant at the Reichsbank took the regime to task for its passivity. Not without a measure of respect, he pointed to the English, who "have combated inflation with enviable success by gradually tightening taxes—without damage to the economy or other disadvantages."[13]

German financial methods were the monetary equivalent of the blitzkrieg. The only hope was quick success. Unlike in World War I, Reichsbank vice president Emil Puhl reasoned in late 1942, Germany's financial strategy entailed a grave "point of danger," having been "bought and paid for" by "transferring to the end of the war [the task of addressing] the currency problem by curbing consumer spending power."[14] As Puhl was making this statement, Germany was being defeated at Stalingrad, a setback that shook the Reich's reliance on silently financing the war. The Nazi regime had, with the active help of the general public and the private financial sector, perpetrated a huge swindle that could remain concealed only if Germany brought the war to a victorious conclusion. Resounding victory alone would allow the regime to satisfy consumer demand at home while paying off its war debts. The longer the war lasted, the harsher the Reich's campaign of plunder became and the more brutal and inhuman its treatment of its "enemies."

From the perspective of domestic politics, the technique of silently financing the war was characteristic of the Reich's whole approach to power. The Nazi leadership avoided any sort of public referendum on the war—which the issuing of long-term war bonds might have led to, had they sold poorly. An economist who was involved with war finances at the time later wrote: "Because Hitler didn't want Reich finances to become the subject of public discussion, he prohibited [us] from publicly taking out loans both in the rearmament phase and during the war itself." Hitler lacked what postwar German chancellor Ludwig Erhard would call the stature to inform "the people about the enormity of the sacrifice necessary" and "the courage of responsibility." Hitler, Erhard wrote, favored "games of hide-and-seek" and "disguise."[15] His fear of calling on Germans to make material sacrifices was shared by his ally Mussolini. In 1944, even the German occupiers criticized Il Duce for "never having been able to decide to test the trust of the populace with a loan."[16]

The Nazi regime avoided enlightening the German people about even a fraction of the true costs of the war. Early on, the leadership tailored its policies to the traditional willingness among Germans to submit to rule from above, as long as they think they are being well taken care of. Unlike Churchill, Hitler could not afford to deliver "blood, toil, tears, and sweat" speeches. The much celebrated, seemingly omnipotent Führer never saw himself in a position to demand openly that his people entrust him with their savings for five, ten, or twenty years in return for the glorious future he promised. Seen from this perspective, the unity between the German people and the Nazi leadership was an illusion that could not withstand real challenges. If Hitler's was a dictatorship of consent, that consent was not based on an ideological conviction held by the majority of Germans. It was bought and paid for through the systematic bribery of social welfare payments and services. Most of the burdens were borne by foreigners and those deemed foreign to the *Volk*. But in the end, those who accepted the bribes had to bear the costs, too.

Savings and Trust

As it did with its food provision measures, the Nazi leadership used tax and currency policies to strengthen public trust in the regime, which was by no means stable. Today one would say that the government was "fighting for its credibility." This was a daily struggle, as Goebbels's diary and the records of many of Hitler's decisions attest.

To gauge the public mood during the Third Reich, historians usually rely on reports by Security Service informants, private letters, notations made by Nazi functionaries in their personal diaries, and similar sources. But a more precise way of measuring the highs and lows of public confidence is to look at the rates at which Germans saved money—a social-historical parameter that has been largely neglected as a source of information. This approach not only reflects changes within short spans of time and differences from region to region but also distinguishes between the morale of various social classes over the course of the Third Reich. The data is relatively easy to collect through records at the Reichspost (which had a savings division), local savings institutions, large banks, and life insurance companies; collating it with major speeches by Hitler and watershed political and military events offers a complex, methodologically sound picture of public opinion. For example, savings, which had been in decline, shot up after the attempted assassination of Hitler by Claus Schenk von Stauffenberg's group on July 20, 1944. They declined again immediately as of August 1, when it became clear that the coup d'état had failed.

Just as government-compiled statistics on the number of Germans who formally renounced ties to established religions provide a good indication of whether people were prepared to put their full trust in the state, an examination of rates of savings yields precise demographic snapshots. In December 1943, the Security Service carried out such an examination—but it used public opinion surveys instead of the more reliable hard data showing exactly how much money people were depositing in banks for the future.[17] A detailed look at the savings rates during World War II is beyond the scope of the present investigation, but a few general conclusions are warranted. Indeed, it is possible to fix the moment at which public confidence in the Hitler regime finally evaporated.

In 1940 and 1941, Germans deposited around one billion marks per month in savings accounts. In 1942, that figure rose to more than 1.5 billion per month.[18] The increase can be seen as both a consequence of limited consumer spending opportunities during the war and an expression of basic trust in Hitler's leadership. In the space of a few years, the amounts in German savings accounts more than tripled, from 15.2 billion to 51.2 billion reichsmarks by 1942. This increase represented "by far the largest amount of growth that Germany ever experienced."[19] Life insurance policies provide an indicator of upper-class Germans' faith in the future: the total amount of premiums paid annually rose from 1.7 billion to 4.2 billion marks between 1939 and 1941.[20]

The voluntary savings that paid a significant portion of the daily costs of war were earmarked, in the plans of many Nazi strategists, to bring about "a better balanced structure of wealth in the future," after Germany had won the war. The money would help "achieve a truly socialist division of personal assets."[21] Here, too, the tendency can be observed within the Nazi state to favor social equality for Germans. The Nazi leadership was also at least partly motivated by a desire to concentrate postwar assets in the hands of workers, so as to take as much consumer spending power as possible off the investment market. Of course, Germans saved their money—whether in the form of savings accounts, supplementary pension plans, or other annuities—for their own purposes. Individual Germans were concerned with putting enough money aside to be able to fulfill their lifelong dreams after the war ended.

Dreams for the future notwithstanding, the savings figures show how much money low-income earners had at their disposal and the extent to which they were, at least implicitly, entrusting it to the Nazi state. In 1942, Deputy Finance Minister Fritz Reinhardt concluded with satisfaction: "There can be no more unambiguous proof of the faith our *Volk* comrades have in the National Socialist leadership and in the stability of the currency than this large increase in savings."[22] Bank representatives saw the trend as an expression of "the will to save in wartime, to save in the interests of victory."[23] One slogan of German banks was "Fight, work, and—save!"[24] The huge success of campaigns encouraging ordinary Germans to save their money is all the more impressive considering that interest rates on savings accounts were continually being lowered.[25] Although ordinary Germans were kept in the dark about the silent transformation of their savings into artillery, those who chose to invest their money this way must have maintained at least a vague hope that Germany would win the war.

With the reversal of Germany's military fortunes, mistrust arose between the Reich and its citizens. In the second half of 1943, the rate of growth in savings fell for the first time. The Reich Finance Ministry explained the decline as a by-product of the aerial bombardments, citing the fact that the largest reductions came in hard-hit northwest German cities, while the savings rate had remained constant in the relatively untouched east.[26] But it was an alarming development all the same. Instead of decreasing, willingness to save should have grown faster than in the previous year, since German military setbacks had reduced the availability of goods for consumers to spend money on.

In 1943, while the Finance Ministry was registering the initial loss of trust, the Security Service, possibly at the behest of the finance minister, began to devote its attention to the topic of popular confidence and the retreat into investments. Security Service analysts localized the mistrust "as being, now as ever, primarily among the better-situated classes of society." Informants reported that many of their wealthier *Volk* comrades "were unscrupulously putting their capitalist proclivities into public practice." Such behavior was followed closely in less well-situated circles. "*The capitalist*," one Security Service report proclaimed, "is becoming a '*bad example*' in the eyes of the *broad masses* on the issue of the value of money." The Security Service offered a sobering conclusion: "A loss of confidence in the value of money has unmistakably occurred in certain social classes and is being translated everywhere into words and deeds. However, we can still observe the willingness to save as an expression of the general confidence in the value of money; the amount of money saved in the past few months is not proportionate to increased levels of income, past and future, especially among certain segments of the populace."[27]

In March 1944, Economics Minister Funk was forced to reassure low- and moderate-income savers by publicly declaring that the Reich "would never call upon the contents of savings accounts to pay off wartime debts."[28] Despite the incipient nervousness, and allowing for variations between types of banks and between regions, the level of savings remained impressively constant in the first half of 1944. But "toward the end of the year, the growth rate in savings slowed significantly." From August 1944 onward, average wage earners in Germany hoarded their money in cash form. The affluent had been somewhat quicker to react: the number of new life insurance policies was already declining dramatically by March 1944.

On September 15, the Reichsbank complained about "the withdrawal of large amounts of cash by the public."[29] Otto Ohlendorf, state secretary at the Economics Ministry, remarked in January 1945 that the "amount of cash held by people" had "hugely increased" and that the Reich "would have no choice but to print more money." The amount of money in circulation had increased from 38.5 to 48.5 billion reichsmarks between September and December 1944 alone—an increase more than three times greater than the average in the preceding twelve months.[30] One financial expert remarked dryly that a "general need for liquidity" had arisen "as the political and military situation came to a head."[31]

The behavior of consumers had a direct influence on the policies of German banks. The finance minister complained: "Contrary to expectations, credit institutions are less and less willing to take on long-term government promissory notes." Beginning in August, Reichsbank resources had to be increasingly shifted and "significant contributions made to prop up the value of Reich bonds."[32] On August 3, 1944, for instance, the previously obedient Savings Bank of Salzburg had decided "in the interest of greater liquidity" to refrain temporarily "from buying Reich bonds."[33] That decision, as the Reichsbank immediately noted, reflected a general wariness of treasury bonds from the German state.[34] Banks were reacting to their customers, who were by then—belatedly—making a clear statement against the war and withdrawing credit from their political leadership.

In August 1944—after the Allies had landed in Normandy, the Red Army had defeated the Army Group Center on the Eastern Front, and the Stauffenberg coup d'état had come to naught—confidence in both the Reich leadership and the reichsmark collapsed completely. It had been gradually declining, judging by savings figures, since the spring of 1943. The affluent were quicker to lose faith than the less well situated. Against this backdrop of growing skepticism toward the Nazi political leadership, the attempted coup d'état, which is often depicted as a lost cause, might have had a chance of popular success.

This sort of skepticism, however, arose only toward the end of the war. Public support for the Nazi state may have been based on mutual illusions, but for most of the duration of the Third Reich its politicians consistently succeeded in renewing trust in their leadership capabilities. In a historically unprecedented fashion, they created the preconditions for the modern social welfare state. Punitive violence, which made an example of rebellious individuals within the *Volk*, cannot be ignored. But neither should its importance be overestimated. State violence became a major means of control only during the second half of the war. Out of the 16,000 death sentences against German civilians, 15,000 were handed down after the crisis of winter 1941–42. Much the same was true in the military. The 253rd Infantry Division is a case in point: eighteen of its soldiers were executed during the war. Between 1939 and 1942, none were put to death; there were eight executions in 1943, six in 1944, and four in 1945. In total, in the course of the war, some 20,000 death sentences were carried out on German soldiers.[35]

The combination of the state's general concern for the welfare of the masses and its exemplary punishment of those defamed as "*Volk* parasites" did not convert the majority of Germans into rabid Nazis. It made them conformists, eager to enjoy the daily advantages the state offered them. The passive loyalty created among the populace was sufficient to guarantee that the state could do pretty much as it wanted until the summer of 1944.

Virtual War Debts

Germany's purely speculative techniques for financing the war meant that the only option for the Third Reich was total victory. Hitler's government could not afford any sort of compromise or partial defeat. From the very first day of the conflict, the government banked on "the enormous additional capacities that Germany could exploit in the territories it occupied—without having to use the German people's own assets." In the immediate wake of victory over France, Germany was brimming with confidence. As the author of a 1941 dissertation on wartime finances proclaimed, "within the sphere of influence from uppermost Norway to the Bay of Biscay," heavily indebted Germany now had "the riches of almost all of Europe at its disposal."[36]

Germans were kept passive and generally content by a lavish social welfare system that was paid for by these riches. The improvement in the public mood that came with increases in people's material welfare explains such policies as the tax benefits aimed at German workers in the fall of 1940, the hike in pensions of 1941, and the government's refusal to impose any broad, direct wartime levies in the years that followed. Once Germany invaded the Soviet Union, the public was only confirmed in its belief that Germany's rearmament and war debts existed merely on paper. In 1942, Fritz Reinhardt published a pamphlet, intended to reassure public opinion, entitled *What Is Happening with Our Money?* In it, he drew attention to the "reordering of things in the East" and promised Germans that they would reap the fruits of victory. German war debts, he tried to lull his readers into thinking, were "actively counterbalanced by access to resources and sources of wealth that amount to many times more than the debt run up by the Reich."[37]

Leading German economists saw the situation exactly the same way. Addressing a conference on wartime finances in the fall of 1941, the economist Rudolf Stucken posed a rhetorical question: "Are debts really a problem after the war? Won't former enemies who still have production capacities support us in all important areas with reparations and the like?"[38] (After 1945, Stucken claimed to have consistently opposed Nazi finance policies.) The financial expert Hero Moeller preferred to emphasize "the sale of land that has freely come to us and that we have conquered, as well as other new state property acquired without cost" as factors that would "provide significant relief."[39]

In the summer of 1942, Moeller's colleague Bernhard Benning came out in favor of "using the reprivatization of Reich property in annexed eastern territories" and "the steady income from the 'channeling profits' of cheap goods imported from occupied eastern territories" as "additional resources for paying off debt."[40] In an earlier lecture, he expanded on his ideas of "utilizing foreign economies": "That includes significant amounts of real value that have fallen into the hands of the Reich through the occupation of foreign countries, especially in what was formerly Poland and in Russia."[41]

What economists meant by "channeling profits" was the difference between the price of Russian grain in Russia and the price it fetched when it was sold in Germany. "If, for example, the going price for a ton of rye is 80 reichsmarks on the Russian market," Reinhardt explained at a meeting of leading technocrats, "the difference between the 180 reichsmarks it fetches on the German market and the original 80 marks plus transportation and storage costs flows into the Reich treasury in the form of channeling profits." According to the minutes of this meeting, Reinhardt's audience, which consisted of senior officials from the Wehrmacht, the Ministry of Food, the Ministry of Economics, and the Ministry for the Occupied Eastern Territories, "were unanimously of the opinion that that was exactly how things should develop."[42]

Against the express wish of Heinrich Himmler in his capacity as Reich commissioner for settlement projects, the deputy interior minister successfully insisted that looted foreign assets be handed over to the treasury and not be allocated to German settlers. "The territories in question," he argued, "have been conquered by armed campaigns as part of a war waged by all Germans [so that] the fruits of this victory may benefit the entire German people."[43] The Finance Ministry eagerly seconded that argument. In the words of one civil servant, "the Reich was the one that originally acquired possession of these great sources of wealth by occupying foreign territory."[44] Members of the administration of the Four-Year Plan used similar arguments to counter the appeals of local functionaries in occupied Poland, who wanted the funds given to the settlers. For the plan's staff, it was self-evident that "the value of conquered Polish assets belongs to the German Reich."[45]

Civil servants in various ministries repeatedly emphasized that the Reich was only interested in receiving equivalent values for the assets it had seized, not in retaining possession of them. From the very beginning, the idea was to reprivatize what had been conquered by the state. Reinhardt and other officials considered issuing and selling "people's stocks" in order to soak up the savings of ordinary Germans after the end of the war and to protect the consumer-goods market from being overrun by eager purchasers. The stocks would "place shares in industrial plants, for example, or in mines in occupied eastern territory at consumers' disposal," as one official proposed. In this way military expenditures could be made even more productive. Such expenditures, the official wrote, "have to be seen as part of an equation balanced by the enormous real value assets that have been won by the German sword."[46]

A document most likely prepared by the financial expert Otto Donner entitled "General Principles for Economic Policies in the Newly Occupied

Eastern Territories" was officially endorsed by Göring on November 8, 1941. It neatly summarized the Reich's system of exploitation: "Via cheap [agricultural] production and by maintaining the low standard of living of the native populace, maximum surplus production is to be achieved so as to supply the Reich and the remaining countries of Europe. In this way, along with covering European needs for food and raw materials as much as possible, a source of income can be opened up for the Reich, which will allow it to cover a significant portion of the war debts incurred during the conduct of the war, while transferring much of the burden from German taxpayers."[47]

A few weeks later, Göring's state secretary, Paul Körner, declared: "The newly won territories in the East must contribute to paying off our war debts. For this reason, wages and prices in eastern territories must remain as low as possible." In response to what must have been an attempt by Körner to take credit for the idea, the Finance Ministry retorted coolly that this was the course that Reinhardt "had always been advocating."[48]

In fact, well before Göring, Schwerin von Krosigk had advanced his own financial and economic vision for Germany's eastern expansion. In early September 1941, in consultation with subordinates responsible for Russia, he suggested that "property formerly belonging to the Russian state"—which thanks to Communism amounted to pretty much everything in Russia—should be "placed at the disposal of the Reich as government property." In 1942, he pushed for "a significant amount of the burdens of war, especially interest and principal payments, to be met via price differences between the Reich and Eastern Europe."[49] Some time later, his deputy, Reinhardt, seconded the idea: "The Reich's debt has risen because it has built up its armed forces and waged war. If our current standard of living is to be maintained, the German people cannot be burdened with payments on the interest and principal of this debt. . . . Woe to him who threatens the corresponding wage and price policies in the eastern territories." Reinhardt estimated the total revenues that the Reich treasury could gain by selling off conquered fields and forests, natural resources, and factories at "several hundred billion reichsmarks."[50]

In January 1942, after a months-long trip through occupied Ukraine,

Reich agricultural adviser Hanns Deetjen declared in an address before an exclusive audience at the German Gentlemen's Club in Berlin: "According to statements from the highest offices, Ukraine will be made to 'pay for the war.' Our policies toward the local population are designed with that goal in mind. Ukraine is to provide cheap labor both for the Reich and for the exploitation of agriculture and natural resources in that country itself. . . . The standard of living there has to be kept low. Only then can the necessary surpluses be produced for Europe."[51]

Addressing Nazi gauleiters on December 12, 1941, Hitler spoke not only about the "Final Solution" but also about Germany's war debts and social issues.[52] For the postwar period, he promised "to take a resolute approach toward carrying out a generous and comprehensive social program, one that will include both German workers and German farmers." Millions of Slavic slave laborers were to help carry out his program, he declared. Otherwise there would be no way for him to achieve his social-political goals and pay off the loans taken out for the war. To decline to go down "such novel paths," Hitler said, would be to invite a repeat "of inflation and, inevitably, of economic catastrophe."

In March 1942, Hitler drew attention to "our enormous arms buildup," which had "consumed sums that thus far have not been covered." He saw two diametrically opposed possibilities for reducing debt. "Either the tax burden will have to be gradually transferred to our ethnic comrades in the Reich or it will be defrayed by potential profits from the occupied eastern territories."[53] In August 1942, "directly" after visiting Hitler, the Reich commissioner and gauleiter for Ukraine, Erich Koch, issued the following instructions to his subordinates: "If the Ukrainian people work ten hours a day, eight of those hours should be for us. All sentimental concerns are to be put aside."[54] With political cover provided by higher authorities, civil servants in the Finance Ministry—who had at an earlier stage conceived of an imperialist form of debt reduction that would benefit ordinary Germans—now spoke of "the Führer's long-term financial-political goals" and proposed that Ukraine become "an object of exploitation for this purpose."[55]

One theme appears repeatedly in the statements of leading Nazi academics and politicians: that the exceptionally cruel regimes installed by Germany in occupied parts of the Soviet Union were justified by a concern for the future standard of living of ordinary Germans, even if it meant starvation, poverty, forced labor, and death for the local populace. In long-term practice, this strategy proved unworkable. Proceeds from the occupied territories failed to live up to expectations, and resistance among the besieged people grew from day to day, becoming impossible to suppress. Much to his consternation, Goebbels discovered in January 1943 that "furtive German slogans about the inferiority of the Slavic people and the need to eliminate them have come to the attention of the broad Russian public." That strengthened Stalin's hand when he urged: "It's better to die on our feet than survive on our knees!"[56]

German plans for ruthless, unrestrained exploitation of Eastern Europe foundered on the resistance of Soviet soldiers and partisans. The medium-range German strategy was to use foreign resources to refinance war debts and raise the general German standard of living in one stroke. In the short term, the Reich sought to cover German food needs as fully as possible. Germany was able to realize only the latter goal, and even then its success was only partial. But the conclusion to be drawn from the historical evidence is inescapable: concern for the welfare of Germans was the decisive motivation behind policies of terrorizing, enslaving, and exterminating enemy groups.

Nazi Socialism

Expertise and Policy

Long before September 1, 1939, the Reich had reshaped public finances so
that state debts would be covered by resources from a war of imperialistic
plunder. A significant number of German financial experts, Reichsbank
managers, and civil servants in government ministries supported this
policy. As early as 1935, the country's aristocratic finance minister,
Schwerin von Krosigk—a traditional German conservative—described
himself as someone who worked "with courage and faith" and who would
not let his "vision for the enormous greatness of the time" be clouded by
the minor difficulties of everyday money matters.[1] Von Krosigk's devotion
to duty illustrates the remarkable convergence of interests between the
Nazi true believers and "apolitical" civil servants, a convergence that influ-
enced every aspect of their cooperation during the war. The historical distinction between "party ideologues," who rabidly persecuted Jews, and
officials such as von Krosigk and his staff, who have too often been credited with offering some form of "resistance," is outmoded and should be
discarded once and for all.[2]

The preceding chapters have sketched out some of the practices by
which Germany dispossessed those deemed to be enemies of the state.
The overall picture, though it may be incomplete, suffices to give an idea
of the techniques used in what amounted to a state-sponsored campaign

of grand larceny. This campaign would not have succeeded without the active cooperation of career bureaucrats, many of whom did not share the anti-Semitic hatred of Nazi ideologues. The Reich Finance Ministry maintained numerous accounts between which money could be pushed back and forth and mixed so as to conceal where it came from. At the very least, von Krosigk and his chief civil servants can be accused of having repeatedly procured and laundered money, using methods prohibited under international law, in support of a criminal regime. The same accusation can be leveled at the leadership and the financial experts at the Reichsbank, the Reich Credit Banks, and the Wehrmacht directorates.

WITHIN GERMANY, the government pursued policies to redistribute wealth, including strict price controls. The public widely considered these policies fair. Outside Germany, Wehrmacht soldiers were encouraged to enrich themselves. From the perspective of the finance minister, the best thing for the German economy was to convert excess consumer spending power at home into foreign currency to be spent on goods abroad. "Send me whatever money you have," Heinrich Böll wrote to his parents at the start of the war, and the message was unmistakable. In this way, family purchasing power that could not· be converted into goods within the German welfare state could be siphoned off. Politicians responsible for wartime finances exploited foreign supplies of consumer goods to render harmless "the few potentially malignant billions" in excess consumer capital, which might have led to shortages, inflation, and popular dissatisfaction.[3] The Nazi regime profited from the basic satisfaction of ordinary Germans, regardless of whether they felt a sense of attachment to or—in the case of Böll and Wolf Goette—distance from the party ideology.

The practical details of how Germany financed World War II vividly illustrate the relationship between financial experts and the political leadership. This relationship required that the sometimes arcane, specialist considerations of career bureaucrats be balanced against political limitations. Often, the two sides worked together to achieve a common goal, such as the dispossession of Jews in Salonika, Belgium, and France.

Wehrmacht intendants and civil servants within the Finance Ministry were delighted at the additional revenues flowing their way—either directly, as in Belgium, or via budgets for occupation costs, such as those levied on France. Together with the directors of the Reichsbank, they hoped the additional resources would combat the short-term inflation caused by the Reich's own presence in occupied countries and thus, in the longer term, stabilize the reichsmark.

There was clear consensus, too, between experts and the political leadership that subjugated peoples should be forced to cover a significant proportion of the day-to-day costs of war. They agreed that the vanquished would pay off the supplementary loans taken out to finance German military campaigns. To quote the discreet language used by the guardians of the reichsmark: "To protect the integrity of the German currency, the Reichsbank stands by the basic principle of satisfying, wherever possible, the monetary needs of German offices in occupied territories by availing itself of payment from the countries concerned."[4]

From the fall of 1941 onward, the political leadership blocked all proposals by finance experts to levy supplementary wartime taxes on the wages and everyday consumer spending of average Germans. They had no such scruples about taxing the upper classes. In the case of the real estate inflation tax, the Reich commissioner for price controls worked together with the German Labor Front, Hitler's Party Chancellery, and the conservative-led Prussian Finance Ministry to see that the originally steep tax rates were doubled. Nazi functionaries supported the hike in the interest of securing the loyalty of the masses. The financial experts involved advocated it as a politically viable way of slowing the increase in wartime debt.

In other situations, the experts clearly took the initiative. Their actions caused the delicate psychological balance between the aims of Nazi politicians and the policies considered desirable by specialists to be constantly recalibrated. The system of RKK certificates, for example, was the independent invention of civil servants at the Finance Ministry and the Reichsbank. As if to prove the truth of Brecht's famous dictum "It is easier to rob by setting up a bank than by holding up a bank clerk," the Reich Credit Banks became the backbone of the remarkably effective—and even elegant—procedures by which Germany plundered much of Europe. The civil servants at the credit banks, recruited almost exclusively from the Reichsbank itself, conducted lucrative business dealings with non-German money—and the heist was pulled off in the name of currency policy. (The occupied parts of the Soviet Union represent an exception. There, money played a significant role, but it was secondary to various methods of terrorizing and subjugating the populace.)

The finance minister did not have to be ordered to stop transfers of forced laborers' wages to their families abroad and to have them paid in local currencies instead. He was quite willing to do so unbidden. Nor did he have to be commanded to extend the same procedure—forcing payment in local currency—to monetary institutions and businesses that bought foreign goods or securities. The market prices paid in reichsmarks for those commodities disappeared into the Reich's clearing account, and they were then added to the annual budget to the benefit of the general German population. The populations of the occupied countries were the ones who had to pay for the German state's unscrupulous business deals. It is inconceivable that Hitler, a financial layman, could have issued orders detailed enough to set up such complex systems. He didn't have to. Instead, he gave Germany's financial experts free rein—with the mandate to do whatever was necessary to benefit the German people. It was hardly an accident that some of the Reichsbank's stationery bore a stamp with a swastika and the honorary designation "Exemplary National Socialist Enterprise."[5]

Differences of opinion arose chiefly around the questions of how quickly and by which means Europe could be robbed penniless. Financial experts tended to be concerned with maximizing medium-term profits. They stressed a certain degree of sustainability, preferring, as it were, to milk the cow for an extended time rather than leading it directly to the slaughter. Schwerin von Krosigk insisted on pursuing what he called "the military-economic optimum," which involved "preventing countries whose potential we want to use from premature collapse."[6]

Nazi ideology may have been guided by grandiose visions of the future, but the party's leaders thought in terms of everyday political survival.

They made their fiscal decisions, whatever the ultimate costs, in order to get through the next couple of weeks or, at most, months.

THE CHAPTERS of this book about Hitler's "satisfied thieves" and those dealing with the large-scale corruption among German civilians in Ukraine shed ample light on the contradictory priorities of the Third Reich's financial experts and its political leadership. The permanent conflict over how much to tax the income of the German masses split along the same fault lines. In both cases, political opportunism overruled expert financial opinion.

At the beginning of this book, the question was posed as to how the Nazi regime was able to achieve such a high level of domestic political stability. In practice, the uneasy marriage of sophisticated financial expertise and the politics of popular opinion oriented around the welfare of the masses proved remarkably fruitful. The Nazi leaders were constantly handing out benefits to ordinary Germans, keeping them remarkably well fed and well supplied. At the same time, those who possessed the financial know-how compensated as best they could for the state's generosity. They kept increasing taxes on Germany's wealthy, not because they thought that made the most sense but because it was the only option for raising taxes at all within the country. They forcibly introduced means of non-currency payment into occupied countries to restrict the amount of cash in circulation and whenever possible imposed new taxes on foreign citizens. Professional considerations prompted them to encourage the dispossession of Europe's Jews in order to put the brakes on inflationary pressure.

A similar decision-making process governed policies on food rationing. With the war disrupting shipments from overseas, food suddenly became scarce in occupied countries such as Norway, Greece, and Holland. Significantly more food is needed to keep a combat army active than is required for an equivalent number of civilians. Moreover, millions of forced laborers suddenly had to be provided for, while resources in broad stretches of Europe decreased due to the effects of war and, later on, inflation.

Experts were responsible for rationing food and determining which items would be subject to control in Germany. They also decided which groups should be allocated very few provisions—or none at all. Jews, Soviet POWs, and psychiatric patients were the first groups to suffer from rationing policies, followed by residents of certain besieged cities. The decisions were made on the basis of political and military expediency.

One example serves to illustrate the general mechanism behind the system, although its particular effects may appear marginal. In 1940, in the interest of stretching supplies of grain and meat, civil servants in the Reich Food Ministry proposed prohibiting people from keeping house pets that did not serve some practical purpose, such as cats on a farm. The food saved would have immediately allowed the Reich to feed additional hundreds of thousands of people. Hitler quashed the ban, fearing that Germans would find the emotional loss unacceptable. The prohibition was, however, put in place for Jews, who were barred from keeping birds, cats, and dogs.

Civil servants in the Food Ministry stopped supplies of milk to Jewish children and introduced special, vastly inferior Jewish food rations, while ensuring that Germans with the right racial pedigree were kept as well fed as possible. These bureaucrats foresaw the mass murder of Jews as a way of increasing food supplies that could be extracted from Poland. In 1942, citing the needs of the German populace and their attitude toward the war, Minister Herbert Backe refused to deliver supplemental food rations to German troops fighting in Russia. In the competition over food reserves between the Eastern Front and the home front, he put the well-being of German civilians first. To ensure there would be enough food in Germany, Göring stressed the following point to agricultural commissioners working in occupied Soviet territories: "The war must sustain the war! That is now to be completely emphasized."[7]

Backe and his subordinates acted without scruple, propagating mass murder both through verbal commands and in writing. Schwerin von Krosigk's degree of culpability is open to debate. Thus far, no documents have been uncovered to link him to any of the specific decisions described here. In a modern state apparatus organized according to principles of division of labor, a prized specialist would not necessarily have been concerned with such issues. But it is beyond question that the finance minister personally, and with a great degree of thoroughness, made sure that everything taken from those who were murdered—including the gold from their teeth and the shirts off their backs—was handed over to the state. He then sold off whatever was received, from precious metals and jewels to garments fit only for rag collectors. Finally, he recorded the proceeds under general administrative revenues in the Reich's annual budget in an effort to obscure their origins.

Whatever Schwerin von Krosigk may have personally thought about Jews in general, he assumed that they would disappear, never to be seen again. Long before the decision was taken to proceed with the Holocaust, Krosigk, Reinhardt, and other leading civil servants at the Finance Ministry were busy inventing new ways of gradually impoverishing Jews so that in the end they would become "burdens on the state." Financial specialists in the Finance and Economics Ministries were the ones who, with their ever more stringent regulations on currency export and ever more draconian techniques of expropriation, made it impossible for many Jews to flee Nazi Germany. Overriding the will of the SS, they also prohibited Jews deported to the General Government of Poland from taking any significant cash reserves with them—money with which the deportees might have been at least minimally able to support themselves.

The financial experts represented a counterweight to the Nazi regime, which, owing to its tendency toward heedless action and, of course, to the character of the Führer himself, was often unstable. The collaboration between the two was makeshift and improvised, but it was efficient enough to support nearly twelve years of rearmament, violence, and annihilation. Even when the experts opposed the politically expedient course of action—as on the issue of what German soldiers could bring back home while on leave—their activities helped maintain the precarious equilibrium between the people and the political leadership. National Socialism did not derive its strength exclusively or even primarily from ideological indoctrination.

Our picture of the Third Reich as an authoritarian *Führerstaat* is misleading. Notwithstanding the state terror inflicted on its putative enemies, the system tolerated remarkably lively differences in opinions and policy between political leaders and professional specialists. The result was creative tension. Without the corrective influence of experts, the political functionaries would have been swamped by a financial crisis caused by currency devaluation and mounting debts. If the politicians had not restrained the experts and allowed political viability to trump financial wisdom on individual issues, the regime would have lost the loyalty of the masses.

Only the uneasy cooperation of both of these policy-making camps ensured that equilibrium would be maintained. Realism and apolitical expertise merged with a racist ideology bent on creating a welfare state for the benefit of ethnically "pure" Germans. It was in the interaction of these two elements—neither of which would have functioned on its own—that National Socialism developed its destructive potential.

Just Like in the Movies

The Nazi government bought the domestic loyalty of the German people through initially irresponsible, then outright criminal financial practices. In 1935, Hitler prohibited the Reich budget from being published. (He had good reason, since the following year his policies would come to depend more and more on mortgaging future assets.) The necessary result was an internal impetus toward war and conquest. The constant Nazi talk of needing more space and colonies, of Germany's place on the world stage and eastward expansion, as well as of the imperative of "de-Jewification," was aimed at hastening a rise in the German standard of living, which the domestic economy alone could never have supported.

In their propaganda, the Nazi leadership boasted of laying the cornerstone of a thousand-year Reich. But on the level of routine decision making, they didn't know how they were going to pay their bills from one day to the next. In January 1938, after reading a memorandum from the Finance Ministry, Goebbels wrote with a hint of bravado: "The situation is worse than I imagined. But no people have ever perished of debt—far more have died from a lack of weapons."[8] Two months later, he noted, after reviewing the draft Reich budget: "We may have a huge deficit, but we've got Austria." In December 1939, an eyewitness described the thrust of Hitler's strategy: "The Führer realizes that we can't hold out in a drawn-out war. . . . All bets have to be placed on a single card."[9]

Nonetheless, after every military victory, no matter how quick and relatively painless for German forces, the same problems with finances and food supplies kept cropping up. However vast the amounts of loot and the size of territories annexed, the revenues derived fell short of expectations. The Nazi state could never develop and cultivate what it had conquered.[10] The political consequences of issuing bad checks (in the form of short-term Reich promissory notes and "floating debts") meant that the Nazi leaders had to push ahead with further military expansionism. Any hesitancy would have led to the end of the regime. They couldn't afford to content themselves with preserving a status quo, even after the victorious military campaigns against France and other rivals in 1939–40 had united Europe's "German soil" (*Volksboden*)—including all disputed regions, vast resources of coal, and the "bread basket" of Poland—within the Reich.

Consolidating what had been won in land and resources would have meant that the Reich would have had to take responsibility for the money it had borrowed to create jobs on the home front and rearm itself, to build architectural monuments, and to expand its territory. The dispossession of Jews, the sale of "enemy assets," and ultimately the murder of hundreds of thousands of "useless mouths to feed" allowed the enlarged Reich to close some of its financial gaps. But these vast crimes would not have helped the Nazi regime pay off its massive debts. If the government had heeded Carl Friedrich Goerdeler's prognosis in the summer of 1940, immediately after Germany's triumph over France, the Reich would have yielded to the bitter necessity of consolidating its finances. But as Goerdeler himself recognized, that was not going to happen. Those in charge, led by a public-opinion-conscious Adolf Hitler, had decided "to take the easier path of self-deception."[11]

Given the political circumstances in the summer of 1940, war was not only the easier of two paths but the only one still open to the German leadership. By the fall of that year, once Churchill had thwarted Germany's colonial ambitions in Africa, the sole option was to invade the Soviet Union. A few days prior to the start of that campaign, Goebbels wrote of the common bond linking popular opinion, crimes against humanity, and the political leadership: "The Führer says that, right or wrong, we have to achieve victory. That is the only way. And it is just, moral, and necessary. Once we've achieved victory, no one will ask how we did it. We have so much on our conscience anyway that we have to be victorious. Otherwise our people and those of us in the leadership will be wiped out, along with everything that is precious to us. So let's get to work!"[12] By the winter of 1941–42, the political leadership had succeeded in convincing a majority of Germans that all bridges had been burned. While they may have supported individual Nazi measures, ordinary Germans also considered it increasingly difficult to change the direction that had been taken. This realization led many of them in the last years of the war to prefer sacrificing themselves for a hopeless cause rather than capitulating.

Undoubtedly there were skeptics in Germany during the war years. But their voices went largely unheard. Most of those who supported National Socialism did so because one or another of the Nazis' vaguely formulated goals appealed to them. Some followed the party's lead because its efforts were directed against Germany's archenemy, France, others because the relatively youthful Nazi leadership broke traditional moral conventions. Catholic clergymen gave their blessing to weapons' being used in the crusade against godless Bolshevism, even as they objected to the seizure of monasteries and the Nazi euthanasia campaigns. *Volk* comrades from a socialist background, on the other hand, enthusiastically supported the party's anticlericism and antielitism. Later, when the fighting was over, the fateful collaboration of millions of Germans vanished, as if by magic, to be replaced by a wildly exaggerated—and historically insignificant—record of resistance to Hitler. Opposition to the Nazis, too, was based on shifting affiliations and allegiances.

The actor Wolf Goette, cited in the chapter on Hitler's satisfied thieves, maintained the same distance from Nazi ideology as the writer

Heinrich Böll. Nazi politics, wrote Goette, always made him "want to puke," evoking a "feeling of terrible shame," when he saw those "branded with yellow [stars]." In contrast to Böll, though, Goette saw the pro-euthanasia propaganda film *Ich klage an* (*J'accuse*) as representing a "pure and respectable outlook," as a moving work of art whose "cinematic excellence" demonstrated the "necessity" of euthanasia "in certain cases of hopeless decrepitude." On occasions he felt pangs of conscience as to what might happen if "this idea were propagated by a state ruled by arbitrariness." Yet no matter how Goette stood on individual political issues, as a resident of the "fairy-tale city of Prague," he relished the prospects for advancing his career and bettering his standard of living that Germany's rule by force offered him. Preoccupied as he was with maximizing his own small, personal advantage, he was politically neutralized.[13]

Hitler moved quickly to stabilize an explosive compound of highly diverse interests and political attitudes. This was the political alchemy of his leadership. The sheer speed of decisions and events kept his regime from falling apart. He preserved the dynamic element of the Nazi Party as a *movement*. He was more supportive of erstwhile street fighters who had become gauleiters and other local Nazi leaders than he was of his governmental ministers. Hitler's triumph in organizing his regime after 1933 was not to let the all-powerful party decay into an ancillary apparatus of the state. On the contrary, unlike the communists in the former East Germany, he was able to mobilize the apparatus of state extraordinarily successfully, using its creativity to support his own goals of a "national uprising" and to stretch the resources of the country to the point of collapse. The majority of Germans succumbed first to the giddiness, then to the full-blown intoxication of history's being made at breakneck pace. Later, after the German defeat at Stalingrad, the relentless pounding of aerial bombardments, and the rise in punitive acts of state terrorism, those people fell into an equally benumbed state of shock. The air raids produced more indifference than fear, leading to fatalistic resignation. The mass deaths of German soldiers on the Eastern Front encouraged those at home to reduce their concerns to everyday needs—and to their hopes of getting at least one more letter from their sons, husbands, or lovers.[14]

Germans experienced the twelve short years between 1933 and 1945 as a perpetual state of emergency. Spinning on the carousel of events, they lost their sense of both balance and proportion. "Everything seems like a film to me," remarked a business associate of Victor Klemperer's during the Sudeten crisis of 1938.[15] A year later, nine days before the German invasion of Poland, Göring assured the workers at the Rheinmetall-Borsig factory in Berlin that they could rely on a leadership that "is positively racing with energy."[16] Entries in Goebbels's diary from February 1941 echoed that sentiment. "The whole day a marvelous tempo," reads one. "Now the pace of life on the offensive is resuming." And in a fit of glee at German military successes against Britain: "I spent the whole day in a feverish state of happiness."[17]

Within his inner circle, Hitler often alluded to the possibility that he might die young as justification for the accelerated pace of his rule. Speed, he explained, was necessary if he was to achieve his political goals. Hitler was like an amateur tightrope walker who can maintain his balance only by taking ever faster steps—and who inevitably falls from the wire. Hitler's political and military decisions are best interpreted in the light of his motivation at the moment, despite all his thundering rhetoric about the future.

Race Conscious and Class Conscious

Along with the radical revisions to the Treaty of Versailles, discussed early on in this book, a major key to the National Socialist German Workers Party's success was its spontaneous, almost adolescent acceleration of the pace of political decisions and action. The war intensified the emphasis on rapidity and radicalism. Military force wiped out borders, and territories that Germany had been obliged to cede after World War I were reacquired, seemingly for all eternity. In 1941, German historians were already pondering the possibilities of "winning back the free county of Burgundy [Franche-Comté]" and the "Low Countries," which had "slipped out of the Reich federation" during the Middle Ages. In two years of blitzkrieg warfare, the tempo increased with every large-scale military action. Attacks on the Norwegian city of Narvik and on Rotterdam followed the one on Warsaw. Campaigns in Crete, the Caucasus, and northern Africa came hot on the heels of victory over France.

The third fundamental pillar of Hitler's popular support was his promise of equality for all members of the racially defined *Volk*. In the policies of wartime socialism that came into effect as of September 1, 1939, many Germans saw a credible vision of a more just social order. The war accelerated the obliteration of class barriers. The Nazi leadership was at pains to ensure that "in these times of shortages every individual *Volk* comrade will be provided for equally with the necessities of life, regardless of his social position and income." The only privileges were for people who did particularly strenuous physical labor or had special needs. In early 1940, an observer from the Social Democratic Party reported from Berlin: "The working classes thoroughly welcome the fact that 'the better off ' have, in practical terms, ceased to be that."[18] Egalitarian rationing policies increased the popularity of the regime.[19]

Hitler claimed to be a man of the people who had risen to the top of society thanks to talent and hard work. He promulgated the idea that his government would guarantee gifted individuals the opportunity to better their lot, no matter how poor and uneducated they had grown up. One of his credos was that "the constricting of upward mobility must be opposed." He promoted Nazi-founded secondary schools, so-called national-political educational establishments, and *Adolf-Hitler-Schulen* as institutions that would correct social inequities in both a material and a pedagogical sense, "so that even the poorest youth can rise to any position, as long as he has what it takes."[20] A number of leading figures in the postwar Federal Republic of Germany were graduates of such institutions, which did not charge tuition, as most schools did. In 1938, Hitler proclaimed: "With the type of help our institutions offer, it should now be possible for any child of a worker or a farmer, if blessed by God with talent, to rise to the highest echelons of our new Germany."[21] In October 1942, as mass German casualties on the Eastern Front forced the Wehrmacht to open its officer ranks to those without higher education, Germans reacted "with enthusiasm," seeing the development as the "realization of a main goal of the party program."[22] As of 1933, the same program had forbidden Aryans from carrying on romantic liaisons with Jews. Now, for the first time in German history, an officer was allowed to marry a working-class woman, provided the two could prove their ethnic hygiene and get a marriage license.

On January 16, 1945, as the Third Reich was being overwhelmed by the Allied armies and reduced to ruins, Fritz Reinhardt offered a final vision of what had become a lost cause. In a statement to a newspaper, he declared that the government was spending more than a billion reichsmarks a year on children and education—an extraordinarily large sum for the time. "Soon after the conclusion of the war," he added, "the next step toward redistribution of family burdens will be the eradication of school fees, tuitions, and costs of educational materials for all children and all types of schools, including trade schools and universities." With this step, a "strong, economically and financially healthy Germany" would become "the first [truly] social state on earth."[23]

Upward mobility for the common people—in various forms and not infrequently at the cost of others—was one of the fundamental political innovations of the twentieth century. The Nazi brand of socialism was part of this tradition. Though based on an odious and thoroughly discredited vision of racial superiority, the Nazi devaluation of individual freedom and indifference toward personal autonomy did not radically deviate from many other forms of egalitarianism. The Nazi movement represented the drive to couple social equality with national homogeneity, a concept that was popular not only in Germany. From this powerful formulation, Hitler's welfare state derived its criminal energies.

In the fall of 1939, most Germans had little desire to go to war again purely to serve the cause of patriotism. It was a political necessity for the Nazi leadership to cut them in, as quickly as possible, on a significant portion of the spoils. Social policy and racial appeals were conjoined for the first time, and the resulting appeasement renewed the public's trust in the state. For this reason, the German public clung to the obviously utopian promises of National Socialism, even after its contradictions and moral dishonesty became evident to all. It is also why those active within the system were so willing to destroy the livelihoods and lives of tens of millions of people.

NOTHING LESS than massive popular greed made it possible for the regime to tame the majority of Germans with a combination of low taxes, ample supplies of consumer goods, and targeted acts of terror against social outsiders. The best strategy in the eyes of the public-opinion-conscious Nazi leadership was to keep all Germans happy. Goebbels was fond of saying that public optimism was "a weapon crucial to the war effort."[24]

The Nazi leadership did not transform the majority of Germans into ideological fanatics who were convinced they were part of the master race. Instead it succeeded in making them well-fed parasites. Vast numbers of Germans fell prey to the euphoria of a gold rush, certain that the future would be a time of unbridled prosperity. As the state was transformed into a gigantic apparatus for plundering others, average Germans became unscrupulous profiteers and passive recipients of bribes. Soldiers became armed couriers of butter.[25]

Men from the simplest walks of life suddenly owned things they hadn't known existed a few years previously. On its own, that was hardly sufficient motivation. But the war itself gave those who fought it a taste of luxuries to come: as German soldiers conquered today, so would all Germans live tomorrow. Underlying this heady sensation, however, was the nagging pull of bad conscience, an uneasy feeling that one was damned to either total victory or total destruction. In late 1943, the Security Service summarized the views of Germans who, like millions of other people, regularly deposited their money in savings accounts: "If we win the war, the money will stand us in good stead. If we lose the war, then it doesn't matter whether we have saved money or spent it on things and property. Everything will be lost."[26]

IN APRIL 1945, a German-born British officer named Julius Posener returned to his former homeland, traveling from the lower Rhine region to the bombed-out city of Cologne. He had previously fought on the Italian front, "where in the hard winter of 1944–45 Neapolitans had starved to death on the streets by the hundreds" and where the people, "even from the upper echelons of society, were broken, pale, and hopeless." The war had been relatively benign in France, Posener wrote, "but that was nothing compared with the rows of lovely girls dressed in white" in Germany, "taking an evening stroll past the ruins of the city."

Although the extent of damage exceeded his expectations, Posener, who was a construction engineer in civilian life, had been prepared for the destruction of cities. What surprised him was the way the people looked: "The people did not fit the destruction. They looked good. They were rosy cheeked, happy, well groomed, and very well dressed. An economic system that had been propped up by millions of foreign hands and the total plunder of an entire part of the world was here displaying what it had achieved."[27]

A Note on Calculations

The publication of this book in Germany in 2005 prompted a number of questions from two British historians, Richard Overy and Adam Tooze, pertaining to the calculations I used to establish the financial burden borne by Germans during the war. In *The Wages of Destruction: The Making and Breaking of the Nazi Economy*, which appeared as this English edition was going to press, Tooze, on a number of occasions, praises and draws on my work, both my previous books on National Socialism and the present volume. But in a note he writes of "serious misreadings that undermine [my] central thesis,"* namely, that the regime went easy on German taxpayers in order to secure their loyalty.

At issue are the statistics concerning Germany's revenues and wartime debt. I argue that the percentage of Germany's wartime revenues derived from external sources—that is, revenues extracted from occupied countries, forced labor, and persecuted Jews—is about 70 percent.† Tooze objects that

---

*Adam Tooze, *The Wages of Destruction*, p. 772, n. 86.

†As yet unpublished research supports my conclusion regarding the high percentage of German revenues from external sources. See Filippo Occhino, Kim Oosterlinck, and Eugene N. White, "How Occupied France Financed Its Own Exploitation in World War II," discussion paper, Oct. 2005 (http://emlab.berkeley.edu/users/webfac/eichengreen/e211_fa05/white.pdf). I am grateful to Dorothea Hauser for alerting me to this source. The U.S. National Archives has recently provided the Federal German Archive with a series of photocopies of substantial documents from the Reich Finance Ministry, the Reichsbank, the Reich Economics Ministry, and other Nazi institutions responsible for wartime finances, occupation costs, and the dispossession of Jews. I was unable to include this material in the present book, yet the information contained there confirms my conclusions. The relevant catalog codes are: PS-2150, PS-2251, PS-2216, PS-2265, PS-2266, PS-2267, PS-2268, PS-2287, PS-2850, PS-3562, PS-3948, PS-3949, PS-3915.

it amounted to around 25 percent of the actual costs of war. Most of the discrepancy can be easily explained. My focus is on revenues received during the actual period of the war; my critic is talking about total, comprehensive war expenditures, including those financed on credit—debts that came due after Germany's defeat.

The Third Reich spent around 620 billion reichsmarks during World War II. We can subtract approximately 20 billion reichsmarks annually—or a total of 110 billion reichsmarks—as money that would also have been spent in peacetime for the basic needs of the Third Reich. That leaves around 510 billion reichsmarks used by Germany for the purpose of waging war. Approximately one-half of these expenditures were covered by ongoing revenues—an extraordinarily high proportion when we look at other historical examples. The remaining funds needed were obtained, to some extent, by printing more money. But the lion's share was financed on credit, from medium- and especially short-term bonds issued by the Reich on the German financial market. There is presumably no disagreement between Tooze and me about these facts, although I question Overy's assertion (which Tooze accepts) that foreign sources—that is, revenues extracted from occupied countries—accounted for a mere 12 percent of the revenues in Germany's total wartime budget.* (Purposely or not, that assertion served postwar Germany's own interests.)

Our major area of disagreement is rather over the question of how much of the cost of the war was borne by Germans during the war itself. Tooze's calculations would put the percentage of budget costs shouldered by Germany considerably higher than my own. This dispute is rooted in the issue of where one starts one's calculations. When attempting to explain Hitler's popular success, in contrast to merely tallying up pluses and minuses in the ledger sheets, it is wrong to include German debts for which repayment began after the end of the war. Tooze and others add up their figures on the German war economy in reverse, starting from the point of Germany's defeat. Thus, while the figures they arrive at may be mathematically correct, the results are historically irrelevant since they

*Richard J. Overy, "'Blitzkriegswirtschaft.' Finanzpolitik, Lebensstandard und Arbeitseinsatz in Deutschland 1939–1942," *Vierteljahresschrift für Zeitgeschichte* 36 (1988), pp. 396–435.

don't adequately reflect the political context in which those debts were incurred.

In contrast, the starting point for my investigation is the question of how Hitler, together with his ministers, gauleiters, and advisers, managed to maintain domestic stability within the Reich between 1940 and 1943. As is also the case in today's Germany, average citizens were only marginally interested in the level of state indebtedness. The loans taken out during the war placed no burden on the populace during the Nazi regime, and indeed Germans as a whole were indifferent to them. They were more likely to protest if the government raised their taxes or cut back on benefits and entitlements. Conversely, state generosity, especially in hard times, created public goodwill. That is my main thesis. This book is concerned with the interaction between a people and its leadership and with what gave Nazi Germany internal stability, not with the burdens Germans faced after 1945.

In arguing against Tooze, one could well cite historian Hans-Ulrich Wehler. Wehler writes, correctly, that post-1939 Nazi financial policy "was completely dominated by and irresponsibly fixated on the idea of passing on its own burdens to the states it had conquered."* I do not, as Tooze claims, ignore the domestic debt the Nazi regime took on in the name of all Germans. On the contrary, I discuss this topic in depth in the section of chapter 12 titled "Virtual War Debts." These wartime debts were, of course, passed on to the taxpaying German populace, but again, only with the Third Reich's defeat in World War II. During the war, ever mindful of popular opinion, Hitler never confronted his subjects with the real level of state debt he was accruing. In fact, a lot of effort went toward assuaging popular fears about debt-driven inflation. In 1942, the Reich Finance Ministry told the public that wartime debts were actively counterbalanced by access to resources and other sources of income worth several times more than the Reich's elevated debt. The plan, at the end of the war, was to eradicate this debt with the help of "the significant amount of real value" assets that had been won by the German sword—

*Hans-Ulrich Wehler, *Deutsche Gesellschaftsgeschichte, vom Beginn des Ersten Weltkriegs bis zur Gründung der beiden deutschen Staaten. 1914–1949*, vol. 4, Munich, 2003, p. 927.

or, to use the more polite language of financial experts back then, by "utilizing foreign economies."

Tooze, in the interest of "symmetry," calculates the debts accrued by nations like France to pay wartime tributes to Germany in the same fashion as he reckons the Reich's wartime debts to German banks, building societies, and insurance companies. He concludes, correctly, that both were forms of credit. But such formal criteria are irrelevant both here and in a number of other cases. The historical problem concerns something different. French contributions to Germany, regardless of how they were collected within France, represented real revenues for the Third Reich, from which ordinary Germans profited. Credit taken out on the German capital market to finance the war postponed the real burden upon the German people, and the goal was to transfer that burden, as quickly as possible, to enslaved peoples. This is why my calculations refer, as explicitly stated, to the Reich's wartime revenues and not to its total expenditures.

AFTER I responded to his review of the German edition of this book,* Tooze wrote an article, citing Hitler's finance minister von Krosigk to the effect that one could not use credit secured by the state to "defer" the burdens taken on by a borrowing country in times of war. At first glance, this seems a reasonable statement. Unlike a private borrower, who can, for example, buy a car on cheap credit and thus maintain his level of consumption basically unaffected, a nation waging war must restrict civilian consumption to compensate for credit-financed military consumption. But the hardships of war on the domestic front were significantly alleviated by selling off the belongings of dispossessed and murdered Jews, as well as of deported Poles and French citizens. Göring's decrees of October 1940 lifting restrictions on what German soldiers could bring and send home from abroad also helped ease the situation. Every time soldiers used available spending money abroad and then sent the wares they

*For the complete exchange, see Adam Tooze, "Einfach verkalkuliert," *Die Tageszeitung*, March 12, 2005; Götz Aly, "Nicht falsch, sondern anders gerechnet. Eine Antwort auf J. Adam Tooze," *Die Tageszeitung*, March 15, 2005; Tooze, "Doch falsch gerechnet—weil falsch gedacht," *Die Tageszeitung*, March 16, 2005; Tooze, *Wages of Destruction*, p. 647, n. 88.

bought back to Germany, they raised the real standard of living for their families.

It is hardly accidental that one of Germany's leading postwar authors, Siegfried Lenz, should write in his 1966 essay "I, for Example: Characteristics of a Generation" that "everyone had a father, a brother or a brother-in-law in the war. Packages came with enchanting soaps from Paris, canned goods from Poland, reindeer ham from Norway and currants from Greece. The war was far away. It was going well and appeared as though it would be profitable. Our only taste of war, initially, was in such packages."* Historians like Tooze and Overy, who focus only on Germany's formal economy, ignore the phenomenon Lenz describes. Both treat the economic statistics for wartime Germany as if we were dealing with a transparent economy instead of one based on collective larceny.

For example, German ration cards for clothing provided 100 points per year. That was just about enough for a pair of shoes and a dress—not much and without a doubt less than what people enjoyed in Great Britain. But as we have seen throughout this book, soldiers often sent back quantities of clothing that greatly exceeded the official yearly allotment. It is thus misleading when Overy uses the nominal purchasing power of wartime ration cards as a measure of the standard of living in Germany. Using retail statistics, Overy concludes that the index of real per capita consumption fell by 30 points between 1938 and 1944, compared with only 12 points for Great Britain. That may be true, but a single home-leave visit by a heavily laden Wehrmacht soldier, a series of packages sent back from the front, and the state-sponsored auctions of Aryanized household effects easily sufficed to make up some of the difference. Some German soldiers and their families were even better off during the war than in peacetime. These factors may not show up in official statistics, but their significance cannot be denied.

My aim is to uncover the kleptocratic character of and the larcenous mechanisms within the National Socialist economy. Only when one does so, can one see how Nazi Germany shored up state revenues, domestic

---

*Siegfried Lenz, *Essays 1, 1955–1982* (vol. 19 of Lenz's complete works), Hamburg, 1997, p. 23. I would like to thank Markus Barth for alerting me to this source.

consumption, and public morale with policies of mass murder and state-organized plunder and terror. The consumer statistics cited by Overy do not reflect the day-to-day reality of the Nazi community of larceny, and thus objections raised to this book on the basis of those numbers are groundless. Overy and Tooze are more interested in the official statistics of Nazi Germany than in the de facto level of goods available to the German populace, which on the whole maintained its standard of living. In choosing to focus their work this way, they obscure rather than illuminate the way Germans actually lived during World War II.

Currency Exchange Rates

Rates of exchange set by Germany, 1939–45*

Albania	100 Albanian francs	81 reichsmarks (RM)
Belgium	100 belgas (= 500 belgian francs)	40 RM
	from 1943 on:	25 RM
Bulgaria	100 leva	3.1 RM
Croatia	100 kuna	5 RM
Denmark	100 crowns	52.3 RM[†]
Finland	100 marks	5.1 RM
France	100 francs	5 RM
General Government of Poland	100 zlotys	50 RM
Greece	100 drachmas	1.67 RM (the value of the mark constantly increased)
Great Britain	100 pounds	991 RM
Hungary	100 pengö	60.9 RM
Italy	100 liras	13.2 RM
	from September 1943 on:	10 RM
Luxembourg	100 francs	10 RM[‡]
Netherlands	100 guilders (or Dutch florins)	132.7 RM
Norway	100 crowns	56.9 RM[§]
Protectorate of Bohemia and Moravia	100 crowns	10 RM
Romania	100 lei	1.67 RM[**]
Switzerland	100 francs	58 RM

Serbia	100 dinar	5 RM
Slovakia	100 crowns	8.6 RM
Ukraine	100 karbowanez	10 RM
USA	100 dollars	250.2 RM
USSR	100 rubles	47.2 RM
	from June 22, 1944, on:	10 RM

Official price of gold during World War II

Gold	$35 per fine ounce = $1,125.00 per kilogram
	= 4,869.80 Swiss francs per kilogram = 2,784 RM[tt]
1 gold pound	$10 = 25 RM

*Kretzschmann, "Reichskreditkassen," pp. 116–17; *Reichszollblatt* 27 (1942), no. 32, ed. A, p. 56; Zahlungsregelungen für die Wehrmacht in den ausserdeutschen Ländern von 1941 und 1944 [Payment Regulations for the Wehrmacht in Non-German Countries from 1941 to 1944], BA R 2501/7101.

[t]At the beginning of the occupation, 100 Danish crowns were worth 50 RM. For a while, the rate was 100 to 49, and in the end it was 100 to 52.3. On the discussion concerning this exchange rate, see BA R 2/60244.

[‡]Also, for a time, 12.5.

[§]Originally 60 RM, then 56.9 RM.

**An agreement between the main administration of the Reich Credit Bank and the Casa Autonoma de Finantare si Amortizare in Bucharest in January 1941 set the internal exchange rate at 100 lei = 2 RM. See BA R 2/30703.

[tt]*Goldtransaktionen im Zweiten Weltkrieg*, p. 4.

List of Abbreviations

AN Archives Nationales, Paris

AOK Armeeoberkommando (Army Headquarters)

ASBI Archivio Storico Banca d'Italia, Rome

AWA Allgemeines Wehrmachtamt (General Wehrmacht Office)

AWI Arbeitswissenschaftliches Institut der DAF (Labor-Scientific Office of the German Labor Front)

BA Bundesarchiv (Berlin-Lichterfelde and Koblenz) .

BA-MA Bundesarchiv-Militärarchiv, Freiburg im Breisgau

BA–DH Bundesarchiv, Dahlwitz-Hoppegarten

DAF Deutsche Arbeitsfront (German Labor Front)

DSK Devisenschutzkommando (Currency Protection Command)

DVO Durchführungsverordnung (implementation ordinance)

DW Dienststelle Westen des RMfbdO (Western Office of the Reich Ministry for the Occupied Eastern Territories)

F (Lese-)Film (Microfiche)

FfW Forschungsstelle für Wehrwirtschaft (Research Group for Military Economics)

F.H.Q. Führerhauptquartier (Hitler's Main Office)

GBW Generalbevollmächriger für die Kriegswirtschaft (general envoy for the war economy)

GG General Government of Poland

HA Hauptabteilung (Main Division)

HAdDB Historisches Archiv der Deutschen Bundesbank, Frankfurt am Main

H.V.Bl. Heeresverordnungsblatt (Registry of Army Ordinances)

HZÄ Hauptzollämter (Main Customs Office)

Int. (intendant)

Kdo Kommando(sache) (command affair)

Kom. Kommandantur (Commandant's Office)

KVR Kriegsverwaltungsrat (Wartime Administration Counsel/Council)

KWVO Kriegswirtschaftsverordnung (Wartime Economic Ordinance)

LArch Landesarchiv

LR Legationsrat (legation councilor)

Lt. Leitender, Leutnant (managing lieutenant)

MB, MBfh, Mil.Befh. Militärbefehlshaber (military commander)

MBB/NF Militärbefehlshaber in Belgien und Nordfrankreich (military commander in Belgium and northern France)

MBiF Militärbefehlshaber in Frankreich (military commander in France)

MOL Magyar Országos Levéltár, Budapest (Hungarian State Archive)

MVB/NF Militärverwaltung Belgien und Nordfrankreich (military administration in Belgium and northern France)

MVAChef Militärverwaltung, Amtschef (military administration, office head)

MVOR Militärverwaltungsoberrat (military administration, superior counsel/council)

NA National Archives (and Records Administration), College Park, Maryland

NS Nationalsozialist (National Socialist)

NSB Nationaal-Socialistische Beweging (in den Niederlanden) (National Socialist Movement of the Netherlands)

NSDAP Nationalsozialistische Deutsche Arbeiterpartei (National Socialist German Workers Party)

OB Oberbefehlshaber (commander in chief)

OFP Oberfinanzpräsident (chief financial officer)

Okdo Oberkommando (High Command)

OKH Oberkommando des Heeres (Army High Command)

OKM Oberkommando der Kriegsmarine (Navy High Command)

OKVR Oberkriegsverwaltungsrat (Superior Wartime Administration Counsel/Council)

OKW Oberkommando der Wehrmacht (Wehrmacht High Command)

OLG Oberlandesgericht (superior local court)

PA AA Politisches Archiv des Auswärtigen Amts, Berlin (Political Archive of the German Foreign Office)

PK Parteikanzlei Hitlers (Hitler's Party Chancellery)

RB (Deutsche) Reichsbank

RFM Reichsfinanzministerium, Reichsminister der Finanzen (Reich Finance Minister/Ministry)

RGBl. Reichsgesetzblatt (Reich Legal Registry)

RH Rechnungshof des Deutschen Reichs (Reich General Auditor's Office)

RHK Reichshauptkasse (Reich treasury)

RK Reichskommissar, Reichskommissariat, Reichskanzlei, Reichskanzler

(Reich commissioner, Reich Commissioner's Office, Reich Chancellery, Reich chancellor)
RKG Reichskredit Gesellschaft AG (Reich Credit Union)
RKK Reichskreditkasse (Reich Credit Bank)
RKU Reichskommissariat Ukraine (Reich Commissioner's Office for Ukraine)
RMfdbO Reichsministerium für die besetzten Ostgebiete (Reich Ministry for the Occupied Eastern Territories)
RMI Reichsministerium des Inneren, Reichsminister des Inneren (Reich Interior Ministry/Minister)
RR Regierungsrat (government counsel/council)
RStBl. Reichssteuerblatt (Reich tax journal)
RTO Reichstarifordnung (Reich Tariff Ordinance)
RWM Reichswirtschaftsministerium (Reich Economics Ministry)
SAEF Service des archives économiques et financières, Savigny-le-Temple
SD Sicherheitsdienst der SS (Security Service of the SS)
Seetra Seetransport (-stelle) (Naval Transport Office)
SKL Seekriegsleitung (Directorate of Naval Warfare)
StA Staatsarchiv (state archive)
StS Staatssekretär (state secretary/deputy)
TB Tätigkeitsbericht(e) (progress report/s)
VO Verordnung (Decree/Ordinance)
VOBlF Verordnungsblatt des Militärbefehlshabers in Frankreich (Register of Ordinances by the Military Commander in France)
VOBlRProt Verordnungsblatt des Reichsprotektors in Böhmen und Mähren (Register of Ordinances by the Reich Protector in Bohemia and Moravia)
WaKo Waffenstillstandskommission (Armistice Commission)
WB, WBfh. Wehrmachtbefehlshaber (Wehrmacht commander)
WFStb Wehrmachtführungsstab (Wehrmacht Chiefs of Staff)
Wi Wirtschafts- (economic)
WO Wirtschaftsoffizier (economics officer)
ZFÄ Zollfahndungsämter (Customs Investigation Offices)
ZF Zollfahndung (customs investigation)
ZFS Zollfahndungsstelle (Customs Investigation Center/s)
ZNU Zentralnotenbank Ukraine (Central Currency Bank of Ukraine)

Notes

The prefixes PS, NG, NID, NO, and NOKW refer to transcripts of the Nuremberg trials, facsimile reproductions of which are available in most major research libraries. ET refers to Eichmann trial protocols and documents, similarly available.

PREFACE

1. Grätz, *Geschichte der Juden*, vol. 8, pp. 49ff.

PART I: POLITICAL OPPORTUNISTS IN ACTION

Chapter I: The Dream of a "People's Empire"

1. Speech by Hitler to the workers at the Rheinmetall-Borsig factory in Berlin, Oct. 10, 1940; *Völkischer Beobachter*, Oct. 11, 1940; Hitler, speech on Dec. 10, 1940 ("Rede," p. 361); Boelcke, *Kosten*, p. 122; Goebbels, *Tagebücher*, Dec. 11, 1940 (hereafter referred to as Goebbels's diary).
2. Goebbels's diary, April 19, 1943.
3. These are comments inscribed in the guest book of the author's family's summer home in the southern Black Forest by Ernst Aly (b. 1912) and Hermann Aly (b. 1910).
4. Bongs, *Strasse*, p. 7.
5. Ilse Prüssmann, Hochschule für Lehrerbildung, Hamburg, Bericht über den Lehrereinsatz Sommer 1940 [Report on Summer Deployment, 1940], BA R 49/appendix 1/20, pp. 8–10.
6. Hachmeister, *Schleyer*, p. 86.
7. Schuster to Hellmut Becker, Jan. 28, 1942, and March 23, 1943, Becker estate, Berlin; on Schuster's dissertation, see Aly, *Rasse*, p. 14.

8. Aly, *Macht*, p. 149; Harald Hansen, interview with author, August 1983.

9. Goebbels's diary, June 6 and 17, 1941.

10. Aly, *Rasse*, pp. 141–51.

11. Hillers, *Skizze meines Lebens* (1935), BA R 55/20176.

12. On the change in sensibility of intellectuals with a socialist background, see Bisky, "Jungen"; Zuckmayer, *Geheimreport*.

13. Hitler to Army High Command, Nov. 23, 1939, PS-789 (NA RG 238/case XI/microfiche 33).

14. Reinhardt to Schwerin von Krosigk, June 18, 1940, NA T 178/15, microfilm 041.

15. On Belgrade, see p. 371, n. 13; Survey of the Westerbork and Vught Camps by Main Auditing Office, BA R 2/30666.

16. Aly and Heim, *Vordenker*, pp. 300–30, 383, and passim.

17. Grimm described German script as "a shapeless affront to the eye" (*Wörterbuch*, vol. 1, p. liii).

18. DAF/NS-Gemeinschaft, "Kraft durch Freude," Gau Berlin, in *Dein Urlaub* (Berlin, 1938); Hitler, speech on Dec. 10, 1940 ("Rede," p. 343).

19. DAF/AWI, Kriegsfinanzierung über die Altersversorgung? [Financing the War via the Pension System?] (Nov. 1939), NA T 178/15, microfilm 668.

20. Hansen, "Rechtsgestaltung."

21. "Gedanken zur Neugestaltung."

22. Ranetsberger, "Gerichtsvollzieher."

23. " 'Fall Köppen.' "

24. Kundrus, *Kriegerfrauen*, pp. 316ff.

25. See Ziche, "Zwangsvollstreckungsrecht."

26. Bissinger, *Das musst du wissen!*, p. 26; *Deutsche Gerichtsvollzieher-Zeitung* 60 (1940), pp. 173–74; Sebode, "Regelung."

27. RFM, Ideensammlung zur steuerlichen Behandlung von Nichtariern [Collection of Ideas Concerning Tax Policy toward Non-Aryans], Aug. 21, 1935, BA R 2/56009, vol. 1, pp. 2–39, passim.

28. RFM (Zülow, Kühne), April 25, 1938, in Friedenberger et al., *Reichsfinanzverwaltung*, pp. 53–54.

29. Goebbels's diary, Aug. 10, 1943, and March 30, 1944.

30. RFM (Ludwig), March 18, 1939, BA R 2/9398, p. 308.

31. Woitkowski, "Graf Schwerin von Krosigk."

32. Reich Labor Office (Zschimmer) to PK, Sept. 11, 1941, BA R 2/31093, pp. 60ff.

33. Schöpf, "Reinhardt"; Schönknecht, "Ausbildung."

34. Goebbels's diary, Feb. 15, 1942.

35. Hamann, *Wien*, pp. 160–68; "Sturm des Jubels und der Freude. Die alte Kaiserstadt huldigt dem Gründer des neuen Reiches," *Völkischer Beobachter*, April 2, 1938; Zitelmann, *Hitler*, p. 80.

36. Hitler, *Mein Kampf*, p. 712.

37. Hitler speech to Army High Command, Nov. 23, 1939, PS-789.

38. Aly, *Voss*, p. 28.

39. For 1937–38, see Abelshauser, "Kriegswirtschaft," p. 526.

40. Wolfgang Aly, "Das Leben eines deutschen Professors. Erinnerungen und Erfahrungen," MS, Freiburg im Breisgau, 1961.

41. Köppen, note, Sept. 18, 1941, BA R 6/34a.

42. Aly and Heim, *Vordenker*, pp. 398–401.

43. One of those children was a future professor of mine, Wolf-Dieter Narr; see Böll, *Briefe*, p. 972.

44. Haupt to Cobitz, Institut für Deutsche Ostarbeit, Cracow, June 27, 1944; Mau, "Vom neuen Land im Osten," Jan. 13, 1944, National Anthropological Archives, Smithsonian Institution, Washington, D.C., Institut für Deutsche Ostarbeit, box 1 (thanks to Margit Berner).

45. Rösle, "Sterblichkeitsverhältnisse," p. 28.

46. Benning, "Expansion und Kontraktion der Geldmenge," March 25, 1943, p. 32, BA R 8136/3810; Bayrhoffer, "Reichsbank," p. 99; Hirschfeld et al., *Enzyklopädie*, pp. 579ff.

47. Krüger, *Lösung*, pp. 30ff.

48. RFM (Hedding) to Reinhardt, June 16, 1937, BA R 2/31097. (On Dec. 4, 1939, the draft law was tabled with the notation "superseded by the Jewish income contribution.")

49. "Kampf dem Weltjudentum," *Deutscher Wochendienst*, May 21, 1943.

50. Banken, "Goldreserven," p. 51.

51. RKG, "Die deutsche Inflation," July 28, 1937, BA R 8136/3803; Bayrhoffer, "Reichsbank," p. 99; Hoffmann, "Probleme," p. 574; Bark, "Kriegsfinanzierung," pp. 74ff.

52. Lütge, "Kriegsfinanzierung," p. 248; Terhalle, "Geschichte," p. 282.

53. Epmeier, "Kriegspotential," p. 49; Jecht, *Kriegsfinanzen*, p. 59.

54. Bark, "Kriegsfinanzierung," pp. 37–38.

Chapter 2: The Accommodating Dictatorship

1. Economics division, RKG, "Die deutsche Wirtschaft im ersten Quartal 1937," BA R 8136/3802, p. 15.

2. Benning (RKG), "Die öffentliche Finanzlage," April 2, 1936, pp. 16–17, and RKG, "Deutschlands wirtschaftliche Lage," July 1939, p. 23, BA R 8136/3804; DAF/AWI, "Die lohnpolitische Lage" (Oct. 1939), in Mason, *Arbeiterklasse*, p. 1266.

3. Finanz- und wirtschaftsstatistische Zahlen. Stand May 31, 1944 (Nur für den Dienstgebrauch!) [Financial and Economic Statistics as of May 31, 1944 (for internal use only)], Berlin, BA R 2/24250, p. 23. See also Christoph Buchheim, "Der Keim des Zusammenbruchs," *Frankfurter Allgemeine Zeitung*, Feb. 8, 2003.

4. Aly, *Voss*, pp. 24–25.

5. Schöllgen, *Brandt*, p. 54.

6. Prion, *Finanzwunder*, passim.

7. See, for example, Günter Schmölders in *Bank-Archiv*, 1939, and *Europäische Revue*, 1940, BA PK/965, microfilm 1628ff. Schmölders joined the Nazi Party in 1933 and was an SS training director from 1933 to 1937.

8. Benning, "Die öffentliche Finanzlage," pp. 4, 10, 13–14 (MS, April 2, 1936), BA R 8136/3804.

9. Reinhardt, *Geld*, p. 27; Stucken, *Geld- und Kreditpolitik*, p. 149; RGBl. I/1936, p. 701, and I/1938, p. 952. The rise in corporate taxes in 1938 was originally supposed to stay in effect only until 1940. See Voss, *Steuern*, p. 106; Blümich, *Körperschaftsteuer-Gesetz*, p. vi.

10. Hohrmann and Lenski, *Körperschaftsteuer*, p. 19.

11. Boberach, *Meldungen*, vol. 2, p. 193.

12. Reinhardt, "Gemeinschaftsbedarf," p. 987.

13. Reinhardt cited the same figures for Germany's prewar debts in 1942. See Goebbels's diary, Feb. 25, 1942. The exaggerated figure of 60 billion reichsmarks is often claimed for German rearmament expenditures prior to the war. See also Benning (RKG), "Reichsschuld," Oct. 24, 1940, BA R 8136/3795, p. 4; on rearmament costs, see Oertel, "Kriegsfinanzierung," p. 685; and Abelshauser, "Kriegswirtschaft," pp. 515–16.

14. Goebbels's diary, Dec. 24, 1937, and March 2, 1939.

15. RB directors, Jan. 7, 1939; Hansmeyer and Caesar, "Kriegswirtschaft," pp. 380ff.

16. RFM, July 7, 1939, NG-4062; Goerdeler, memorandum of Sept. 10, 1938, Goerdeler, *Schriften*, p. 755.

17. Goerdeler, *Schriften*, pp. 773, 784–85.

18. Reinhardt to Backe, Riecke, Schlotterer, Meyer, and Hanneken [1942], BA R 2/30675. Emphasis in original.

19. Goerdeler, *Schriften*, p. 789.

20. Letter of appointment (Frick, Göring), March 19, 1938; Göring to Keppler, March 19, 1938, NG-2503.

21. On the specifics, see Stucken, *Geld- und Kreditpolitik*, pp. 149ff.

22. RFM (Schwerin von Krosigk), Richtlinien für die künftige Rüstungsfinanzierung [Principles for the Future Financing of Armaments], March 10, 1938, NG-5553.

23. Krüger, *Lösung*, p. 211.

24. RWM to Foreign Office, Berlin, Nov. 21, 1938, PA AA Inland II A/B 26; Leeuw, "Griff," p. 221; Krüger, *Lösung*, p. 70.

25. Ordinance on the Registration of Jews' Wealth, April 26, 1938, RGBl. I, p. 414; Ordinance Based on the Ordinance on the Registration of Jews' Wealth, April 26, 1938, RGBl. I, p. 415. The legal situation created for Jewish assets in Greater Germany in 1938 was duplicated in the ordinances issued by the Reich protector in Bohemia and Moravia, June 21, 1939, VOBlRProt 1939, p. 45. Similar ordinances were issued in almost all Nazi-occupied countries.

26. RWM edict, May 14, 1938.

27. Leeuw, "Griff," pp. 216–17.

28. RMI (Frick), June 14, 1938, NG-3937; RWM (Brinkmann), Dec. 27, 1938, BA R 2/3847, p. 188.

29. Schwerin von Krosigk to Hitler, Sept. 1, 1938, IMG, vol. 36, pp. 492ff.

30. Conference on the Jewish Question, chaired by Göring, Nov. 12, 1938, IMG, vol. 2, p. 501; RMI conference, Dec. 16, 1938. See also Heim and Aly, *Bevölkerungsstruktur*, pp. 15–21.

31. Foreign Office, Berlin (Schumburg), Jan. 25, 1939, PS-3358.

32. Heim and Aly, "Ordnung," pp. 392, 398; Heim and Aly, *Bevölkerungsstruktur*, pp. 15–21.

33. Göring's decree, Dec. 10, 1938, in Leeuw, "Griff," p. 219.

34. Conference on the Jewish Question, Nov. 12, 1938, IMG, vol. 2, p. 539.

35. RWM, Sept. 25, 1938, PA AA Inland II A/B 26.

36. Foreign Office, Berlin (Richard Buzzi), BA-DH ZA ZE 6175.

37. RFM memorandum (Schwerin von Krosigk), July 5, Sept. 1, Dec. 8, 1938; Reichsbank board of directors, Dec. 29, 1938, to RFM (Bayrhoffer), BA R 2/3847, pp. 139ff., 180–81, 190ff.

38. RWM, Statistik und Begleitbericht [Statistics and Accompanying Report] [end of 1938], BA R 7/4740, pp. 36ff.

39. Foreign Office, Berlin (Woermann), Nov. 18, 1938, on a speech by Göring the previous day, IMG, vol. 32, pp. 411ff.

40. Ordinance on the Atonement Payment for German Jews, Nov. 12, 1938, RGBl. I, p. 1579; DVO, Nov. 21, 1938, RGBl. I, pp. 1638–40.

41. Friedenberger et al., *Reichsfinanzverwaltung*, p. 30.

42. Government counsel W. Donandt, Berlin, RFM, "Die Judenvermögensabgabe, Januar 28, 1939," quoted in Friedenberger et al., *Reichsfinanzverwaltung*, pp. 67–68.

43. Gestapo, Bielefeld, to Gestapo, Berlin, Nov. 26, 1938, in Stöber, *Nation*, p. 209.

44. Schwerin von Krosigk, *Staatsbankrott*, p. 279.

45. RGBl. I/1939, p. 2059; Friedenberger et al., *Reichsfinanzverwaltung*, p. 21; Review of the Economic and Financial Measures Taken against the Jewish Populace, Carried Out at the Request of Mr. Kagan by the Archive of the Federal Finance Minister (Siegert), Aug. 14, 1951, BA R 2/appendix/52, pp. 9–11.

46. BA R 2/appendix/52, pp. 9–11. Emphasis in the original. There were extensive continuities between the postwar Federal Republic of Germany and the Third Reich. Numerous civil servants who worked for the Reichsbank and the various ministries discussed in this book carried their attitudes with them into postfascist Germany.

47. All quotations concerning the cooperation between private banks and the Reich government are from RKG-Akte, BA R 8136/3692 (21 pp.).

48. Decree, Dec. 3, 1938, RGBl. I, p. 1710, secs. 11, 12; Schwerin von Krosigk to the Reich Finance Offices, Dec. 10, 1938, NG-4902.

49. Deutsche Bank memorandum to local branches, Dec. 13, 1938, BA R 8119/10563, pp. 99, 180.

50. RFM, Dec. 13, 1941, NG-5067; RFM, Sept. 1, 1942, NG-5040; RFM, Sept. 14, 1942, NG-5000; Krüger, *Lösung*, pp. 371ff. Even as late as 1944, the Prussian State Bank recorded numerous transactions concerning "Payments for Securities from Jewish Assets Contributions," BA R 2/31802. For 1938–39: 14695, 14696, 14697, 14698; for 1940: 14700; for 1941: 14710, 14711; for 1942: 31801; for various other issues: 14699, 14701, 14702. See also "Ein 'circulus,' " *Berliner Börsen-Zeitung*, Feb. 9, 1939.

51. Preussische Staatsbank to RFM (Bussmann), March 6, 1942, BA R 2/31800, p. 99.

52. Reichsbank, Securities Statements 272.1941, April 10, 1942, NA AJ 40/1125B. Together with his superior Walther Bayrhoffer, senior government adviser Walther Bussmann was the administrator responsible for managing war finances. As of 1939, Bayrhoffer ran the Main Bureau for General Finance and Credit Affairs in the Finance Ministry. On Feb. 1, 1939, he was charged

with representing that ministry on the Reichsbank board of directors. His responsibilities there encompassed general legal and economic issues, cash transactions, and public finances. See Bayrhoffer testimony, Feb. 5, 1948, NID-14444.

53. GBW (Wohlthat), Dec. 1937, NA RG 238/case XI/microfiche 32.

54. Reich Labor Office (Rettig) to Reichsbank, Aug. 29, 1936; see Mason, *Arbeiterklasse*, pp. 986ff.

55. GBW (Posse, Reinhardt, Kretzschmann, Michel, Tischbein, Neumann, Kadgien, and others), May 30, 1939, PS-3562.

56. Boelcke, "Kriegsfinanzierung," p. 37.

57. To clarify the KWVO, the Reich High Court issued a ruling on Sept. 22, 1941 (5 D 355/41), *Deutsches Recht*, 1941, p. 2441. VO zur Ergänzung der KWVO [Supplementary Ordinance to the KWVO], March 25, 1942, RGBl. I, p. 147. The ordinance outlawed the hoarding of currency, although it imposed no specific penalties. These were added three years later.

58. RGBl. 1939/I, pp. 1609ff.; Recker, *Sozialpolitik*, pp. 43–44, which cites Mason, *Arbeiterklasse*. The figures on exemptions vary. Recker writes of a 2,500 reichsmarks cutoff, others of 3,000. The discrepancies can be explained by the extremely low tax rates on monthly incomes between 220 and 245 reichsmarks and the tax-exempt status of certain premiums on wages. See Oermann and Meuschel, *Kriegssteuern*, p. 146.

59. Begründung zur VO über Kriegszuschläge [Rationale behind the Ordinance on Wartime Surcharges] [1943], NA T 178/15, microfilm 098. According to statistics from 1937, members of Germany's working class earned less than 2,400 reichsmarks per year, as did 53 percent of the country's 3.7 million white-collar employees. Low-level civil servants, many of whom worked for the post office and the railroad, almost certainly did not earn that much, either, so very few German wage earners were required to pay direct wartime taxes.

60. Economics division of the RKG, "Probleme der Kriegsfinanzierung," Oct. 3, 1939, p. 13, BA R 8136/3809. In 1936, 90 percent of all employed people earned less than 3,000 RM a year. See Donner, "Grenzen," p. 205.

61. Reich Defense Council, June 26, 1935, NA RG 238/case XI/microfiche 28; Boelcke, *Kosten*, p. 99.

62. Bayrhoffer, "Reichsbank," p. 100.

63. Jessen, *Kriegswirtschaftsverordnung*, p. 26.

64. Bark, "Kriegsfinanzierung," p. 55; Hitler, speech on Dec. 10, 1940, "Rede," pp. 348–49.

65. Recker, *Sozialpolitik*, pp. 34–35.

66. RFM, Dec. 8, 1943, BA R 2/56205, p. 1.

67. Grosa, *Zielsetzungen*, p. 38; Recker, *Sozialpolitik*, p. 34.

68. VO zur Lenkung der Kaufkraft [Ordinance on Control of Consumer Spending], RGBl. 1941/I, p. 664. According to Grosa, *Zielsetzungen*, concerns about social stability—"the need to restrain excessive demands for intoxicants"—and not financial ones motivated the second hike (p. 40).

69. Oermann and Meuschel, *Kriegssteuern*, pp. 101, 123ff.

70. RGBl. I/1939, p. 2254; Ressortbesprechung [division meeting], Nov. 10, 1939, in Mason, *Arbeiterklasse*, pp. 1183ff.

71. RGBl. I/1939, p. 2403 (ordinance of Dec. 12, 1939, taking effect on Jan. 1, 1940).

72. Recker, *Sozialpolitik*, pp. 51ff.

73. Schwerin von Krosigk, *Staatsbankrott*, p. 299; original quotation, NA T 178/15, microfilm 898.

74. Goebbels's diary, March 15, 1940.

75. Recker, *Sozialpolitik*, pp. 53–56.

76. Bissinger, *Das musst du wissen!*, p. 22; RFM, Schwerin von Krosigk to RK (Lammers), June 28, 1943, BA R 2/32096. On the limits on tax exemptions for overtime pay and the moderate reductions in wages for workers during the final months of the war, see Recker, *Sozialpolitik*, pp. 275–76.

77. Reinhardt to Schwerin von Krosigk, June 18, 1940, NA T 178/15, microfilm 041–044.

78. Benning, "Expansion und Kontraktion der Geldmenge," March 25, 1943, BA R 8136/3810.

79. Head, Finance Office, Grevenbroich, to OFP, Düsseldorf, Dec. 1, 1939, BA R 2/56917.

80. Gauleiter, Magdeburg, to PK, Aug. 15, 1941, BA R 2/31093, p. 103.

81. Wirtschaftspressekonferenz, geh. Mitteilung [economic press conference (secret communiqué)], July 29, 1941, BA R 8136/3990. Prior to the law of July 24, 1941 (RGBl. I, pp. 443–44), a Dec. 1937 law improving pension payments (RGBl. I, p. 1393) had already bettered the lot of German senior citizens.

82. Recker, *Sozialpolitik*, pp. 206ff., 282–83.

83. Schwerin von Krosigk to Göring, Jan. 20, 1940, NA T 178/15, microfilm 896–902. On the discussions surrounding the reform, the arguments concerning the financing of the war, and German "socialism of deeds," see DAF (Ley) to RFM, RWM, etc., Jan. 19, 1940, and Ley to Hitler, Dec. 28, 1939,

NA T 178/15, microfilm 735ff.; Recker, *Sozialpolitik*, p. 115. A modest version of the reform was begun by German occupiers in Hungary as late as 1944; see Gerlach and Aly, *Kapitel*, pp. 198–99, 228.

84. Recker, *Sozialpolitik*, pp. 283–84.

85. Hupfauer (DAF) to Gündel (RFM) after a meeting with Ley, April 15, 1943, BA R 2/31092.

86. Schwerin von Krosigk, *Staatsbankrott*, pp. 300–01; Recker, *Sozialpolitik*, pp. 217–23.

87. BA R 2/20405a; emphasis in original.

88. Klein, *Lageberichte*, p. 249.

89. Benning, "Expansion und Kontraktion der Geldmenge," March 25, 1943, BA R 8136/3810.

90. Schwerin von Krosigk to Göring, May 6, 1943, BA R 2/20405a.

91. Benning, "Expansion und Kontraktion," pp. 15–16.

92. Goebbels's diary, May 7, 1943.

93. Goebbels to Bormann, July 14, 1943; notes on conversation, June 30, 1943; NSDAP (Gündel) to Bormann, June 25, 1943 (Reinhardt's handwritten notes); PK (Bormann), July 3 and 7, 1943, BA R 2/20405a.

94. Goebbels's diary, September 7 and 10, 1943.

95. Lammers to Schwerin von Krosigk, Sept. 29, 1944, BA R 2/14553, p. 256.

96. Schwerin von Krosigk to Lammers, Dec. 22, 1943, NA T 178/15, microfilm 078ff.

97. Recker, *Sozialpolitik*, pp. 218–19.

98. Goebbels's diary, November 5, 1944.

99. Goebbels's diary, March 3 and 28, 1945; on Goebbels's role as patron and protector of the lower and middle classes, see Federau, *Weltkrieg*, pp. 27–28.

100. E. W. Schmidt (economics division, Deutsche Bank), "Die Entwicklung des deutschen Bankwesens im Kriege," 1944; Schmidt, "Gewinnabführung und Preissenkung," BA R 8119/10883/10935; Oertel, "Kriegsfinanzierung," pp. 699–700.

101. GewinnabführungsDVO [Implementation Ordinance on Profit Taxes], March 31, 1942, RGBl. I, p. 162; Zweite VO zur Durchführung der GewinnabführungsVO [Second Implementation Ordinance on Profit Taxes], Aug. 24, 1942, RGBl. I., p. 536; RFM, VO über die Gewinnabführung 1943 (Entwurf), Begründung [Draft Implementation Ordinance on Profit Taxes, 1943, rationale], BA R 2/32104; Meimberg, "Gewinnabführung."

102. Gewinnabführungserklärung [Declaration on Profit Taxes], 1943, RStBl., Sept. 27, 1944, p. 585.

103. RGBl. I/1941, p. 510 (SteueränderungsVO [Ordinance on Changes to Tax Legislation]).

104. Hohrmann and Lenski, *Körperschaftsteuer*, pp. 2–3; RGBl. I/1941, pp. 510, 515; I/1942, p. 162.

105. Benning, "Expansion und Kontraktion," p. 212.

106. Oertel, "Kriegsfinanzierung," p. 735, table.

107. Directors of J. F. Lehmann, Munich, to employees in the field ("Heil unserer Wehrmacht, Heil unserem Führer"), April 2, 1942, private newspaper collection, G. Aly, W. Lehmann estate.

108. Louis Adlon, OFP, RFM, Berlin-Brandenburg, BA R 2/56903; on the relation between profit and risk, see Erhard, *Kriegsfinanzierung*, pp. 51–52ff.

109. See Donner, "Staatsform."

110. Benning, "Der Versuch des Wiederaufbaus der deutschen Volkswirtschaft und sein Scheitern 1929/31," Jan. 30, 1945, BA R 8136/3797; Schmidt, "Bilanz."

111. RGBl. I/1931, p. 706; I/1936, p. 992.

112. "Der mögliche Erfolg einer Ablösung der Industrieumlage," *Bankwirtschaft*, 1943, pp. 38–39; "Das Ergebnis der Hauszinssteuerablösung," *Bank-Archiv*, 1943, pp. 32–33; BA R 2/57964, pp. 5–8, 90–91.

113. Begründung zur VO über Kriegszuschläge [Rationale behind the Ordinance on Wartime Surcharges] [spring 1943], NA T 178/15, microfilm 096.

114. Tribius (Reichsbund der Haus- und Grundbesitzer [Association of Property and Real Estate Owners]), in conversation with Uhlich (RFM), March 7, 1942, BA R 2/57964, p. 166.

115. Benning, "Kriegsfinanzierung," 1944, BA R 8136/3809, p. 17; Erhard, *Kriegsfinanzierung*, pp. 104, 104a–i.

116. Klein, *Lageberichte*, pp. 81–82. Similar articles were printed in *Das schwarze Korps* on Nov. 19 and 26, 1942.

117. Price Commissioner (Fischböck) to Gauleiter, spring 1942; Schwerin von Krosigk to Fischböck [May 1942], BA R 2/31681. On the Nazi campaign against "the privilege of property owners," see *Völkischer Beobachter*, May 15, 1942, and *Berliner Börsen-Zeitung*, May 14, 1942. With Goebbels's support, the Finance Ministry succeeded in suppressing the campaign; see Klopfer to Bormann, May 22, 1942, BA R 2/31681.

118. Meeting, Dec. 11, 1941, BA R 2/31681, pp. 39ff.; RFM (Uhlich), Jan. 31, 1942, pp. 82–83; Popitz to Schwerin von Krosigk, March 26, 1942, p. 219; high-level meeting, April 17, 1942, pp. 248ff.; meeting, Feb. 11, 1942, pp. 106ff. See also BA R 2/14017.

119. Göring in the Reich Defense Council, Nov. 18, 1938, notes of Woermann, Foreign Office, Berlin, IMG, vol. 32, pp. 411–15 (PS-3575).

120. "Wieder Spekulationssteuer für Aktiengewinne," *Sparkasse* 61 (1941), p. 9.

121. Schwerin von Krosigk to Funk, Feb. 25, 1941, BA R 2/14007, pp. 84–86.

122. Meeting with Reichsbank vice president Lange, July 22, 1941, BA R 2/14685, pp. 22ff., 55.

123. "Die andere Seite der Aktienkäufe," *Rheinisch-Westfälische Zeitung*, Sept. 21, 1942.

124. RFM, Meeting (RWM), Sept. 29, 1942, BA R 2/14686, pp. 154ff.

125. Oertel, "Reichsbank," p. 38.

126. RWM (Martini) to RB, RFM, Jan. 28, 1943, BA R 2/14688, p. 12.

127. RFM, Aug. 13, 1941, BA R 2/14685, p. 39; RWM (Martini) to Reich protector, Nov. 16, 1942, LArch, Berlin, B Rep. 039–01/313, pp. 153, 252.

128. Dietrich, *Verordnung*, "Börsenwesen: Steuerung der Aktienkurse," *Wirtschaftsblatt der Berliner Börsen-Zeitung*, Dec. 31, 1942; BA R 2/14688, p. 60; Schriftwechsel zu den genannten VO [correspondence on the abovementioned ordinance], BA R 2/14689, pp. 153ff., R 2/14687.

129. RB (Lange), Börse [Stock Market], Sept. 16, 1941, BA R 2/14685, pp. 47ff.

130. Stucken, *Geld- und Kreditpolitik*, pp. 184–85. Similar tendencies can also be observed in the occupied countries; see Warschau Bankaufsichtsstelle des GG [Warsaw Bank Supervisory Office of the General Government] to RWM (Martini), Jan. 23, 1943, Archiwum Akt Nowych, Warsaw, Reg. GG/1297, p. 26.

131. Boberach, *Meldungen*, p. 4556 (Dec. 7, 1942).

132. Friedenberger et al., *Reichsfinanzverwaltung*, pp. 88–89; BA R 1501/1838, p. 21.

133. "Kursstopp und Dividendenzuwachs," *Bankwirtschaft*, 1943, p. 85; RB, Verwaltungsbericht 1941 [Reichsbank administrative report, 1941], Berlin, 1942, pp. 7–8.

134. Reichsbankausweis [Reichsbank disclosure], May 31, 1944, BA R 2/13480, p. 204; Funk, "Wirtschaftspolitik der stabilen Währung," *Berliner Börsen-Zeitung*, Feb. 13, 1943.

135. Funk to Schwerin von Krosigk, April 16, 1943, NA T 178/15, microfilm 116.

136. *Finanzarchiv*, 1943, pp. 246–72; RKG, Schmölders on "Steuerumbau als Aufgabe für heute" ["The Revision of the Tax Code as a Pressing Task"], BA R 8136/3804. See also Boberach, *Meldungen*, pp. 2297ff., 2555ff.

137. Wicküler-Küpper-Brauerei AG, Wuppertal, to RFM, Reduktion der Gewinnsteuer [Reduction of Profit Taxes], May 14, 1943, BA R 2/14689, pp. 24ff.

138. Franz Schultz (former mayor of Altona) to RFM, Feb. 7, 1945, BA R 2/14690.

139. "Die Gewinnabführung 1943," *Bankwirtschaft*, 1944, pp. 234–36; "Steuerung der Überfülle," *Sparkasse* 62 (1942), pp. 1–4; GewinnabführungsVO [Ordinance on Profit Taxes], March 31, 1942; Erste DVO [First Implementation Ordinance], March 31, 1942, RGBl. I/1942, p. 162; Dritte VO zur Durchführung der GewinnabführungsVO [Third Ordinance on the Implementation of the Profit-Tax Ordinance], March 28, 1943, RGBl. I/1943, p.160; "Die verschärfte Gewinnabführung 1942," *Bankwirtschaft*, 1943, pp. 37–38.

140. Albrecht, "Unterstützung."

141. Reich Chancellery press secretary to Prussian Interior Ministry, Sept. 13, 1918, Stöber, *Nation*, p. 284. In general, see Kundrus, *Kriegerfrauen*.

142. RGBl. I/1939, p. 1531; *Familienunterhaltswesen*, pp. 99ff.

143. *Familienunterhaltswesen*, pp. 10–11.

144. Ibid.

145. Ibid., p. 61.

146. "Sicherung des Familienunterhalts," "Vorbildliche Fürsorge," press clippings, Oct. 20–21, 1939, BA R 2/29986, pp. 24–25.

147. Rass, *"Menschenmaterial,"* p. 249.

148. RGBl. I/1940, p. 911.

149. *Familienunterhaltswesen*, p. 13.

150. Bissinger, *Das musst Du wissen!*, p. 33.

151. Hauser, *Einsatz-Familienunterhaltsgesetz*, p. 48.

152. *Familienunterhaltswesen*, p. 75.

153. Kundrus, *Kriegerfrauen*, p. 434; Rass, *"Menschenmaterial,"* pp. 238ff.

154. Schielin, "Familienunterhalt," p. 458. Dietrich Eichholtz interprets the family support payments as an antidoctrinaire measure, as a "concession to the populace made by the ruling classes"; see *Kriegswirtschaft*, vol. 1, pp. 83–84.

155. Oertel, "Kriegsfinanzierung," p. 689.

156. Kundrus, *Kriegerfrauen*, p. 434.

157. RFM, Statistics Office, Haushaltsausgaben [Household Expenditures] 1938–1943, Nov. 1944, BA R 2/24250, p. 182.

158. Funk to Lammers, April 16, 1943, BA R 2/20405a; Funk on wartime tax surcharges, July 2, 1943, NA T 175/15, microfilm 083–84.

PART II: SUBJUGATION AND EXPLOITATION

Chapter 3: With Unwavering Efficiency

1. Recker, *Sozialpolitik*, p. 53.

2. Donner, "Grenzen," p. 205.

3. RFM (Berger), Debatte um den Kurs der dän. Krone mit Vertretern von RB, VJP, AA und RWM [Debate on the Rate of the Danish Krone with Representatives of the Reichsbank, Four-Year Plan, Foreign Office, and Economics Ministry], Nov. 22, 1941, BA R 2/60244.

4. RFM (Rottky) to Finance Division, RKU (Arlt), May 22, 1944, BA R 2/14592, p. 21.

5. RB, Dienstreise (Lange, Kretzschmann), to Athens, Salonika, Sofia, Bucharest, Belgrade, and Budapest, May 24–30, 1941, BA R 29/1, pp. 215–20; Schlarp, *Wirtschaft*, p. 185.

6. Schlarp, *Wirtschaft*, pp. 381ff.; BA R 2/14138/14570.

7. Spindler to Frank, Feb. 28, 1940, in Präg and Jacobmeyer, *Diensttagebuch* (hereafter referred to as Frank's diary), p. 137; Frank to Reinecke (Wehrmacht Administration Office), July 15, 1942, BA-MA RW 7/1710/a, pp. 69–70; Paersch to Frank, March 23, 1942, Frank's diary, p. 235.

8. Senkowsky to Frank, March 17 and 25, 1942, Frank's diary, pp. 180, 234–35; RFM (Bussmann), Erhöhung des Kriegsbeitrags im Generalgouvernement [Increase in War Contributions in the General Government], March 22, 1943, BA R 2/14580, pp. 133–34; RFM (Schwerin von Krosigk) to Frank, July 23, 1943, BA R 2/14580, pp. 191ff. See also "Gen. Gouvernement Polen, Wehrbeitrag," BA R 2/5085.

9. RFM, Matrikularbeitrag des GG [Contribution of the General Government], Oct. 11, 1941, BA R 2/30511.

10. Paersch to Frank, March 10, 1942, Frank's diary, p. 155.

11. Central bank of Poland, Geschäftsbericht und Jahresabschluss für 1942 [Final business report for 1942], BA R 2/14552, pp. 258–69.

12. RFM (Bussmann), Kriegsbeitrag des GG [War Contribution of the GG], March 22, 1943, BA R 2/14580, pp. 133–34; RFM (Burmeister), Oct. 3, 1941, BA R 2/5085, pp. 41–42.

13. Frank, Senkowsky, Bühler, Jan. 19, 1943, GG budget talks, Jan. 26, 1943, Frank's diary.

14. Discussion in RWM on arms finances in the GG, March 4, 1944, Archiwum Akt Nowych, Warsaw, Reg. GG/1351.

15. "Der Kriegshaushalt des Reiches," *Bankwirtschaft*, 1944, p. 15.

16. Devisen für Zahnersatz [Currency for Dentures], 1943, BA-MA RW 7/1710b, p. 20.

17. Lemkin, *Axis*, pp. 50–65.

18. Boisanger to Hemmen, Nov. 4, 1941, PS-1741.

19. RFM, Steuerung der Geldmittel und Waren, Bewirtschaftung der deutsche Wehrmacht in Dänemark [Control of Money and Goods, Supplying the Wehrmacht in Denmark] (Litter), Oct. 2, 1944, PA AA R 105210.

20. Material expenditures included soldiers' pay, expense money, clothing replacement allowances, and transfer and travel costs. BA-MA RW 38/146, pp. 14ff., 147, 148.

21. Ibid., pp. 36, 22.

22. Reich envoy in Denmark, liaison of the main administration of the RKK, Copenhagen, Oct. 1, 1944, PA AA R 105211.

23. Foreign Office, Berlin, conference with Schnurre, May 14, 1941, PA AA R 105298.

24. RB to central bank, July 19, 1940; on similar procedures, see Archiwum Akt Nowych, Warsaw, Emissionsbank/154.

25. Senkowsky to Frank, March 9 and April 21, 1942, Frank's diary, pp. 152, 394.

26. Reich commissioner for the occupied territories of the Netherlands (Rinkefeil) to RFM (Breyhan), Besatzungskosten [Occupation Costs], Nov. 21, 1940, BA R 2/11433, pp. 3–4; RFM (Breyhan), Finanzpolitik des Reiches [Reich Financial Policies], June 1944, BA R 2/267, pp. 25ff. See also R 2/30602.

27. BA R 2/24250.

28. Boelcke, "Kriegsfinanzierung," p. 31; Jecht, Kriegsfinanzen, p. 29; Wiel, Krieg, p. 115.

29. "Der Kriegshaushalt des Reiches," Bankwirtschaft, no. 1 (1944), p. 15.

30. Chmelda-Bericht, p. 18, NID-14615; "Der Druck auf die französische Währung," Bank-Archiv, 1942, pp. 484–85; Rass, "Menschenmaterial," p. 240.

31. Benning, "Die sogenannte 'Stabilität' der Währungsrelationen in Europa," Feb. 12, 1944, BA R 8136/3773, pp. 68–69.

32. Reichsbank vice president Puhl, Nov. 22, 1941, BA R 2/60244.

33. Platow circular, Feb. 25, 1943, BA R 2/30703.

34. Main administration of the RKK on German clearing debts, Sept. 11, 1944, BA R 2/14553.

35. RFM (Litter), Preparations for Peace Treaties, Oct. 2, 1942, BA R 2/12158, p. 99.

36. "Mahnung an die Clearingpartner," Die Bank 36 (1943), pp. 106–07.

37. RKK administrative council, Nov. 13, 1941, pp. 231–34; OKH General Staff (Kössler) to General Quartermaster (Waldhecker), Feb. 5, 1942, BA R 29/111.

38. Four-Year Plan (Roethe) in meeting with OKW (Kersten), Sept. 8, 1943, BA R 2/14553, pp. 69–74.

39. Meinen, *Wehrmacht*, pp. 76–77. On bordello visits, see also Böll, *Essayistische Schriften*, pp. 260–76 (Brief an einen jungen Katholiken).

40. Kasten, "Reichskreditkassen," p. 10.

41. Pfleiderer, "Reichskreditkassen," p. 385.

42. RKK administrative council, Aug. 10, 1942, BA R 29/4, p. 121.

43. Ordinance of the Army High Command, May 18, 1940, VOBlF 1 (1940), p. 23; president of Deutsche Zentralgenossenschaftskassen [Central Comrados Bank] to RFM (Bayrhoffer), Sept. 18, 1939, BA R 2/30915.

44. Arnoult et al., *La France*, p. 39.

45. "Der Reichskreditkassenschein," *Deutscher Reichsanzeiger*, Jan. 15, 1944, BA R 2/56045, p. 69.

46. Kretzschmann, "Reichskreditkassen," p. 586; Kasten, "Reichskreditkassen," p. 134.

47. OKW, Zurückziehung der RKK-Scheine in Frankreich [Withdrawal of RKK certificates in France], Sept. 8, 1943, BA R 2/14553, pp. 69–74; compare Lt. Int., MBiF (Lenz) to OKW, etc., July 27, 1943, BA R 2/267, pp. 6ff.

48. "Reichskreditkassenscheine in Frankreich aus dem Verkehr gezogen," *National-Zeitung*, Dec. 1, 1943, BA R 2/56059, p. 165; MBiF (Michel) to Association professionelle des banques, Nov. 25, 1943, Archive de la Banque de France 1067199401/15. At this point there were only 5 billion francs' worth of RKK certificates in circulation; see Banque de France archive and Margairaz, *Banques*, pp. 39ff.

49. Holzhauer, *Barzahlung*, pp. 44, 108, 110.

50. Kasten, "Reichskreditkassen," pp. 10–11.

51. Petrov, *Money*, pp. 15–16.

52. Holzhauer, *Barzahlung*, pp. 44ff.

53. Kasten, "Reichskreditkassen," pp. 14, 30–34. Kasten cites two other studies: Georg Süss, *Das Geldwesen im besetzten Frankreich* (Munich, 1920), and Walter Wiese, "Geld und Notenbankpolitik im Generalgouvernement Warschau während der deutschen Besetzung," dissertation, University of Breslau, 1922.

54. Holzhauer, *Barzahlung*, pp. 66ff.

55. German Armistice Commission, Paris, to Foreign Office, Berlin, August 4, 1942, BA R 29/4, pp. 93–96; Materialsammlung für eine Chronik der RKK [Collection of Material for a History of the Reich Credit Bank], BA R 29/113.

56. Oertel, "Reichsbank," p. 69; Kasten, "Reichskreditkassen," p. 28; Kretzschmann, "Reichskreditkassen," pp. 113–14, 120ff. German copper and aluminum-bronze coins were withdrawn from circulation in 1941 and replaced by zinc ones; RFM (Bayrhoffer), May 7, 1941, BA R 29/2, p. 79.

57. Consequently the institution that distributed the certificates "necessarily had to be called the Reich Credit Bank," RB (Kretzschmann, Bayrhoffer) to RFM, Dec. 2, 1939, BA R 2/13499, p. 89.

58. On the bank's founding and the initial skepticism surrounding it, see RFM (Bayrhoffer) to RWM (Holtz), Sept. 19, 1939, NA T 1139/53, NG-5326.

59. Kasten, "Reichskreditkassen," pp. 37–41; Kretzschmann, "Währungshilfe," p. 1. On the credit issued by the main administration of the Reich Credit Bank to promote German interests in the occupied parts of the Soviet Union, see BA R 2/14631. Petrov offers a mistake-ridden and laudatory account in *Money*, pp. 32–40, but he is right when he asserts that "Reich officials were not uniformly the madmen they were depicted to be by wartime propaganda."

60. RKK administrative council, June 10, 1941, BA R 29/1, pp. 208–14; notation (Waldhecker), June 10, 1941, p. 221.

61. Kretzschmann, "Reichskreditkassen," pp. 118–19.

62. Kasten, "Reichskreditkassen," p. 26.

63. Holzhauer, *Barzahlung*, p. 89.

64. Kasten, "Reichskreditkassen," pp. 113–14.

65. Ibid., p. 49.

66. Questionnaires, June 14, 1940, Archive de la Banque de France, 1065199801/46; General Confiscation Ordinance, May 20, 1940, spezielle DevisenVO [special currency ordinance], Aug. 1, 1942, VOBlF, no. 73, Aug. 10, 1942, pp. 425–30. A senior customs official named Hartmann was in charge of the DSK in France.

67. Belege zum Verwahrungsbruch [Evidence on the Tampering with Articles in Government Custody], AN AJ 40/1027.

68. DSK, France, Erfolgsübersicht [progress report] (June 15, 1940–April 30, 1941), AN AJ 40/1027 (file "Entwürfe").

69. Goldaufkommen bei der RB aus ehemals einverleibten und vorübergehend von deutschen Truppen besetzten Gebieten [Gold Supplies at the Reichsbank from Formerly Annexed Territories and Those Temporarily Occupied by German Troops], no date, HAdDB B 331-BAY/678, p. 29.

70. *Mitteilungsblatt des Reichskommissars für das Ostland* [Announcement Circular of the Reich Commissioner for Eastern Europe], ed. B, 2 (1942), Nov. 20, 1942, p. 225.

71. Such records belie historian Jonathan Steinberg's assertion that RKK transfers of gold from the victims of Nazi persecution can neither be proved nor disproved. See Steinberg, *Bank*, pp. 37–38, 101ff.

72. The deportation took place on April 22, 1942. See Pätzold and Schwarz, *Auschwitz*, p. 129.

73. RKK administrative council, Aug. 13, 1941, BA R 29/2, pp. 54–60.

74. RKK administrative council, Jan. 19, 1942, BA R 29/3, pp. 69–74; Feb. 16, 1942, BA R 2/13502, pp. 39ff.

75. RKK administrative council (Puhl), April 27, 1942, BA R 2/13502, pp. 54ff.

76. Puhl, "Der Arbeitseinsatz für die Reichskreditkassen," Feb. 28, 1941, in Oertel, "Reichsbank," p. 101.

77. Kasten, "Reichskreditkassen," pp. 88ff., 121ff.

78. RKK administrative council, April 11, 1942, BA R 29/3, pp. 151–54.

79. Bohn, *Reichskommissariat*, pp. 154–55.

80. Kretzschmann, "Reichskreditkassenscheine"; Kretzschmann, "Reichskreditkassen," pp. 138, 113.

81. State secretary of French Finance Ministry to president of French delegation to Armistice Commission, Feb. 1, 1941, SAEF B 0060937.

82. "Konzept eines neuen Staatsaufbaus" (fall 1941), in Goerdeler, *Schriften*, pp. 790–91, 1006–07.

Chapter 4: Profits for the People

1. Böll, *Briefe*, pp. 14–15, 90, 102, 111. The quotations that follow are taken from the more than three hundred single-spaced pages of Böll's letters. Böll's wife, Annemarie, edited out numerous passages, many of which seem to have been about gifts that her husband sent or brought back home from the front.

2. Feldpostamt 405, BA-MA RH 24/5/181; progress report no. 1 of intendant, MBB/NF (Fritsch), July 1–Dec. 31, 1940, BA-MA RW 36/118, p. 88.

3. German Commissioner of the Central Bank of the Netherlands (Wohlthat), Material für den Januarbericht an Hitler [Material for the January Report to Hitler], Feb. 10, 1941, BA R 2/30701.

4. RFM (Breyhan) to MBB/NF (Wetter), Aug. 9, 1941, BA R 2/274, pp. 142–43.

5. Reichsbank board of directors to RFM, Nov. 21, 1940, BA R 2/56061, p. 469.

6. Reichsbank office, Rostock, to Reichsbank board of directors, May 16, 1941, BA R 2/56058, p. 48.

7. MBB/NF to OKH, Dec. 1, 1941, BA R 29/3, pp. 36–62.

8. RKK administrative council, July 21, 1942, BA R 29/4, pp. 59–60.

9. Managing intendant, MBB/NF, progress report no. 6, July 1–Dec. 31, 1942, BA-MA RW 36/127, p. 16; final report of MVB/NF, Währung und Finanzen [Currency and Finances], winter 1944–45, pp. 13–14, 18, BA-MA RW 36/225.

10. July 6, 1942, BA-MA RW 36/95.

11. The information was gathered as part of a survey carried out by the author among elderly women in his circle of relatives and acquaintances.

12. Adelheid B. to G. Aly, May 20, 2003.

13. Dennler, *Passion*, p. 31 (October 1940); Chmela Report, NID-14615.

14. Wolf Goette (1909–1995) to his family and to A., July 6, Dec. 20, 1940; June 13, Oct. 5, Oct. 31, Nov. 17, 1941; April 28, 1942, Stiftung Archiv der Akademie der Künste, Berlin, Wolf-Goette-Archiv, Prague, 1939–42, Goettes Briefe/I, p. 157; Goettes Briefe/II, pp. 192, 210, 316; Goettes Briefe/III, pp. 23, 51, 65; 2./Familienbriefe Prag, vol. 4, pp. 213ff. The author is grateful to Gisela Riff-Eimermacher for alerting him to this source material.

15. Umbreit, "Kontinentalherrschaft," p. 236; Latzel, *Soldaten*, pp. 135–38.

16. Böll, *Briefe*, pp. 845, 874, 902–03.

17. Ibid., pp. 619, 663, 694, 765, 833.

18. Ibid., pp. 738, 798.

19. Michel, *Paris*, pp. 298–99.

20. Liselotte S. to G. Aly, May 25, 2003.

21. Confiscated letters of the soldier Schwabe (Dec. 2, 1939–June 16, 1940), BA R 2/56100, pp. 54–61. On mass theft by German soldiers in Poland, see Böhler, *Auftakt*.

22. RKK administrative council, Dec. 16, 1941, BA R 29/3, pp. 18–23.

23. RWM, Conference on Currency Regulations for the Occupied Soviet Territories, Sept. 8, 1941, BA R 2/56060, pp. 18–30. The regulation was issued on Sept. 16, 1941, ibid., p. 102.

24. Reichsbank board of directors to RFM, Aug. 17, 1942, ibid., pp. 118, 143ff.

25. Bräutigam, *Überblick*, pp. 53–54; Oertel, "Reichsbank," p. 159; Heilmann, "Kriegstagebuch," p. 140.

26. Marlene F. to G. Aly, Nov. 14, 2003; on the comparable situation in Belarus, see Gerlach, *Morde*, pp. 260–65.

27. Böll, *Briefe*, pp. 924, 975, 986ff., 999–1000.

28. Schmitt and Gericke, "Feldpost," p. 62; Ziegler, "Erinnerungen," p. 48. On the positive supply situation of German troops in the second and third winters of the war, see Rass, "*Menschenmaterial*," p. 246.

29. Customs Regulations for Members of the Wehrmacht, BA R 2/58094.

30. Wehrmacht commander, Norway, Shipping and Personal Carrying of Wares, July 14, 1941, BA R 2/58094, pp. 155–56.

31. The reason for the measure was the intervention of Swedish customs, since the leave transports passed through Swedish territory, Wehrmacht Chiefs of Staff, Jan. 9, 1943, BA R 2/58094, p. 260.

32. Progress report of chief intendant, Norway (Jan. 1–March 31, 1944), BA-MA RW 7/1711b, p. 87.

33. Ibid. (April 1–June 30, 1944), p. 243.

34. Ibid. (Oct. 1–Dec. 31, 1943), p. 6.

35. RKK administrative council, July 1, 1942, BA R 29/3, pp. 223–24; SS Main Office (Klumm) to Reichsführer Brandt, Nov. 9, 1944, in Petrik, *Okkupationspolitik*, pp. 215–16.

36. Schmitt and Gericke, "Feldpost," pp. 3–4.

37. Oberleitner, *Feldpost*, pp. 190–91.

38. RFM (Schwerin von Krosigk) to chief of the OKW, Oct. 24, 1944, BA R 2/14554, p. 2; R 2/323. At the start of Germany's occupation of northern Italy, Field Marshal Rommel had issued restrictions on "the bringing of goods back to Germany," Sept. 21, 1943, BA R 2/30601.

39. Lt. Int., MBiF, to OKH, July 27, 1943, BA R 2/14553, pp. 46–53.

40. RFM to OFP, Würzburg, June 12, 1940, BA R 2/56059, p. 33.

41. Customs authority, RFM (Siegert), Kontrolle der Wehrmachtangehörigen (durch die Hand des Herrn Staatssekretärs dem Herrn Minister) [Monitoring of Wehrmacht Members (hand-delivered by the state secretary to the minister)], June 13, 1942, BA R 2/56061, p. 28.

42. Feldpostamt 406, July 1940, BA-MA RH 24/6/319; Gericke, *Feldpost*, pp. 61–62.

43. OKW, Oct. 10, 1940; conference chaired by Göring on the economic exploitation of occupied territories, Oct. 7, 1940, LArch, Berlin, A Rep. 92/105, pp. 106–08. Umbreit merely alludes to the decree in "Kontinentalherrschaft," p. 236.

44. OKW (Reinecke), Über den Versand und die Beschlagnahme von Feldpostpäckchen [On the Shipment and Confiscation of Military Mail Packages], July 14, 1942, LArch, Berlin, A Rep. 92/105, p. 115.

45. Hitler, *Monologe*, pp. 363–64 (Aug. 25 and 26, 1942).

46. Ibid., p. 346 (Aug. 16, 1942).

47. *Hitlers Tischgespräche*, p. 182 (July 17, 1942).

48. Keitel, Aug. 16, 1942, LArch, Berlin, A Rep. 92/105, p. 116. On Sept. 17, 1942, the Finance Ministry declared that Hitler's decree also applied to those entering from wartime allied and friendly states.

49. Göring to StS, RK, and Mbfh., Aug. 6, 1942, IMG, vol. 39, pp. 388, 391.

50. Seydelmann, *Balance*, pp. 105, 130, 182.

51. ZFS, Kiel, progress report, Aug. 1, 1942–Jan. 31, 1943, BA R 2/56104, p. 53.

52. Reinhardt to the OFP responsible for eastern borders, Jan. 28, 1942. The decree was later extended for the Reich's northern, western, and southern borders, Oct. 7, 1942, BA R 2/31099.

53. Foreign Office, Berlin (Wiehl), to RFM, Hamsterkäufe in Dänemark [Hoarding in Denmark], April 27, 1940, BA R 2/56058, p. 13.

54. RKK main administration to Reichsbank board of directors, Oct. 5, 1940, BA R 2/56045, p. 14.

55. MBiF, army field postmaster, diary (July 1–Dec. 31, 1940, and Jan. 1–June 30, 1941), BA-MA RW 35/1390, p. 26; 1391, p. 18.

56. H.V.Bl., Nov. 4, 1940; Frank to Keitel, Nov. 25, 1940, BA-MA RW 7/1710a, pp. 85–86; RKK administrative council, Feb. 16, 1942, BA R 29/2, p. 234.

57. Böll, *Briefe*, pp. 108, 114 (Sept. 4 and 15, 1940), 264, 372, 526.

58. Böll, *Essayistische Schriften*, pp. 261–76.

59. OKW, Jan. 21, 1942, BA-MA RW 36/126. An identical text was drafted by the OKW/AWA, Oct. 6, 1941, BA R 2/58094, p. 411.

60. RFM (Wucher), July 25, 1942, LArch, Berlin, A Rep. 092/105; *Reichszollblatt*, ed. B, 37 (1942), p. 309.

61. Göring to the state secretary, treasury, and military commander, Summary of Results (Klare), Aug. 6, 1942, IMG, vol. 39, pp. 391, 410.

62. Göring to Schwerin von Krosigk, Aug. 24, 1942, BA R 2/58091.

63. RFM (Reinhardt) to OFP, Oct. 7, 1942, BA R 2/31099; RFM (Reinhardt), Sept. 28, 1942, R 2/58094, p. 476; OFP, Hamburg, to the HZÄ, Oct. 8, 1942, BA R 2/58088, p. 277.

64. Göring to MBiF, Nov. 3, 1943, BA R 2/14553, p. 56.

65. RFM (Litter), Geldmittel in Dänemark [Monetary Instruments in Denmark], Oct. 2, 1944, PA AA R 105210.

66. Böll, *Briefe*, vol. O, pp. 407, 363, 406, 816, 417, 738, 908.

67. ZFS, Nuremberg, to RFM (Galleiske), Sept. 3, 1943, progress report of the ZFS (1943–44), BA R 2/56045/56105, pp. 56, 111, 127.

68. Hundreds of similar examples can be found in the reports by ZFÄ to the OFP, BA R 2/56103–6.

69. Final report of the military administration, Belgium, BA-MA RW 36/257, p. 155.

70. NA RG 242 T 454/92, microfilm 973–78 (BA R 6/81). Thanks to Wendy Lower for alerting the author to this source; see also Gerlach, *Morde*, p. 212.

71. Hitler, *Monologe*, p. 63 (Sept. 17 and 18, 1941).

72. Hillgruber, *Staatsmänner*, vol. 2 (conversation with the Croatian ambassador, Feb. 14, 1942).

73. Hitler, *Monologe*, p. 331 (Aug. 6, 1942).

74. Handwritten note from conference in Rowno (Lt. von Engelbrechten), Aug. 26–28, 1942, BA R 6/243, pp. 20–22.

75. Kaufmann in retrospect to Göring, Sept. 4, 1942, in Bajohr, "Gefühlsduseleien," p. 13.

76. OFP, Cologne (Kühne), to OLG president, Cologne, Nov. 4, 1941; Rummel and Rath, *Reich*, pp. 356ff.

77. Longerich, *Politik*, pp. 705–06.

78. OFP, Cologne, to OLG president, Cologne, Nov. 4, 1941; Rummel and Rath, *Reich*, p. 189.

79. OFP, Westphalia, to finance offices on the start of deportations of Jews, Dec. 8, 1941; Dressen, *Betrifft*, pp. 78ff.; Beer, *Kriegsalltag*, p. 157.

80. Schwerin von Krosigk to Rosenberg, March 14, 1942; Woitkowski, "Schwerin von Krosigk," p. 251 (LArch, Berlin, A Rep. 093–03/54611).

81. RFM (Maass) to OFP, Aug. 14, 1942; Rummel and Rath, *Reich*, p. 423.

82. Dressen, *Betrifft*, pp. 149ff.

83. Rosenberg to MBiF, telex, Jan. 29, 1942, BA R 2/14567, p. 197.

84. Report on "M-Aktion," Aug. 7, 1944, LArch, Berlin, B Rep. 039–01/358, pp. 244ff.

85. RFM (Litter), Massnahmen gegen Juden in Frankreich [Measures against Jews in France], Feb. 13, 1942, BA R 2/14867, pp. 200–01.

86. Rosenberg to Hitler, Dec. 18, 1941; Lammers to Keitel, Dec. 31, 1941; Rosenberg to Utikal, Jan. 14, 1942; Task Force to MBiF, Feb. 4, 1942; DW, Zwischenbericht [Interim Report] [fall 1942], NG-3058; German embassy, Paris (Schleier), to Foreign Office, Berlin, Jan. 30, 1942, NG-5018.

87. Utikal to Göring's adjutant (Major von Brauchitsch), April 21, 1943, NA RG 238/case XI/45, microfilm 1017.

88. German embassy, Paris (Abetz), to Foreign Office, Berlin (Rademacher), Jan. 31, 1942, NG-5018.

89. Göring conference at Berchtesgaden, April 28, 1943, NA RG 238/case XI/ microfiche 28 (NG-3392).

90. Wehrmacht commander of WaKo, Besatzungskosten [Occupation Costs], April 18, 1943, PA AA R 107415.

91. Rosenberg to Hitler, Nov. 17, 1943, NA RG 238/case XI/45, microfilm 964–67.

92. Business Audit of the Western Office, Paris, Sept. 15, 1943; Dressen, *Betrifft*, pp. 54ff.; Dreyfus and Gensburger, *Camps*.

93. Rummel and Rath, *Reich*, p. 192.

94. Abschlussbericht über den Grossangriff auf Köln [Final Report on the Major Offensive against Cologne], May 30–31, 1942 (Grohé); Rüther, *Köln*, pp. 198–214.

95. Western Office, Comprehensive Report, June 8, 1944; Dressen, *Betrifft*, pp. 50ff.

96. DW, Aug. 7, 1944, LArch, Berlin, B Rep. 039–01/358, pp. 244–46; RMfbO, Koeppen to Zölffel, July 16, 1943; Dressen, *Betrifft*, p. 205. On the Ruhr region, see Blank, "Ersatzbeschaffung."

97. Führer's Chancellery to OFP, Vienna, Veräusserung des dem Dt. Reich zugefallenen jüdischen Vermögens [Disposal of Assets Ceded to the German Reich by Jews], Aug. 21, 1942, BA R 2/31096, pp. 156ff.

98. United Restitution Organization, "M-Aktion," pp. 140, 148, 156.

99. PK of the NSDAP, June 5, 1942; OFP, Köln (Kühne), to RFM (Gündel), June 9, 1942, BA R 2/31096, pp. 41ff.

100. Rüther, *Köln*, pp. 93ff.

101. A. J. van der Leeuw, Die Behandlung des in den Niederlanden lagernden Umzugsgutes ausgewanderter Juden [The Handling of Goods Left Behind by Jewish Emigrants from the Netherlands], July 20, 1959, LArch, Berlin, B Rep. 039–01/321; United Restitution Organization, "M-Aktion," p. 4.

102. Ebbinghaus et al., *Heilen*, p. 68.

103. Rummel and Rath, *Reich*, p. 193.

104. *Ein offenes Geheimnis*, pp. 125–26.

105. Aalders, *Geraubt*, p. 360.

106. Progress report of the Treuhandstelle [Escrow Agency], Prague [ca. March 1943], LArch, Berlin, B Rep. 039–01/314; sworn testimony of Ludvik Engel, Prague (Oct. 4, 1963), LArch, Berlin, B Rep. 039–01/313, pp. 162–63. On the Ruhr region, see Blank, "Ersatzbeschaffung"; on Cologne, see Dressen, *Betrifft*, p. 201, and Adler, *Mensch*, pp. 597–98.

107. On Kaliningrad (Königsberg), see Aly, *Tunnel*, p. 137; on Düsseldorf, see Pätzold and Schwarz, *Auschwitz*, pp. 129–30, and Zimmermann, "Deportation," pp. 134–35.

108. Bajohr, *"Arisierung,"* pp. 331ff.

109. Seydelmann, *Balance*, pp. 105–06; Bajohr, *"Arisierung,"* p. 335.

110. Aalders, *Geraubt*, p. 364.

111. Annotations to the Report on the Western Office's Performance for 1943, Jan. 8, 1944; United Restitution Organization, "M-Aktion," p. 185.

112. RMfdbO (Meyer) to RKU, Nov. 9, 1942; RFM (Eckhardt), Dec. 1, 1942, BA R 2/30585.

113. Foreign Office, Berlin (Maltzan), Schwarzkäufe in Frankreich [Black Market Purchases in France], Nov. 26, 1941, PA AA R 107060; MBiF, April 22, 1943, BA R 2/14552, p. 292.

114. A.W. (Morett), June 15, 1946, SAEF B 5701, 5.

115. Four-Year Plan (Veltjens), Second Operating Report of the Delegate for Special Tasks (July 1–Nov. 30, 1942), PS-1765.

116. Aalders, Geraubt, p. 44.

117. MBiF (Lenz) to OKH, July 22, 1942, BA R 29/4, pp. 118–19; Lenz to RKK, Paris, Aug. 22–Oct. 27, 1942, pp. 130–71; OKW, Secret Commando Affairs, (Biehler), Nov. 20, 1942, BA R 2/14552, p. 70.

118. RFM (von Manteuffel) to Four-Year Plan (Legler), Feb. 22, 1943, NA RG 238/case XI/44, microfilm 435.

119. Diary of the Reich Delegate for Economic and Financial Questions to the French Government (Hartlieb), Feb. 1945, HAdDB B 330/4600, p. 9. Since the goods were bought on the black market at five times the normal prices, Hartlieb claimed Germans were "forfeiting" 80 percent of the total sum, as those "amounts entered the French economy as profits of war."

120. Göring, Aug. 6, 1942, IMG, vol. 39, pp. 390–91, 395.

121. Boberach, Meldungen, Oct. 5, 8, 12, and November 9, 1942, pp. 4279ff., 4483; see also p. 4355.

122. Goebbels's diary, Dec. 24, 1942.

123. F.H.Q. (Bormann), Dec. 25, 1942, BA R 2/31093, pp. 44–45.

124. Göring conference at Berchtesgaden, April 28, 1943, NG-3392.

125. Four-Year Plan (Gramsch) to RFM (Breyhan), Aug. 28, 1943, BA R 2/67, pp. 16ff.; RFM (Bussmann), Oct. 8, 1943, BA R 2/14552, pp. 324–25. See also Lindner, who tries to justify German policies on the management of "enemy" assets (Reichskommissariat).

Chapter 5: The Mainstay: Western Europe

1. Böll, Briefe, pp. 250–51, 264, 502.

2. Abschlussbericht Wirtschaftslenkung in Belgien [Final Report on Economic Control in Belgium] (Lampe), BA-MA RW 36/257, p. 157.

3. Göring conference at Berchtesgaden, April 28, 1943, NA RG 238/case XI/microfiche 28 (NG-3392).

4. Progress report no. 1 of MBB/NF intendant, July 1–Dec. 31, 1940, BA-MA RW 36/118, pp. 92–93.

5. MBB/NF memorandum, Oct. 2, 1941, BA-MA RW 36/123. Alexander von Falkenhausen (b. 1878) was an infantry general who functioned as the German military commander in Belgium from May 1940 to July 18, 1944. He was arrested on July 20, 1944.

6. Reichsbank economics division on progress report of MVB/NF (June 1–Sept. 1, 1942), Oct. 24, 1942, BA R 2/14552, pp. 66–67; "Elastische Staatsfinanzierung in Belgien," *Bank-Archiv* (1942), p. 68.

7. Progress report no. 2 of MBB/NF intendant, Jan. 1–March 31, 1941, BA-MA RW 36/119, p. 111; Foreign Office, Berlin (Maltzan), Besatzungskosten Belgien [Occupation Costs in Belgium] [March 1942], PA AA R 105284.

8. RKK administrative council, July 3, 1941, BA R 29/1, pp. 247–52.

9. Währung und Finanzen [Currency and Finances], p. 1, BA-MA RW 36/225.

10. The flyer was discovered on Feb. 6, 1941 in Brussels. BA R 2/274, pp. 46ff.

11. RFM (Eckardt), Besatzungskosten in Belgien [Occupation Costs in Belgium], May 16, 1941, BA R 2/274, pp. 109ff.

12. Conference of military commanders of all three branches of the armed forces and economic experts in Belgium, Oct. 29–30, 1941, progress report no. 4 of MBB/NF intendant, July 1–Dec. 31, 1941, BA-MA RW 36/123, p. 96.

13. RKK administrative council, Aug. 13, 1941, BA R 29/2, pp. 54–60; RKK, Brussels (Schulte), Nov. 31, 1941, ibid., pp. 84–85; MBB/NF to OKH, Währungslage in Belgien [Currency Situation in Belgium], Dec. 1, 1941, BA R 29/3, Bl. 36–62; MBB/NF, Besatzungskosten Belgien [Occupation Costs in Belgium], June 1941–Sept. 1942, appendix 3, Oct. 28, 1942, BA R 29/4, p. 197.

14. MBB/NF, Belgiens Leistungen für die deutsche Kriegswirtschaft [Belgium's Contributions to the German War Economy], March 1, 1942, BA-MA RW 36/250, pp. 2–23.

15. Progress report no. 5 of MBB/NF intendant, Jan. 1–June 30, 1942, BA-MA RW 36/125, p. 53, appendix 5.

16. Währung und Finanzen, p. 7, BA-MA RW 36/225.

17. Wirtschaftslenkung und Wirtschaftskontrolle in Belgien [Economic Guidance and Monitoring in Belgium] (Lange), BA-MA RW 36/257, pp. 149–50; progress reports nos. 6 and 7 of MBB/NF intendant, July 1, 1942–June 30, 1943, BA-MA RW 36/127 and 129, pp. 32ff. and 37–38.

18. RKK administration council, March 3, 1941, BA R 29/1, pp. 104–08; for the agreement on transport, see pp. 6–19.

19. Meeting between Neumann and deputy head of wartime administration von Craushaar in Brussels, Feb. 16, 1941, BA R 29/1, p. 202.

20. RKK administrative council, July 3, 1941, BA R 29/1, pp. 247–52.

21. RKK administrative council to RKK main administration, June 1 and 12, 1942, BA R 29/3, pp. 192ff., 202; Four-Year Plan (Neumann) to OKW (Tischbein, Thomas), appendix, July 8, 1942, NA RG 328/case XI/44, microfilm 546–50.

22. Während und Finanzen, p. 3, BA-MA RW 36/225; MBB/NF (von Falkenhausen) to Four-Year Plan (Neumann), May 14, 1942, BA R 2/14552, pp. 20ff.

23. RFM to the German commissioner of the Belgian National Bank (von Becker), Oct. 9, 1942, BA R 2/14552, p. 26.

24. Wiehl (Foreign Office) to von Weizsäcker and von Ribbentrop, NG-2181.

25. One such transfer, on May 27, 1943, amounted to 21.6 tons of gold. See Customs Border Command in France (Mangold) to German currency commissioner in France (Michel), AN AJ 40/1012, vol. 2, p. 296.

26. Four-Year Plan (Gramsch) to German currency commissioner in France (Michel), Sept. 15, 1942, AN AJ 40/1012, vol. 1, p. 311.

27. Während und Finanzen, pp. 5ff., BA-MA RW 36/225.

28. RFM (Breyhan), Besatzungskosten [Occupation Costs], Oct. 13, 1942, BA R 2/14552, pp. 52–53.

29. Progress report of chief intendant, Netherlands, Oct. 1–Dec. 31, 1943, BA-MA RW 7/1710, p. 125.

30. "Einkommensteuer erhöht," Wirtschaftlicher Pressespiegel, Nov. 23–29, 1942, PA AA R 107904.

31. "Die niederländische Staatsschuld," Wirtschaftliche Tageschronik, May 15, 1942, PA AA R 107903. This mimeographed information circular was put out by the press division of the Reich Commission for the Maintenance of German Ethnicity. As of June 21, 1942, it was called the Wirtschaftlicher Pressespiegel.

32. "Die niederländische Staatsschulden," Wirtschaftlicher Pressespiegel, Sept. 28–Oct. 3, 1942, Jan. 25–31, 1943, PA AA R 107904, 106869.

33. RKK administrative council, Jan. 15, 1941, BA R 29/1, pp. 38–46.

34. Rinkefeil to RFM (Breyhan), May 21, 1942, BA R 2/30666.

35. Reichsbank economics division (Kretzschmann), Besatzungskosten in den nord- und westeuropäische Ländern [Occupation Costs in Northern and Western European Countries], Aug. 26, 1941, BA R 29/2, pp. 71–77.

36. RWM, monthly status report on the general and economic situation abroad (March 1944), NA T 71/59, microfilm 785–99.

37. RWM, monthly status report for the Netherlands (Hoffmann), March 10, 1944, NA T 71/59, microfilm 761–62.

38. RFM (Litter), Gefährdung der Guldenwährung [Threats to the Guilder], April 6, 1944, BA R 2/56059, p. 205.

39. "Wirtschaftsprüfstelle," *Tägliche Wirtschaftsbeobachtung*, Sept. 19, 1940, PA AA R 107901.

40. "Steuerdruck auf das Wirtschaftsleben," *Wirtschaftliche Tageschronik*, May 6, 1942, PA AA R 107903.

41. *Correspondentie*, vol. 1, pp. 816–28.

42. *Nieuwe Rotterdamsche Courant*, May 8 and 11, 1942.

43. RFM (Breyhan), meeting with Schwerin von Krosigk, Feb. 6, 1942, BA R 2/14552, pp. 165ff.; RK, Feb. 9, 1942; the Netherlands were to pay the contribution to the war against Bolshevism retroactively from July 1, 1941, ibid., p. 168; Göring to Schwerin von Krosigk, April 20, 1942, ibid., p. 176. The Reichsbank received bars of gold from Holland and transferred 2,784 reichsmarks for every kilogram of refined gold. On May 16, 1942, the Reichsbank's board of directors informed the finance minister that "a first shipment of 767 bars of gold has been delivered from the Nederlandschen Bank N.V., Amsterdam, as a contribution of the Dutch government to the eastern campaign." The shipment weighed 9,420 kilograms and had a value of more than 26 million reichsmarks (ibid., pp. 178, 182–83). The files also contain records of further transactions.

44. Herbert, *Best*, pp. 251–322.

45. On Michel's support for the rebate law of 1933, see Aly, *Rasse*, pp. 61–63. In 1938, together with the Gestapo and the NSDAP, Michel was responsible for appointing military-economic leaders; see RWM (Michel) to local and government presidents, Dec. 7, 1938, NI-12513 (NA RG 238/case XI/microfiche32).

46. RWM (Funk) to Foreign Office, Berlin, Oct. 10, 1940, AN AJ 40/1019 (the German currency commissioner in France, p. 27).

47. For Scheffler's biography, see Gerlach and Aly, *Kapitel*, pp. 215ff.

48. RFM (Berger) to Foreign Office, Berlin, Sept. 9, 1940, NA RG 338/case XI/F44, microfilm 884–85.

49. RKK administrative council, Feb. 27, 1943, BA R 2/13502, p. 110.

50. Göring conference at Berchtesgaden, April 28, 1943, NA RG 238/case XI/microfiche 28 (NG-3392). Michel was among the participants.

51. French note on German-French relations [April 1941], PA AA (BA) 61136; German embassy, Paris (Gerstner), to Foreign Office trade division, July 3, 1941, AN AJ 40/1021, pp. 49–50.

52. Schachtschnabel, "Finanzwirtschaft; Der französische Staatshaushalt," *Bank-Archiv* (1943), p. 76; RWM, monthly status report for France, Feb. 10, 1944, NA T 71/59, pp. 750–52. In 1942, according to German reports, 157.5 billion francs were siphoned off from the French budget for occupation costs and clearing advances. This amount was more than the total "expenditures for French purposes" (153.9 billion francs). In 1943, these expenditures fell to 143.4 billion, while occupation costs and clearing advances rose to 281.6 billion francs—that is, 200 percent of French state expenditures. Progress report (Schaefer), April 5, 1944, PA AA R 106959, pp. 2–3; aide-mémoire (Hartlieb and Hemmen), Französiche Finanzlage und Vorschläge zur Deckung der Ausgaben [The French Economy and Suggestions for Covering Expenditures], May 7, 1943, Archive de la Banque de France 1397199501/12.

53. Archive de la Banque de France 1397199501/12, p. 1; progress report (Hartlieb), Feb. 1945, HAdDB B 330/4600, pp. 7, 15.

54. Französiche Finanzlage [The French Financial Situation] (Germany embassy, Madrid), Jan. 21, 1945, PA AA R 106959.

55. Progress report (Hartlieb), Feb. 1945, HAdDB B 330/4600, pp. 65, 76ff.

56. Ibid., p. 5; Évolution de la trésorerie et des dépenses publiques 1938–1945, SAEF B 0060911/1.

57. Arnoult, "Finances," p. 39.

58. Foreign office trade division (Reinel), Nov. 7, 1942, BA R 2/14552, p. 68; OKW (Kersten) to Foreign Office, Berlin, Nov. 6, 1942, PS-1741.

59. RFM (Berger) to Four-Year Plan (Gramsch), Jan. 15, 1941, BA R 29/1, pp. 25–26. On the actual uses of the money, see RKK main administration to RFM, Feb. 21, 1941, ibid., p. 89; Umbuchungen [transfers] 1941, BA R 29/2, pp. 82, 163ff.; RFM (Bayrhoffer) to RVM, Dec. 10, 1940, AN AJ 40/1124 (Besatzungskosten A IV [Occupation Costs Account A IV]); Feindvermögen [Enemy Assets], AN AJ 40/589, p. 42.

60. RFM (Mayer), Result of Calculations 1941, Aug. 6, 1942, R 2/24250.

61. Account A VI of the RKK, Paris, 1941, AN AJ 40/1124; WaKo, May 24, 1941, NG-3630.

62. RFM, Oct. 14, 1942, Reich secret, BA R 2/14552, p. 15; MBiF, intendant director to OKW, Jan. 18, 1943, pp. 114ff.

63. Progress report (Hartlieb), Feb. 1945, HAdDB B 330/4600, pp. 6, 11.

64. RFM, Primetex, Nov. 30, 1942, BA R 2/14553, pp. 35–36.

65. Papiers Monange, Postwar Investigations, SAEF B 57045.

66. Aufbau, Aufgaben und bisherige Tätigkeit der Roges [Expansion, Mandate, and Current Activity of Roges] [Feb. 1942], BA R 2/30536, pp. 3–4.

67. RFM (Bussmann) to RHK, Oct. 24, 1940, AN AJ 40/1124. (There are hundreds of examples of these practices in this unpaginated file.) Heinz Schmid-Lossberg, Rüstungskontor GmbH, etc., June 8, 1945, SAEF B 57045, p. 12.

68. DSK, France to all bank auditors, Ankauf von ausländischen Wertpapieren durch Deutsche Interessengruppen [Purchase of Foreign Securities by German Groups], Oct. 18, 1941, AN AJ 40/1027 (DSK 2.5); RWM (Schlotterer) to Bank der deutschen Arbeit and other banks, Oct. 24, 1940, ibid. (chief customs inspector Kambartel).

69. DSK, France, shares of the Compagnie Française des Mines de Bor, Feb. 21, 1941, AN AJ 40/1027 (chief customs inspector Kambartel).

70. DSK, France (Hartmann), to the Banque de Paris et des Pays Bas, Dec. 1, 1941, AN AJ 40/1027 (DSK 2.5).

71. RFM to RHK, Dec. 6 and 9, 1940, AN AJ 40/1124.

72. Besatzungskosten-Kto. Frankreich A I [Occupation Costs Account France A I], Finance ministry announcements (Oct. 15, 1940–April 5, 1943), AN AJ 40/1124. (Numerous other examples can be found here.)

73. RFM to RHK, Oct. 17, 1940, NA AJ 40/1124.

74. Umbreit, "Kontinentalherrschaft," p. 239.

75. Progress report (Hartlieb), Feb. 1945, HAdDB B 330/4600, p. 17.

76. Foreign Office, Berlin (Rahn), Vorschläge zum deutschen-italienischen Clearingverkehr [Suggestions on German-Italian Clearing Transactions], Nov. 1, 1943, BA R 2/30601.

77. For the broader context, see Klinkhammer, Bündnis; "Das neofaschistische Sozialisierungsprogramm," Neue Zürcher Zeitung, Oct. 31, 1944, BA R 8119F/10883.

78. Agent general of the Wehrmacht in Italy, Jan. 27, 1944, BA R 2/30597, p. 104.

79. RFM, BA R 2/30597, pp. 143–44.

80. RFM, Wirtschaftsbeziehungen zu Italien [Economic Relations with Italy], Nov. 20, 1943, BA R 2/30601.

81. Bernhuber and Orgera, ASBI, Azzolini archive, Ufficio speciale di coordinamento, 00520010155ff.; Banca d'Italia Conto No. 5019 intestato al ministero Dr. Rodolfo Rahn, Nov. 2, 1943–April 4, 1946, ASBI, Banca d'Italia segreteria particolare 493/5, pp. 17ff.

82. German embassy, Italy, finance division (Schmidt) to RFM (Berger), June 29, 1944; Agent general of the Wehrmacht in Italy, status report (July 16–August 15, 1944), BA R 2/30598, pp. 94ff., 135ff.

Chapter 6: Room for Expansion: Eastern Europe

1. Monthly report of the commissioner of the National Bank of Belgium, March 9, 1943, appendix, p. BA-MA RW 36/363.

2. Lemkin, *Axis*, p. 62; MBiF to OKH general quartermaster, Dec. 7, 1940, BA R 2/14601, pp. 5ff.; RFM (Breyhan), Lohntransfer der in Deutschland beschäftigten ausländischen Arbeiter [Transfer of Wages for Foreign Workers Employed in Germany], May 1944, BA R 2/30909.

3. Tätigkeitsbericht des Delegierten der Reichsregierung für Wirtschafts- und Finanzfragen bei der Französischen Regierung [Activities Report of the Delegate of the Reich Government for Economic and Financial Questions to the French Government] (Hartlieb), Feb. 1945, HAdDB B 330/4600, p. 9.

4. RFM (Breyhan), Lohntransfer ausländischer Arbeiter [Transfer of Wages for Foreign Workers], May 1944, BA R 2/30909.

5. Foreign Office, Berlin (Rahn), Vorschläge zum deutschen-italienischen Clearingverkehr [Suggestion on German-Italian Clearing Transactions], Nov. 1, 1943; RWM (Süsskind-Schwendi), position paper, Nov. 10, 1943, BA R 2/30601.

6. AOK 16, quartermaster general to local commission, Jan. 21, 1942, BA R 29/111.

7. BA R 2/31097.

8. VO zur Sozialausgleichsabgabe [Ordinance of Social Equity Levy], RGBl. I/1940, p. 1077.

9. See Reichstarifordnung für polnische Landwirt. Arbeiter [Decree for Polish Agricultural Workers], Jan. 8, 1940, in Oertel, "Kriegsfinanzierung," p. 702, and (though inadequate) Herbert, *Fremdarbeiter*, p. 107. The commensurately low tax revenues for the Reich amounted to a state subsidy for both small farmers and large agricultural firms, a policy that, in turn, kept German food prices low.

10. Discussion of decree, Geheimes Preussisches Staatsarchiv, Berlin, Rep. 77/307/4, 141, pp. 148–53.

11. Gesetze zur Änderung des Einkommensteuergesetzes [Laws to Alter the Income Tax Law], RGBl. I/1938, p. 99, RGBl. I/1939, pp. 283ff.

12. Aly, *Tunnel*, pp. 64–65; Kaemmel and Bacciocco, *Einkommensteuergesetz*, p. 498.

13. Frank's diary (Präg and Jacobmeyer), pp. 293, 297; Finance Division of the GG (von Streit), Discussion with the General Governor, Oct. 4, 1940, AAN Reg.GG/796, pp. 292ff.

14. PK der NSDAP to Reinhardt, May 26, 1942, BA R 2/56926.

15. RFM, Einkommensteuerliche Sonderbehandlung der Juden, Polen und Zigeuner [Special Income Tax Treatment of Jews, Poles, and Gypsies], June 11, 1943, contribution to the discussion by Hunsche (Reichssicherheitshauptamt [Reich Central Security Office]), BA R 2/56926.

16. According to the ordinance on the taxation and labor-law situation of eastern workers (RGBl. I/1942, pp. 42, 86, 419–20; RStBl. 1942, pp. 265, 705), maximum weekly net wages were set at 17 reichsmarks. But hardly any eastern workers earned the gross weekly wage of 70 reichsmarks needed to reach that sum. See Abzügetabelle für Ostarbeiter [Deduction Table for Eastern Workers] (Reich Labor Ministry), June 1942, NG-1952.

17. VO über die Einsatzbedingungen der Ostarbeiter [Ordinance on the Conditions for the Use of Eastern Workers], June 30, 1942, sections 8, 13.

18. "Das Sparsystem für Ostarbeiter," Bank-Archiv (1942), pp. 339–40; RKK main administration, Ostarbeiter-Sparen [Eastern Workers' Savings], June 2, 1942, BA R 29/112; Oertel, "Kriegsfinanzierung," pp. 702–03.

19. Oertel, "Kriegsfinanzierung," pp. 702–03; Eichholtz, Geschichte, vol. 2, pp. 217ff.

20. RFM (Breyhan), Gehalts- und Lohntransfer der in Deutschland beschäftigten ausländischen Angestellten und Arbeiter [Wage Payment Transfer of Foreign Workers Employed in Germany] (1941–1943), May 1944, BA R 2/30909. The table in this document does not include foreign workers and forced laborers, but it does indicate a general rise.

21. Wirtschaftliches Merkblatt (zur Unterrichtung der Truppe) [Economic Circular (on the Education of the Troops)], May 20, 1942, BA-MA RW 7/1711a, pp. 241–42.

22. Buchheim, "Länder"; Gerlach, Morde, pp. 240ff.

23. RKK administrative council, June 10, 1941, BA R 29/1, pp. 208–14.

24. RKK administrative council to RFM (Bayrhoffer), BA R 29/1, pp. 195–96.

25. RKK administrative council to RFM, Aug. 20 and 29, 1941, BA R 29/2, pp. 52, 62; Oertel, "Reichsbank," p. 187.

26. RWM, Wirtschaftsstab Ost [Eastern Economics Staff], Aug. 28, 1941, BA R 29/2, pp. 68–69.

27. RKK administrative council, June 10, 1941, BA R 29/1, pp. 208–14.

28. RFM (Bussmann), June 16, 1941, on the conference of June 10 and the notation (Reichsbank director Winter) of June 9 about a conversation with Schlotterer, BA R 2/14588, pp. 119ff.

29. RKK administrative council, Dec. 16, 1941, BA R 29/3, pp. 18–23; RB, Bernhuber to Wilhelm, Oct. 20, 1941, BA-DA ZA Z-E 10237, vol. 1, p. 315; Schwerin von Krosigk, Feb. 17, 1942, BA R 2/30915.

30. RKK administrative council, May 14, 1942, BA R 29/3, pp. 180–82.

31. RKK administrative council, Aug. 15, 1942, BA R 29/4, pp. 120–23.

32. Frank to Schwerin von Krosigk and vice versa, July 1942, BA R 2/14588, Bl. 175ff.; Oertel, "Reichsbank," p. 175.

33. RKK administrative council, March 3, 1941, BA R 29/1, pp. 104–08.

34. Schwerin von Krosigk to Frank, April 16, 1940, Frank to Schwerin von Krosigk, May 31, 1940, RFM (Bussmann) to Central Bank, Cracow, July 25, 1940, BA R 2/5102, pp. 95ff., 122, 136.

35. "Eine Notenbank für die Ukraine," Bank-Archiv (1942), pp. 123–24.

36. RFM (Eckhardt), Umtausch von Rubeln in Karbowane [Conversion from Rubles to Karbowanez], April 30, 1942, BA R 2/14591, p. 96. (This file is concerned with the founding and operational procedure of the ZNU.)

37. Wehrmachtkosten in der Ukraine, R 2/30586; RKK administrative council, Feb. 27, 1943, BA R 2/13502, p. 112.

38. RKU, Hauptabteilung Finanzen [Main Division Finances], Feb. 16, 1943, BA R 2/30585.

39. Verwaltungsbericht [Administrative Report] der ZNU für 1942, p. 3, ibid.

40. Göring to Backe, Nov. 29, 1938, NG-235.

41. Reichsministerium für die Ernährung and Landwirtschaft [Reich Ministry for Food and Agriculture] (Moritz), Getreidelagerräume, Oct. 28, 1938, BA R 2/18157.

42. Sworn testimony by Kurt Kozuszek, Feb. 25, 1947, NA RG 238/case XI/F34, microfilm 211–14 (NID-14478).

43. De Beauvoir to J.-L. Bost, Aug. 28, 1939, Frankfurter Allgemeine Zeitung, July 3, 2004.

44. Göring, Aug. 6, 1942, IMG, vol. 39, p. 385.

45. Wirtschaftspol. RL f.d. Wirtschaftsorg. Ost, Gr. Landwirt., May 23, 1941, IMG, vol. 36, pp. 135–57.

46. Gerlach, Morde, p. 258.

47. All quotations, unless otherwise indicated, are from Aly and Heim, Vordenker, pp. 381–83.

48. Wehrmacht (exhibition catalog), p. 311.

49. Ibid., quoted in Aly, Rasse, p. 132.

50. OKW, Rücksendung eigener Winterbekleidung durch die im Osten eingesetzten Truppen [Return of Winter Clothing by Troops Deployed in the East], April 30, 1942, LArch, Berlin, A Rep. 92/105, p. 110.

51. OFP, Hamburg, to RFM, June 5, 1942, BA R 2/58094, pp. 486–87.

52. RMfdbO to OKW, Dec. 9, 1942, BA R 2/30585.

53. RFM, Haushalt [Budget] der Ukraine für 1942, BA R 2/30585; on the difficulties with package operations, see Goebbels's diary, Oct. 1942.

54. Göring, Aug. 6, 1942, IMG, vol. 39, pp. 385–86.

55. Benzler (Belgrade) to Foreign Office, Berlin, Sept. 13, 1942, NA T 120/1174,
microfilm 70ff.

56. Discussions, Backe/Bonnafous, March 1, 1943, statistics on German demands, 1943–44, SAEF B 49478/1; MBiF, July 19,1944. On the exchange
of goods between Germany and France, SAEF B 57046 (Rapports allemands).

57. Conference in Rowno (von Engelbrechten, chair), Aug. 26–28, 1942, NA
242/24, p. 13 (DW files, Foreign Office).

58. Conference (Backe), June 23, 1942, in Gerlach, Krieg, p. 192.

59. Ibid., p. 220.

60. Witte, "Funkspruch."

61. Gerlach, Morde, pp. 796–813.

62. Goebbels's diary, Oct. 5 and 15, 1942; Boberach, Meldungen, p. 4309; Boelcke, Kosten, p. 288.

63. RFM, Bedeutung der besetzten Ostgebiete nach der deutsche Ein- und Aus-
fuhrstatistik [Significance of Occupied Eastern Territories for German Import and Export Statistics] (Ostbilanz), July 30, 1943, BA R 2/30675. For
annual calculations involving food, a year was measured as the period between harvests. Grain statistics include animal feed. Oils and margarine
also include oil seed.

64. Statistisches Handbuch, pp. 124ff., 231.

65. Finanz- und Wirtschaftsstatistische Zahlen (Geheim) [Financial and Economic Statistical Figures (Secret)], May 31, 1944, BA R 2/24250.

66. Aly and Heim, Vordenker, p. 372.

67. Letter by an employee of the I. G. Farben factory in Premnitz to his director, June 14, 1942, in Kundrus, Kriegerfrauen, pp. 318–19.

68. Wette, Jahr, pp. 241ff.

69. Burkert, Tage, p. 47.

PART III: THE DISPOSSESSION OF THE JEWS

Chapter 7: Larceny as a State Principle

1. "Für Juden nur ein Konto. Massnahmen zur Sicherung des jüdischen Vermögens," Krakauer Zeitung, Nov. 26–27, 1939.

2. "Tätigkeit der Treuhandstelle für das Generalgouvernement," Die Ost-
wirtschaft, no. 1 (1941), BA R 2/5100, p. 8.

3. Finance division of the GG (Spindler) to Department of the Interior, Jan. 15, 1941, BA R 2/5100, p. 5.

4. Plodeck to Frank, Jan. 19, 1942, Frank's diary, pp. 74ff.

5. Finance division of the GG (Spindler) to directors of other main divisions, April 24, 1941, AAN Reg.GG/574, pp. 22, 33; Spindler, Jan. 15, 1941, AAN Reg.GG/1257, p. 1; Treuhänderisch verwaltete Vermögensobjekte [Trustee-managed Assets] (Plodeck), Aug. 3, 1940, ibid., pp. 21ff.; Treuhandstelle GG, general director no. 11 (Plodeck), Nov. 8, 1940, ibid., pp. 17ff., 86; Einzelfälle, ibid., Reg.GG/1255.

6. RFM (Litter) to Foreign Office, Berlin, Oct. 7, 1942, PA AA R 111208.

7. Reichsbank economics division, Besatzungskosten in den nord- und westeuropäischen Gebieten [Occupation Costs in the Northern and Western European Territories], Aug. 26, 1941, BA R 29/2, pp. 71–77.

8. RKK administrative council, Oct. 16, 1941, BA R 29/2, pp. 199–203.

9. Progress report no. 3 of intendant WBB/NF (April 1–June 30, 1941), BA-MA RW 36/121, p. 97.

10. RFM (Eckardt), Besatzungskosten in Belgien [Occupation Costs in Belgium], May 16, 1941, BA R 2/274, pp. 89ff., 109ff.

11. Bernhuber to Orgera, Nov. 23, 1944, ASBI, Archivo Azzolini, Ufficio speziale di coordinamento, corr. Bernhuber e Nehlsen, 520010263; ASBI, Vigilanza sulle aziende di credito 669/1/1, p. 26.

12. Aalders, *Geraubt*, p. 182.

13. Übersicht über Massnahmen gegen Juden in den besetzten Gebieten [Survey of the Measures against Jews in the Occupied Territories] (Rademacher), May 23, 1942, PA AA R 103285, p. 1. An appendix of September 17, 1942, to the investigative report of the General Auditor's Office suggests that the ghettoizing and murder of Serbian Jews cost 33,500,000 dinars, BA R 26/VI/602, p. 23; Bericht über die Verwaltung des Judenvermögens in Serbien [Report on the Management of Jewish Assets in Serbia] (Gurski), Dec. 1, 1944, BA R 26/VI/470, p. 51.

14. BA R 26/VI/470, p. 51, and RH (Müller) to GBW, Verwaltung des Judenvermögens [Management of Jewish Assets], June 3, 1942, BA R 26/VI/602, pp. 2–9.

15. Notation (Rademacher), PA AA, Pol. Abteilung Judenfragen 36/1 (Serbien) [Political Division for Jewish Questions 36/1 (Serbia)], pp. 629–32.

16. Schlussbericht der Kommissarischen Verwaltung des jüdischen Haus- und Grundbesitzes [Final Report of the Administrative Commission for Jewish Real Estate and Property], June 22, 1943, BA R 26/VI/359, p. 87.

17. GBW (Gurski) to RH, Sept. 8, 1942, BA R 26/VI/602, pp. 12–20.

18. RFM (Breyhan), May 22, 1942, BA R 2/30132.

19. Trade division of the Foreign Office (Pamperrien), June 20, 1942, PA AA R 111255. The meeting also touched on liquid Jewish assets, RFM (Breyhan), July 1, 1942, BA R 2/330, p. 33.

20. Treuhandverwaltung und Judenvermögen [Escrow Account Administration and Jewish Assets], March 23, 1945, pp. 14–15, BA F 627 P.

21. Four-Year Plan (Gramsch) to Foreign Office, Berlin, June 20, 1942, BA F 627 P.

22. Gurski report, Dec. 1, 1944, BA R 26/VI/470, pp. 51–52.

23. Foreign Office agent with military command in Serbia to Foreign Office, Berlin, Sept. 13, 1941; see also Nov. 5, 1942, PA AA R 111208.

24. Gurski, Oct. 16, 1944, BA R 26/VI/470, p. 68; Gurski to Gramsch (Four-Year Plan), April 30, 1943, ibid., vol. 364, pp. 345–57; Schlarp, Wirtschaft, pp. 294–95. The actual profit would have been less; see Schlarp, Wirtschaft, pp. 297ff. Gotthardt's report (RWM), of Jan. 15, 1944, BA R 2/14553, pp. 204–06, shows how inflation and occupation costs developed in Germany; the Finance Ministry (Breyhan) estimated Jewish assets in Serbia as totaling 150 million reichsmarks (or 3 billion dinars), May 22, 1942, BA R 2/30132.

25. Schlarp, Wirtschaft, p. 302.

26. Woermann (Foreign Office) to von Rintelen (Foreign Office), Lage in Serbien [Situation in Serbia], Sept. 24, 1942, based on a telegram from Benzler (Belgrade), Sept. 19, 1942, NA T 120/1174, microfilm 093ff.

27. For the details, see Gerlach and Aly, Kapitel.

28. Institut für Zeitgeschichte, Munich, report (Fauck), Nov. 28, 1960, LArch, Berlin, B Rep. 039–01, pp. 17ff.

29. Gerlach and Aly, Kapitel, pp. 227–28; RFM (Patzer) to Reich protector, Prague, July 8, 1942, LArch, Berlin, B Rep. 039–01/313, pp. 232–33.

30. Deutsche Bundesbank to Landgericht [local court], Berlin, Feb. 11, 1963, LArch, Berlin, B Rep. 039–01/313, p. 169.

31. Protocol (von Jüterbog) "über Versorgung der Truppen und Dienststellen der Deutschen Wehrmacht in Ungarn," BA-MA RW 7/1711b, pp. 40–47.

32. Schwerin von Krosigk to Keitel, April 4, 1944, BA R 2/14553, pp. 107–08.

33. Discussion (Belatiny and Scheffler), April 29, 1944, MOL Z 9 (Hungarian National Bank, secret presidential writings), box 39. Such, at least, is the picture I was able to put together from documents at the Hungarian State Archive before January 2004, when an official there prohibited me from continuing my line of inquiry. Fortunately, other sources provide a sketch of how the story continued.

34. RWM, Division III (Schlotterer, director), May 23, 1944, and minutes (Schomaker), May 31, 1944, Gerlach and Aly, *Kapitel*, p. 230.

35. RWM (Schomaker), military commander for Hungary, June 13, 1944, NA T 71/59, microfilm 237–40.

36. Otto Donner (Ff W), early October 1944, BA R 2/30679.

37. NA RG 238/case XI/F24, microfilm 308.

38. RFM (Trapp), March 17, 1941, BA R 2/59888, pp. 67–71. The final text read: "Abandoned assets should be directed toward furtherance of solving the Jewish question" (RGBl. I/1941, p. 722).

39. For example, Preussische Staatsbank [Prussian State Bank] to RFM (Radebach), Sept. 24, 1942, BA R 2/3180; RFM, chronicle (Parpatt), Aug. 31, 1945, NA T 1139/53, NG-5294.

40. Hitler's Decree on the Utilization of Wealth Confiscated from Enemies of the Reich, May 29, 1941, RGBl. I/1941, p. 303; procedural orders and numerous individual cases, BA R 1501/1838 (RMI); RFM (Office of State Secretary), 1942, BA R 2/31098, pp. 53–65.

41. RFM (Burmeister) to Finance Division of the GG (von Streit), May 22, 1942, BA R 2/5056, p. 7.

42. RFM (Bayrhoffer) to financial administrators of local governments, Sept. 26, 1942, NA T 1139/50, NG-4997. In January 1942, changes had been made in how Jewish assets were recorded. Until that point they were entered in Individual Measures XV, chapter 3, part 10. RFM (Maedel), Jan. 6, 1942, Conference (Maedel, Patzer, Matthaeus, Pape), Dec. 23, 1941, NA T 1139/50, NG-5001; RFM, Vereinfachung des Rechnungswesens [Simplification of Accounting Procedures] (Maedel), Jan. 26, 1945, BA R 2/56201, pp. 51, 62. German stocks, mining shares, and government bonds were transferred to the Prussian State Bank, and all other securities to the Reichsbank, RFM (Patzer) to OFP, Cologne, May 11, 1942, NA T 1139/51, NG-5059; RFM (Schwerin von Krosigk), Haushaltsführung im Reich im Rechnungsjahr 1945 [Reich Finances in the Fiscal Year 1945], Jan. 2, 1945, BA R 2/56201, p. 14.

43. RFM (Maedel), Jan. 17, 1944, on the visit of the ministers to the alternate location of Sigmaringen, NG-5338.

44. Memorandum to head of SS administration, Lublin, and administrative director, Auschwitz (Frank), Sept. 26, 1942, NO–724 (NA RG 238/case XI/39, microfilm 548f.); calculations of gold, currency, fountain pens, watches, and "other valuables" collected in the death camps up until Feb. 3, 1943, can be found in IMG, vol. 33, pp. 60ff. (PS-4024).

45. Thoms statement, May 8, 1946, NA RG 238/case XI/39, microfilm 551–56; Thoms interrogation, IMG, vol. 13, pp. 661–78; RB on worth of jewelry, etc.,

March 31, 1944, PS-3947; SS Main Office of Economic Administration (Frank) to RFM, July 24, 1944, NA RG 238/case XI/44, microfilm 383–84; Patzer (RFM) to Gossel (RHK), Nov. 16, 1944, NG-5544; IMG, vol. 33, pp. 577–81.

46. Emil Puhl, declaration, May 3, 1946, in Baden-Baden, NA RG 238/case XI/39, microfilm 594–95.

47. RHK (Gossel) to RFM (Patzer), Sept. 7, 1944, NG-4094; Patzer to Gossel, Nov. 16, 1944, NG-5544.

48. Chief of Security Police and Security Service to AOK 11, Feb. 12, 1942, NOKW-631.

49. ZFS (Scheplitz, Dolderer) to OFP, Berlin, April 1, 1941, Verwertung von Juwelen und Edelmetall [Utilization of Jewels and Precious Metals], BA R 2/appendix/80, pp. 11–18; Zuständigkeits-Verordnung [Jurisdiction Regulations], RGBl. I/1939, p. 37; Leeuw, *Griff*, p. 226.

50. Four-Year Plan, Geschäftsgruppe Devisen [Currency Business Group], June 24, 1943, LArch, Berlin, B Rep. 039–01/304, p. 17; BA R 2/56240, pp. 265ff.

51. RFM, March 26, 1941, NG-4063.

52. Kwiet, "Pogrom," pp. 564–65.

53. Möllenhoff and Schlautmann-Overmeyer, *Familien*, vol. 2, pp. 793–94.

54. Ibid., vol. 1, pp. 669ff.

Chapter 8: Laundering Money for the Wehrmacht

1. Einziehung jüdischen Vermögens [Confiscation of Jewish Wealth] (Quisling), Oct. 28, 1942, to the head of the Norwegian State Police, copy to the Finance Department, LArch, Berlin, B Rep. 039–01/381, pp. 3aff. The letter was preceded by a cabinet decision, Hilberg, *Vernichtung*, pp. 538–39; Reisel and Bruland, *Report*, p. 10.

2. Übersichtsbericht u.a. zur Beschlagnahme jüdischen Eigentums in Norwegen [Summary Report on the Confiscation of Jewish Property in Norway], LArch, Berlin, B Rep. 039–01/381.

3. The Finance Ministry (Maedel) got involved on Jan. 29 and May 26, 1943, in the administration of "Jewish Wealth in Norway," BA R 2/30513.

4. RH (Müller) to Reich commissioner for Norway and RFM, Nov. 18, 1943, BA R 2/11444, pp. 62ff.

5. Liquidation Office to administrator of housing, no date, LArch, Berlin, B Rep. 039–01/381, p. 54a.

6. Reich commissioner for Norway, Finance Department (Korff) to RFM, Nov. 3, 1943, BA R 2/357, pp. 55ff. Reich commissioner Bohn did not mention the Liquidation Office.

7. This command was apparently issued simultaneously in both Belgium and France after the meeting in the Ritz Hotel in Paris (see p. 214). My account is based on the Final Report of MVB/NF, section 16, Treuhandvermögen, III Abschnitt: Judenvermögen [Trustee Wealth, Division III: Jewish Wealth] (MVOR, Dr. Pichier), pp. 108–09, BA-MA RW 36/227, subsequently cited as Treuhandvermögen.

8. Treuhandvermögen, pp. 128–29, 164–65; Doorslaer, "Raub," pp. 137–38.

9. Treuhandvermögen, pp. 119–20.

10. Finance Ministry excerpt from the diary of the military commander in Belgium and northern France, Feb. 1941, BA R 2/274, pp. 129ff.

11. Doorslaer, "Raub," pp. 135–36.

12. Treuhandvermögen, pp. 119ff.

13. Währung und Finanzen [Currency and Finances], pp. 15–16. BA-MA RW 36/225.

14. Doorslaer, "Raub," p. 140.

15. RFM, Sept. 27, 1944, BA R 2/305, p. 37.

16. Commander of the Security Police and the Security Service, Netherlands, June 21, 1941, in Leeuw, "Reichskommissariat," p. 239.

17. Verwaltung des Judenvermögens in den Niederlanden [Administration of Jewish Assets in the Netherlands] (Friedrich), Dec. 11, 1943, BA R 2/11443b, pp. 74–97.

18. Aalders, Geraubt, p. 311.

19. The Customs Investigation Office [Zollfahndungsstelle] in Lübeck (1943–44, BA R 2/56101, pp. 82–95) documented the corruption of civil servants working in Holland.

20. See Dreyfus, "Enteignung," pp. 50–54. In gauging the value of property seized by the Reich from Jews and others, it is wrong to use the totality of liquidated securities. A distinction must be drawn between compulsorily and voluntarily acquired state securities, on the one hand, and stocks in private companies, on the other. Whereas stocks first had to be sold off before they could be used to bolster state finances, state bonds did not need to be— since the state was already in possession of their monetary value. In terms of currency policies, it made no difference whether assets converted into government securities continued to exist in the names of their involuntarily dispossessed owners or whether they disappeared into anonymous funds.

21. Aalders, Geraubt, pp. 189, 191, 244, 272.

22. Rauter to Himmler, Sept. 24, 1942, LArch, Berlin, B Rep 039–01/320, pp. 174ff. On February 2—that is, before the final dispossession ordinances—

the director of the Rosenberg Task Force in Amsterdam (an SS group leader named Schmidt-Stähler) reported on the "Jewish question" that "the German authorities do not think the time is ripe for mandatory evacuation to the East." Ibid., p. 168.

23. "Arisierung des niederländischen Wirtschaftslebens," *Wirtschaftliche Tageschronik*, April 21, 1942, PA AA R 107903.

24. Verwaltung des Judenvermögens in den Niederlanden [Administration of Jewish Assets in the Netherlands] (Friedrich), Dec. 11, 1943; BA R 2/11443b, pp. 74–97.

25. Compare Aalders, *Geraubt*, p. 393. I find the sums for the burdens of occupation estimated there too low and therefore the Jewish portion too high.

26. MBiF, Report by Group Wi I/2 on the Treatment of Enemy Wealth in the Area of Responsibility of the Military Commander in France (Oct. 20, 1940–Aug. 15, 1944), AN AJ 40/589, p. 6 (Feindvermögen).

27. Ibid., p. 10.

28. Ibid., pp. 24, 28.

29. Ibid., pp. 71–72, 100. (French securities, jewelry, table silver, and works of art were not confiscated from enemies of the state.)

30. Ibid., pp. 35, 41.

31. Luftgaukommando Westfrankreich, unbarer Zahlungsverkehr [Noncash Payments for Transactions], Jan. 21, 1941, AN AJ 40//1106 (Luftwaffe money transfers).

32. Hartlieb and Coquelin, Sept. 9, 1943, aide-mémoire, May 7, 1943, Archive de la Banque de France 1397199801/12.

33. DSK, France, to Association professionnelle des banques, Nov. 14, 1941, AN AJ 40/1027 (DSK 2.5, Verfügungen).

34. Memorandum (Hemmen) to Laval, Dec. 15, 1942, PS-1741.

35. Laskier, *Jewry*, p. 74.

36. Discussions, Dec. 11–12, 1942, with Lt. Int. Pichier (MBB/NF) and Maedel (RFM), NG-5369.

37. Fräulein Stiller (private bank in Vienna) in a discussion with Maedel (RFM), Jan. 28, 1943, ET T 37/218.

38. Discussion, Oct. 16, 1940, BA-MA RW 35/772.

39. Herbert, *Best*, pp. 262–63.

40. Military commander in France, Economic Division [to Decree/Ordinance], MBiF, Wirtschaftsabt. zur VO, Oct. 14, 1940, BA-MA RW 35/772.

41. Account by Department Wi I/1(fragment), AN AJ 40/614 (5).

42. Correspondence, MbiF/Sipo, AN AJ 40/616; Steur, *Dannecker*, p. 81. As of June 1942 the permanent representative of the man Adolf Eichmann had

put in charge of Paris, Theodor Dannecker, was the wartime administrative counselor Heinz Röthke. The Wehrmacht appointed him to head up both the Security Police and the Security Service in France. He was also promoted to Dannecker's post—that is, directly under Eichmann—when Dannecker left Paris in August 1942.

43. MBiF (Michel), Economic Report, Oct. 1940, BA R 2/265, pp. 73–74. See also Nov. 1940, R 2/14566, pp. 270ff.; MBiF (Michel) to RWM (Klesper, Joerges), Sept. 22, 1941, AN AJ 40/615 (Deutsche Beteiligungen. Allgemeines).

44. Compte-rendu de la réunion de liaison finances-production, Feb. 25, 1942, SAEF B 0060936.

45. MBiF (Michel) to RWM, Sept. 22, 1941, SAEF 57046.

46. Abetz to Gelich (WaKo, Italy), July 3–4, 1942; Carpi, Between, p. 220.

47. Niedermeyer (MBiF) to MBiF (Drueke), July 4, 1942, BA-MA RW 35/1188; MBiF, Niedermeyer, Report no. 1, Nov. 20, 1944, BA-MA RW 35/1191, p. 14.

48. MBiF (Bargatzky), Aug. 26, 1940; Herbert, Best, p. 263.

49. AN AJ 40/619, file 1941; ibid., 621, vol. 2. On Gerstner, see Aly, Rasse, pp. 210–15.

50. VOBlF, no. 49 (Dec. 20, 1941).

51. "Grundsätze Judenfrage," Vermerke ["Fundaments of the Jewish Question," notations], 1943, AN AJ 40/591; four draft letters (Michel) on the "Collection of the Atonement Payment" to the Central Department, Union des Israélites, general commissioner on Jewish questions (Vallat), French Finance Ministry, Dec. 15, 1941, AN AJ 40/615 (file 12, pp. 116–17); VO über eine Geldbusse der Juden [Ordinance on an Atonement Payment for Jews], Dec. 17, 1941, VOBlF, no. 49 (Dec. 20, 1941), pp. 325–26; MBiF (Stülpnagel) to OKH, Dec. 5, 1941, NG-117.

52. RFM (Litter), Massnahmen gegen die Juden in Frankreich [Measures against the Jews in France], Feb. 13, 1942, Haushalts- und kassenmässige Behandlung der Judengeldbusse in Frankreich [Budget and Treasury Treatment of the Atonement Payment in France], April 24, 1942, BA R 2/14567, pp. 200ff.; OKW to RFM, Sicherstellung der Mittel aus der vom MBiF auferlegten Judenbusse usw. [Securing Funds from the Atonement Payment Imposed by the Military Commander in France], April 8, 1943, p. 311; MBiF, status report, beginning 1943, BA-MA RH 2/592, pp. 52–53.

53. NG-4882, NA RG 238/case XI/38, microfilm 734–37.

54. Rahn to Megerle (Foreign Office, Berlin), April 6, 1943, NG-2737, NA RG 238/case XI/38, microfilm 741.

55. Article 15 of the legislative decree of the Duce, "Nuove disposizioni concernenti i beni posseduti dai cittadini di razza ebraica," Jan. 4, 1944, Gazzetta

Ufficiale, no. 6, pp. 7–12, was explicitly about confiscating Jewish money. On Hungary, see Gerlach and Aly, *Kapitel*, pp. 235–36.

56. *Wehrmacht. Dimensionen*, p. 155. According to the military commander's report, city administrators "confiscated the apartments left behind by Jews and sold them off to needy local residents."

57. On the anti-Semitic legislation, the MBiF, and the French government, see Tables des textes concernant la situation des biens juifs, SAEF B 47361.

58. Account by Department Wi I/1 (fragment), AN AJ 40/614 (5). Michel's subordinates in the "de-Jewification" campaign worked for the OKVR (Dr. Blanke) and the KVR (Stenger, Dr. Mangold).

59. VOBlF, no. 79 (Dec. 9, 1942), pp. 451–52; ibid., no. 97 (Sept. 27, 1943), pp. 553–54; Dreyfus, *Pillages*, pp. 107ff.

60. Economics division, MBiF, military commander in France to the delegate of the military commander in France responsible for German assets in occupied French territories, June 4, 1942, AN AJ 40/616.

61. Niedermeyer, July 4, 1942, BA-MA RW 35/1188.

62. See, for example, the communiqués of the Aero Bank, Paris (a branch of the German Aviation Bank in Berlin), where Niedermeyer set up his general accounts and depots, AN AJ 40/621, vol. 5. Niedermeyer, too, worked primarily with French administrators, and he increasingly liquidated seized businesses (vol. 4).

63. RFM (Litter), Massnahmen gegen die Juden in Frankreich [Measures against the Jews in France], Feb. 13, 1942, BA R 2/14567, pp. 200ff.

64. RFM to MBiF, Settlement Staff, Potsdam, Oct. 11, 1944, BA R 2/305, pp. 9ff.

65. On the evolution of the Treuverkehr Deutsche Treuhand, see AN AJ 40/591 (Treuhandstelle Organization); on its founding, see VOBlF, Jan. 9, 1941, p. 166; Feindvermögen [Enemy Wealth], AN AJ 40/589, p. 89.

66. AN AJ 40/589, p. 90.

67. MBiF (Michel) to Treuverkehr Deutsche Treuhand AG, May 21, 1942, AN AJ 40/591 (Treuhandstelle Organization, p. 37).

68. MBiF, economics division for the head of the military administration, Feb. 25, 1944, AN AJ 40/591 (Treuhandstelle Organization, p. 44). War administration counsel Stenger at least partially served as a representative of the Military Command at the General Commission on Jewish Questions. Ibid., Grundsätzliche Judenfragen [Fundamental Jewish Questions], p. 77.

69. Final report of Treuverkehr Deutsche Treuhand, Paris, 1941, vol. 1, AN AJ 40/591 (Rapports de la Treuhand sur sa propre activité). On the SCAP in general, see Verheyde, "Looting," pp. 71ff., and Baruch, "Perpetrator," pp. 193ff. Thanks to Wolfgang Seibel, who is supervising a thesis by Mar-

tin Jungius on the SCAP, for clearing up misunderstandings about this office.

70. Treuverkehr Deutsche Treuhand, Paris, report for 1941, introduction, March 14, 1942, AN AJ 40/591.

71. Stenger to General Commission for Jewish Questions, Dec. 4, 1942, AN AJ 40/617, bundle 4; see also March 31, 1943, 618A, bundle 2.

72. Scheffler to Union syndicale des banquiers de Paris et de la province, June 21, 1941, AN AJ 40/1027 (File 5).

73. Feindvermögen, AN AJ 40/589, p. 16.

74. Printed in République Française, Spoliation.

75. Feindvermögen, AN AJ 40/589, p. 400. Dreyfus (Pillages, pp. 91ff.) doesn't recognize the clear financial and economic orientation of German policies of "de-Jewification."

76. Final reports of Treuverkehr Deutsche Treuhand, Paris, 1942 and 1943, AN AJ 40/591.

77. Feindvermögen, AN AJ 40/589, pp. 93–94.

78. Anlegung Treuhandgelder [Investment of Escrow Money], AN AJ 40/595A; Revision der Treuhand und Revisionsstelle des MBiF [Review by the Trustee and the Review Office of the Military Commander in France], Oct. 16, 1944 (notarized German translation of French original), LArch Berlin, B. Rep. 039–01/355.

Chapter 9: Subsidies to and from Germany's Allies

1. Speech on Feb. 5, 1939, in Lipscher, Juden, p. 25. On Mach, see Tönsmeyer, Slowakei, pp. 114ff.

2. Kaiser, "Politik," p. 402.

3. Lipscher, Juden, pp. 33–34.

4. Ibid., pp. 40ff.; Tönsmeyer, "Raub," p. 77.

5. Kaiser, "Politik," p. 409.

6. Aly and Heim, Vordenker, pp. 253ff.

7. Lipscher, Juden, pp. 65ff.

8. Final report of the German Army Mission, Slovakia (Herzog), May 10, 1941, BA-MA RH 31/IV/11.

9. Kaiser, "Politik," p. 522; Lipscher, Juden, pp. 77–78; Tönsmeyer, "Raub," p. 78.

10. Annual report of the governor of the Slovakian National Bank (Korvas), Feb. 27, 1943, BA R 2/13492, pp. 356ff.

11. RFM, Nov. 1942, no signature, BA R 2/30703.

12. Lipscher, Juden, p. 119.

13. "Abschöpfungsprobleme."

14. RFM, Nov. 1942, no signature, BA R 2/30703; Boelcke, *Kosten*, p. 120; A. J. van der Leeuw, review (Nov. 8, 1962) of securities seized and delivered to the "Bankhause" Lippmann, Rosenthal & Co. (Fortsetzung I), LArch, Berlin, B Rep. 039–01/322, p. 10.

15. Bescheinigung der kroatischen Juden-Abteilung [Certificate of the Croation Jewish Division], May 17, 1941, für Hermann Bosnjak (Blühweiss) and Cilika Pick über die Beschlagnahme verschiedener Wertgegenstände [On the Confiscation of Various Items of Value], LArch, Berlin, B Rep. 039–01/294, pp. 37ff., 59, 59a; Rückerstattungssachen [Restitution Matters for] Sternfeld und Anica Polic, verw. Ehrenfreund und weitere Fälle [Widowed, and Further Cases], pp. 67ff.

16. Institut für Zeitgeschichte, Munich (Auerbach), to Wiedergutmachungskammer [Reparations Board], Berlin, Oct. 3, 1962, LArch, Berlin, B Rep. 039–01/294, pp. 2–3.

17. *Frankfurter Zeitung*, Jan. 5, 1943, BA R 2/60251.

18. Hilberg, *Vernichtung*, p. 764.

19. Neubacher, *Sonderauftrag*, pp. 58, 66; Aufstellung der Dt. Gesandtschaft Sofia [Disposition of the German Consulate in Sofia] (Feb. 3, 1941), über Reisekostenvorschüsse "an die Mitglieder der Sonderdelegation Gesandter [About Advances of Travel Costs to the Members of the Special Delegation under Envoy] Dr. Neubacher" (classified state secret). Other members of the delegation were Dr. Reinhard Koenning (RFM), Dr. Reinhardt (RWM), Reichsbank director Rudolf Sattler, intendancy counsel Kaltenegger (OKW), Dr. Biehler (OKW), and intendancy counsel Dr. Ullrich (OKW), PA AA 10565 (Neubacher personal file), pp. 57–58, BA–DH, ZA/ZE/6900 (Sattler personal file), pp. 203–05.

20. Administrative council to RKK main administration (Scholz), Feb. 17, 1941, BA R 29/1, p. 90.

21. RKK administrative council (Kretzschmann), March 3, 1941, BA R 29/1, pp. 108ff.

22. RKK administrative council, April 9, 1941, BA R 29/1, pp. 138–47; RKK, Sofia, to Reichsbank (Waldhecker), April 15, 1941, pp. 151–78.

23. RKK, Sofia, to RKK administrative council, June 5, 1941. On April 2, 1942, the credit limit was, according to the Reich Credit Bank, Sofia, 3.4 million leva, BA R 29/3, p. 168.

24. German consulate, Sofia (Richthofen), to Foreign Office, Berlin, May 31, 1940, Feb. 18, 1941, PA AA R 110010.

25. German consulate, Sofia (Beckerle), to Foreign Office, Berlin, Nov. 12,

1942, PA AA R 110010; RKK administrative council, Dec. 16, 1941, BA R 29/3, pp. 18–23.

26. RKK administrative council, Dec. 16, 1941, BA R 29/3, pp. 18–23; Mischaikov, "Bulgarien," p. 52; monthly report, Bulgaria, Feb. 1944, NA T 71/59, microfilm 748–49; Reichsbank economics division (Eicke), July 8, 1944, BA R 2/13502, p. 175.

27. Hillgruber, *Staatsmänner*, pp. 338ff. (Hitler and Bozhilov, Nov. 5, 1943).

28. See the correspondence in BA-MA RW 7/1709a, pp. 77–156; Kontrolle der Ausfuhr von Waren aus Bulgarien [Monitoring of the Export of Wares from Bulgaria], ibid., 1710b, pp. 213–21; war log of the intendant of the German Army Mission, Romania, Oct. 31, 1941, BA-MA RH 31/I/v.156, p. 6.

29. German consulate, Sofia (Beckerle), to Foreign Office, Berlin, March 12, 1942, PA AA R 110010.

30. Assa, *Macedonia*, p. 109; Matkovski, *History*, pp. 117ff.; Mischaikov, "Bulgarien," p. 51; Chary, *Jews*, p. 62.

31. Order of the Bulgarian cabinet council, July 4, 1941, RKK, Sofia, July 5, 1941, PA AA R 110030.

32. Lemkin, *Axis*, pp. 189–90.

33. Chary (*Jews*, p. 62) estimates the total worth of assets owned by Jews in Bulgarian-occupied territory as 1.5 billion leva.

34. Kolonomos and Veskovich-Vangeli, *Jews*, vol. 1, p. 125.

35. *Bulgarisches Amtsblatt*, no. 192, Aug. 29, 1942; German translation, LArch, Berlin, B Rep. 039–01/318.

36. Dannecker to Eichmann, Feb. 23, 1943, ET T 37/54.

37. Hilberg, *Vernichtung*, vol. O, pp. 804–05.

38. War log of economics officer, Sofia (June 1–30, 1943, summary), BA-MA, RW 29/81.

39. Chary, *Jews*, p. 64. (The sum would be 50 percent less if one were to take wartime inflation into account, but that has no significance in this context.)

40. German translation, LArch, Berlin, B Rep. 039–01/342, p. 87.

41. Superior government counsel Dr. Bersch was assigned to the Romanian Finance Ministry, while superior government counsel Schulte was responsible for price controls. With an eye toward the imminent war against the Soviet Union, a road-construction specialist and an agricultural expert named Fachmann were also sent to Romania. Clodius to Foreign Office, Berlin (Schwager), Dec. 13, 1940; Clodius to Neubacher, Oct. 19, 1940, PA AA 10565 (Neubacher personal file), pp. 28–30.

42. RFM (Breyhan), Meeting on Romania of Schlotterer, Landwehr, Reinhardt (RWM), and Neubacher, Oct. 12, 1940, BA R 2/30703.

43. "Das Siedlungswerk von 1942 in Rumänien," *Raumforschung und Raumordnung* 7 (1943), pp. 62ff.; Ancel, "Seizure," p. 46.

44. RFM, Truppenausgaben in Rumänien [Troop Expenditures in Romania], June 1942, BA R 2/60196.

45. RFM (Mayer), Rechnungsergebnis [Result of Calculations] 1941, Aug. 6, 1942, BA R 2/24250; zur Anfangsphase der "Abfindung durch Sachleistung" [On the Initial Phase of the "Compensation by Material Contribution"]; RFM (Bänfer), Ansprüche der umzusiedelnden Volksdeutschen, [Claim of Resettled Ethnic Germans], Oct. 20, 1939, BA R 2/30011, pp. 15ff.

46. RB (Waldhecker), Jan. 16, 1941, BA R 2/30703.

47. Aly, "Endlösung," pp. 130, 257–58.

48. Survey by the Institut für Zegeschichte (S. Fauck) on the persecution of Jews in Romania submitted to the Wiedergutmachungskammer [Reparations Board], Berlin, Sept. 20, 1961, LArch, Berlin, B Rep. 039–01/298, pp. 14ff.; Ancel, "Seizure," pp. 47ff.

49. RFM (Breyhan), Oct. 12, 1940, BA R 2/30703.

50. Sattler personal file, BA-DH, ZA/ZE/6900, pp. 203ff.; Reichsbank (Waldhecker), Jan. 1942, BA R 2/30703.

51. Official trip of Reichsbank vice president Lange and Reichsbank director Kretzschmann to Athens, Salonika, Sofia, Bucharest, Belgrade, and Budapest, May 24–30, 1941, BA R 29/1, pp. 215–20.

52. Memorandum, Nov. 1940, in Goerdeler, *Schriften*, p. 824.

53. Reichsbank (Waldhecker, Trier), Dec. 13, 1940, BA R 2/30703.

54. Währungslage in Rumänien [Currency Situation in Romania] (Blessing), Bucharest, Oct. 8, 1941, abgefasst im Auftrag Neubachers, dem Gouverneur der Rumänischen Nationalbank vorgelegt [Composed at the Behest of Neubacher and Presented to the Governor of the Romanian National Bank], BA-MA RH 31/I/v.66.

55. The military attaché and head of the German Military Economics Mission, Romania, Lei-Beschaffung [Procurement of Lei], Nov. 1941; Hitler to Antonescu, Aug. 14, 1941; Vereinbarung über die Sicherung, Verwaltung und Wirtschaftsauswertung der Gebiete zwischen Dnjestr und Bug (Transnistrien) und Bug und Dnjepr (Bug-Dnjepr-Gebiet) geschlossen am 30.8.1941 in Tighina zwischen dem Königlich Rumänischen Grossen Generalstab (Tataranu) und dem OKH (Hauffe) [Agreement on the Procure-

ment, Administration, and Economic Utilization of the Territories between the Dnjester and Bug Rivers and the Bug and the Dnjeper (Bug-Dnjeper Territory), Concluded on Aug. 30, 1941, in Tighina between the Romanian Royal General Staff and the Army High Command], BA-MA RH 31/I/v.66).

56. Intendant of German Army Mission, Romania, Nov. 1941, BA-MA RH 31/I/v.156, pp. 15ff.; chief intendant, Romania, April 1941, ibid., 233, pp. 148–59.

57. Visit of director general of Romanian Finance Ministry, Nicolae Rasmeritza, to Reichsbank director Wilhelm, July 2, 1941, BA R 2/14585, p. 52; RKK administrative council, Dec. 16, 1941, BA R 29/3, pp. 18–23.

58. Karl Graupner, a leading Reichsbank employee, estimates that the Reichsbank delivered gold with a value of 200 million reichsmarks (i.e., seventy tons) to Romania (Vermerk über Goldabgaben der Reichsbank v. 20.8.1945 [Notation on Gold Deliveries by the Reichsbank from Aug. 20, 1945], appendix 2, HAdDB B 331–BAY/678, p. 48). In contrast, an independent Swiss commission of experts on World War II (Unabhängige Expertenkommission Schweiz Zweiter Weltkrieg, p. 64) put the figure at 134.4 million reichsmarks (p. 55). I have used the Swiss figure. For further details on the gold transactions, see Stellungnahme der RB [Statement by the Reichsbank] (Wilhelm) via Puhl to Funk, Dec. 8, 1941, BA R 2/30703.

59. Economic decree no. 1, 1943 v. 1.1 (Hauffe), BA-MA RH 31/I/v.134.

60. Goebbels's diary, Jan. 10, 1943; transcript, M. Antonescu and Ribbentrop, Jan. 11, 1943 (Reich secret), BA-MA RW 7/1711a, pp. 176–77.

61. Hauffe on trip of Romanian delegation to F.H.Q., Jan. 8–14, 1943, BA-MA RH 31/I/v.134.

62. German Army Mission, Bucharest (Hansen), to OKW/AWA (Reinecke), Feb. 3, 1943, BA-MA RH 31/I/v.134; Hansen to OKW (WFSt), March 5, 1943, ibid. The gold transactions were recorded in the registry of expenditures at the Goldkammer der Deutschen Reichsbank, HAdDB, BSG 10/62.

63. RKK administrative council, Dec. 5, 1942, and Feb. 27, 1943, BA R 2/13502; Goebbels's diary, Feb. 5, 1943.

64. *Türkische Post*, May 11, 1943, BA R 2/60198.

65. Transcript, M. Antonescu and Ribbentrop (Reich secret), Jan. 11, 1943, BA-MA RW 7/1711a, pp. 176–77. Germany soon drastically increased its demands. See Ergänzungsprotokoll [Supplemental Protocol] (Clodius and M. Antonescu), July 17, 1943, pp. 178–79. In their talks on January 10, 1943, Hitler and Antonescu touched only briefly on the topic of financial prob-

lems. See Hillgruber, *Staatsmänner*, p. 201. German finance experts regarded the governor of the Romanian National Bank, Al Ottolescu, as a "notable financial politician" who would accept a drastic increase in the amount of money in circulation as long as he had sufficient gold reserves. RKK, Bucharest (Seiffert), to RKK main administration, Dec. 7, 1941, BA R 29/3, pp. 14–17. The Economics Ministry, on the other hand, had objected to Ottolescu's "orthodox policies on gold and currency" and had wanted him to be replaced with a more compliant partner. That happened only in February 1944. Monthly report, Romania, April 1940, NA T 71/59, microfilm 962–67.

66. RFM (Breyhan), Wehrmachtfinanzierung in Rumänien 1944, BA R 2/30916; RWM, Monthly report, Romania, July 1944, NA T 71/59, microfilm 287–90.

67. Transcript, Privy Council, March 19, 1944, LArch, Berlin, B Rep. 039–01/281, p. 42.

Chapter 10: The Trail of Gold

1. *Documents*, introduction; *Jüdisches Lexikon*, s.v. "Salonica" and "Griechenland."

2. Reich Statistics Office, Greece, Öffentliche Verwaltung und Finanzen [Public Administration and Finances] (Status, April 6, 1941), PA AA R 110262.

3. In general, see Hilberg, *Vernichtung*, pp. 737–55.

4. Reich envoy (Schiedlausky) to RWM (Landfried), March 21, 1942, PA AA R 110306. In 1942, tobacco accounted—in terms of value—for two-thirds of all (compulsory) Greek exports to Germany. Reich envoy (Altenburg) to Foreign Office, Berlin, May 4, 1942, PA AA R 110264.

5. Max Merten's sworn testimony, May 2, 1970, LArch, Berlin, B Rep. 039–01/342, pp. 267ff.

6. Reich envoy (Schulte) on price problems in Greece, Nov. 27, 1942, to Foreign Office, Berlin, via Neubacher, PA AA R 110321.

7. RFM, July 15, 1942, BA R 2/30936.

8. Mackensen (Rome) to Foreign Office, Berlin, Sept. 26, 1942, NA T 120/1174, microfilm 801–02.

9. RFM to Foreign Office trade division, OKW, RWM, Reich Ministry for Food and Agriculture, and Four-Year Plan (copy, Sept. 23, 1942), BA R 2/014552, pp. 30–31; Statement by Reichsbank economics division, Sept. 12, 1942, ibid., pp. 33–34.

10. OKW to RKK main administration, Sept. 14, 1942, BA R 29/4, p. 149.

11. Economic Defense Staff, Greece, Finanzierung der Wehrmachtbeschaffungen [Financing of Wehrmacht Procurements], June 10, 1944, BA-MA RW 29/116, p. 3.

12. Fleischer, *Kreuzschatten*, p. 116.

13. "Das Kinderelend in Griechenland (Bildbericht)," *Neue Zürcher Zeitung*, May 30, 1943. On rates of mortality in Greece between 1940 and 1942, see Apostolou, "Exception," p. 169.

14. Währungspläne für Kreta [Currency plans for Crete], March 8, 1942, PA AA R 110283.

15. Commander in chief in the Southeast and commander in chief of the Twelfth Army, military mail survey, Jan. 2, 1942, BA-MA RW 40/198.

16. Hahn, *Währung*, p. 27.

17. Reich envoy (Altenburg) to Foreign Office, Berlin, Oct. 29, 1942, PA AA R 110263; war log of economics officer, Athens, Oct. 24 and 27, 1942, BA-MA RW 29/98.

18. Nov. 27, 1942, p. 14, PA AA R 110321.

19. Ordinance of commander in chief in the Southeast, Jan. 30, 1943, BA-MA RW 29/100; Reichsbank, newspaper clippings on Greece, BA R 2501/4795. In early 1943, Germany also considered forcing investors to raise additional capital. See E. W. Schmidt (Deutsche Bank) to Walter Tron (Creditanstalt-Bankverein, Vienna), Feb. 24, 1943, BA R 8119/10880, pp. 266–69.

20. See PA AA R 27320, BA R 2/30680; Neubacher, *Sonderauftrag*, p. 85; economics officer, Athens, war log, 1942, appendix 10, BA-MA RW 29/98.

21. OKW chief intendant (Kersten) to Foreign Office, Berlin, March 10 and 23, 1943, BA-MA RW 7/1710b, pp. 165ff.; final report of military commander, Southeast, B: Greece (draft, early 1945), NA T 501/258, microfilm 97; Palairet, *Ends*, pp. 33–34; Höffinghoff, "Wirtschaft"; RFM, July 17, 1943, BA R 2/14580, pp. 182ff. On Swedish aid shipments, see BA-MA RM 7/1909; Reichsbank economics division, Inflation in Griechenland, Sept. 12, 1942, BA R 2/14552, pp. 33–34; Roediger, "Hilfsaktion."

22. Wappler, "Grundzüge," p. 56.

23. RFM, Besatzungskosten Griechenland [Occupation Costs Greece], Nov. 26, 1942; Reichsbank directors to RFM (Bussmann), March 3, 1943, BA R 2/14569, pp. 174, 184, 190.

24. Clodius and Mackensen (Rome) to Foreign Office, Berlin, Oct. 5, 1942, NA T 120/1174, microfilm 785ff.

25. According to Paul Hahn, German commissioner at the Bank of Greece, he was "required" to destroy all the files in his office (*Währung*, p. 50). His ac-

count is supported by a memo written by the head of the military administration in southeastern Europe: "In the final months of occupation, orders were issued to sort out and destroy great numbers of files." To OKH quartermaster general (Malitzky), April 1945 (fragment), BA-MA RW 40/115, p. 5. On the destruction of files in general, see Hartlaub, *Umriss*, vol. 1, p. 199.

26. Reichsbank (Wilhelm), Oct. 21, 1942, BA R 2/14552, p. 32.

27. Travel expense account, Aug. 4, 1943, according to directive of Oct. 17, 1942, PA AA (personal file, von Thadden), monetary file, pp. 129–30; Vermerk, Nov. 18, 1942, ibid., p. 121. On March 15, 1943, Thadden was appointed to Neubacher's staff (p. 126). Thadden later claimed his activities had been purely "economic" in nature. See, for example, Vernehmung in Düsseldorf, May 7, 1961, http://www.nizkor.org/hweb (Sept. 1, 2002).

28. Ritter, "Neubacher," pp. 125–26; Mazower, *Greece*, pp. 71–72.

29. *Kriegstagebuch*, vol. 3, p. 109.

30. Altenburg to Foreign Office, Berlin, Jan. 26, 1944, PA AA Inl. Ig 190, p. 60. On Logothetopoulos's "resistance," see Apostolu, "Exception," pp. 180–81.

31. Facsimile in Molho, *Memoriam*. Six days later Wisliceny specified that "the Jewish identification is to consist of a six-pointed star, 10 centimeters in diameter."

32. Commander of the Security Police and the Security Service, Greece, to special envoy for the Southeast, Aug. 2, 1944, PA AA R 27318, p. 3. The Greek law was issued on May 29, 1943. In June 1944, the newspaper *Deutsch-Griechische Wirtschaftsnachrichten* (vol. 2, p. 67) reported with reference to the belongings of Athens's Jews: "The Greek Finance Ministry ·has announced that the Office for the Management of Jewish Assets is located at 10 Thiseos Street. All interested parties should get in touch with that address."

33. Testimony of Nikolaos Tzavaras, Sept. 11, 1945, LArch, Berlin, B Rep. 039–01/342, pp. 237ff.

34. German consul general (Schönberg) to Foreign Office, Berlin, March 15, 1943, in Seckendorf, *Okkupationspolitik*, pp. 226–27.

35. Hilberg, *Vernichtung*, p. 745.

36. From a telegram, decoded by the British military, from Wisliceny to Eichmann, in Apostolou, "Exception," p. 182.

37. Travel expenses, Aug. 4, 1943, PA AA (personal file, von Thadden), monetary file, p. 130.

38. Elias Douros, Bericht über die Verwaltung der israelitischen Vermögen von Nord-Griechenland (Gerichtsübersetzung) [Report on the Administration of Israelite Wealth from Northern Greece (notarized translation)], July 1, 1945, LArch, Berlin, B Rep. 039–01/344.

39. Mazower, *Greece*, p. 248.

40. Österreichischer Rundfunk, Aug. 9, 2000, http://magazine.orf.at/report/int/sendungen/000823/000823 3.htm (Aug. 31, 2002). The historian Polychronis Enepekidis, too, considers Merten the central figure in the persecution of Greek Jews: "All major documents left behind by the civilian division of the military administration bear the signature Dr. Merten." See "Die 'Endlösung' in Griechenland zum ersten Male ins Licht gerückt. Die Ausrottung von 70000 Juden" (translation, MS), p. 23, LArch, Berlin, B Rep. 039–01/345.

41. "Rush Is On for Nazi Gold in Greek Sea," *New York Times*, July 31, 2000.

42. Fleischer, *Kreuzschatten*, p. 365.

43. Mackensen (Rome) to Foreign Office, Berlin, Oct. 21, 1941, Foreign Office (Hudeczek), Oct. 16, 1942, NA T 120/1174, microfilm 752ff.

44. *Kriegstagebuch*, vol. 4, p. 665; vol. 3, p. 109.

45. Economics officer, Salonika (Müller), Beschäftigung von Juden [Employment of Jews], Oct. 30 and Nov. 14, 1942, BA-MA RW 29/109, pp. 25, 75.

46. Yahil, *Shoa*, p. 560; Safrian, *Eichmann-Männer*, pp. 238ff.; Molho, *Memoriam* (1981), vol. 1, p. 48; Athens court, trial of Max Merten, March 24, 1958, pp. 28ff., LArch, Berlin, B Rep. O58/839, vols. 15–18.

47. BA-MA RW 29/110, appendix 12; Drissner, "Deportation," p. 69.

48. Testimony of Merten, Feb. 27, 1959, LArch, Berlin, B Rep. 039–01/347.

49. RWM (Pasel) to RFM, Aug. 9, 1943, BA R 2/310, p. 117.

50. Molho, *Memoriam* (1981), vol. 1, p. 79.

51. LArch, Berlin, B Rep. 039–01/346, pp. 124ff.

52. Declaration of the Central Board of the Jewish Communities of Greece, May 12, 1948, NA RG 59 (1945–49), box 4255 (thanks to Martin Dean). This estimate corresponds to the figures provided by Hahn.

53. Special envoy (Graevenitz) to Foreign Office, Berlin, March 26, 1944, BA R 2/30674.

54. Commander, Salonika-Aegean (Merten), June 15, 1943, LArch, Berlin, B Rep. 039–01/342, p. 92.

55. Merten, testimony before Reparations Office, Berlin, Feb. 3, 1964, LArch, Berlin, B Rep. 039–01/346, pp. 94ff.; unreliable contrary testimony, vol. 347.

56. Sworn statement by Wisliceny, June 27, 1947, LArch, Berlin, B Rep. 039–01/247, pp. 243–48; testimony of Wisliceny (Nuremberg), Jan. 3, 1946, ET T 37; Mazower, *Greece*, p. 243.

57. Transportation Ministry (Rau) to OKH, March 1, 1944, PA AA R 110285. All information provided in the final report of the southeastern military commander (early 1945) on the subject of "Jewish assets" is false, NA T 501/358, microfilm 546ff.

58. Stroumsa, *Geiger*, pp. 38–39.

59. RKK administrative council, Nov. 5, 1942, BA R 29/4, pp. 174–77; Schaefer to directors, Landeszentralbank Bayern, Oct. 17, 1948, HAdDB Pers 101/20.335; RB (Wilhelm), Oct. 21, 1942, BA R 2/14552, p. 32.

60. *Berliner Börsen-Zeitung*, Feb. 1, 1943, BA R 2501/7098, p. 25; Hahn, *Währung*, p. 5.

61. Final report of commander for the Southeast (early 1945), NA T 501/358, microfilm 503; Mazower, *Greece*, p. 357.

62. The otherwise instructive studies by Wappler ("Grundzüge," pp. 56–57) and Rondholz ("Geschichte") fail to recognize how the gold was used.

63. Undated protocol (OKW to chief intendant, Wehrmacht command, Southeast, Salonika) [June 15, 1943], BA-MA RW 7/1710b, pp. 176ff.

64. Telegram, Oct. 5, 1943, LArch, Berlin, B Rep. 039–01/343, p. 390.

65. Status report of military commander, Greece, for military commander, Southeast, for Nov. 1943, BA-MA RH 2/685, p. 53.

66. Envoy of the Foreign Office with the Wehrmacht command, Serbia, to Foreign Office, Berlin (for envoy Neubacher), Nov. 13, 1943, PA AA R 110358; military commander, Greece, to military commander, Southeast, Dec. 10, 1943, BA-MA RW 7/1711a, pp. 3–41.

67. Reichsbank directors, Gold für Griechenland, Dec. 1, 1943–May 25, 1944, BA R 2/14553, pp. 131–43; Foreign Office, Berlin (Fischer), to special envoy, Southeast, March 1, 1944, PA AA R 110358; RFM, Währungsfragen Balkan [Currency Questions in the Balkans], Nov. 8, 1942, PA AA R 110285; RFM, transcript (Bayrhoffer und Hahn), Nov. 8, 1943, BA R 2/14569, pp. 194–96; Hahn, *Währung*, pp. 28–35. According to Hahn (p. 29), on January 20, 1944, Göring approved the retroactive "allocation, for six months, of up to 4 million reichsmarks a month" to Greece, Albania, and Serbia; *Goldtransaktionen*, pp. 55, 64 (deliveries to Greece are listed under VI.3 ["Zweigstellen der Dt. Reichsbank"]).

68. Special envoy (Graevenitz) to Foreign Office, Berlin, Nov. 17, 1942, PA AA R 110358.

69. Telegrams (Graevenitz), December 9 and 10, 1943, PA AA R 110285.

70. Gotthardt and Neubacher, Jan. 15, 1944, BA R 2/14553, pp. 204ff.

71. Graevenitz to Foreign Office, Berlin, for RFM (Breyhan), Oct. 4, 1944, PA AA R 110357.

72. Hahn, *Währung*, pp. 41, 30.

73. Neubacher, p. 87.

74. Hahn, *Währung*, pp. 40, 52–53.

75. Smaller revenues on Feb. 5 and Nov. 15, 1943, were likely allocated for special expenditures such as military spying. Hahn, *Währung*, p. 55, appendix 5, p. 2.

76. Hahn, *Währung*, p. 51; Palairet (*Ends*, p. 36) offers no evidence for his assertion that the gold was delivered months earlier by the Reichsbank and then stored in Athens until November. Oertel ("Reichsbank," p. 224) provides an apologetic account; Masower's depiction (*Greece*, p. 72) lacks context.

77. Final report of military administration in Greece (early 1945), p. 73, BA-MA RW 40/116b. The information on "Jewish assets" (pp. 81ff.) is purely fictitious.

78. Reichsbank economics division, Aug. 1944, BA R 2/14569, pp. 224–28. The Reichsbank calculated that, after November 1943, 66 to 75 percent of German occupation costs had been paid in gold. That gold came from Germany, but the larger amounts that were employed in the first six months of 1943 had most likely been delivered from Salonika.

79. Palairet, *Ends*, pp. 125–26; special envoy in Athens (Graevenitz), March 26, 1944, BA R 2/30674.

80. Rates of the gold pound in Athens (March 19, 1943–Aug. 31, 1944), BA R 2501/7098, pp. 4–8; Reichsbank economics division, March 23, 1943, BA R 29/105, p. 19; military commander, Greece, status report of the military administration for Nov. 1943, NOKW-1794; progress reports of chief intendant to commander in chief, Southeast (Jan. 16–Sept. 4, 1943), BA-MA RW 7/1709b, pp. 155–62. Fleischer (*Kreuzschatten*, pp. 452ff.) is very much an apologist. Eckert ("Ausplünderung," p. 265) reports, contrary to source information, that as of March 1943 the inflation rate "once again rose dramatically." Xydis (*Economy*) and Boelcke ("Kriegsfinanzierung," pp. 23–24) also miss the main point.

81. RFM (Berger), April 24, 1943, to chief intendant to commander in chief, Southeast, BA-MA RW 7/1710b, pp. 170–71; RFM (Berger) to Foreign Office, Berlin (Wiehl), May 12, 1943, BA R 2/30674.

82. OKW to chief intendant to commander in chief, Southeast, June 15, 1943, BA-MA RW 7/1710b, pp. 176ff. There was a similar dispute with Göring; see Neubacher, *Sonderauftrag*, p. 93.

83. Economics officer Athens, July 16, 1943, BA-MA RW 29/103, p. 15. According to Hahn, "gold deliveries arrived" on Aug. 3 and 7, 1943.

84. Neubacher, *Sonderauftrag*, p. 89.

85. Palairet (*Ends*) doesn't even acknowledge that the assets of Greek Jews were liquidated.

86. Neubacher, *Sonderauftrag*, pp. 80, 88ff.

87. Secret command affairs for chief, OKW, Wirtschaftslage und Wehrmachtfinanzierung in Griechenland [Economic Situation and Wehrmacht Finances in Greece], June 20, 1944, BA-MA RW 7/1712, pp. 105–06; final report of military commander, Southeast, NA T 501/358, microfilm 538.

88. Hahn, *Währung*, pp. 52ff.

89. Final report of military commander, Southeast, NA T 501/358, microfilm 538–39.

90. "Simon Wiesenthal verklagt den griechischen Staat," *Tagesspiegel*, Nov. 13, 1970; Merten to Landgericht [local court], Berlin, Nov. 13, 1970, LArch, Berlin, B Rep. 039–01/342, p. 275.

91. "Hunt for Sunken Jewish Treasure," Aug. 11, 2000, http://news.bbc.co.uk/1/hi/world/europe/875376.stm (Sept. 1, 2002); "Divers End Search for Greek Jewish Gold," Aug. 15, 2002, http://www.cnn.com/2000/WORLD/briefs/08/12/europe.1208 (Sept. 1, 2002).

92. Fleischer, "Griechenland," p. 267.

93. Rosh and Jäckel, *Tod*, p. 82.

94. Bernhuber to Oregera, Bernhuber to Pelligrini, Aug. 9, 1944, ASBI, Azzolini archive, Ufficio speziale di coordinamento/00520010114/005200101160.

95. Chief of OKW, May 10, 1944, BA-MA RM 7/239, pp. 341ff.

96. SKL to Navy Group South, June 9, 1944; Navy Group South to OKM, June 10, 1944, BA-MA RM 7/239, pp. 320–21; Moll, "*Führer,*" pp. 417–18.

97. SKL to Navy Group South, June 20 and July 3, 1944, BA-MA RM 7/239, pp. 365–72.

98. Navy Group South to OKW/WFStb, June 26, 1944, BA-MA RM 7/239, pp. 382ff.

99. Fleischer, "Griechenland," p. 265.

100. War log, head of sea transport, Aegean, July 1–15, 1944, NA T 1022/2543.

101. Navy Group South to SKL, July 9, 1944, BA-MA RM 7/239, p. 393; Navy Group South to OKM/SKL, Sept. 24, 1944, p. 542; Rücktransportleistung Ägäis [Return Transport Performance in the Aegean], Aug. 23–Oct. 21, 1944, pp. 656–57; Kriegsschauplatz Ägäis [The Theater of War in the Aegean], no date, no signature, no letterhead (late Sept. 1944), BA-MA RM 7/1418, pp. 42–49.

102. Secret command affair, Wehrmacht Needs in Greece (Kersten), July 31, 1944, BA-MA RW 7/1712, pp. 108–09.

103. War log, head of sea transport, Aegean, Aug. 1–31, 1944, NA T 1022/2543.

104. War log, Naval Transport Office, Rhodes, Sept. 1–30, 1944, NA T 1022/2528.

105. Wappler, "Grundzüge," pp. 165ff.

106. Die Verkehrslage Griechenlands während der deutschen Besatzungszeit 1941–1944 [The Transport Situation in Greece during the German Occupation] (Winter 1944–45), BA R 2/30680; on the transport situation in the northern part of the route to Auschwitz, see Gerlach and Aly, *Kapitel*, pp. 271–74.

107. SKL to Navy Group South, Aug. 27, 1944; OKW/WFStb to Navy Group South, Aug. 27, 1944; commanding admiral, Aegean, Aug. 28, 1944, NA T 1022/2635; SKL to commanding admiral, Aegean, Sept. 13, 1944, BA-MA RM 7/239, p. 515; Wappler, "Grundzüge," p. 175.

108. Order of High Command, Army Group E (Löhr), Nov. 24, 1944, BA-MA RM 7/239, p. 542. High Command, Army Group E (Löhr), Sept. 22–23, 1944, to commandant, Crete, and Sturmdivision Rhodes, NA T 1022/2635, is identical.

109. Ordinance no. 30 (Kleemann), July 13, 1944, called for Rhodes's Jews to be concentrated in the city of Rhodes and the villages of Trianda, Kremasti, and Villanova by July 17, NOKW-1802. Kleemann (1892–1963), a general in the armored forces of the Werhmacht, was stationed on Rhodes from September 1943 to August 31, 1944.

110. War log, Naval Transport Central Office, Portolago, July 1–31, 1944, NA T 1022/2527.

111. Sturmdivision Rhodos, secret order of July 16, 1944 (Kleemann), NOKW-1801; Hilberg, *Vernichtung*, p. 754.

112. War log, Naval Transport Central Office, Portolago (Probst), (July 16–30, 1944), NA T 1022/2527. The MS *Störtebeker* had a capacity of only 200 tons; the *Horst* and *Merkur*, 300 tons each. They had been redeployed in May 1944, together with twenty-one other lightweight cargo ships, from the Black Sea to the Aegean. War log, head of sea transport, Aegean, May 1–June 30, 1944, NA T 1022/2543.

113. War log, Naval Transport Central Office, Portolago, July 16–31, 1944, NA T 1022/2527. Earlier the problem was solely one of replenishing supplies. War log, April 1–June 30, 1944, NA T 1022/2511.

114. War log, Naval Transport Central Office, Piraeus, July 16–31, 1944, NA T 1022/2527; War log, Naval Transport Central Office, Portolago, Aug. 1–15, 1944, ibid.

115. Molho, *Memoriam* (1948), vol. 2, pp. 75–76. For a detailed description of the deportation, see Varon, *Juderia*, pp. 36–58.

116. Angel, *Jews*, p. 152; Franco, *Martyrs*. (The figures they provide differ only slightly.)

117. *Documents*, p. 363.

118. War log, commanding admiral, Aegean, July 1–15, 1944, NA T 1022/3955.

119. RKK administrative council, Oct. 9, 1944, BA R 2/13502, pp. 184–86.

120. Molho, *Memoriam* (1981), p. 288. Molho is mistaken when he asserts the material was destined for Germany. Testimony by Pepo Recanati (alias Konstantin "Costas" Rekanatis), given on November 20, 1967, is not credible (LArch, Berlin, B Rep. 039–01/342, pp. 104ff.). On Recanati's lies, see Edward Kossoy to Landgericht (local court), Berlin, March 3, 1968, ibid., p. 111; Franco, *Martyrs*, p. 57.

121. District command, Rhodes city, to Sturmdivision Rhodos, Aug. 4, 1944, NOKW-1795.

122. Gilbert, *Holocaust*, p. 707.

123. Rosh and Jäckel, *Tod*, p. 85.

124. Hilberg, *Vernichtung*, p. 687.

125. Secret command affair, Wehrmacht Needs in Greece (Kersten), July 31, 1944, BA-MA RW 7/1712, pp. 108–09.

126. Military commander, Greece, June 17, 1944, in Wappler, "Grundzüge," p. 146.

127. Sturmdivision Rhodos (Kleemann), July 16, 1944, NOKW-1801.

128. War log of district command, Rhodes (Aug. 1944), Sept. 3, 1944, NOKW-1795.

129. Testimony of Erwin Lenz, May 10, 1947, NOKW-1715; Institut für Zeitgeschichte, Munich, report (I. Arndt), March 21, 1967; with reference to NOKW-1715, LArch, Berlin, B Rep. 039–01/342, pp. 101–02.

PART IV: CRIMES FOR THE BENEFIT OF THE PEOPLE

Chapter 11: The Fruits of Evil

1. Treuhandverwaltung und Judenvermögen [Escrow Account Administration and Jewish Assets], March 23, 1945, p. 4, BA F 627 P (also NA T 175/410).

2. Wehrmacht Administration Office, Besprechungspunkte [Speaking Points], May 1943, NA RG 238, box 26 (Reinecke files).

3. Gerlach and Aly, *Kapitel*, pp. 212–13.

4. Boelcke, *Kosten*, pp. 110–11.

The first document used is a report by the Research Group for Military Economics (Forschungsstelle für Wehrwirtschaft, or FfW) entitled "The Financial Contributions of the Occupied Territories as of Late March 1944." It was published in 1986 by Christoph Buchheim ("Besetzte Länder," pp. 123–45). The Research Group had begun compiling statistics in 1940–41 and continually updated the figures (BA R 2/3847, pp. 285–94). The group was part of the brain trust within Göring's Four-Year Plan, and it was headed from 1939 to 1945 by the finance expert Otto Donner (Aly and Heim, *Vordenker*, pp. 54ff.). The 1944 version of the report used here is relatively clear in its organization. The authors tried to adjust individual countries' occupation contributions—some of which (for example, in Greece) had become distorted by hyperinflation—in order to draw meaningful comparisons. They were open about the methodological problems in their calculations and assumptions. In line with the de facto situation, Göring's advisers included clearing advances as part of the Reich's revenues.

The second document originated in the General Office of the Reich Finance Ministry. The authors presented it on November 6, 1944, as a secret communiqué to the finance minister and his deputy. The report balanced the revenues, expenditures, and state debts of the preceding five years of war. It includes data up to August 31, 1944, and thus goes five months beyond the FfW study. In contrast to that report, this one does not adjust figures for inflation. The authors classified clearing advances as Reich debts and included contributions to the war made by Germany's allies—including Spain—under the heading "occupation costs." That was, in fact, where they belonged. Since the FfW study does not include payments made by Croatia and the Mussolini-led Republic of Salò, which was formally allied with Germany, as contributions from occupied countries, the total figures have been corrected with the help of those from the Finance Ministry. (The document can be found in BA R 2/24250. The file is unbound and unpaginated. I paginated my own copy; the table from the Statistics Office is drawn from pages 152–78.)

The third primary source came from the Statistics Office of the Finance Ministry. Entitled "Statistical Overview of Reich Budgetary Calculations, 1938–1943," it was prepared in November 1944 and was also secret (BA R 2/24250, pp. 179–92 [my pagination]). In contrast to the General Office, which used the fiscal year (September 1 to August 31), the Statistics Office used the calendar year. As there were no dramatic changes in tax revenues in the first six months of 1944, we can apply the figures up to August 31, 1944. After that, the war entered its chaotic final phase and statisticians were only sporadically able to track the Reich's finances. This document provides a reasonable answer to the question of how the burdens of war were distributed among various social classes.

The fourth document was prepared by the economics division of the Reichsbank. It concerns clearing balances on June 30, 1944, and confirms the data from the other three documents. It also explicitly shows the extent to which Holland, the General Government, and the Protectorate of Bohemia and Moravia were forced to buy Reich bonds, as well as how many Bulgaria voluntarily purchased. The figures include more than 500 million reichsmarks in clearing debts that Germany owed Switzerland. Surrounded by the Wehrmacht, Switzerland was in no position to consistently refuse German demands or to insist on immediate payment in gold or hard currency. Because all these cases concerned de facto revenues, the relevant figures were entered under the heading "Clearing." (Economics division [Eicke], July 8, 1944, BA R 2/13502, pp. 175–76; see also Clearingverschuldung nach der Saldenausweisung der Deutschen Verrechnungskasse [Clearing Debt after the Settlement of Balances by the German Settlement Bank], Sept. 7, 1944, BA R 2/267, p. 59.)

5. As part of their general administrative revenues, the Finance Ministry recorded sums of reichsmarks taken in as a result of soldiers' exchanging currency abroad. Revenues also arose, as we saw in chapter 5, when German companies purchased goods or services abroad. They paid the prices they had agreed on with their foreign business partners in reichsmarks to the German Settlement Bank, which transferred the money to the treasury. Foreign creditors were then paid with funds from their respective countries' occupation-costs budgets or from clearing accounts. Also part of the Reich's general administrative revenues were profits earned from deliveries of supplies with which the Soviet Union, Italy, and Romania compensated the Reich for ethnic Germans who had been resettled. Similar revenues arose when representatives of German government offices made purchases abroad using foreign currency and sold off the goods within the Reich on behalf of the treasury. Such was the case both with consumer goods available for private citizens to purchase at Christmas and with raw materials, armaments, and food. All sums of money resulting from such transactions were recorded as general administrative revenues, as were all monies generated by the "furniture operation" and the sale of Jewish assets in Germany and the territories it annexed.

6. Conservative estimates are used to avoid any chance of exaggeration, although the institutions owed the sums in question, a good 4 billion reichsmarks between 1939 and 1945, to increased usage of their services during the war.

7. Estimates for the period between Sept. 1, 1944, and May 8, 1945, have been calculated as 50 percent of the sums for the previous fiscal year.

8. RFM (Statistics Office), Einkommenbesteuerung [Income Taxes], 1938–43, Nov. 1944, BA R 2/242500, p. 187; Milward, *Der Zweite Weltkrieg*, p. 138.

Chapter 12: Speculative Politics

1. Geh.RL aus der Pressekonferenz der Reichsregierung [Secret Directives from the Press Conference of the Reich Government], Jan. 26, 1940, BA R 8136/3990.

2. NSDAP, Hamburg (Kaufmann), to Reich Leader Bormann, telex, Feb. 10, 1942, BA R 2/31681.

3. Donner (Ff W), Finanzlage in Ungarn [Financial Status in Hungary], early Oct. 1944, BA R 2/30679; Busch, "Finanzaufgaben."

4. Federau, Weltkrieg, p. 19.

5. Chmela Report, p. 89, NID-14615.

6. MBiF, economics division (Rinke), Jan. 20, 1944, BA R 2/14552, pp. 317ff.; status report (Rinke), July 5, 1943, BA R 2/30123.

7. RGBl. I, p. 963.

8. Währung und Wirtschaft, p. 405.

9. Benning, "Kriegsfinanzierung," 1944, BA R 8136/3809.

10. Benning, "Expansion und Kontraktion der Geldmenge," March 25, 1943, BA R 8136/3810, p. 18.

11. Ibid.

12. Boelcke, "Kriegsfinanzierung," pp. 34, 36.

13. BA R 2501/7007, pp. 330ff.; Oertel, "Reichsbank," p. 191.

14. RKK administrative council, Dec. 21, 1942, BA R 2/13502, p. 102. In 1944, Ludwig Erhard spoke of the need for a "retroactive consolidation of heretofore nontransparent processes and movements on the capital market" (Kriegsfinanzierung, pp. 11ff., 44); see also Boelcke's apologist account, Kosten, p. 94.

15. Federau, Weltkriẹg, p. 16; Erhard, Kriegsfinanzierung, pp. 13, 212.

16. Status report of general agent of the German Wehrmacht in Italy, July 16–Aug. 15, 1944, BA R 2/30598, pp. 128–29.

17. BA R 2/24250.

18. For 1940: "Die Sparleistung des Jahres 1940," Sparkasse 61 (1941), pp. 109–11 ("a total of almost 11 billion reichsmarks"); for 1941–42: Reinhardt, Geld, pp. 48–49; RFM, General Office, Dec. 9, 1943, BA R 2/24250. Growth rates were particularly impressive at the post office's savings division. 1939: 100 million reichsmarks; 1941: 1.3 billion reichsmarks; 1942: 2.8 billion reichsmarks, Dr. B[enning], "Das Zinsproblem in der Kriegsfinanzierung," June 10, 1943, p. 3, BA R 8136/3809.

19. Benning, "Expansion," p. 214.

20. "Der Sparinhalt der Lebensversicherung," Sparkasse 63 (1943), pp. 4–6.

21. Rath, "Aufgaben," p. 514; Bark, "Kriegsfinanzierung," p. 109.

22. Reinhardt, *Geld*, p. 49.

23. "Zum 30. Januar 1943," *Sparkasse* 63 (1943), vol. 2, p. 15.

24. *Die Bank* 33 (1940), pp. 17–18.

25. Dr. F., "Die Deutsche Girozentrale berichtet," *Sparkasse* 61 (1941), pp. 68–69; on the problem of interest, ibid., p. 87.

26. RFM, General Office, Dec. 9, 1943, BA R 2/24250.

27. Security Service report on domestic economic questions ("Auf Anforderung des [ungenannten] Empfängers"), Dec. 13, 1943, BA R 2/24250; emphasis in original.

28. "Tilgung der Kriegsschulden," *Bankwirtschaft*, 1944, pp. 135–36.

29. Reichsbank disclosure statement, Sept. 15, 1944, BA R 2/13480, p. 213.

30. RWM, War Finances (presentation for Ohlendorf), Jan. 3, 1945, BA R 26/36, p. 19.

31. Keiser, "Das fünfte Kriegsjahr"; presentation, Jan. 3, 1945, BA R 25/36, pp. 27–28.

32. Schwerin von Krosigk to K. H. Frank, Nov. 30, 1944, NA RG 238/case XI/microfiche 33.

33. Seminar, "Die Finanzierung des Zweiten Weltkriegs" (G. Aly, University of Salzburg, 2002–03); Walter Pichler, *Zur Rolle der Sparkassen*.

34. Reichsbank disclosure statement, Aug. 31, 1944, BA R 2/13480, p. 210.

35. Friedrich, *Brand*, pp. 449ff.; Rass, *"Menschenmaterial,"* pp. 293ff.

36. Bark, "Kriegsfinanzierung," pp. 23, 28.

37. Reinhardt, *Geld*, p. 38.

38. Akademie für Deutsches Recht, Oct. 17–18, 1941; Janssen, *Nationalökonomie*, p. 493.

39. Moeller, "Grenzprobleme," p. 116.

40. Benning, "Expansion," pp. 227–28. (Benning retracted his previous opposition to policies of debt repayment that were predicated on military victory.)

41. Benning, "Aufbringung der Kriegskosten, Kapitalfreisetzung und Geldüberfluss," June 9, 1942, pp. 1, 36, BA R 8136/3809.

42. Four-Year Plan, Reinhardt presentation for Backe, Riecke, Schlotterer, Meyer, and Hanneken [1942], BA R 2/30675.

43. RMI (Stuckart), Einziehung reichsfeindlichen Vermögens in Slowenien [Procurement of Enemy Wealth in Slovenia], Sept. 11, 1941, NG-4764; RFM, July 30, 1942, NG-4919.

44. RFM (Schlüter) to RMI, April 9, 1942, NG-4766.

45. Four-Year Plan (Körner) to RFM, June 17, 1941, NG-4912.

46. Arbeitstagung der Gauwirtschaftsberater [Working Conference of Regional Economic Advisers] (Braun, Kurhessen), Feb. 19, 1942, BA R 2/31681.

47. Eichholtz, "Richtlinien."

48. RFM/NSDAP (Gündel) to Reinhardt, April 17, 1942, BA R 2/31681.

49. RFM (Breyhan), meeting with Schwerin von Krosigk, Sept. 6, 1941, BA R 2/14586, pp. 23–24; Schwerin von Krosigk to ministerial colleagues, Sept. 4, 1942, R 2/352, pp. 31–40.

50. Four-Year Plan, Reinhardt presentation for Backe, Riecke, Schlotterer, Meyer, and Hanneken [1942], BA R 2/30675.

51. RKG (Benning), Jan. 18, 1943, presentation (Deetjen), Jan. 15, 1943, BA R 8136/3734, pp. 2–3; Aly, *Rasse*, pp. 114–20.

52. On the significance of the speech, see Gerlach, *Krieg*, pp. 85–166; Goebbels's diary, Dec. 13, 1943.

53. *Hitlers Tischgespräche* (Bormann), p. 136 (March 25, 1942).

54. Conference in Rowno (von Engelbrechten), Aug. 26–28, 1942, NA 242/24, p. 13.

55. RKU, finance division (Höll), to RFM (Eckardt), Feb. 21, 1942, BA R 2/30584.

56. Goebbels's diary, Jan. 10, 1943.

Chapter 13: Nazi Socialism

1. Schwerin von Krosigk, "Finanzpolitik," p. 16 (lecture, Nov. 27, 1935).

2. For example, see Genschel, *Verdrängung*.

3. "Abgabenpolitik im Kriege," *Bankwirtschaft* (1944), p. 74.

4. *Verwaltungsbericht der Deutschen Reichsbank für das Jahr 1942*, p. 6.

5. Archiwum Akt Nowych, Warsaw, Emissionsbank/145.

6. RFM (Schwerin von Krosigk), July 15, 1942, BA R 2/30909; Keitel to chief and Wehrmacht intendants, March 6, 1942, BA-MA RW 7/1711b, pp. 158–59.

7. Aug. 6, 1942, IMG, vol. 39, p. 397.

8. Goebbels's diary, Jan. 14 and March 27, 1938.

9. War log, Economic Defense Staff, Dec. 4 and 6, 1939, BA-MA RW 19/164.

10. As we can observe in the example of resettlement, the logic of the Nazi system encouraged "projective" solutions to conflicts. The more the Nazi state encountered material difficulties, the more radically its leaders and ideologues, having maneuvered themselves into a position where compromise was impossible, restricted their policies to campaigns of plunder and murder. In 1995, I identified the same underlying rationale for the "ethnocrats" responsible for Nazi population policies as obtained for specialists on issues

like finances, currency, and food. One of the main characteristics of Nazi politics was that "even when the agents of individual institutions represented opposing, mutually exclusive interests, they were willing to overcome the contradictions that their divergent conceptions (especially concerning the speed of implementation) produced with plunder, slave labor, and annihilation." This basic conception was linked with the seductively formulated hope that Germany could once and for all overcome its chronic scarcity of resources with the next big victory, freeing itself from all restraint and scruples in developing its national socialism, at the cost of "enemies" and "inferiors." See Aly, "*Endlösung,*" pp. 250–55; 394–400.

11. Goerdeler, *Schriften*, pp. 785ff.

12. Goebbels's diary, June 16, 1941.

13. See chapter 4, note 14 (p. 356).

14. Kundrus, *Kriegerfrauen*, p. 315.

15. Klemperer, *Zeugnis*, p. 410 (May 25, 1938).

16. *Völkischer Beobachter*, Sept. 11, 1939.

17. Goebbels's diary, March 5, April 6, and April 14, 1941.

18. *Deutschland-Berichte*, vol. 7, p. 176 (March 7, 1940).

19. Bark, "Kriegsfinanzierung," pp. 48–49.

20. *Hitlers Tischgespräche*, pp. 201–02 (Jan. 27, 1942); Hitler, "Rede," p. 350.

21. Zitelmann, *Hitler*, p. 135.

22. Boberach, *Meldungen*, p. 4331.

23. "Inflation völlig ausgeschlossen. Reinhardt sprach über wichtige Finanzierungsprobleme," *Der Angriff*, Jan. 17, 1945.

24. Goebbels's diary, Sept. 7 and 17, 1941. These are only two of many such passages.

25. The phrase "armed couriers of butter" comes from a letter to me by Michael Naumann in response to my article "Hitlers zufriedene Räuber," in *Die Zeit*, May 8, 2003.

26. Security Service report on domestic questions, Dec. 13, 1943, BA R 2/24250; Kundrus, *Kriegerfrauen*, pp. 314–21.

27. Posener, *Deutschland*, p. 18.

Bibliography

Aalders, Gerhard. *Geraubt! Die Enteignung jüdischen Besitzes im Zweiten Weltkrieg.* Cologne, 2000.

Abelshauser, Werner. "Kriegswirtschaft und Wirtschaftswunder. Deutschlands wirtschaftliche Mobilisierung für den Zweiten Weltkrieg und die Folgen für die Nachkriegszeit." *Vierteljahrshefte für Zeitgeschichte* 47 (1999), pp. 503–38.

"Abschöpfungsprobleme auch in der Slowakei," *Bank-Archiv,* 1943, pp. 114–15.

Adler, H. G. *Der verwaltete Mensch. Studien zur Deportation der Juden aus Deutschland.* Tübingen, 1974.

Albrecht, G. "Bericht über die deutsche Kriegsfinanzierung." *Finanzarchiv N.F.* 7 (1940), pp. 517–32.

———. "Die Unterstützung der Familien Einberufener. Entwicklung und gesetzliche Grundlagen." *Jahrbücher der Nationalökonomie und Statistik* 151 (1940), pp. 66–84.

Aly, Götz. *"Endlösung": Völkerverschiebung und der Mord an den europäischen Juden.* Frankfurt am Main, 1995.

———. *Im Tunnel. Das kurze Leben der Marion Samuel 1931–1943.* Frankfurt am Main, 2004.

———. *Macht, Geist, Wahn. Kontinuitäten deutschen Denkens.* Berlin, 1997.

———. *Rasse und Klasse. Nachforschungen zum deutschen Wesen.* Frankfurt am Main, 2003.

———, ed. *Das Posener Tagebuch des Hermann Voss.* In *Biedermann und Schreibtischtäter,* Beiträge zur nationalsozialistischen Gesundheits- und Sozialpolitik, vol. 4. Berlin, 1987. Pp. 15–66.

Aly, Götz, and Susanne Heim. *Vordenker der Vernichtung. Auschwitz und die deutschen Pläne für eine neue europäische Ordnung.* Hamburg, 1991.

Ancel, Jean. "Seizure of Jewish Property in Romania." In *Confiscation of Jewish Property in Europe, 1933–1945: New Sources and Perspectives.* United States Holocaust Memorial Museum, Symposium Proceedings. Washington, 2003. Pp. 43–56.

Angel, Marc D. *The Jews of Rhodes: The History of a Sephardic Community.* New York, 1980.

Apostolou, Andrew. "The Exception of Saloniki: Bystanders and Collaborators in Northern Greece." *Holocaust and Genocide Studies* 14 (2000), pp. 165–96.

Arnoult, Pierre, et al. *La France sous l'occupation.* Paris, 1959. See esp.: Arnoult, "Les finances de la France sous l'occupation," pp. 39–56.

Assa, Aaron. *Macedonia and the Jewish People.* Skopje, 1994.

Azzolini, Vicenzo. "Die Technik der Finanzierung der italienischen Kriegswirtschaft." *Bank-Archiv,* 1942, pp. 44–47.

Bajohr, Frank. "Arisierung," in *Hamburg: Die Verdrängung der jüdischen Unternehmer 1933–1945.* Hamburg, 1997.

————. "... 'dann bitte keine Gefühlsduseleien': Die Hamburger und die Deportationen." In *Die Deportation der Hamburger Juden 1941–1945.* Hamburg, 2002.

Banken, Ralf. "Die deutsche Goldreserven- und Devisenpolitik 1933–1939," *Jahrbuch für Wirtschaftsgeschichte* 1 (2003), pp. 49–78.

Bankier, David. *Die öffentliche Meinung im Hitler-Staat: Die "Endlösung" und die Deutschen. Eine Berichterstattung.* Berlin, 1995.

Bark, Harry. "Quellen und Methoden der Deutschen Kriegsfinanzierung im Weltkriege und heute." Dissertation, University of Göttingen, 1941.

Baruch, Marc Olivier. "Perpetrator Networks and the Holocaust: The Spoliation of Jewish Property in France, 1940–1944." In Feldman and Seibel, *Networks,* pp. 189–212.

Bayrhoffer, Walther. "Die alte und die neue Reichsbank." In *Deutsche Geldpolitik.* Schriften der Akademie für Deutsches Recht. Gruppe Wirtschaftswissenschaft, no. 4. Ed. Reichsminister Dr. Hans Frank, Präsidenten der Akademie für Deutsches Recht. Berlin, 1941. Pp. 88–102.

Beer, Wilfried. *Kriegsalltag an der Heimatfront: Alliierter Luftkrieg und deutsche Gegenmassnahmen zur Abwehr und Schadensbegrenzung, dargestellt für den Raum Münster.* Bremen, 1990.

Benning, Bernhard. "Der Anstieg von Besteuerung und öffentlicher Verschuldung im Ausland und in Deutschland." *Bank-Archiv,* 1940, pp. 39–41.

————. "Abschöpfung durch Anleihebegebung." *Bankwirtschaft,* 1943, pp. 117–21.

————. "Expansion und Kontraktion der Geldmenge," *Weltwirtschaftliches Archiv* 58, no. 2 (1943), pp. 205–44.

Benz, Wolfgang, ed. *Die Juden in Deutschland 1933–1945. Leben unter national-sozialistischer Herrschaft.* Munich, 1989.

Bisky, Jens. "Wenn Jungen Weltgeschichte spielen, haben Mädchen stumme Rollen." *Süddeutsche Zeitung,* September 24, 2003.

Bissinger, Edgar, ed. *Das musst du wissen! Arbeitsrecht, Sozialversicherung, Familienunterhalt usw. im Kriege.* Berlin, 1941.

Blank, Ralf, "Ersatzbeschaffung durch 'Beutemachen': Die 'M-Aktion'—ein Beispiel nationalsozialistischer Ausplünderungspolitik." In *Verfolgung und Verwaltung. Die wirtschaftliche Ausplünderung der Juden und die westfälischen Finanzbehörden.* Ed. Alfons Kenkmann and Bernd A. Rusinek. Münster, 1999. Pp. 87–101.

Blümich, Walter. *Einkommensteuergesetz. Mit Durchführungsverordnungen und Verwaltungsanweisungen.* Berlin, 1943.

————. *Körperschaftsteuer-Gesetz vom 16. Oktober 1934 in der Fassung der Änderungsgesetze von 1936 und 1938, mit Durchführungsverordnungen und Verwaltungsanweisungen.* Berlin, 1939.

Boberach, Heinz, ed. *Meldungen aus dem Reich 1938–1945. Die geheimen Lageberichte des Sicherheitsdienstes der SS.* Herrsching, 1984.

Boelcke, Willi A. "Die Finanzpolitik des Dritten Reiches. Eine Darstellung in Grundzügen." In Bracher et al., *Deutschland,* pp. 95–117.

————. *Die Kosten von Hitlers Krieg. Kriegsfinanzierung und finanzielles Kriegserbe in Deutschland 1933–1948.* Paderborn, 1985.

————. "Kriegsfinanzierung im internationalen Vergleich. Globale Wesenszüge der Kriegsfinanzierung unter theoretischen Aspekten." In *Kriegswirtschaft und Rüstung 1939–1945.* Ed. Friedrich Forstmeier and Hans-Erich Volkmann. Düsseldorf, 1977. Pp. 14–72.

————. "Veränderungen im Aktivgeschäft der Sparkassen während der Zeit des Nationalsozialismus." *Zeitschrift für bayerische Sparkassengeschichte* 13 (1999), pp. 29–51.

————, ed. *Wollt Ihr den totalen Krieg? Die geheimen Goebbels-Konferenzen 1939–43.* Herrsching, 1989.

Böhler, Jochen. *Auftakt zum Vernichtungskrieg. Die Wehrmacht in Polen 1939.* Frankfurt am Main, 2005.

Bohn, Robert. *Reichskommissariat Norwegen. "Nationalsozialistische Neuordnung" und Kriegswirtschaft.* Munich, 2000.

Böll, Heinrich. *Briefe aus dem Krieg 1939–1945.* 2 vols. Ed. Jochen Schubert. Foreword Annemarie Böll. Afterword James H. Reid. Cologne, 2001.

————. *Essayistische Schriften und Reden 1, 1952–1963.* Vol. 7 of *Werke.* Ed. Bernd Balzer. Cologne, 1978.

Bongs, Rolf. *Harte herrliche Strasse nach Westen.* Berlin, 1942.

Bracher, Karl Dietrich, Manfred Funke, and Hans-Adolf Jacobsen, eds. *Deutschland 1933–1945. Neue Studien zur nationalsozialistischen Herrschaft.* Düsseldorf, 1992.

Bräutigam, Otto. *Überblick über die besetzten Ostgebiete während des Zweiten Weltkrieges.* Tübingen, 1954.

Buchheim, Christoph. "Die besetzten Länder im Dienste der deutschen Kriegswirtschaft während des Zweiten Weltkriegs." *Vierteljahrshefte für Zeitgeschichte* 34 (1986), pp. 117–45.

Bundesarchiv. "Der Verbleib der Unterlagen der Deutschen Reichsbank. Ein Recherchebericht." MS. Berlin, August 1998.

Burkert, Hans-Norbert, ed. *900 Tage Blockade Leningrad. Leiden und Widerstand der Zivilbevölkerung im Krieg.* Part 2: *Text, Quellen, Dokumente.* Berlin, 1991.

Burkheiser, Karl. "Quellen und Methoden der Kriegsfinanzierung." *Finanzarchiv* N.F. 8 (1941), pp. 29–69.

Busch, Alfred. "Finanzaufgaben der Banken im Kriege." *Bankwirtschaft,* 1944, pp. 4–8.

Carpi, Daniel. *Between Mussolini and Hitler: The Jews and the Italian Authorities in France and Tunisia.* Hanover, 1994.

Chary, Frederick B. *The Bulgarian Jews and the Final Solution, 1940–1944.* Pittsburgh, 1972.

Chemnitz, Walter. *Frauenarbeit im Kriege.* Berlin, 1926.

Ciano, Count Galeazzo. *The Ciano Diaries, 1939–1943.* Ed. Hugh Gibson. New York, 1946.

Clausen. "Deutsches Vollstreckungswesen im Dritten Reich." *Deutsche Gerichts vollzieher-Zeitung* 54 (1934), pp. 360–62.

Correspondentie van M. M. Rost van Tonningen. Vol. 1: *1921–mei 1942.* Rijksinstituut voor Oorlogsdocumentatie. Bronnenpublicaties Documenten, no. 1. Ed. E. Fraenkel-Verkade and A. J. van der Leeuw. The Hague, 1967.

Correspondentie van M. M. Rost van Tonningen. Vol. 2: *Mei 1942–mei 1945.* Rijksinstituut voor Oorlogsdocumentatie. Bronnenpublicaties Documenten, no. 1. Ed. E. Fraenkel-Verkade and A. J. van der Leeuw. The Hague, 1993.

Dennler, Wilhelm. *Die böhmische Passion.* Freiburg im Breisgau, 1953.

Deutschlandberichte der Sozialdemokratischen Partei Deutschlands (Sopade). Vol. 7 (1940). Frankfurt am Main, 1980.

Deutsches Geld- und Bankwesen in Zahlen 1976–1975. Ed. Deutsche Bundesbank. Frankfurt am Main, 1976.

Dietrich, Hugo. *Zur Verordnung über den Aktienbesitz und ihre Durchführungsverordnungen. Soziale Praxis* (1942), pp. 519–31.

Documents on the History of the Greek Jews: Records from the Historical Archives of the Ministry of Foreign Affairs. Ed. Ministry of Foreign Affairs of Greece; Department of Political Science and Public Administration, University of Athens. Researched and ed. Photini Constantopoulou and Thanos Veremis. Athens, 1998.

Donner, Otto. "Die deutsche Kriegswirtschaft." *Nauticus. Jahrbuch für Deutschlands Seeinteressen* 27 (1944), pp. 397–431.

————. "Grenzen der Staatsverschuldung." *Weltwirtschaftliches Archiv* 56 (1942), pp. 183–266.

————. "Staatsform und Staatsverschuldung." *Bankwirtschaft,* April 1, 1943, pp. 1–5.

————. "Valutapolitik im Kriege. Ein Beitrag zur aussenwirtschaftlichen Problematik fester Wechselkurse bei unstabilen Kaufkraftparitäten." *Weltwirtschaftliches Archiv* 58 (1943), pp. 27–50.

Doorslaer, Rudi van. "Raub und Rückerstattung jüdischen Eigentums in Belgien." In Goschler and Ther, *Raub und Restitution,* pp. 134–53.

Dörner, Bernward. *"Heimtücke." Das Gesetz als Waffe. Kontrolle, Abschreckung und Verfolgung in Deutschland 1933–1945.* Paderborn, 1998.

Dressen, Wolfgang, ed. *Betrifft: "Aktion 3." Deutsche verwerten jüdische Nachbarn. Dokumente zur Arisierung.* Berlin, 1998.

Dreyfus, Jean-Marc. "Die Enteignung der Juden in Westeuropa." In Goschler and Ther, *Raub und Restitution,* pp. 41–57.

————. *Pillages sur ordonnances. Aryanisation et restitution des banques en France 1940–1943.* Paris, 2003.

Dreyfus, Jean-Marc, and Sarah Gensburger. *Des camps dans Paris. Austerlitz, Léviatan, Bassano, juillet 1943–août 1944.* Paris, 2003.

Drissner, Ulrike. "Die Deportation der Thessaloniker Juden während der Zeit der deutschen Besatzung von April 1941 bis August 1943." Master's thesis, University of Stuttgart, 1990.

Ebbinghaus, Angelika, Heidrun Kaupen-Haas, and Karl Heinz Roth, eds. *Heilen und Vernichten im Mustergau Hamburg. Bevölkerungs- und Gesundheitspolitik im Dritten Reich.* Hamburg, 1984.

Eckert, Rainer. "Die wirtschaftliche Ausplünderung Griechenlands durch seine deutschen Okkupanten vom Beginn der Besetzung im April 1941 bis zur Kriegswende im Winter 1942/43." *Jahrbuch für Wirtschaftsgeschichte* 36 (1988), pp. 233–66.

————. *Vom "Fall Marita" zur "wirtschaftlichen Sonderaktion." Die deutsche Besatzungspolitik in Griechenland vom 6. April 1941 bis zur Kriegswende im Februar/März 1943.* Frankfurt am Main, 1992.

Eggenkämper, Barbara, Marian Rappel, and Anna Reichel. "Der Bestand Reichswirtschaftsministerium im 'Zentrum für die Aufbewahrung historischdokumentarischer Sammlungen' ('Sonderarchiv') in ₊Moskau," *Zeitschrift für Unternehmensgeschichte* 43 (1998), pp. 227–36.

Eheberg, Karl. "Finanzen im Weltkrieg." *Handwörterbuch der Staatswissenschaften.* 4th ed. Vol. 4. Pp. 75–86.

Eichholtz, Dietrich. *Geschichte der deutschen Kriegswirtschaft 1939–1945.* 3 vols. Berlin, 1984–99.

———, ed. "Die Richtlinien Görings für die Wirtschaftspolitik auf dem besetzten sowjetischen Territorium vom 8. November 1941." "Zweiter Weltkrieg." Special issue of *Bulletin des Arbeitskreises,* nos. 1–2 (1977), pp. 73–111.

Epmeier, Ernst. "Das finanzielle Kriegspotential Deutschlands und Englands. Ein Vergleich und seine Problematik." Dissertation, University of Innsbruck, 1942.

Erhard, Ludwig. *Kriegsfinanzierung und Schuldenkonsolidierung; Faksimiledruck der Denkschrift von 1943/44.* Frankfurt am Main, 1977.

Etmektsoglou-Koehn, Gabriella. *Axis Exploitation of Wartime Greece, 1941–1943.* Ann Arbor, 1995.

"Der 'Fall Köppen' und seine Lehren." *Deutsche Gerichtsvollzieher-Zeitung* 54 (1934), pp. 341–43.

Familienunterhalt. Ed. Oberbürgermeister der Stadt der Reichsparteitage Nürnberg, Abteilung für Familienunterhalt. May 1940.

Das Familienunterhaltswesen und seine praktische Handhabung. Systematische, erläuternde Darstellung. Ed. Deutscher Verein für öffentliche und private Fürsorge. Leipzig and Berlin, 1943.

Fasse, Norbert, et al. *Nationalsozialistische Herrschaft und Besatzungszeit. Historische Erfahrung und Verarbeitung aus niederländischer und deutscher Sicht.* Münster, 2000.

Faulstich, Heinz. *Hungersterben in der Psychiatrie 1914–1949. Mit einer Topographie der NS-Psychiatrie.* Freiburg im Breisgau, 1998.

Federau, Fritz. *Die deutsche Geldwirtschaft.* Berlin, 1949.

———. "Die deutsche Geldwirtschaft in der Jahreswende 1940/41." *Deutsche Sparkassen-Zeitung,* February 20, 1941, pp. 1–2.

———. "Kriegsfinanzierung aus dem Geldmarkt." *Der Deutsche Volkswirt* 14 (1939–40), pp. 1912–13.

———. *Der Zweite Weltkrieg. Seine Finanzierung in Deutschland.* Tübingen, 1962.

Feldman, Gerald D., and Wolfgang Seibel. *Networks of Nazi Persecution: Bureaucracy, Business, and the Organization of the Holocaust.* New York and Oxford, 2005.

Fleischer, Adolf. *Kriegsfinanzierung unter Einschluss des totalen Krieges*. Berlin, 1939.

Fleischer, Hagen. "Griechenland." In Wolfgang Benz, ed., *Dimension des Völkermords. Die Zahl der jüdischen Opfer des Nationalsozialismus*. Munich, 1991. Pp. 241–74.

———. *Im Kreuzschatten der Mächte. Griechenland 1941–1944 (Okkupation, Résistance, Kollaboration)*. Frankfurt am Main, 1986.

Franco, Hizkia M. *The Jewish Martyrs of Rhodes and Cos*. Harare, 1994.

Friedenberger, Martin, Klaus-Dieter Gössel, and Eberhard Schönknecht, eds. *Die Reichsfinanzverwaltung im Nationalsozialismus. Darstellung und Dokumente*. Bremen, 2002.

Friedrich, Jörg. *Der Brand. Deutschland im Bombenkrieg 1940–1945*. Munich, 2002.

"Gedanken zur Neugestaltung des Vollstreckungsrechts." *Deutsche Gerichtsvollzieher-Zeitung* 54 (1934), pp. 147–53.

Genschel, Helmut. *Die Verdrängung der Juden aus der Wirtschaft im Dritten Reich*. Göttingen, 1966.

Gericke, Bodo. *Die deutsche Feldpost im Zweiten Weltkrieg. Eine Dokumentation über Einrichtung, Aufbau, Einsatz und Dienste*. Archiv für deutsche Postgeschichte, vol. 1, 1971.

Gerlach, Christian. *Kalkulierte Morde. Die deutsche Wirtschafts- und Vernichtungspolitik in Weissrussland 1941 bis 1944*. Hamburg, 1999.

———. *Krieg, Ernährung, Völkermord. Forschungen zur deutschen Vernichtungspolitik im Zweiten Weltkrieg*. Hamburg, 1998.

Gerlach, Christian, and Götz Aly. *Das letzte Kapitel. Ideologie, Realpolitik und der Mord an den ungarischen Juden 1944–1945*. Stuttgart, 2002.

Gilbert, Martin. *The Holocaust: A History of the Jews of Europe during the Second World War*. New York, 1987.

Gillingham, John. "The 'Deproletarianization' of German Society: Vocational Training in the Third Reich." *Journal of Social History* 19, no. 3 (1986), pp. 423–32.

Goebbels, Joseph. *Die Tagebücher, Teil I und II*. Ed. Elke Fröhlich. Munich, 1993–2005.

Goerdeler, Carl Friedrich. *Politische Schriften und Briefe*. 2 vols. Ed. Sabine Gillmann and Hans Mommsen. Munich, 2003.

Goldtransaktionen im Zweiten Weltkrieg: Kommentierte statistische Übersicht. Ein Beitrag zur Goldkonferenz in London, 2.–4. Dezember 1997, ausgearbeitet von der unabhängigen Expertenkommission Schweiz—Zweiter Weltkrieg. Bern, December 1997.

Goschler, Constantin, and Philipp Ther, eds. *Raub und Restitution.* *"Arisierung"* *und Rückerstattung des jüdischen Eigentums in Europa.* Frankfurt am Main, 2003.

Göttel, Heinrich. *Steuerrecht.* Leipzig, 1939.

Grätz, Heinrich. *Geschichte der Juden.* Leipzig, 1890.

Grimm, Jacob, and Wilhelm Grimm. *Deutsches Wörterbuch.* Vol. 1. Leipzig, 1854.

Grosa, Karl. *Die wirtschaftspolitischen Zielsetzungen der deutschen Steuergesetzgebung unter besonderer Berücksichtigung ihrer betriebswirtschaftlichen Auswirkungen.* Vienna, 1942.

Guillebaud, Claude W. *The Social Policy of Nazi Germany.* Cambridge, 1941; New York, 1971.

Hachmeister, Lutz. *Schleyer. Eine deutsche Geschichte.* Munich, 2004.

Hahn, Paul. *Die griechische Währung und währungspolitische Massnahmen unter der Besetzung 1941–1944.* Studien des Instituts für Besatzungsfragen in Tübingen zu den deutschen Besetzungen im 2. Weltkrieg, no. 10. Tübingen, 1957.

Halder, Franz. *Kriegstagebuch. Tägliche Aufzeichnungen des Chefs des Generalstabes des Heeres 1939–1942.* 3 vols. Ed. Hans-Adolf Jacobsen. Stuttgart, 1962–64.

Hamann, Brigitte. *Hitlers Wien. Lehrjahre eines Diktators.* Munich, 1996.

Handbuch über die Beamten der Deutschen Reichsbank 1941, abgeschlossen mit den Personalveränderungen vom 12. Juni 1941. Berlin, 1941.

Hansen. "Nationalsozialistische Rechtsgestaltung in der Zwangsvollstreckung." *Deutsche Gerichtsvollzieher-Zeitung* 55 (1935), pp. 262–65.

Hansmeyer, Heinrich-Karl, and Rolf Caesar. "Kriegswirtschaft und Inflation (1936 bis 1948)." In *Währung und Wirtschaft in Deutschland 1976–1975.* Ed. Deutschen Bundesbank. Frankfurt am Main, 1976.

Hartlaub, Felix. *In den eigenen Umriss gebannt. Kriegsaufzeichnungen, literarische Fragmente und Briefe aus den Jahren 1939 bis 1945.* 2 vols. Ed. Gabriele Liselotte Ewenz. Frankfurt am Main, 2002.

Hassell, Ulrich von. *The Von Hassell Diaries, 1938–1944.* Garden City, 1947.

Hauser, Josef. *Einsatz-Familienunterhaltsgesetz vom 26. Juni 1940.* Munich, 1942.

Heiber, Beatrice, and Helmut Heiber, eds. *Die Rückseite des Hakenkreuzes. Absonderliches aus den Akten des Dritten Reiches.* Munich, 1993.

Heilmann, H. D., ed. "Aus dem Kriegstagebuch des Diplomaten Otto Bräutigam." In *Biedermann und Schreibtischtäter. Materialien zur deutschen Täter-Biographie.* Beiträge zur nationalsozialistischen Gesundheits- und Sozialpolitik, vol. 4. Berlin, 1987. Pp. 123–87.

Heim, Susanne. " 'Deutschland muss ihnen ein Land ohne Zukunft sein.' Die Zwangsmigration der Juden 1933 bis 1938." In *Arbeitsmigration und Flucht.*

Vertreibung und Arbeitskräfteregulierung im Zwischenkriegseuropa. Beiträge zur nationalsozialistischen Gesundheits- und Sozialpolitik, vol. 11. Berlin, 1993. Pp. 48–81.

Heim, Susanne, and Götz Aly, eds. *Bevölkerungsstruktur und Massenmord. Neue Dokumente zur deutschen Politik der Jahre 1938–1945.* Beiträge zur nationalsozialistischen Gesundheits- und Sozialpolitik, vol. 9. Berlin, 1991.

————. "Staatliche Ordnung und 'organische Lösung.' Die Rede Hermann Görings 'Über die Judenfrage' vom 6. Dezember 1938." *Jahrbuch für Antisemitismusforschung,* vol. 2. Frankfurt am Main, 1993. Pp. 378–405.

Henning, Friedrich Wilhelm. "Die nationalsozialistische Steuerpolitik. Programm, Ziele und Wirklichkeit." In Schremmer, *Steuern,* pp. 197–211.

Herbert, Ulrich. *Best. Biographische Studien über Radikalismus, Weltanschauung und Vernunft, 1903–1989.* Bonn, 1996.

————. *Fremdarbeiter. Politik und Praxis des "Ausländer-Einsatzes" in der Kriegswirtschaft des Dritten Reiches.* Berlin, 1985.

Hilberg, Raul. *Die Vernichtung der europäischen Juden: Die Gesamtgeschichte.* 3 vols. Frankfurt am Main, 1980.

Hillgruber, Andreas. *Hitlers Strategie. Politik und Kriegsführung 1940–1941.* Frankfurt am Main, 1965.

————, ed. *Staatsmänner und Diplomaten bei Hitler. Vertrauliche Aufzeichnungen über Unterredungen mit Vertretern des Auslandes 1942–1944.* Frankfurt am Main, 1970.

Hillgruber, Andreas, and Gerhard Hümmelchen. *Chronik des Zweiten Weltkriegs. Kalendarium militärischer und politischer Ereignisse 1939–1945.* Bindlach, 1989.

Hirschfeld, Gerhard, Gerd Krumeich, and Irina Renz, eds. *Enzyklopädie Erster Weltkrieg.* Paderborn, 2003.

Hitler, Adolf. *Mein Kampf.* Munich, 1934.

————. *Monologe im Führerhauptquartier 1941–1944. Die Aufzeichnungen Heinrich Heims.* Ed. Werner Jochmann. Hamburg, 1980.

————. "Rede am 10. Dezember 1940 in Berlin vor Rüstungsarbeitern." In *Vom März 1940 bis 16. März 1941.* Vol. 2 of *Der grossdeutsche Freiheitskampf. Reden Adolf Hitlers.* Ed. Philipp Bouhler. Munich, 1941. Pp. 333–62.

Hitlers Tischgespräche im Führerhauptquartier 1941–1942. Transcribed Henry Picker. Ed. Gerhard Ritter. Bonn, 1951.

Höffinghoff, Hellmuth. "Die griechische Wirtschaft im Kriege." *Deutsch-Griechische Wirtschaftsnachrichten. Mitteilungen der Deutschen Handelskammer in Griechenland* 1 (June 1943), pp. 4–6.

Hoffmann, Walter. "Probleme der englischen Kriegsfinanzierung." *Weltwirtschaftliches Archiv* 51 (1940), pp. 570–94.

Hohrmann, Johannes, and Edgar Lenski. *Die Körperschaftsteuer.* 2nd ed. Bücherei des Steuerrechts, vol. 24. Berlin, 1941.

Holzhauer, Georg. *Barzahlung und Zahlungsmittelversorgung in militärisch besetzten Gebieten.* Introd. H. Rittershausen. Jena, 1939.

IMG [International Military Tribunal]. *Der Prozess gegen die Hauptkriegsverbrecher vor dem Internationalen Militärgerichtshof. Nürnberg 14. November 1945–1. Oktober 1946.* 42 vols. Nuremberg, 1948.

Ioanid, Radu. *The Holocaust in Romania: The Destruction of Jews and Gypsies under the Antonescu Regime, 1940–1944.* Chicago, 2000.

Janssen, Hauke. *Nationalökonomie und Nationalsozialismus. Die deutsche Volkswirtschaftslehre in den dreissiger Jahren.* Marburg, 1998.

Jecht, Horst. *Kriegsfinanzen.* Jena, 1938.

———. "Stand und Probleme der deutschen Kriegsfinanzierung." *Weltwirtschaftliches Archiv* 51 (1940), pp. 464–89.

Jessen, Jens. *Deutsche Finanzwirtschaft.* Hamburg, 1938.

———. "Kriegsfinanzen." *Wörterbuch der Volkswirtschaft.* Jena, 1932. Pp. 674–82.

———. *Die Kriegswirtschaftsverordnung vom 4. September 1939. Erläuterungen.* Berlin, 1939.

Johnson, Uwe. *Jahrestage. Aus dem Leben von Gesine Gresspahl.* Frankfurt am Main, 1983.

Jüdisches Lexikon. 4 vols. Berlin, 1927; rpt. Frankfurt am Main, 1987.

Junz, Helen B. *Where Did All the Money Go? The Pre-Nazi-Era Wealth of European Jewry.* Bern, 2002.

Kaemmel, Ernst, and Eduard Bacciocco. *Einkommensteuergesetz vom 16. Oktober 1934 unter Berücksichtigung aller einschlägigen Vorschriften, Veranlagungsrichtlinien und Verwaltungserlasse.* Munich and Berlin, 1936.

Kaiser, Johann. "Die Eingliederung der Slowakei in die deutsche Kriegswirtschaft." In *Das Jahr 1945 in der Tschechoslowakei.* Ed. Carl Bosl. Munich, 1971. Pp. 115–38.

———. "Die Politik des Dritten Reiches gegenüber der Slowakei 1939–1945. Ein Beitrag zur Erforschung der nationalsozialistischen Satellitenpolitik in Südosteuropa." Dissertation, University of Bochum, 1969.

Kasten, Helmut. "Die Neuordnung der Währung in den besetzten Gebieten und die Tätigkeit der Reichskreditkassen während des Krieges 1939/40." Dissertation, University of Berlin, 1941.

Keiser, Günter. "Das fünfte Kriegsjahr der Banken." *Bankwirtschaft,* 1945, pp. 29–33.

———. "Spareinlagen der Banken," *Bankwirtschaft,* 1943, pp. 77–79.

Keller, Robert von. *Von der Kriegswirtschaft zur Friedenswirtschaft.* Stuttgart, 1940.

Klein, Thomas, ed. *Die Lageberichte der Justiz aus Hessen 1940–1945*. Darmstadt, 1999.

Klemperer, Victor. *Ich will Zeugnis ablegen bis zum letzten. Tagebücher 1933–1941*. Berlin, 1995.

Klingemann, Hellmuth. *Die Biersteuer*. Bücherei des Steuerrechts, vol. 46. Berlin, 1943.

Klinkhammer, Lutz. *Zwischen Bündnis und Besatzung. Das nationalsozialistische Deutschland und die Republik von Salò 1943–1945*. Tübingen, 1993.

Kolonomos, Zhamila, and Vera Veskovich-Vangeli. *The Jews in Macedonia during the Second World War (1941–1945): Collection of Documents*. 2 vols. Skopje, 1986.

Kretzschmann, Max. "Deutsche Währungshilfe in den besetzten Gebieten." *Bank-Archiv*, 1941, pp. 1–3.

———. "Die Reichskreditkassen." In *Deutsche Geldpolitik*. Schriften der Akademie für Deutsches Recht. Gruppe Wirtschaftswissenschaft, no. 4. Ed. Reichsminister Dr. Hans Frank, Präsidenten der Akademie für Deutsches Recht. Berlin, 1941. Pp. 113–39.

———. "Reichskreditkassenscheine als Truppengeld." *Die Bank* 33 (1940), pp. 584–87.

Kriegstagebuch des Oberkommandos der Wehrmacht (Wehrmachtführungsstab) 1940–1945, geführt von Helmuth Greiner und Percy Ernst Schramm. Ed. Percy Ernst Schramm. Frankfurt am Main, 1961–65.

Krug von Nidda, Carl Ludwig. *Familienunterhalt der Angehörigen der Einberufenen*. Berlin, 1941.

Krüger, Alf. *Die Lösung der Judenfrage in der deutschen Wirtschaft. Kommentar zur Judengesetzgebung*. Berlin, 1940.

Krumme, F. "Der Spareinlagenzuwachs im Kriege." *Deutsche Sparkassen-Zeitung*, September 12, 1940, p. 1.

Kundrus, Birthe. *Kriegerfrauen. Familienpolitik und Geschlechterverhältnis im Ersten und Zweiten Weltkrieg*. Hamburg, 1995.

Kwiet, Konrad. "Nach dem Pogrom: Stufen der Ausgrenzung." In Benz, *Juden*, pp. 545–659.

Lanter, Max. *Die Finanzierung des Krieges. Quellen, Methoden und Lösungen seit dem Mittelalter bis Ende des Zweiten Weltkrieges 1939 bis 1945*. Lucerne, 1950.

Laskier, Michael M. *North African Jewry in the Twentieth Century: The Jews of Morocco, Tunisia, and Algeria*. New York, 1995.

Latzel, Klaus. *Deutsche Soldaten—nationalsozialistischer Krieg. Kriegserlebnis—Kriegserfahrung 1939–1945*. Paderborn, 1998.

Leeuw, A. J. van der. "Der Griff des Reiches nach dem Judenvermögen." In Paape, *Studies*, pp. 211–36.

———. "Reichskommissariat und Judenvermögen in den Niederlanden." In Paape, *Studies*, pp. 237–49.

Lemkin, Raphael. *Axis Rule in Occupied Europe: Laws of Occupation, Analysis of Government, Proposals for Redress.* Washington, 1944.

Lindner, Stephan H. *Das Reichskommissariat für die Behandlung feindlichen Vermögens im Zweiten Weltkrieg. Eine Studie zur Verwaltungs-, Rechts- und Wirtschaftsgeschichte des nationalsozialistischen Deutschlands.* Stuttgart, 1991.

Lipscher, Ladislav. *Die Juden im slowakischen Staat 1939–1945.* Munich, 1980.

Longerich, Peter. *Politik der Vernichtung. Eine Gesamtdarstellung der nationalsozialistischen Judenverfolgung.* Munich, 1998.

Lütge, Friedrich. "Die deutsche Kriegsfinanzierung im ersten und zweiten Weltkrieg." In *Beiträge zur Finanzwissenschaft und Geldtheorie. Festschrift für Rolf Stucken.* Ed. Fritz Voigt. Göttingen, 1953. Pp. 243–57.

Maedel, Walter. *Das Reichsbewertungsgesetz.* Berlin, 1941.

Margairaz, Michel, ed. *Banques, Banque de France et seconde guerre mondiale.* Paris, 2002.

Mason, Timothy W., ed. *Arbeiterklasse und Volksgemeinschaft. Dokumente und Materialien zur deutschen Arbeiterpolitik 1936–1939.* Opladen, 1975.

Matkovski, Aleksandar. *A History of the Jews in Macedonia.* Skopje, 1982.

Mazower, Mark. *Inside Hitler's Greece: The Experience of Occupation, 1941–1944.* New Haven, 2001.

Meimberg, Rudolf. "Die Gewinnabführung in Deutschland als Kriegsgewinnsteuer." *Weltwirtschaftliches Archiv* 60 (1944), pp. 349–64.

———. "Kaufkraftüberhang und Kriegsfinanzpolitik." *Weltwirtschaftliches Archiv* 58 (1943), pp. 98–132.

Meinen, Insa. *Wehrmacht und Prostitution während des Zweiten Weltkriegs im besetzten Frankreich.* Bremen, 2002.

Meyer, Fritz. "Die finanzielle Neuordnung in Serbien." *Bank-Archiv,* 1942, pp. 310–12.

Michel, Henri. *Paris Allemand.* Paris, 1981.

Milward, Allan S. *Der Zweite Weltkrieg. Krieg, Wirtschaft und Gesellschaft 1939–1945.* Munich, 1977.

Mischaikov, D. "Bulgariens Wirtschafts-, Finanz- und Kreditsystem unter dem Einfluss des Krieges." *Bank-Archiv,* 1942, pp. 49–52.

Moeller, Hero. "Aktuelle Grenzprobleme kreditärer Mittelaufbringung in der Staatswirtschaft." *Finanzarchiv N.F.* 9 (1943), pp. 95–116.

Molho, Michael, ed. *In Memoriam, gewidmet dem Andenken an die jüdischen Opfer der Naziherrschaft in Griechenland.* Essen, 1981.

————, ed. *In Memoriam. Hommage aux victimes juives des nazis en Grèce.* Thessaloniki, 1948.

Moll, Martin, ed. *"Führer-Erlasse" 1939–1945. Edition sämtlicher überlieferter, nicht im Reichsgesetzblatt abgedruckter, von Hitler während des Zweiten Weltkrieges schriftlich erteilter Direktiven aus den Bereichen Staat, Partei, Wirtschaft, Besatzungspolitik und Militärverwaltung.* Stuttgart, 1997.

Möllenhoff, Gisela, and Rita Schlautmann-Overmeyer. *Jüdische Familien in Münster 1918–1945.* Vol. 1: *Biographisches Lexikon.* Münster, 1995.

————. *Jüdische Familien in Münster 1918–1945.* Vol. 2: *Abhandlungen und Dokumente 1935–1945.* Münster, 2001.

Neubacher, Hermann. *Sonderauftrag Südost 1940–1945. Bericht eines fliegenden Diplomaten.* 2nd ed. Göttingen, 1957.

Oberleitner, Gerhard. *Geschichte der Deutschen Feldpost 1937–1945.* Innsbruck, 1993.

Oermann, Josef. *Die arbeitsrechtliche und steuerrechtliche Behandlung der Ostarbeiter mit den ab 1. April 1944 gültigen Lohnsteuertabellen.* Berlin, 1944.

————. *Die Sozialausgleichsabgabe.* Bücherei des Steuerrechts, vol. 47. Berlin, 1944.

————, and Hans Meuschel. *Die Kriegssteuern.* Bücherei des Steuerrechts, vol. 22. Berlin, 1939.

Oertel, Manfred. "Besteuerung von Zwangsarbeitern als Mittel der Kriegsfinanzierung." *Fremdarbeiterpolitik des Imperialismus* 19 (1988), pp. 71–73.

————. "Die Kriegsfinanzierung." In Eichholtz, *Geschichte,* vol. 3, pp. 681–737.

————. "Über die Deutsche Reichsbank im zweiten Weltkrieg." Dissertation, University of Rostock, 1979.

Ein offenes Geheimnis. "Arisierung" in Alltag und Wirtschaft in Oldenburg zwischen 1933 und 1945. Ed. Werkstattfilm e.V. Oldenburg, 2001.

Ostermann, Josef, and Hans Meuschel. *Die Kriegssteuern.* Bücherei des Steuerrechts, vol. 22. Berlin and Vienna, 1939.

Paape, Abraham H., ed. *Studies over Nederland in oorlogstijd, deel 1.* The Hague, 1972.

Pätzold, Kurt, and Erika Schwarz. *"Auschwitz war für mich nur ein Bahnhof." Franz Novak—der Transportoffizier Adolf Eichmanns.* Berlin, 1994.

Palairet, Michael R. *The Four Ends of Greek Hyperinflation of 1941–1946.* Copenhagen, 2000.

Pantlen, Hermann. *Krieg und Finanzen.* Hamburg, 1936.

Petrick, Fritz, ed. *Die Okkupationspolitik des deutschen Faschismus in Dänemark und Norwegen (1940–1945).* Europa unterm Hakenkreuz, vol. 7. Berlin, 1992.

Petrov, Vladimir. *Money and Conquest: Allied Occupation Currencies in World War II.* Baltimore, 1967.

Petzina, Dietmar. "Soziale Lage der deutschen Arbeiter und Probleme des Arbeitseinsatzes während des Zweiten Weltkrieges." In *Zweiter Weltkrieg und sozialer Wandel. Achsenmächte und besetzte Länder.* Ed. Waclaw Dlugoborski. Göttingen, 1981. Pp. 65–86.

Pfleiderer, Otto. "Reichskreditkassen und Wehrmachtsbedarfsgeld." *Bank-Archiv,* 1942, pp. 385–87.

Pichler, Walter. *Zur Rolle der Sparkassen, Sitzungsprotokolle des Verwaltungsausschusses der Sparkasse Salzburg 1941–44.* Salzburg, 2004.

Posener, Julius. *In Deutschland 1945 bis 1946.* Berlin, 2001.

Präg, Werner, and Wolfgang Jacobmeyer, eds. *Das Diensttagebuch des deutschen Generalgouverneurs in Polen. 1939–1945.* Stuttgart, 1975.

Prion, Willi. *Das deutsche Finanzwunder. Die Geldbeschaffung für den deutschen Wirtschaftsaufschwung.* Berlin, 1938.

Probleme der Kriegsfinanzierung. Vorträge, gehalten auf der ersten Arbeitstagung des Vereines deutscher Wirtschaftswissenschaftler. Jena, 1940.

Puhl, Emil. "Reichsbankarbeit im Kriege." *Die Staatsbank* 10 (1941), pp. 13–19.

———. "Währungsaufbau in Serbien." *Der Vierjahresplan* 58 (1941), pp. 643–46.

Ranetsberger. "Der Gerichtsvollzieher im Dritten Reich." *Deutsche Gerichtsvollzieher-Zeitung* 54 (1934), pp. 115–17.

Rass, Christoph. *"Menschenmaterial": Deutsche Soldaten an der Ostfront. Innenansichten einer Infanteriedivision 1939–1945.* Paderborn, 2003.

Rath, Klaus. "Die produktiven Aufgaben der Kreigsfinanzierung." *Weltwirtschaftliches Archiv* 51 (1940), pp. 490–523.

———. "Schöpferische Kriegsfinanzierung." *Wirtschaftsdienst* 25 (1940), pp. 6–9.

———. "Sozialistische Kriegsfinanzierung." *National-Zeitung,* ed. A (Gross-Essen), no. 47, February 16, 1940.

Ray, Roland. *Annäherung an Frankreich im Dienste Hitlers. Otto Abetz und die deutsche Frankreichpolitik 1930–1942.* Munich, 2000.

"Die Rechtsstellung der Juden in Frankreich." *Deutsch-Französische Wirtschaftszeitschrift (La revue économique Franco-Allemande),* June 1942, pp. 12–14.

Recker, Marie-Luise. *Nationalsozialistische Sozialpolitik im Zweiten Weltkrieg.* Munich, 1985.

Reinhardt, Fritz. "Gemeinschaftsbedarf und seine Finanzierung nach nationalsozialistischen Grundsätzen." *Die Deutsche Volkswirtschaft* 10 (1941), pp. 985–92.

———. "Grundsätze nationalsozialistischer Steuerpolitik." *Reichssteuerblatt,* 1934, p. 1229.

———. *Die neuen Steuergesetze. Einführung in die neuen Steuergesetze, Übersichten über die wesentlichen Änderungen gegenüber dem bisherigen Recht, Wortlaut der neuen Gesetze.* Berlin, 1934.

————. *Passauer Vorträge*. Part 2: *Körperschaftsteuer*. Berlin, 1941.

————. *Passauer Vorträge 1942*. Part 1: *Einkommensteuer*. Bücherei des Steuerrechts, vol. 49. Berlin, 1942.

————. *Was geschieht mit unserem Geld? Finanzen, Kaufkraft, Währung*. Nuremberg, 1942.

Reisel, Berit, and Bjarte Bruland. *The Reisel/Bruland Report on the Confiscation of Jewish Property in Norway during World War II*. Part of Official Norwegian Report, no. 22, June 1997.

République Française. *La spoliation financière*. Vol. 2. Ouvrages de Mission d'étude sur la spoliation des juifs de France. Paris, 2000.

Ritter, Harry R. "Hermann Neubacher and the German Occupation of the Balcans, 1940–1945," Ph.D. dissertation, University of Virginia, 1969.

Roediger, Conrad. "Die internationale Hilfsaktion für die Bevölkerung Griechenlands im zweiten Weltkrieg," *Vierteljahrshefte für Zeitgeschichte* 11 (1963), pp. 49–71.

Rondholz, Eberhard. "Eine längst vergessene Geschichte. Warum Johannes Rau um die Jüdische Gemeinde von Thessaloniki einen so grossen Bogen gemacht hat." *Konkret* 8 (2000).

Rosh, Lea, and Eberhard Jäckel. *"Der Tod ist ein Meister aus Deutschland." Deportation und Ermordung der Juden, Kollaboration und Verweigerung in Europa*. Hamburg, 1990.

Rösle. "Die Geburts- und Sterblichkeitsverhältnisse." In *Deutschlands Gesundheitsverhältnisse unter dem Einfluss des Weltkrieges*. Vol. 1. Ed. Franz Bumm. Stuttgart, 1928. Pp. 3–61.

Royal Institute of International Affairs. *Occupied Europe: German Exploitation and Its Post-War Consequences*. London, 1944.

Rummel, Walter, and Jochen Rath. *"Dem Reich verfallen"—"den Berechtigten zurückerstattet." Enteignung und Rückerstattung jüdischen Vermögens im Gebiet des heutigen Rheinland-Pfalz 1938–1953*. Koblenz, 2001.

Rüther, Martin. *Köln, 31. Mai 1942: Der 1000-Bomber-Angriff*. Cologne, 1992.

Safrian, Hans. *Die Eichmann-Männer*. Vienna, 1993.

Schachtschnabel, Hans G. "Frankreichs Finanzwirtschaft." *Bankwirtschaft* 1 (1943), pp. 74–77.

Schielin, Irma. "Der Familienunterhalt. Anwendung und Bewährung." *Jahrbücher für Nationalökonomie und Statistik* 157 (1943), pp. 435–59.

Schlarp, Karl-Heinz. *Wirtschaft und Besatzung in Serbien 1941–1944. Ein Beitrag zur nationalsozialistischen Wirtschaftspolitik in Südosteuropa*. Stuttgart, 1986.

Schmid, Heinz. *Kriegsgewinne und Wirtschaft. Die Aufgabe einer deutschen Kriegswirtschaftspolitik im Hinblick auf den Kriegsgewinn*. Oldenburg, 1934.

Schmidt, E. W. "Bilanz der Hauszinssteuerablösung." *Bankwirtschaft* 1 (1943), pp. 72–74.

Schmitt, Bruno, and Bodo Gericke. "Die deutsche Feldpost im Osten und der Luftpostdienst Osten im Zweiten Weltkrieg." *Archiv für deutsche Postgeschichte*, vol. 1, 1969.

Schmitt-Degenhardt, Hubert. *Die Vermögensteuer.* Bücherei des Steuerrechts, vol. 26. Berlin, 1941.

Schmölders, Günter. "Probleme der Kriegsfinanzierung (Literaturbericht)." *Finanzarchiv N.F.* 8 (1941), pp. 203–09.

Schöllgen, Gregor. *Willy Brandt. Die Biographie.* Berlin, 2001.

Schönknecht, Eberhard. "Die Ausbildung in der Reichsfinanzverwaltung 1933 bis 1945." In Friedenberger et al., *Die Reichsfinanzverwaltung*, pp. 186–243.

Schöpf, Andreas. "Fritz Reinhardt." In Friedenberger et al., *Die Reichsfinanzverwaltung*, pp. 253–59.

Schremmer, Eckart, ed. *Geld und Währung vom 16. Jahrhundert bis zur Gegenwart. Referate der 14. Arbeitstagung der Gesellschaft für Sozial- und Wirtschaftsgeschichte vom 9. bis 13. April 1991 in Dortmund.* Stuttgart, 1993.

———, ed. *Steuern, Abgaben und Dienste vom Mittelalter bis zur Gegenwart. Referate der 15. Arbeitstagung der Gesellschaft für Sozial- und Wirtschaftsgeschichte vom 14. bis 17. April 1993 in Dortmund.* Stuttgart, 1994.

Schwerin von Krosigk, Lutz. "Nationalsozialistische Finanzpolitik." Kieler Vorträge, gehalten im Inst. für Weltwirtschaft an der Universität Kiel, vol. 41. Jena, 1936.

———. *Staatsbankrott. Die Geschichte der Finanzpolitik des Deutschen Reiches von 1920 bis 1945, geschrieben vom letzten Reichsfinanzminister.* Göttingen, 1974.

———. "Wie wurde der Zweite Weltkrieg finanziert?" In *Bilanz des Zweiten Weltkrieges. Erkenntnisse und Verpflichtungen für die Zukunft.* Oldenburg, 1953. Pp. 313–28.

Sebode, Dr. "Einheitliche Regelung des Pfändungsschutzes für Arbeitseinkommen ab 1.12.1940 auf Grund der Lohnpfändungsverordnung vom 30.10.1940 (RGBl. I, pp.1451f.)." *Deutsche Gerichtsvollzieher-Zeitung*, 1940, pp. 185–92.

Seckendorf, Martin, ed. *Die Okkupationspolitik des deutschen Faschismus in Jugoslawien, Griechenland, Albanien, Italien und Ungarn (1941–1945).* Europa unterm Hakenkreuz, vol. 6. Berlin, 1992.

Seydelmann, Gertrud. *Gefährdete Balance. Ein Leben in Hamburg 1936–1945.* Hamburg, 1995.

Statistisches Handbuch von Deutschland 1928–1944. Ed. Länderrat des Amerikanischen Besatzungsgebiets. Munich, 1949.

Steinberg, Jonathan. *Die Deutsche Bank und ihre Goldtransaktionen während des Zweiten Weltkrieges.* Munich, 1999.

Steur, Claudia. *Theodor Dannecker. Ein Funktionär der "Endlösung."* Essen, 1997.

Stöber, Rudolf. *Die erfolgverführte Nation. Deutschlands öffentliche Stimmung 1866 bis 1945.* Stuttgart, 1998.

Stroumsa, Jacques. *Geiger in Auschwitz. Ein jüdisches Überlebensschicksal aus Saloniki 1941–1967.* Ed. Erhard Roy Wiehn. Konstanz, 1993.

Stucken, Rudolf. *Deutsche Geld- und Kreditpolitik 1914 bis 1963.* 2nd ed. Tübingen, 1964 (the first edition appeared under the title *Deutsche Geld- und Kreditpolitik* in Hamburg in 1937).

Terhalle, Fritz. "Geschichte der deutschen Finanzwissenschaft vom Beginn des 19. Jahrhunderts bis zum Schlusse des Zweiten Weltkrieges." In *Handbuch der Finanzwissenschaft.* Vol. 1. Ed. Wilhelm Gerloff and Fritz Neumark. Tübingen, 1952. Pp. 273–326.

Tönsmeyer, Tatjana. *Das Dritte Reich und die Slowakei 1939–1945. Politischer Alltag zwischen Kooperation und Eigensinn.* Paderborn, 2003.

————. "Der Raub des jüdischen Eigentums in Ungarn, Rumänien und der Slowakei." In Goschler and Ther, *Raub und Restitution*, pp. 71–91.

Tooze, Adam. *The Wages of Destruction: The Making and Breaking of the Nazi Economy.* London, 2006.

Umbreit, Hans. "Auf dem Weg zur Kontinentalherrschaft." In *Organisation und Mobilisierung des deutschen Machtbereichs, Erster Halbband: Kriegsverwaltung, Wirtschaft und personelle Ressourcen 1939–41.* Ed. Bernhard R. Kroener, Rolf-Dieter Müller, and Hans Umbreit. Vol. 5 of *Das Deutsche Reich und der Zweite Weltkrieg.* Ed. Militärgeschichtliches Forschungsamt. Stuttgart, 1988. Pp. 3–345.

————. *Der Militärbefehlshaber in Frankreich 1940–1944* (Militärgeschichtliche Studien, vol. 7). Boppard, 1968.

United Restitution Organization. "M-Aktion. Frankreich, Belgien, Holland und Luxemburg 1940–1944," by Kurt May. 2nd exp. ed., Oct. 30, 1958.

Varon, Laura. *The Juderia: A Holocaust Survivor's Tribute to the Jewish Community of Rhodes.* Westport and London, 1999.

Verheyde, Phillipe. "The Looting of Jewish Property and Franco-German Rivalry, 1940–1944." In Feldman and Seibel, *Networks*, pp. 69–87.

Verwaltungsbericht der Deutschen Reichsbank für das Jahr 1942. Berlin, 1943.

Völkl, Ekkehard. *Der Westbanat 1941–1944. Die deutsche, die ungarische und andere Volksgruppen.* Munich, 1991.

Voss, Reimer. *Steuern im Dritten Reich. Vom Recht zum Unrecht unter der Herrschaft des Nationalsozialismus.* Munich, 1995.

Währung und Wirtschaft. Ed. Deutsche Bundesbank. Frankfurt am Main, 1976.

Wandel, Eckhard. "Die Rolle der Banken bei der Finanzierung der Aufrüstung und des Krieges 1933 bis 1945." In Schremmer, *Geld*, pp. 275–88.

Wappler, Anke. "Grundzüge der Okkupationspolitik des faschistischen deutschen Imperialismus gegenüber Griechenland vom März 1943 bis zum Oktober 1944." Dissertation, Akademie der Wissenschaften der DDR, Berlin, 1986.

Wehrmacht. Dimensionen des Vernichtungskrieges 1941–1944. Ausstellungskatalog, Hamburg, 2002.

Wette, Wolfram, Ricarda Bremer, and Detlev Vogel, eds. *Das letzte halbe Jahr. Stimmungsberichte der Wehrmachtpropaganda 1944/45.* Essen, 2001.

Wiel, Paul. *Krieg und Wirtschaft.* Berlin, 1938.

Witte, Peter. "'. . . Zusammen 1 274 166.' Der Funkspruch des SS-Sturmbannführers Hermann Höfle liefert ein Schlüsseldokument des Holocaust." *Die Zeit,* January 10, 2002.

Woitkowski, Hans-Peter. "Graf Schwerin von Krosigk." In Friedenberger et al., *Reichsfinanzverwaltung,* pp. 246–52.

Xydis, Stephen G. *The Economy and Finances of Greece under Axis Occupation in 1941–1942.* Pittsburgh, 1943.

———. *The Economy and Finances of Greece under Occupation.* New York, 1945.

Yahil, Leni. *Die Shoa. Überlebenskampf und Vernichtung der europäischen Juden.* Munich, 1998.

Zeidler, Manfred. "Die deutsche Kriegsfinanzierung 1914 bis 1918 und ihre Folgen." In *Der Erste Weltkrieg.* Ed. Wolfgang Michalka. Munich, 1994. Pp. 415–33.

Ziegler, Karl. "Erinnerungen an die Feldpost im Kriege 1939–1945." MS, Bonn, 1950 (BA-MA Library).

Ziehe, R. "Das neue Zwangsvollstreckungsrecht seit Kriegsbeginn." *Deutsche Gerichtsvollzieher-Zeitung* 60 (1940), pp. 33–35.

Zimmermann, Michael. "Die Deportation der Juden aus Essen und dem Regierungsbezirk Düsseldorf." In *Über Leben im Krieg. Kriegserfahrungen in einer Industrieregion 1939–1945.* Ed. Ulrich Borsdorf and Mathilde Jamin. Reinbek bei Hamburg, 1989. Pp. 126–31.

Zitelmann, Rainer. *Hitler. Selbstverständnis eines Revolutionärs.* Hamburg, 1987.

Zuckmayer, Carl. *Geheimreport.* Göttingen, 2002.

Zülow, Kurt, Hermann Gaus, and Max Henze. *Die Mehreinkommensteuer.* Bücherei des Steuerrechts, vol. 17. Berlin, 1939.

Zumach, Ernst-Günther. "Die wirtschaftlichen Kriegsmassnahmen Deutschlands im II. Weltkrieg in völkerrechtlicher Betrachtung." Dissertation, University of Erlangen, 1955.

Zumpe, Lotte. *Wirtschaft und Staat in Deutschland 1933 bis 1945.* Vaduz, 1980.

Index

Entries in *italics* refer to charts, illustrations, and tables.

About the Author

One of the most respected historians of the Third Reich and the Holocaust, GÖTZ ALY is the author of *Architects of Annihilation*, among other books. A winner of Germany's prestigious history award, the Heinrich-Mann Prize, Aly has been a visiting fellow at the Holocaust Museum in Washington and currently teaches at the University of Frankfurt. He lives in Berlin.

About the Translator

JEFFERSON CHASE's translations include the Signet edition of Thomas Mann's *Death in Venice and Other Stories* and *The Culture of Defeat* by Wolfgang Schivelbusch. He lives in Berlin.

Made in the USA
Monee, IL
24 June 2020